JOURNAL FOR THE STUDY OF THE NEW TESTAMENT
SUPPLEMENT SERIES
45

Executive Editor, Supplement Series
David Hill

Publishing Editor
David E Orton

JSOT Press
Sheffield

THE
RHETORIC
OF
ROMANS

Argumentative Constraint and Strategy
and Paul's Dialogue with Judaism

Neil Elliott

Journal for the Study of the New Testament
Supplement Series 45

Published by JSOT Press
JSOT Press is an imprint of
Sheffield Academic Press Ltd
The University of Sheffield
343 Fulwood Road
Sheffield S10 3BP
England

Typeset by Sheffield Academic Press
and
Printed on acid-free paper in Great Britain
by Billing & Sons Ltd
Worcester

British Library Cataloguing in Publication Data

Elliott, Neil
    The rhetoric of Romans
    1. Bible. N.T. Romans—Devotional works
    I. Title   II. Series
    227.106

    ISSN 0143-5108
    ISBN 1-85075-261-3

CONTENTS

PREFACE

It would, I confess, be a mark of downright envy to want to compete with scholars such as these, and it never occurred to me to detract in the least from their praise. Let them retain both the favour and authority which, by the confession of all good men, they have earned. It will, however, I hope, be admitted that nothing has ever been so perfectly done by men that there is no room left for those who follow them to refine, adorn, or illustrate their work. I do not dare to say anything of myself, except that I thought that the present work would be of some profit, and that I have been led to undertake it for no other reason than the common good of the church...

When, therefore, we depart from the views of our predecessors, we are not to be stimulated by any passion for innovation, impelled by any desire to slander others, aroused by any hatred, or prompted by any ambition. Necessity alone is to compel us, and we are to have no other object than that of doing good.*

The seeds of this book were sown in J. Christiaan Beker's graduate seminar on Romans at Princeton Theological Seminary in 1983. My initial disappointment at drawing the assignment of no less worked-over a pericope than 1.18–2.16 quickly gave way to fascination with the difficulty many interpreters had in getting out of the text what they knew must be there, namely Paul's rhetorical assault on *the Jew*. The emerging problem, how to integrate the apostrophe to the Jew that begins in Rom. 2.17 within a letter explicitly directed to a Gentile-Christian congregation, became the focus of my

---

*   From the preface to John Calvin's commentary on *The Epistles of Paul to the Romans and to the Thessalonians*, trans. Ross Mackenzie [Grand Rapids: Eerdmans, 1960], pp. 2-3.

PhD dissertation, which now appears in revised form before the reader.

For the growth of that first germ into the present work I have to thank friends and colleagues in the New Testament Colloquium at Princeton, and in particular the two men who have taught me Paul by sharing not only their critical acumen, but also their passion for Paul's Gospel: Professors J. Christiaan Beker and Paul W. Meyer (now emeritus). It was their generous encouragement that prodded me forward, no less when I disagreed with their views than when we agreed, and it was their wisdom that saved me from greater errors that, due to no fault of theirs, remain in what follows. To Dr David Hill, who accepted my manuscript for publication, to Dr David Orton, who has overseen its production with grace and efficiency, and to Professor David Clines, who gave close attention to the accuracy of the Greek, I offer my thanks.

I dedicate this work to the memory of my father, Rodger N. Elliott, whose legacy to me includes the conviction that interpreting the Bible is one of the most important vocations to which one may aspire.

INTRODUCTION

THE STARTING POINT OF ARGUMENTATION
IN ROMANS

1. The 'Historical Problem of Romans' as the Problem of the Letter's 'Double Character'

Why did Paul write Romans? He seems to declare his intentions toward the Roman congregation clearly enough in 1.11-15:

> For I long to see you, that I might impart to you some spiritual gift to strengthen you, that is, that we may be mutually encouraged by each other's faith, both yours and mine. I want you to know, brethren, that I have often intended to come to you (but have thus far been prevented), in order that I may reap some harvest among you as well as among the rest of the Gentiles. I am under obligation both to Greeks and barbarians, both to the wise and to the foolish: so I am eager to preach the gospel to you also who are in Rome (RSV).

Exactly what these statements mean, however, and precisely how they relate to Paul's immediate purposes in writing this letter, are questions that remain controversial today, chiefly because what the apostle says itself seems to defy any single cohesive explanation.

By way of illustration: does Paul's desire to 'strengthen' the Roman congregation (1.11) imply that he perceives that they are somehow deficient in faith? The commendation in 1.8 would seem to contradict such an implication, and the qualification in 1.12 is, for many interpreters, a sign that Paul heard in the phrase a tone more harsh and aggressive than he intended to sound, and immediately sought to soften it. Further: what does the apostle mean when he says that he has long desired to 'reap some harvest' among the Romans (1.13), or to 'evangelize' them (εὐαγγελίσασθαι, 1.15)? Do those phrases bear on his purposes in this letter, or do they declare *past* intentions that are mentioned now only in order to show that Paul has the Romans congregation on his heart?

Such questions about the letter opening have driven many commentators to search for clues to Paul's actual purpose in his *closing* remarks, where he mentions his projected mission in the west (15.23-24) and the anticipated journey to Jerusalem with the collection for the saints (15.25-29), a prospect that fills him with not a little anxiety (15.30-32). But then how is Paul's silence about these concerns in the letter *opening* to be understood? Is he showing an initial circumspection before a congregation that does not know him personally, or does he there betray trepidation before a church that he fears may think the worst of him and his mission; or is there yet another explanation? Furthermore, how do the apostle's purposes, if these are in fact implicit in 1.1-15, relate to what is almost universally considered the announcement of a theological 'theme' in 1.16-17, and to its exposition in the chapters that follow? However that relationship might be construed, why is it not more readily apparent?

The cumulative effect of these questions has been to raise doubts that Romans will submit to the sort of historical explanation that has been so fruitfully applied to the apostle's other correspondence. Clues to a concrete historical situation are evident enough in the epistolary frame (1.1-15; 15.14-32), but their connection with the sustained argument in the intervening chapters is not at all obvious.[1] In fact, some commentators find in the lack of an urgent historical situation prompting the letter a sort of theological windfall: *because* Paul is not constrained by circumstance, he is at some leisure to present a fairly systematic and orderly exposition of the gospel that he preaches.[2]

---

1 Note C.E.B. Cranfield's comment that, although the letter's historical occasion is evident from Paul's remarks in the epistolary frame, it is less clear 'why he included 1.16b–15.13—and this precisely—in the letter' (*The Epistle to the Romans* [ICC; Edinburgh: T. & T. Clark, 1975], I, p. 23).
2 'To the Romans', wrote J.B. Lightfoot, Paul 'writes at leisure, under no pressure of circumstances, in the face of no direct antagonism,

This book seeks to contribute to the ongoing discussion regarding the character and purpose of Paul's letter to the Romans. Despite a wealth of literature on the letter as a 'historical problem',[1] consensus has not yet been reached on a number of fundamental issues.[2] The best avenue of approach to the fundamental problem of interpreting the letter may be found in the conception of the letter's 'double character' offered by W.G. Kümmel:

> Romans manifests a double character: it is essentially a debate between the Pauline gospel and Judaism, so that the conclusion seems obvious that the readers were Jewish Christians. Yet the letter contains statements which indicate specifically that the community was Gentile-Christian.[3]

explaining, completing, extending the teaching of [Galatians], by giving it a double edge directed against Jew and Gentile alike. The matter, which in the one epistle is personal and fragmentary, elicited by the special needs of an individual church, is in the other, generalized and arranged so as to form a comprehensive and systematic treatise' (*Saint Paul's Epistle to the Galatians* [London: Macmillan, 1865], p. 49). F.F. Bruce endorses Lightfoot's judgment in his chapter on 'The Gospel According to Paul', in *Paul: Apostle of the Heart Set Free* (Grand Rapids: Eerdmans, 1977), pp. 325-26; one may compare Cranfield's remarks in *Romans*, II, pp. 816-17.

1 See Walter Schmithals, *Der Römerbrief als historisches Problem* (Gütersloh: Gütersloher Verlagshaus Mohn, 1975); the essays collected by Karl P. Donfried in *The Romans Debate* (Minneapolis: Augsburg, 1977); W.S. Campbell's review articles, 'Why did Paul Write Romans?', *ExpT* 85 (1973–1974), pp. 264-69, and 'Revisiting Romans', *Scr* 12 (1981), pp. 2-10; J. Christiaan Beker, *Paul the Apostle: The Triumph of God in Life and Thought* (Philadelphia: Fortress, 1980), pp. 59-93; H. Boers, 'The Problem of Jews and Gentiles in the Macro-Structure of Romans', *SEÅ* 47 (1982), pp. 184-96; most recently the essays by Sigfred Pedersen, 'Theologische Überlegungen zur Isagogik des Römerbriefes', *ZNW* 76 (1985), pp. 47-67, and Peter Stuhlmacher, 'Der Abfassungszweck des Römerbriefes', *ZNW* 77 (1986), pp. 180-93.
2 As recently as 1981 W.S. Campbell could refer to the perception of 'an increasing confusion rather than clarity in the interpretation of the letter', and cited Ulrich Luz's opinion that 'eine eindeutige Lösung drängt sich aus dem Studium der Sekundärliteratur nicht auf' ('Romans III as a Key to the Structure and Thought of the Letter', *NovT* 23 [1981], p. 22).
3 W.G. Kümmel, *Introduction to the New Testament*, trans. H.C. Kee, rev. edn (Nashville: Abingdon, 1975), p. 309.

But the problem of the letter's 'double character' extends
beyond the perceived incongruity between 'Jewish' topics and
a Gentile-Christian audience to include the oblique connection
between the epistolary frame (1.1-15; 15.14-33), which
includes references to Paul's intentions and travel plans, and
the content of the letter body. Here as well as Kümmel finds
tension:

> Only the external occasion and the immediate aim of the
> letter are accounted for by the announcement of his visit, by
> the clarification of his objectives, and by the enlisting of the
> understanding and help of the Christians in Rome for the
> missionary goals which he is pursuing. The broad theologi-
> cal discussion and the debate with Judaism that pervade the
> letter must have other, deeper grounds.[1]

According to Kümmel, the 'other, deeper grounds' for the
letter's content may include 'false views' of Paul's preaching,
both among Jewish opponents and among 'libertine-antino-
mians' in Pauline churches (and presumably in Rome as
well), and the tension between 'weak' and 'strong' in Rome.
But, he continues, 'it is just as clear... that the most weighty
part of the letter does not lie in such specific polemics but in the
setting forth of the Pauline message of redemption in ongoing
debate with Jewish teaching about redemption'.[2]

For Kümmel, then, Paul's explicit references to the immediate epistolary situation, garnered from the letter frame (1.1-
15; 15.14-32), are insufficient to explain the theological content of the letter body (Paul's 'debate with Judaism'). The connection between discrete historical occasion and compositional
purpose is oblique, and can be recovered only by reading
between the lines, since Paul's purpose in presenting this
'debate with Judaism' before his Roman audience is never
made explicit. To be sure, this does not mean that Kümmel
denies the letter's historical contingency. On the contrary, he
writes that, if Paul's 'debate with Judaism' in Romans can be
said to have a main purpose, it is Paul's self-introduction to the
Roman community:

1 *Ibid.*, p. 312.
2 *Ibid.*, p. 314.

On the other hand, since Paul is seeking ties with the Roman Christians in the interests of his ongoing missionary activity, it is quite appropriate that he presents himself to them and tells them what is the essence of Christianity and what is the content of the gospel that he preaches as apostle to the Gentiles. The desire to introduce himself to the Christians in Rome and to tell them who he is and what he preaches gives Paul the occasion to express himself at some length about the basic truths of Christianity as he sees and teaches it. Though it arose out of concrete necessity for his missionary work, Romans is the theological confession of Paul, which has been appropriately characterized [by G. Bornkamm] as 'the testament of Paul'.[1]

Nevertheless, as the last sentence shows, in Kümmel's view the force that has comprehensively shaped the letter cannot be explained on historical grounds alone.

In broad terms, Kümmel's presentation of the historical problem of Romans is representative of a consensus in scholarship.[2] The outlines of Kümmel's solution have won wide acceptance as well. Once the letter's core (chs. 1–8) has been identified as 'essentially a debate... with Judaism', the historical-critical task has been pursued by extrapolating a plausible occasion for that debate, either from Paul's anxious remarks about his visit to Jerusalem in 15.30-32, or from indications of religious and ethnic tensions within the Roman congregation in chs. 9–11 and 14–15, or from both (see below). Nevertheless, the compositional purpose that has shaped the letter body exceeds the character of a response to the requirements of the concrete situation. The theological exposition (or, in Kümmel's phrase, 'Paul's theological confession') is seen to unfold very much according to the inherent logic of Paul's gospel,[3] which

1 *Ibid.*, pp. 312-13.
2 W. Schmithals (*Römerbrief*, p. 9) adopts the term 'Doppelcharakter' (originally that of P. Feine, *Der Römerbrief* [Göttingen: Vandenhoeck & Ruprecht, 1903]) to introduce his monograph; others have relied on the concept in reviews of research (see Campbell, 'Revisiting Romans', p. 8; A.J.M. Wedderburn, 'The Purpose and Occasion of Romans Again', *ExpT* 90 [1978], pp. 137-41).
3 So, for example, Cranfield (*Romans*, II, p. 81) labels the body 'a serious and orderly summary of the gospel as [Paul] had come to understand it', in the composition of which Paul 'allowed the inner logic of the gospel as he understood it itself to determine, at any rate

is intrinsically and inevitably antithetical to Judaism.[1] The letter's 'double character', then, consists not only in the tension between 'Jewish' subject matter and Gentile-Christian audience, but in the tension between Paul's compositional purpose (*Abfassungszweck*) and the discrete historical circumstances that are no longer in sharp focus, but have become a mere jumping-off point (*Anlassungspunkt*) for that theological exposition.[2]

for the most part, the structure and contents of what was now going to be the main body of his letter'. Similarly, Bruce (*Paul*, pp. 325-38) labels his discussion of Romans 'The Gospel According to Paul'; The *New English Bible* has supplied the same heading for the text of Rom. 1–8.

1 Against challenges to reading Romans as a comprehensive statement of Paul's Gospel, H. Schlier (*Der Römerbrief* [HTKNT 6; Freiburg: Herder, 1974], p. 4, n. 12) asks why Paul should not have sent an introductory letter to the unknown Roman congregation including an exposition of 'what was central to his own preaching, which directed itself against Judaism'. For his part, G. Bornkamm (*Paul*, trans. D.M.G. Stalker [New York: Harper & Row, 1971], p. 95), although he emphasizes the letter's relevance to the upcoming confrontation in Jerusalem, can characterize the letter as Paul's 'exposition of salvation as he understands it and his justification of his gospel for the Gentiles [which is] made through a contrast with the Jews' understanding of [salvation] and their claim to possess it exclusively'. He goes on to declare that 'Paul's opponent is not this or that section in a particular church, but the Jews and their understanding of salvation'; moreover, 'the Jew symbolizes man in his highest potentialities; he represents the "religious man" whom the Law tells what God requires of him...'

2 H. Gamble's comments (*The Textual History of the Letter to the Romans* [Grand Rapids: Eerdmans, 1977], p. 133) on the letter's occasion succinctly express the problem: 'The interpretation of Romans must proceed at the most basic level from these given data: first, Paul's statements about his situation and plans; second, the Roman letter as such. But with these data we are given the problem: how to correlate satisfactorily the content of the letter with its ostensible occasion. Put differently, why did Paul write *this* letter to the Romans?' Compare Cranfield's remark cited in n. 1 p. 10 above; and see J. Knox, *Romans* (IB 9; New York: Abingdon, 1954), p. 358.

2. The 'Double Character' Problem as a Rhetorical-Critical Problem

Any new solution to a problem implies that at least some aspect of the problem remains unsolved apart from the solution offered. Our premise in this work is that despite a number of significant gains in understanding the content and occasion of Romans, a *rhetorically* satisfactory resolution of this central 'double character' problem remains elusive. We contend that the prevailing explanations of the letter's double character are too often purchased at the cost of the letter's rhetorical integrity. Substantiating this assertion is our task in this section of the Introduction.

In inquiring in this Introduction after the 'starting point of argumentation in Romans', we are concerned with the agreement with the audience that persuasive discourse, or rhetoric, always presupposes. We take our cue from C. Perelman and L. Olbrechts-Tyteca's observation that

> from start to finish, analysis of argumentation is concerned with what is supposed to be accepted by the hearers.... When a speaker selects and puts forward the premises that are to serve as foundation for his argument, he relies on his hearers' adherence to the propositions from which he will start.[1]

This observation corresponds to the view that argumentation intends 'to elicit or increase the adherence of the members of an audience to theses that are presented for their consent', proceeding in such a way as 'to modify an audience's convictions or dispositions through discourse' in the attempt to gain 'a meeting of minds'.[2]

These remarks point to rhetorical criticism's interest not only in the *appropriateness* of discourse intended to be per-

---

1 Chaim Perelman and L. Olbrechts-Tyteca, *The New Rhetoric: A Treatise on Argumentation*, trans. John Wilkinson and Purcell Weaver (Notre Dame: University of Notre Dame, 1969), p. 65.
2 Chaim Perelman, *The Realm of Rhetoric*, trans. W. Kluback (Notre Dame: University of Notre Dame, 1982), pp. 9, 11; Perelman and Olbrechts-Tyteca, *New Rhetoric*, p. 45.

suasive in the situation that calls it forth,[1] but to the means by which rhetoric allows the *modification* of the rhetorical situation by *redisposing* the constraints of speaker, audience, and exigence.[2] As Scott Consigny writes in a valuable essay on rhetoric,

> The rhetorical situation is an indeterminate context marked by troublesome disorder which the rhetor must structure so as to disclose and formulate problems... But the rhetorical situation is not one created solely through the imagination and discourse of the rhetor. It involves particularities of persons, actions, and agencies in a certain place and time; and the rhetor cannot ignore these constraints if he is to function effectively... The rhetor must work through what Aristotle calls the *pragmata* of the situation in such a way that an issue emerges from his interactions with the situation; and the rhetor who fails to take these constraints into account, spinning issues from his imagination, may never get in touch with events or his audience, and may rightly be dismissed as ineffective and irrelevant.
>
> ... Through his actions the rhetor attains a 'disposition' of the situation, or a new way of seeing and acting in the situation. He discloses a new 'gestalt' for interpreting and acting in the situation, and thereby offers the audience a new perspective to view the situation.[3]

As a consequence, Consigny considers that the rhetor must meet two requirements: 'integrity', which is 'a "universal"

---

1 'Discourse is rhetorical', declares Lloyd F. Bitzer ('The Rhetorical Situation', *PhR* 1 [1968], p. 6), 'insofar as it functions (or seeks to function) as a fitting response to a situation which needs and invites it'.

2 Bitzer defines the *rhetorical* situation as 'a complex of persons, events, objects, and relations presenting an actual or potential exigence which can be completely or partially removed if discourse, introduced into the situation, can so constrain human decision or action as to bring about the significant modification of the exigence' (*ibid.*). *Exigence* is defined as 'an imperfection marked by urgency; it is a defect, an obstacle, something waiting to be done, a thing which is other than it should be'; a *rhetorical exigence* is specifically an exigence that can be modified through discourse (*ibid.*).

3 Scott Consigny, 'Rhetoric and its Situations', *PhR* 7 (1974), pp. 178-79.

capacity such that the rhetor can function in all kinds of indeterminate and particular situations as they arise', and
'receptivity' to the restrictions of a particular situation.[1] These
functions are served in rhetoric by the selection and development of *topics*, which Consigny defines as devices that allow
the rhetor 'to discover, through selection and arrangement,
that which is relevant and persuasive in particular situations'.[2] The rhetor's choice of topic is to be assessed on the basis
of its success in illuminating a situation, and that success
depends on the rhetor's sensitivity to the situation's particularities. This sensitivity, too, is in Consigny's view an aspect of
the topic, or, we should perhaps say, of the 'topical' (or
'situational') dimension of rhetoric.[3]

Can Romans be understood as rhetoric? In order to answer
that question it will be necessary to examine the letter for the
characteristics of rhetoric suggested in the paragraphs above,
including appropriateness or responsiveness to the constraints
of a rhetorical situation, and an overall argumentative
purpose that moves from a basis of agreement shared with the
audience to consolidate the audience's adherence to the
speaker's theses. Of course, our rhetorical-critical analysis of
Romans cannot have recourse to independent knowledge of
the situation Paul confronted; we must rely on inference from
the letter itself. Thus, this project must be fundamentally
exegetical. A third dimension in our rhetorical approach must
therefore be the *intelligibility* of argumentation in the letter.

1 *Ibid.*, pp. 180-81.
2 *Ibid.*, p. 181.
3 Aristotle distinguished 'specific topics' (ἴδιοι τόποι), consensual
observations in various fields of knowledge that could function as
sources for inference, and 'common topics' (κοινοὶ τόποι), the means
or methods of inference. Precisely the rhetor's creative use of observations accepted by the audience in order to extrapolate, by mutually
accepted means of inference, to an ambiguous or indeterminate situation is the 'topical' dimension of rhetoric that makes persuasion
possible. See Perelman and Olbrechts-Tyteca, *New Rhetoric*, esp.
pp. 65-99; William M.A. Grimaldi, 'The Aristotelian Topics',
Traditio 14 (1958), pp. 1-16, reprinted in K. Erickson, ed., *Aristotle:
The Classical Heritage of Rhetoric* (Metuchen: Scarecrow, 1974),
pp. 176-93.

The first two dimensions of rhetoric, which Consigny has discussed under the categories 'receptivity' and 'integrity', bear a striking resemblance to J. Christiaan Beker's discussion of the 'contingent' and 'coherent' aspects of Paul's hermeneutic. Beker argues forcefully that the 'character of Paul's thought' consists in 'the constant interaction between the coherent center of the gospel and its contingent interpretation'. This hermeneutic allows Paul to 'make the gospel a word on target for the particular needs of his churches without either compromising its basic content or reducing it to a petrified conceptuality'.[1] The key to this hermeneutical interplay of coherence and contingency is the purposefulness of Paul's apostolic responsibility: 'Just because the apostle writes "in order to bring about something", his gospel is necessarily contingent; and just because the gospel itself has as its content the "in order that" of God's coming triumph, it has a coherent core'.[2] Beker's comments suggest that Paul's letters can in fact be understood as rhetoric, i.e., as discourse determined by persuasive purpose within a constraining situation. One of the most important contributions in *Paul the Apostle* is Beker's effort to demonstrate this same hermeneutical interaction of coherence and contingency at work *in Romans*.[3]

We have ventured into the territory of rhetorical criticism in the conviction that focusing on whether Romans can be understood as *rhetoric* puts the *historical* problem of the letter in sharpest relief. To be sure, rhetorical criticism and historical investigation pursue different goals. If historical criticism seeks to establish the historical circumstances lying behind a text, rhetorical criticism asks how a particular speaker (or writer) *perceived* that situation and responded to that perception. Nevertheless, with reference to ancient texts such as Romans, both disciplines must proceed along parallel lines of inference from the text to a hypothetical situation—in the one case rhetorical, in the other historical. Our premise in this work is that the ancient and modern discussions of the

---

1 Beker, *Paul the Apostle*, pp. 11, 12.
2 *Ibid.*, p. 12.
3 *Ibid.*, pp. 59-108.

dynamics of argumentation[1] may help us to evaluate the cogency of some of the inferences that have been made from Romans in 'classical' historical treatments.

The problem with which this Introduction began—the presence of a 'dialogue with Judaism' within a letter addressed to *Gentile Christians*—will be obliterated if we neutralize the letter's persuasive aspect, severing the argumentative theological 'core' of the letter from the discrete situational bearings apparent in the epistolary frame (1.1-15; 15.14-33; ch. 16). Unless interpretation pursues the rhetorical integration and cohesion of message and audience, the conception of Romans as rhetoric will deteriorate into 'mere essay-making, without concern for real life', rhetoric 'addressed to conventional audiences, of which such rhetoric can afford to have stereotyped conceptions'.[2] Of course the possibility that what Paul says in Romans is *not* effective rhetoric—that the letter body does *not* show the dimensions of rhetorical integrity and receptivity to situational constraints tht Consigny describes, and that Beker attributes to Paul's hermeneutic in general— cannot be excluded *a priori*. In fact E.P. Sanders' discussion of Romans 2 implies that Paul's argumentation there is completely inappropriate to the rhetorical situation, and that Paul has relied on traditional formulations and arguments from other contexts that do not say what Paul means to say in

---

1 We have in mind the ancient rhetorical handbooks by Aristotle (*The Art of Rhetoric*), Cicero (*De Inventione; De Oratore; De Partitione Oratoria*), Quintilian (*Institutio Oratoria*), and the *Rhetorica ad Alexandrum* and *Ad Herennium*, all available in the Loeb Classical Library. For modern surveys see George A. Kennedy, *The Art of Persuasion in Ancient Greece* (Princeton: Princeton University Press, 1963); *The Art of Rhetoric in the Roman World* (Princeton: Princeton University Press, 1972); *Classical Rhetoric and its Christian and Secular Tradition from Ancient to Modern Times* (Chapel Hill: University of North Carolina Press, 1980); Heinrich Lausberg, *Handbuch der literarischen Rhetorik: Eine Grundlegung der Literaturwissenschaft*, 3rd edn, 2 vols. (Munich: Max Hueber, 1967); Josef Martin, *Antike Rhetorik: Technik und Methode*, Handbuch der Altertumswissenschaft, 2.3 (Munich: C.H. Beck, 1974); and modern essays in rhetorical theory such as Perelman and Olbrechts-Tyteca's *New Rhetoric* and William Brandt's *The Rhetoric of Argumentation* (New York: Bobbs-Merrill, 1970).
2 Perelman and Olbrechts-Tyteca, *New Rhetoric*, p. 20.

Romans.[1] It is not our intention to protect the apostle from the charge of being 'idiosyncratic',[2] or a 'bad rhetor'; rather, it is our intention to examine whether or not the argumentative movement within Romans justifies those characterizations.

To point the issue sharply, we contend that the 'double character' problem of Romans is in fact a rhetorical-critical problem to the extent that *historical* solutions put the letter's *rhetorical* integrity in question. On the premise that the letter body (and especially chs. 1–8) consists largely of a 'dialogue' or 'debate with Judaism', interpreters have taken one of two paths. Either they have sought to identify the Jewish *animus* of that debate within the letter's historical context (as when interpreters focus on possible antagonism toward Paul among Jewish Christians in Rome or Jerusalem), or else what is perceived as Paul's 'debate with Judaism' has been attributed to factors independent of the historical circumstances surrounding the letter (as when interpreters speak of Paul's *earlier* debates with Jews, or of the Pauline gospel's *inherent* antithesis to Judaism). On either reading, Paul launches an offensive against 'the Jew' early in the letter without indicating what, if anything, this offensive has to do with his Gentile Christian readers in Rome (cf. 1.6, 13, 14-15).

The rhetorical-critical problem becomes acute at the 'hinges' that connect the epistolary frame (1.1-15; 15.14-32) to the letter body, and especially at the begining of what is widely considered Paul's offensive against 'the Jew' in 1.18–2.29. The abrupt transition from the letter opening to the beginning of Paul's 'debate with Judaism' puts Paul's rhetorical 'receptivity' (Consigny) in doubt (as when interpreters speak of the Roman audience 'dropping from view' in these early chap-

---

1 See E.P. Sanders, *Paul, the Law, and the Jewish People* (Philadelphia: Fortress, 1983), pp. 125ff.
2 James D.G. Dunn ('The New Perspective on Paul', *BJRL* 65 [1983], p. 101) remarks that Sanders has replaced the 'Lutheran Paul' with an 'idiosyncratic Paul who in arbitrary and irrational manner turns his face against the glory and greatness of Judaism's covenant theology and abandons Judaism simply because it is not Christianity'. Beker ('Paul's Theology: Consistent or Inconsistent?' *NTS* 34 [1988], pp. 364-77) speaks in similar fashion of 'Paul the muddled and self-contradictory thinker', in Sanders' interpretation.

ters). It is just here that the letter's historical problem becomes
an acute rhetorical-critical problem; for although there is no
dearth of explanations that integrate Paul's 'debate with
Judaism' with a historical situation that includes the Roman
congregation, these proposals fall short of explaining how the
argumentation moves in 1.16–2.29 to modify the rhetorical
situation established in 1.1-15. More often, in fact, Paul's
positive statements of intention in the letter opening become a
hermeneutical liability as interpreters balance the letter's
rhetorical weight on the fulcrum of Paul's anxiety regarding
Jerusalem (15.30-32).

The following brief survey of explanations concerning the
letter's occasion is intended to highlight the rhetorical-critical
problems left outstanding in prevailing historical explanations
of the letter.

a. *Romans as an Exposition of Paul's Gospel*
We have already referred to Kümmel's view that Romans
provides Paul's theological self-introduction to the Roman
congregation. The conception of the letter body as a relatively
self-contained theological treatise is not dissimilar to
Melanchthon's characterization of the letter as a com-
pendium *doctrinae christianae*. We have seen that for some
modern scholars this view is not inconsistent with a historical-
critical perspective, since in their view the letter gives no indication of being determined by contingent circumstance
(Lightfoot; Bruce; with more nuance, Cranfield). What is distinctive in historical-critical essays like Kümmel's is the
attempt to coordinate that treatise with an occasion to which it
can be seen as the fitting response. So Romans can serve as
something of a missionary dossier with which Paul hopes to
gain the Romans' support for his work in the west (Kümmel,
et al.), by presenting a sample of his preaching (Scroggs) or
teaching activity (Stowers). Alternately, the letter is seen as a
rehearsal of the 'defense' Paul will make for his Law-free
mission in Jerusalem, provided to garner the Romans'
support in prayer (Jervell) or with political influence (Brown).
Or again, the letter encapsulates the gospel which provides the

apostolic foundation that should constitute the Roman communities as a church (Klein, Minear, Schmithals).[1] The risk in any view that reads the letter body (1.16–15.13) as a relatively self-contained and independent theological essay is that these chapters of the letter may come to be read not as argumentation but as the monological showpiece by means of which Paul hopes to gain support, *not* for the propositions he advances, but for *himself* as their advocate; the weight of interpretation would then shift from εὐαγγέλιον (1.16) and the stated intention to 'evangelize' the Romans (εὐαγγελίσασθαι, 1.15) to Paul's supposed concern to exonerate himself as εὐαγγελιστής. Campbell has rightly protested that 'it is not consistent with what we know of Paul from his other letters that he would feel obliged to outline his Gospel for the approval of the Roman Christians'.[2] Günter Klein raises a protest much to the same point:

> Already, the far-reaching intention with which [in Kümmel's treatment] Paul's theological deliberations are credited seems unlikely. Paul could hardly have moved in a more indirect way than to write a letter including his most fundamental ideas and systematic concepts, not because he wanted to deal with these issues directly, but because he had essentially other goals in mind, i.e. the organization of the infra-structure of his missionary strategy. Seldom is it realized what an enormous insinuation actually underlies such a statement, viz., that the intention of the message and its

1 References: R.E. Brown and J.P. Meier, *Antioch and Rome: New Testament Cradles of Catholic Christianity* (New York: Paulist, 1983); Bruce, *Paul*, pp. 325-26; Cranfield, *Romans*, II, pp. 816-17; J. Jervell, 'The Letter to Jerusalem', trans. in Donfried, *The Romans Debate*, pp. 61-74; G. Klein, 'Paul's Purpose in Writing the Epistle to the Romans', trans. in Donfried, *The Romans Debate*, pp. 32-49; Lightfoot, *Galatians*, p. 49; Philipp Melanchthon, 'Römerbriefkommentar, 1532', in *Melanchthon's Werke in Auswahl*, V, ed. R. Stupperich (Gütersloh: C. Bertelsmann, 1965); P. Minear, *The Obedience of Faith* (London: SCM, 1971); W. Schmithals, *Römerbrief*; R. Scroggs, 'Paul as Rhetorician: Two Homilies in Romans 1–11', in *Jews, Greeks, and Christians*, ed. R. Hamerton-Kelly and R. Scroggs (Leiden: E.J. Brill, 1976), pp. 271-99; S.K. Stowers, *The Diatribe and Paul's Letter to the Romans* (Chico: Scholars Press, 1981)
2 'Why did Paul Write Romans?', p. 264.

content would no longer be interrelated; in fact, there would be such an irreconcilable contradiction that one would no longer be able to conclude one from the other. Thus, theology would be reduced to merely a means to an end; nothing but grist for his apostolic calling card. As a further consequence, no matter how pure his motives, Paul would have to be viewed as having only ulterior motives, viz., that his theological statements serve primarily as a means to benefit his own prestige. According to such a position, even though the theme of the justification of the godless appears throughout the epistle, Paul does not treat it in a consistently serious manner since he uses it essentially as a suitable medium of communication with the Roman Christians.[1]

These criticisms are to the point. But when Klein turns to a positive solution to the problem, he betrays the same fundamental conception of the letter body as a tool to be applied unilaterally rather than as argumentation within a dialogical context:

> Briefly stated, Paul, despite his epistolary habits, addresses the Romans with a theological treatise which in most parts seems free of any reference to a concrete situation... Paul does not artificially construct the Romans' need; instead, for him it results from their objective situation, which shows them still lacking the fundamental *kerygma*... The fact that Paul writes to the Romans in the form of a theological treatise is indicative of an occasion which calls for the normative message of the apostle and demands that his theological reflections be raised to a new level of general validity.[2]

The letter body thus retains a 'general' and 'systematic' character: historical circumstances has only prompted Paul to issue a copy of 'his gospel' to the kerygmatically deficient Roman church. It is hardly surprising at last when Klein exults that this hypothesis 'would confirm from a new angle the fact that the primary content of Romans—the justification of the godless—also constitutes the center of Pauline theology'.[3]

---

1 Klein, 'Paul's Purpose', p. 37.
2 *Ibid.*, pp. 48-49.
3 *Ibid.*

b. *Romans as an Encyclical Letter*
A number of interpreters have fastened on discrepancies between remarks made in the letter opening (1.1-15) and in the closing (15.14-32) as clues to Paul's compositional purposes. For example, in Rom. 1.1-15 the Romans are in the center of vision. It is to them that Paul is eager to come and 'preach the gospel'. There is no other indication of the apostle's plans, however, and even this positive declaration seems to be qualified by the profuse *captatio benevolentiae* in 1.8, as by the expansion (or correction?) of his purpose in 1.12. In 15.14-33, by contrast, Paul supplies abundant details about his plans. He has run out of area in the east and looks to mission fields in the west, specifically in Spain (15.22-24), and now his remarks seem to make of Rome not a destination but a way station, or as some have conjectured, a prospective base of operations in the west.[1] His interest in Rome now appears to be purely strategic. He has gathered the collection from Achaia and Macedonia, and voices his apprehension about the mission to Jerusalem (15.25-26, 30-32) as he asks for the Romans' support in prayer. In this chapter Paul also declares his policy of evangelizing 'where Christ is not named, lest I build on another's foundation' (15.20), a verse that seems to stand in definite tension with the intention, stated in 1.15, of evangelizing the Romans.

Some scholars have resolved these inconsistencies by denying that Romans was written originally *for the Romans*. On the contrary, in this view an original encyclical letter, drafted by Paul to present his theological convictions systematically to a new church audience (thus the 'evangelical' language in 1.12, 13, 15), has been particularized for dispatch to Rome by inserting the place name 'Rome' at 1.7 and 1.15[2] and by adding 15.14-33, in which the reference to evangelization in 1.15, inappropriate for Rome, has been recanted (15.20). By appending the greetings in what is now ch. 16, the same letter

---

1 Notably G. Schrenk, 'Der Römerbrief als Missionsdokument', in *Studien zu Paulus*, ATANT 26 (Zürich: Zwingli-Verlag, 1954), pp. 81-106.
2 The phrase ἐν Ῥώμῃ is missing from 1.7, and τοῖς ἐν Ῥώμῃ from 1.15, in G (9th century).

was dispatched to Ephesus.[1] This view has now been reversed by Gamble's study of the text-history of Romans which concludes that the textual variants at the beginning and end of the letter are the result of a *later* process of 'catholicizing' the Pauline corpus.[2]

c. *Jerusalem as Target: Rome as Mediator*

For other scholars the interpretive fulcrum lies in recognizing that the inconsistent remarks about Rome in chs. 1 and 15 cancel each other out. Rom. 15.24 and 28 make it clear that Paul's principal concern is not the Roman congregation; the concern expressed for them in 1.11-15 must, therefore, be a rhetorical device for eliciting their good will and has little or no direct bearing on Paul's actual purposes. Attention is to be

1 In T.W. Manson's view ('Saint Paul's Letter to the Romans—and Others', *In the Romans Debate*, p. 15), 1.1–15.13 served then as 'a manifesto setting forth [Paul's] deepest convictions on central issues, a manifesto calling for the widest publicity, which the apostle did his best—not without success—to give it'. Some years after Manson's article and his own commentary on Romans had appeared, John Knox expressed a similar view in 'A Note on the Text of Romans', *NTS* 2-3 (1955-56), pp. 191-93. Knox's only express 'reservation' about his hypothesis, that it does not explain the form of Romans ending with 14.23, is neatly answered by Origen's report that Marcion lopped off the last two chapters of the letter (so Manson, 'To the Romans—and Others', p. 9). Robert Funk ('The Apostolic Parousia: Form and Significance', in *Christian History and Interpretation: Studies Presented to John Knox*, ed. W.R. Farmer, C.F.D. Moule, and R.R. Niebuhr [Cambridge: Cambridge University Press, 1967], p. 268) concurs with this assessment in his treatment of what he has identified as a form-critical *Gattung*, the 'apostolic *parousia*': 'The double treatment of the apostolic *parousia* and the position of the particularized form (15.14-33) at the end of the letter lend considerable weight to this suggestion, in my opinion: Paul needed only to fill in the address and, if the occasion required it, add a personalized form of the apostolic *parousia* at the end, in order to be able to dispatch this generalized summary of his gospel to yet another church. The customary form of the Pauline letter could scarcely be modified so easily, and the presence of the generalized apostolic *parousia* in the thanksgiving made it possible for him to send off another copy without doing more than adding his name.'

2 Gamble, *Textual History*; see also his essay, 'The Redaction of the Pauline Letters and the Formation of the Pauline Corpus', *JBL* 94 (1975), pp. 403-18.

focused rather on Paul's concern regarding Jerusalem
(15.25-32). That this concern is not voiced in 1.1-15 is taken as
a measure of the apostle's anxiety.[1] The letter's exigence is
thus located not in Rome but in Jerusalem. Jervell represents
this view when he concurs with Knox that 'whenever Paul
speaks about his work in Rome he himself is uncertain as to
what he wants to do there': therefore the Roman situation is a
false lead for interpreters.[2] Jervell argues that the letter's argumentation is not
directed at the Romans. The letter's subject matter itself
indicates that 'we are not dealing with a debate Paul is having
with the church in Rome, but with objections he is anticipating
in Jerusalem'.[3] Romans is, then, a rehearsal of the defense he
will make before the Jerusalem Christians. The Roman
address is hardly incidental, however, for the letter is directed
to securing the cooperation and support of the Roman congregation against possible adversaries in Jerusalem.[4] The signifi-

1 John Knox (Romans, pp. 358-63) remarks that Paul 'seems to give
one explanation [of his purpose] in 1.1-15 and another in 15.18-29'
and concludes that 'he is not sure of the reception he will receive
there and is uncertain how he can most tactfully explain his
coming'. The 'consistently irenic tone' of the whole letter betrays
Paul's anxiety toward the Roman church, an anxiety justified in
Knox's opinion by the 'conservative', by which he means the Jewish
or Judaizing, cast of Roman Christianity. Along a similar vein,
Ernst Käsemann (Commentary on Romans, trans. G.W. Bromiley
[Grand Rapids: Eerdmans, 1980], p. 390) interprets the 'advance' in
ch. 15 over the 'obscurities, reservations, and retractions' of the 1.8-
15 in terms of 'an apologetic tendency'. It is only in ch. 15 that
Paul's real motivations for writing the letter come out: 'To that
extent the whole epistle prepares the way for this "epilogue"'. Yet
Käsemann is unwilling to speak of Paul's 'uncertainty' in Rom 1,
but instead characterizes the apostle's reticence as 'high diplomacy'. Although 'materially Paul surrenders nothing' of his
gospel, his tone is 'unusually mild and accommodating to Jewish-
Christians' (p. 405; cf. pp. 16-21).
2 Jervell, 'Letter to Jerusalem', p. 67. Jervell contends that 'the letter
itself states clearly that its raison d'être does not stem from the situation of the Roman congregation, but is to be found in Paul himself
at the time of writing' (p. 62).
3 Ibid., p. 71.
4 'Paul has only one objective: to ask the Roman congregation for solidarity, support, and intercession on his behalf' (ibid., pp. 64-65).

cance of the παρακαλῶ-clause in 15.30 is taken to confirm the fundamental importance of Jerusalem for understanding the letter.[1] Paul's concern for the journey to Jerusalem with the collection 'for the saints' and his intention that the Romans should share that concern are obvious. There are nevertheless two problems with Jervell's proposal. First of all, he focuses attention *exclusively* on Paul's anxiety about Jerusalem (15.30-32) as 'the reason for writing Romans'. Other indications of Paul's intentions toward the Romans are neutralized: the recapitulation of the letter in 15.14-16 is not discussed,[2] and the statements of intent in 1.1-15 are dismissed as inconsistent with Paul's 'principle never to preach at a place where others already taught before him (15.20)'.[3] The last point, which plays an important role in Klein's essay as well, has been disputed by Sigfred Pedersen, who shows that Paul's supposed 'working principle' in 15.20 never precluded cooperative effort in the mission field elsewhere (e.g., Corinth).[4] As to Paul's references to 'strengthening' and 'evangelizing' the Romans in ch. 1, it would seem preferable to *balance* these indications of purposes relating to the letter's explicit audience with Paul's concern regarding Jerusalem, rather than to simply cancel them out or collapse them into the Jerusalem 'target'.[5]

---

1 *Ibid.* Käsemann (*Romans*, p. 405) concurs that the Roman congregation plays a 'mediating role' with regard to Jerusalem, as do a number of other scholars who emphasize both the 'political' importance of the Roman congregation and the possibility of considerable Jewish or Judaizing sentiment within it, which would account for the apostle's supposed apologetic posture; so also Wedderburn, 'Purpose and Occasion', pp. 140-41.
2 Rom. 15.15 is mentioned only in connection with the letter's ultimate target, Jerusalem (Jervell, 'Letter to Jerusalem', p. 66).
3 *Ibid.*, p. 67.
4 Pedersen, 'Theologische Überlegungen', pp. 51-53.
5 Wilhelm Wuellner ('Paul's Rhetoric of Argumentation in Romans', in *The Romans Debate*, p. 512; again in 'Toposforschung und Torah-interpretation bei Paulus und Jesus', *NTS* 24 [1977-1978], p. 477) has suggested that Paul's mention in 1.13 of 'being hindered' from coming to Rome is in fact a cryptic reference to 'past *and present* obstacles': 'It is this latter point which reappears in 15.22 as past hindrance, and in 15.30-31 as gloomy prospect'. In this way

The second problem with Jervell's proposal is that, while he is able to integrate the letter's presumed exigence (Jerusalem) with its explicit address (Rome) by reliance on 15.30-32, he is unable to demonstrate this integration from the first part of the letter, where Paul's treatment of Judaism begins. On the contrary, he argues that 'actual letter style can only be found in the introduction and conclusion of the letter.... However, between 1.18 and 11.36 the recipients are no longer in focus'.[1] In a strikingly similar passage, Bent Noack, who holds that the 'current' of Paul's argument in chs. 1–11 is intended to justify his trip to Jerusalem before he turns to visit the Gentile Christians of Rome, finds the transition in 1.13-18 enigmatic, and labels the section that it introduces (1.18-3.8) 'backwater'.[2] It is evident from these statements that this solution to the letter's double character is purchased at the cost of the rhetorical integration of letter frame and body at the crucial hingepoint 1.15-18.

d. *The Roman Congregation as Target*
A fourth avenue of explanation finds the primary target of Paul's rhetoric within the Roman audience themselves. Günter Klein finds a 'major problem' in the fact that 'on the one hand, Paul unmistakably makes known to us his intention to preach the gospel to the Romans; on the other hand, he states [in 15.20] his principle of noninterference', a problem Klein is not willing to solve by relaxing the import of 1.11 or of 1.15. Rather, he concludes that 'Paul can consider an apostolic effort in Rome because he does not regard the local Christian community there as having an apostolic foundation'.[3] His argument rests in part on the judgment,

Wuellner seeks to relate Paul's intentions regarding the Romans to what he takes to be the letter's real exigence, anticipated Jewish opposition in Jerusalem. But neither in 1.13 nor in 15.22 does Paul characterize this 'hindrance' as *inimical*, as Wuellner suggests. If 1.13 is indeed a reference to Paul's anxieties regarding Jerusalem, it is too cryptic to be meaningful.

1 Jervell, 'Letter to Jerusalem', p. 70.
2 Bent Noack, 'Current and Backwater in the Epistle to the Romans', *ST* 19 (1965), pp. 161-62.
3 Klein, 'Paul's Purpose', pp. 36, 44.

Introduction 29

based on 1 Cor. 3.1, that for Paul 'laying the foundation' of an ἐκκλησία is an exclusively apostolic prerogative, and on the absence of the word ἐκκλησία from 1.1-6. As Pedersen has shown, these arguments are overdrawn.[1] Nevertheless, the focus on what Paul perceived to be the needs of the Roman community has become increasingly attractive to interpreters.

In his monograph on *Der Römerbrief als historisches Problem*, Walter Schmithals takes as his starting point the observation that Paul clearly addresses the Romans as *Gentile* Christians, and seeks to discover a *unified* solution to the letter's 'double character' by identifying a single audience (*'eine* angeredete Leserschaft') to which all of the letter's argumentation is appropriate. He argues quite plausibly that the earliest Gentile Christians in Rome, as elsewhere in Paul's missionary world, were converted Godfearers (i.e., former adherents to the synagogue), so that Paul can address them (in 1.6, 13) explicitly as Christians 'from among the Gentiles'.[2]

1 See n. 4 p. 2 above; Käsemann, *Romans*, p. 18.
2 So Schmithals, *Römerbrief*, p. 83. Despite recent attacks on the notion, epigraphic remains corroborate the literary indications in Luke–Acts and Josephus that Gentile sympathizers were widely recognized and could be distinguished from Jews by use of several terms translatable as 'Godfearers' (φοβούμενοι/σεβόμενοι τὸν θεόν). Admittedly such use was not always either precise or technical, although an inscription from Aphrodisias (2nd or 3rd century CE) seems clearly to distinguish Jews, προσήλυτοι and θεοσεβίς (sic): Jews also could be called 'Godfearers', as in an inscription from the theater in Miletus (τόπος ⟨E⟩'ιουδ⟨έ⟩ων τῶν καὶ θεοσεβ⟨ίο⟩ν), as could proselytes (τῶν σεβομένων προσηλύτων, Acts 13.43). But 'the specific name or title of a group of Gentile "sympathizers" is far less important than the question concerning evidence from this period which might indicate that Jewish communities of the Diaspora had included such a group of Gentiles in their life and worship' (J. Andrew Overman, 'The God-fearers: Some Neglected Features', *JSNT* 32 [1988], p. 22). Such evidence is abundant. For references and discussion see Louis H. Feldman, 'Jewish "Sympathizers" in Classical Literature and Inscriptions', *TAPA* 81 (1950), pp. 200-208; F. Siegert, 'Die "Gottesfürchtige" und Sympathisanten', *JSJ* 4 (1973), pp. 109-64; Emil Schürer, *The History of the Jewish People in the Age of Jesus Christ*, rev. and ed. G. Vermes, F. Millar, M. Goodman (Edinburgh: T. & T. Clark, 1985), III, pp. 150-76, esp. pp. 166-72; John G. Gager, *The Origins of Anti-Semitism* (New

Paul can presuppose that his Gentile audiences have a substantial acquaintance with the Septuagint precisely because
they have come out of the synagogue. As Schmithals himself
admits, however, even the powerful attractions of Judaism
and Judaizing[1] could not persuade the vast majority of Gentile
sympathizers to the ultimate commitment to Judaism. Such
enlightened pagans, in Schmithals' view, would have found
Gentile Christianity attractive precisely because it allowed
them to embrace all that they found attractive in Judaism
without becoming Jews,[2] and without enduring the second-

York: Oxford University Press, 1985), pp. 67-88; Overman, 'God-
fearers'. It is clearly inaccurate, however, to characterize these
'God-fearers' as a regularized class of 'semi-proselytes' or 'semi-
converts', despite that idea's popularity (so recently Lawrence
Schiffman, *Who Was a Jew? Rabbinic and Halakhic Perspectives on
the Jewish-Christian Schism* [Hoboken: KTAV, 1986], p. 37; see
against it G.F. Moore, *Judaism in the First Centuries of the
Christian Era: The Age of the Tannaim* [Cambridge, Mass.:
Harvard University Press, 1927-1930], I, pp. 339-40). There is no
evidence that ancient Judaism anywhere held out an alternative,
more 'open', 'lenient', or 'relaxed' standard of covenant
membership for Gentiles (Schürer, *History*, III, p. 169; Käsemann,
Romans, p. 72; John Nolland, 'Uncircumcised Proselytes?', *JSJ* 12.2
[1981], pp. 173-94; John Collins, *Between Athens and Jerusalem:
Jewish Identity in the Hellenistic Diaspora* [New York: Crossroad,
1983], p. 167). To speak as does Martin Hengel (*Judaism and
Hellenism*, trans. John Bowden [Philadelphia: Fortress, 1975], I,
p. 313) of Judaism having to 'stoop to constant and ultimately
untenable compromises' regarding Gentiles is tendentious. The
celebrated account of Izates, king of Adiabene (Josephus, *Ant.* 20.34-
48), is the exception that proves the rule, for Izates demurred from
circumcision on purely political grounds; his Jewish instructor,
Ananias, supported this decision out of fear that if Izates converted
publicly, he himself might be blamed (by the king's subjects) for the
king's 'unseemly practices'. We can hardly gather from this story
that 'one might become a Jew in a lesser degree without being circumcised' (L. Feldman, 'The Omnipresence of the God-fearers',
BAR 12.5 [1986], p. 61; *pace* Nolland, 'Uncircumcised Proselytes?').

1 Schmithals (*Römerbrief*, p. 73) lists among these attractions Jewish
belief in one creator God, the 'rein geistige' conception of God, the
Mosaic *moral* law, and Judaism's renowned antiquity. See also
Schürer, *History*, III, pp. 153-76, and Gager, *Origins*, pp. 35-88.
2 Schmithals (*ibid.*, p. 75) declares that these Gentile adherents were
attracted to Jewish morality, familiar with Jewish eschatological
expectation, at home in the Old Testament, acquainted with the con-

class status accorded them by the Jewish claim to salvation-historical prominence which, Schmithals says, 'drove' the Godfearers into the church.[1] It is precisely this lucid and convincing characterization of converted Godfearers as those who enjoy the heritage of Judaism *without becoming Jews* that casts doubt on Schmithals' subsequent explanation of the 'double character' of Romans. He writes,

> Der Doppelcharakter des Römerbriefes wird von daher zunächst *grundsätzlich* verständlich. Die Gemeinde setzt sich aus ehemaligen Heiden zusammen, so dass Paulus ihre Glieder als Christen aus den Heiden ausdrücklich anreden kann. Zugleich aber sind diese Heiden in einem gewissen Masse vom Judentum beeinflusst, mit jüdischen Problemen befasst, durch jüdischen Ansichten gebunden, so dass prinzipiell begreiflich wird, wenn Paulus mit ihnen Fragen diskutiert, für die man jüdische Gesprächspartner voraussetzt.[2]

It is at just this point, where Schmithals must hypothesize some distinctly *Jewish animus* provoking Paul's 'debate with Judaism', that his discussion of 'Godfearers' and 'Jewish'-Gentile Christianity takes an unsatisfying turn. In order to explain the letter's 'double character', he postulates an ethnically *Gentile* congregation who, because of their earlier associations with the synagogue, continue to think like *Jews*.

This description of the letter's audience is as inconsistent with Schmithals' earlier discussion as it is historically improbable. To illustrate: Schmithals describes the content of chs. 1 – 11 as follows: 'Paulus bestreitet jeglichen Vorzug des Judentums angesichts der Glaubensgerechtigkeit. Der Weg zum eschatologischen Heil ist für ihn in keiner Weise mehr der Weg zum empirischen Judentum'.[3] But one may well ask why Paul should have had to tell *the Romans* this; for, accord-

cept of the Messiah; but were not willing to step outside of their social environment and their nation to become Jews; as Godfearers, they did not need to abandon their 'pagan' environment, and yet were able to enjoy what they valued of Judaism.
1 *Ibid.*, p. 75.
2 *Ibid.*, p. 83.
3 *Ibid.*, p. 84.

ing to Schmithals' own statements earlier in the study, precisely these assertions would have *attracted* the letter's readers to Gentile Christianity in the first place. Furthermore, it is curious that although Schmithals acknowledges a separate theme in chs. 9–11, i.e., Paul's warning that the Gentiles not gloat over an apparently defeated Israel, he insists that this theme is only a corollary to Paul's *main* argument, which is 'dass es keinen Vorzug des empirischen Israel mehr gibt'.[1] To explain why *this* message needs so urgently to be proclaimed to the Roman Christians, Schmithals relies on Klein's argument that the Roman community lacks the apostolic foundation that this exposition of Paul's 'universal' gospel is to provide, and then suggests that some, at least, of the former Godfearers in Rome have not fully broken with the synagogue, but are still under the influence of Jewish propaganda. Paul therefore writes to constitute them as an ἐκκλησία by informing them that 'empirical Israel' has lost its place in the history of salvation. As we have seen, however, this aspect of Schmithals' hypothesis cannot be supported from Romans.[2]

Schmithals' hypothesis of a 'Jewish'-Gentile Christianity in Rome, comprised of former adherents to the synagogue, has been endorsed by J. Christiaan Beker, who nevertheless rightly argues that the Roman congregation also included Jewish Christians.[3] Schmithals' concentrated argument for a single addressed readership is refracted in Beker's treatment into a 'convergence of motivations' and, one may add, of presumed audiences: Paul has his eye on the Jerusalem confrontation before him; he looks as well to future mission work in the west; past conflicts in Corinth and Galatia are on his mind, and his letter to the Galatians may have secured opponents there and in Jerusalem.[4] In contrast to Schmithals, Beker sees in ch. 14 direct evidence of ethnic tensions between Jewish and Gentile Christians in Rome, responsibility for which he lays squarely with the latter group. Paul may write

1 *Ibid.*
2 See n. 4 p. 27, n. 1 p. 29 above.
3 Beker, *Paul the Apostle*, pp. 74-76.
4 *Ibid.*, p. 73.

in part, then, to assist 'Jewish Christians who are being oppressed by Gentile Christians'.[1] But Beker does not exploit this insight, following instead the argument advanced by Kümmel: 'This cannot explain the whole letter... To the contrary, the main body of the letter confronts Judaism'.

In his discussion of a 'convergence of motivations', Beker locates the 'Judaism' confronted in Romans alternately in Jewish and Jewish-Christian opposition to Paul's mission (both earlier, in Corinth and Galatia, and anticipated, in Jerusalem); in the non-Christian synagogue;[2] in Jewish Christians in Rome; and in Jewish sentiments among recent Gentile converts from the synagogue (with Schmithals). This constellation of motives from Jerusalem, from Rome, from Galatia, and from within Paul himself impel the Apostle 'to contemplate the proper role of Judaism in salvation-history'.

To the extent that Beker endorses Schmithals' location of the Jewish *animus* behind Romans in a congregation of Gentile Christians who 'think like Jews', the preceding criticisms of Schmithals would apply to Beker's work as well. Beyond this, however, it must be asked whether Beker's proposal of a 'convergence of motivations' does not surrender what Schmithals has rightly tried to hold fast, namely, a *unified* understanding of the letter's argumentative coherence. To be sure, this does not preclude the possibility that more than one factor is at work in the rhetorical situation, or indeed that the audience contains more than one 'sub-audience'. One thinks, for example, of the diversity of groups specified in 1 Corinthians, and even within ch. 7 of that letter. On the other hand, Romans does not show the sort of clear

1 *Ibid.* p. 75. Beker's description (*ibid.*) of an aggressive, 'triumphalist' Gentile Christianity in Rome has the advantage, not shared by Schmithals' portrayal, of evident confirmation in the letter (Rom. 11.13, 17-24), and in fact is more consistent with what one would expect to find in a congregation of Schmithals' former 'Godfearers'. This picture is corroborated, as Beker briefly indicates, by the history of anti-Jewish rhetoric in early Christianity (cf. Beker's essay, 'The Faithfulness of God and the Priority of Israel in Paul's Letter to the Romans', *HTR* 79 [1896], pp. 15-16).

2 Beker (*Paul the Apostle*, p. 89) asks, 'If Paul's concern is the unity of Jewish and Gentile Christians in the church, why does he carry on a dialogue with synagogue Jews in Romans?'

shifts in argumentation that punctuate 1 Corinthians, and on any of the readings of the audience that Beker provides, we are left with the integrative problem discussed above with reference to 1.15-18.

This matter of the letter's rhetorical integrity, involving coherence across the 'hinges' that connect epistolary frame and letter body as well as the cohesiveness of the presumed audience addressed, appears particularly vexing for just those interpreters who, like Schmithals and Beker, locate the letter's target in Roman Christianity. Paul S. Minear, for example, finds no fewer than five distinct communities or 'cells' addressed in 14.1–15.13, and sections the rest of the letter into supporting argumentation aimed at one or another of these sub-audiences. Although this approach is attractive for anchoring the letter firmly in a historical situation, it can do so only by breaking up the letter into discrete chunks.[1] Thus, for example, Paul breaks off his address to all the Roman Christians in 1.1-17 and turns to one group, 'the weak', in 1.18–4.15. It is evident that the neatness of this approach is purchased at the cost of the letter's rhetorical coherence.

In his recent monograph Francis Watson has forwarded a sociological reading of Romans that has much in common with the preceding interpretations. Like Beker, Watson denies that 1.6 and 15 require a *Gentile*-Christian audience, and finds indications of Gentile-Jewish tension within Roman Christianity in chs. 14 and 15. He concludes, like Beker and Minear, that the letter does not have a single cohesive audience, and is written in part to reconcile antagonistic parties in Rome. Watson's treatment of the letter's purpose also effectively situates the letter's perceived anti-Jewish *animus*; Paul writes

> to defend and explain his view of freedom from the law (i.e.
> separation from the Jewish community and its way of life),
> *with the aim of converting Jewish Christians to his point of*

---

1 Minear, *Obedience of Faith*; see the responses by R.J. Karris, 'Romans 14.1–15.13 and the Occasion of Romans', and K.P. Donfried, 'False Presuppositions in the Study of Romans', in *The Romans Debate*, pp. 77ff, 125ff.

view so as to create a single 'Pauline' congregation in Rome. At the same time, he encourages Gentiles to be conciliatory towards their Jewish fellow-Christians, since the union for which Paul hopes will not be possible without a degree of tact and understanding on the part of the Gentile Christians.[1]

Despite Watson's claim to bring a new perspective to bear on Romans, his sociological reading raises many of the same questions about the letter's rhetorical coherence that have been discussed with regard to Klein, Schmithals, Beker, and Minear. These views may be seen to represent two sides of a dilemma: to insist on one cohesive audience–the Gentile Christians evidently addressed in 1.6, 13, and 15 (Schmithals)–can mean compromising the integrity of that audience (Gentile Christians think like Jews, except when they do not); on the other hand, to assign each section of the letter to a rhetorically appropriate audience may mean surrendering the letter's coherence (Beker, Minear, Watson).

It deserves note here that Watson has raised an additional question, what we should call that of rhetorical *plausibility*, in an important digression from his main argument. Contending that ch. 2 represents a 'denunciation of the Jewish view of the covenant' designed to move Jewish Christians to break out of the orbit of the Roman synagogue once and for all, Watson asks whether such a denunciation ' would have been convincing to the Roman Jewish Christians':

> This is an important point, because if the argument could be shown to be utterly unsuitable to such an audience, it would cast doubt on the present view of the purpose of Romans. It might be suggested that Rom 2 presents such a travesty of the authentic Jewish view of the covenant that it cannot have been intended as a serious argument for Jewish Christians.[2]

Watson's answer, that ch. 2 indicts especially Jewish *teachers*, and that just this indictment would have appealed to the

1 Francis Watson, *Paul, Judaism, and the Gentiles* (Cambridge: Cambridge University Press, 1986), p. 98; emphasis added.
2 *Ibid.*, p. 113; cf. pp. 113-15. See now W.S. Campbell, 'Did Paul Advocate Separation from the Synagogue? A reaction to Francis Watson: *Paul, Judaism, and the Gentiles: A Sociological Approach*', *SJT* 41 (1988), pp. 1-11.

Jewish Christian rank and file in Rome, seems frail support
for the weight Watson must put on ch. 2. But we are more
interested here in the question he has asked, not only because
rhetorical plausibility will be an important criterion for our
exegesis below, but also because it serves as an evaluative
principle with regard to other interpretations of Romans.

For example, in a series of essays Lloyd Gaston has insisted
that what Paul says about the Law in his letters to Gentile-
Christian congregations must be interpreted against the
background of what ancient Judaism said about the Law *'as it
relates to Gentiles'*.[1] This approach, insightful and fundamentally sound as it is, is flawed by Gaston's *presupposition* concerning the purpose of Romans. Rather than determine that
purpose exegetically, Gaston 'claims' that 'Paul's central theological concern'—in Romans as well as in other letters—'was
a positive justification of the status of Gentile Christians';[2] the
principal question yet to be determined is simply 'why other
Jews opposed his activities'. Following Gaston's lead, John
Gager seeks to delimit the contours of 'Paul's argument with
the Jews' in Romans without first establishing the letter's
intended audience or purpose exegetically; Gaston's general
characterization of the letter is accepted.[3] The result in both
cases is a dramatic reinterpretation of Paul's thought that
suffers from the lack of a corresponding exegetical reexami-
nation *of Paul's purposes in Romans*. Unquestionably innovative answers are being given to traditional questions ('what
was the nature of Paul's argument with Judaism') without

1 Lloyd Gaston, 'Paul and the Torah', in Alan T. Davies, ed., *Anti-
  Semitism and the Foundations of Christianity* (New York: Paulist,
  1979), p. 56, now in Gaston, *Paul and the Torah* (Vancouver: University of British Columbia Press, 1987), p. 23.
2 Gaston, *Paul and the Torah*, p. 32; again, in his essay on 'Abraham
  and the Righteousness of God', Gaston (*ibid.*, p. 57) declares that he
  'understands' this to be Paul's major theological concern; in yet
  another essay focusing on the exegesis of Romans (*ibid.*, p. 116),
  Gaston begins by positing that the 'inclusive πᾶς-language in
  Romans' should be understood 'to include the formerly excluded,
  namely, the Gentiles'. It is surprising that so monumental a reinterpretation of Paul as Gaston proposes is undertaken without more
  interest in determining the letter's purpose exegetically.
3 Gager, *Origins*, pp. 213-25, 247-64.

testing those traditional questions against a rhetorical-critical exegesis; and thus the prior, rhetorical question, what is the function of Paul's purported 'argument with Judaism' within the argumentation of *this* letter, is neglected.

One other treatment of the letter's audience, a recent essay by Daniel Fraikin, merits our attention because of its concentrated effort to describe a single, cohesive situation behind the letter. Like Schmithals and Beker, Fraikin holds that the warning in ch. 11 is peripheral to Paul's overall purpose in writing. The main thrust of Paul's argument is, as Fraikin rewrites 1.16, '*not only* the Jews *but also* the Gentiles'.[1] Fraikin understands 1.18–3.20 to function within the letter as 'an argument addressed to Jews, for the benefit of the Gentile Roman audience'. The 'complacent tirade against the Gentiles' in 1.18-32 is crafted to lure Paul's Jewish dialogue partner into an attitude of judgment against the Gentile, and then to lead 'the Jew, who has the law and who judges on its basis, to admit that he is in the same predicament as the Gentile before the judgment'.[2]

This interpretation, to be sure, has already been advanced by Beker, who contends that 1.18-32 and 2.17-29 are not equal indictments of Jew and Gentile. Rather Paul 'invites Jewish agreement with his description of [the Gentile] world and its vices because he intends to set a trap for the Jewish auditor: he is in the same condemnable condition before God as is the Gentile world in Jewish eyes'.[3] It is Fraikin, however, who more carefully spells out how such a 'trap' functions in a letter addressed *to Gentiles*:

> We are faced, then, with the interesting fact that Paul, in a discourse whose goal is to strengthen the Gentiles in the gospel, provides them with the arguments by which he would make his understanding of the gospel and its consequences credible to Jews. It is not simply that the theological categories used by Paul are Jewish (what other theological

---

1 Daniel Fraikin, 'The Rhetorical Function of the Jews in Romans', in *Anti-Judaism in Early Christianity 1: Paul and the Gospels*, ed. Peter Richardson with David Granskou (Waterloo: Wilfrid Laurier, 1986), p. 96; emphasis added.

2 *Ibid.*, p. 97.

3 Beker, *Paul the Apostle*, p. 79.

framework could we expect Paul to use?), but that it is important for the Gentiles that their position be credible in the eyes of Jews.[1]

Fraikin goes on to argue that the material in chs. 1–8 is provided to the Gentile Christians in Rome as a potential defense to be used against a hostile Judaism that 'would accuse the Gentiles, deny their inheritance as sons of Abraham, their being chosen and loved'.[2] Chapters 9–11 are added as an explanation not of Jewish rejection of the gospel per se, but of Jewish opposition to Gentile acceptance of the gospel.[3]

Fraikin's essay, like Schmithals', has the attraction of providing a single comprehensive explanation for the 'double character' of Romans. It is an improvement over Schmithals' treatment in that it more plausibly explains how Paul's 'dialogue with the Jew' in chs. 2–3 functions within a letter addressed to Gentiles, inasmuch as Fraikin does not require us to believe that Paul's Gentile audience will identify instinctively with the 'Jew' addressed in 2.17.

But against the view shared by Fraikin, Schmithals and Beker, one notes that there is no explicit evidence in Romans that Paul addresses Christians enthralled by the synagogue, or cowed by the impressive salvation-historical claims of Israel. On the contrary: Paul's warning in ch. 11, dispensed with as an incidental digression by Schmithals, presents a very different picture of the Gentile Christianity that Paul would address.[4] Far from being overwhelmed by Jewish claims of privilege, they run the risk, in Paul's estimation, of holding God's mercy in contempt by boasting of having 'replaced' Israel (cf. 11.17-24). In light of this *explicit*

---

1 Fraikin, 'Rhetorical Function of the Jews', p. 98.
2 *Ibid.*, p. 100.
3 'The rejection of the gospel and of Christians by Israel is a blow to the credibility of the movement, and is a special threat to the Gentile Christians' (*ibid.*, p. 102).
4 Thomas Schmeller (*Paulus und die 'Diatribe'* [Münster: Aschendorff, 1987], pp. 226-27) rightly states that, while there were 'probably' a number of former Godfearers in the Roman audience, 'dennoch dürften sie gegenüber Heidenchristen, die ohne vorangehenden Anschluss an das Judentum Christen wurden, die Ausnahme gewesen sei (vgl. bes. 6.19; 11.13-24, 25, 28, 31)'.

information about the audience Paul intends to persuade, and in the absence of definite evidence that the Roman Christians were tempted, as were the 'Judaizers' of Galatia, to defect to the synagogue, this part of Schmithals' hypothesis appears to be an elaborately argued but fundamentally flawed mirror-reading from what he takes to be the 'debate with Judaism' in chs. 1–8. Against Fraikin in particular: it would seem that Paul could easily have identified his theological essay as a defense to be offered to Jewish adversaries. Why did he not do so? Was he really more interested in his subject matter than in rhetorical clarity?

W.S. Campbell has objected to Schmithals' and Beker's view that the Gentile Christianity in Rome was characterized by a tendency to Judaize. He argues, to the contrary, that 'there is no question of back-sliding to the synagogue here—it is not too much Judaism that Paul fears but too little an appreciation of the Jewish roots of the church... There are [in Rome] no Judaizers, and therefore there is a lack of clarity [in modern interpretation] as to what Romans as a "Dialogue with Jews" really means.' In Campbell's view, the studies by Schmithals and Beker represent an attempt to take the letter's address to a Gentile-Christian audience seriously, without calling into question the perception of the letter as a debate with Judaism:

> It has been the tradition to see Romans as a polemic against Judaizers. When these disappear from the scene to be replaced by Jewish influenced Gentile Christians, the problem is how are we to explain the age old problem of the double character of Romans? It is apparently addressed to Gentile Christians but argues about Jewish themes in a Jewish manner. I suspect that Beker's designation of Romans as a dialogue with Judaism is designed to meet this problem.[1]

Beker's view of a convergence of motivations for Romans offers yet another way to understand the letter's double character by way of the question, what can the 'debate with Judaism' mean for the Gentile-Christian audience in Rome? By paraphrasing one of the dominant themes in Romans, Beker implies its relevance for these former Godfearers:

1 Campbell, 'Revisiting Romans', p. 8.

'Above all, what is the unity and continuity of salvation-history? Is the God of Christ a faithful or an arbitrary God? If he has ceased to be faithful to *Israel's* promises, how can he be trusted by the Gentiles?'[1] This suggests that Paul's 'debate with Judaism' is intended primarily to affirm God's faithfulness to the covenant with Israel, despite the apparent failure of the Jews, *for the sake of Gentile Christian readers* who might otherwise see in the Jewish 'failure' a threat to their own place in salvation history. In fact, Beker makes this suggestion explicit in a subsequent essay:

> It is essential for Paul to maintain the priority of the Jew in the gospel, not only for the sake of the Jew, but especially for the sake of the Christian. What is at stake is nothing less than the faithfulness of God. If it could be argued that God has rejected the people of the election, Israel, and that therefore God's promises to Israel have become null and void, how are the Gentiles to trust the confirmation of these promises to them through God's righteousness in Christ?[2]

But against Beker's view it must be pointed out that there is no evidence in the apostolic or post-apostolic period that Gentile Christians perceived the general Jewish rejection of the gospel to jeopardize *their own* place in the divine economy of salvation. On the contrary, the conviction that, by their obedience to Christ, Gentiles had come to occupy the favored position that the Jews, by their 'disbelief' in Jesus, had forfeited—the 'replacement' theory that has persisted throughout Christian history—arose very early in the Gentile mission,[3] and is in fact

---

1 Beker, *Paul the Apostle*, p. 77.
2 Beker, 'Faithfulness of God', p. 14. One may note that a comparable understanding of Gentile-Christian *anxiety* provoked by Israel's apparent salvation-historical failure has been read out of Lukan theology: see Hans Conzelmann, *The Theology of St. Luke*, trans. Geoffrey Buswell (Philadelphia: Fortress, 1961), p. 212; Nils Dahl, 'The Purpose of Luke–Acts', in *Jesus in the Memory of the Early Church* (Minneapolis: Augsburg, 1976), p. 95; idem, 'The Story of Abraham in Luke–Acts', *ibid.*, pp. 66-86.
3 On the 'replacement' theory in early Christianity see J. Gnilka, *Die Verstockung Israels: Isaias 6.9-10 in der Theologie der Synoptiker* (Munich: Kösel, 1961); Peter Richardson, *Israel in the Apostolic Church* (New York: Cambridge University Press, 1969); Marcel Simon, *Verus Israel: A Study of the Relations between Christians*

already the object of Paul's attack in Romans 11.13-32, as Beker himself affirms.[1]

Indeed, one of the most puzzling ironies in Romans scholarship is this determination on the part of scholars like Kümmel, Schmithals and Beker, who recognize Paul's warning against Gentile-Christian arrogance in this letter to a Gentile-Christian congregation, not only to deny this warning more than a peripheral role in the apostle's purposes, but to go on to hypothesize a Gentile-Christian audience in terms quite inconsistent with this warning; in such a way, that is, as to locate within this congregation some *Jewish* animus, antithetical to Paul's gospel of justification by faith.[2] In light of Beker's plea for the letter's situational contingency, the possibility presents itself that the theological position to which, in Beker's view, Paul is responding ('if [God] has ceased to be faithful to Israel's promises...') might be situated in a particular social context

and Jews in the Roman Empire, trans. H. McKeating (New York: Oxford University Press, 1986); W.H.C. Frend, *The Rise of Christianity* (Philadelphia: Fortress, 1984), pp. 119-60.

1 Beker, *Paul the Apostle*, pp. 74-75. Fraikin ('Rhetorical Function of the Jews', p. 101) writes that 'somehow, at some point, the rejection of the gospel by individual Jews or synagogues has led to the theological conclusion that Israel has rejected the gospel. It remained only to explain the 'fact'. The fact, of course, is the result of an interpretation. When it came about, and who is responsible for it, are difficult questions to answer, but that it should be considered a major theological event is clear'. This theological 'fact' is already 'one of the presuppositions' of Rom. 9–11.

2 Of course this generalization is not meant to deny differences between various reconstructions. Beker (*Paul the Apostle*, p. 76), for example, discusses Paul's argument 'for the sake of the [Gentile] Christian' without directly attributing such salvation-historical anxiety as we have described to the Christians in Rome (although this is the implication of his appeal to Schmithals. For his part, Schmithals (*Römerbrief*, p. 83) understands the Gentile-Christian diffidence in the face of Jewish claims to express itself in a propensity to Judaize. Other scholars have recognized the significance of Paul's warning against Gentile Christians, but without relating this concern to the theological argumentation in chs. 1–8 (cf. H.W. Bartsch, 'Die antisemitischen Gegner des Paulus im Römerbrief', in W. Eckert et al., eds., *Antijudaismus im Neuen Testament?* [Munich: Kaiser, 1967]; *idem*, 'Die historische Situation des Römerbriefes', *SE* 4/*TU* 102 [1968], pp. 282-91).

on Paul's missionary landscape. Beker has argued convincingly that Romans is a profound and eloquent response to the premise of Israel's rejection. Can that insight be coordinated with an understanding of the letter's Gentile-Christian audience? Campbell has pointed toward a solution in this direction. He protests that, although 'Judaizing Jewish Christians have virtually disappeared' from historical reconstructions of the letter's situation, 'there remains a tendency to replace these with Gentile Christians strongly under the influence of the synagogue. This tendency is an effort to explain the phenomenon that Romans reads like a dialogue with Jews or Judaism'. Campbell suggests that a start be made from the 'growing consensus, of which Beker is typical', that chs. 9–11 'are the climax of the discussion in the body of the letter', and that these chapters, which comprise an apology for Israel, are 'directed against Gentile Christian boasting... The apologetic nature of the letter, which Beker himself notes, points to a better solution'.[1]

It remains to be seen how Paul's arguments in chs. 1–8, where scholars have found the apostle's 'debate with Judaism', might be related to the apocalyptic admonition of ch. 11 in one cohesive rhetorical situation. Campbell calls into question the wide perception that in this section of the letter Paul addresses objections, real or anticipated, from *Jews* or *Jewish Christians*, and instead relates the implicit Christian audience of 6.1ff to the Gentile-Christian audience in ch. 11, asking whether 'Paul is opposing non-Jewish or not specifically Jewish misinterpretations of Christian life'. The same question is extended to ch. 3, where Paul may be 'taking up positions adopted by the Roman Gentile Christians'.[2]

Our examination of argumentation in chs. 2–3 in Chapter 2 will take up this hypothesis again. At this point it is appropriate to focus attention on the other pole of the 'double

1 Campbell, 'Revisiting Romans', p. 8; see *idem*, 'The Freedom and Faithfulness of God in Relation to Israel', *JSNT* 13 (1981), pp. 27–45; and Campbell's University of Edinburgh dissertation, 'The Purpose of Paul in the Letter to the Romans: A Survey of Romans 1–11 with Special Reference to Chapters 9–11'.
2 Campbell, 'Romans III', p. 31.

character' problem, the circumstances of the Christian congregation in Rome, and to set out what *can* be ascertained about the historical situation at the time the letter was written.

3. *The Historical Background of the Roman Christian Community*

In recent scholarship, the hypothesis has found wide support that tensions between Gentile and Jewish Christians in Rome in the wake of the return of Jews exiled under Claudius constitute at least part of the letter's historical context, although the extent to which those tensions can explain the letter's content is a matter of question. This aspect of the letter's situation can be related to one pole of the 'double character' problem.

Our sources allow us to sketch briefly the history of Judaism in ancient Rome as the context for the origins of Christianity there; Romans provides additional clues to the makeup of the Christian congregations addressed. It is therefore possible to establish, at least in a preliminary way, part of the historical context of the letter.

The origins of Judaism in Rome are obscure.[1] Outside of diplomatic embassies from the Hasmonean dynasty, Jews first appear in a confused reference to Jewish sojourners banished from Rome for proselytizing, around 139 BCE.[2] In any case a

---

1 For the history of Judaism in ancient Rome, see the discussion in Schürer, *History*, III, pp. 73-81; M. Stern, 'The Jewish Diaspora', in *The Jewish People in the First Century*, ed. S. Safrai and M. Stern (Philadelphia: Fortress, 1974), I, pp. 160-68; George LaPiana, 'Foreign Groups in Rome during the First Centuries of the Empire', *HTR* 20 (1927), pp. 341-93; and H.J. Leon, *The Jews of Ancient Rome* (Philadelphia: Jewish Publication Society of America, 1960); for the relation of that history to the nascent Christian congregations in Rome, Brown and Meier, *Antioch and Rome*, pp. 87-127; W. Wiefel, 'The Jewish Community in Ancient Rome and the Origins of Roman Christianity', in *The Romans Debate*, pp. 100-19.

2 Valerius Maximus, according to the epitomist Julius Paris, refers to the expulsion from Rome of Jews who 'attempted to contaminate the morals of the Romans with the worship of Jupiter Sabazius'. Obviously the Phrygian deity has been confused either with the Jewish Sabbath, or with the name Sabaoth; but it seems probable enough that Jewish sojourners were expelled from Rome for some

substantial Jewish comunity must have predated Pompey's triumphal return to Rome from his Judean campaign (61 BCE); for although it was Philo's later impression that most of the Jewish population of Rome were descendants of the slaves brought back in train (*Leg.* 155), only two years later (?) Cicero spoke of the Jews in his audience as a potent political presence in Rome (*Flac.* 67).[1] These early references reflect two persistent aspects of the Jewish community's high visibility in Rome: first, a fairly aggressive posture toward the surrounding culture, evident in perseverance in Jewish customs despite intermittent hostility, and in continued proselytizing activity (which met with substantial success in the early imperial period); second, an apparent high level of organization that allowed for remarkable consolidation and mobilization of the community at critical occasions.[2] Both aspects point

sort of religious propaganda, as is evident from a second epitome by Ianuarius Nepotianus (so Schürer, *History*, III, pp. 74-75). These propagandists are probably not to be related to Maccabean embassies to Rome in the first century BCE (Leon, *Jews*, pp. 2-4). Leon points out that the Jews were forced 'to go back to their own homes', and therefore were not native to Rome at any rate.

1 See Leon, *Jews*, 4-8; text and discussion in M. Stern, *Greek and Latin Authors on Jews and Judaism*, 3 vols. (Jerusalem: Israel Academy of Sciences and Humanities, 1974-1984), I, pp. 196-201.

2 The Jews of Rome collected funds for the Jerusalem Temple (Philo, *Leg.* 156-57); they may have helped secure the manumissions of their Judean brethren brought to the city as slaves by Pompey (Leon, *Jews*, p. 5); eight thousand of them supported the embassy from Judea asking that Archelaus be deposed (Josephus, *Wars* 2.80-81; *Ant.* 17.300-301). These concerted actions point to a level of organization transcending the local synagogue, as LaPiana ('Foreign Groups', p. 362) remarks: 'On general grounds a central organ of government coordinating the activities of the several synagogues, supervising the general administration, and having definite authority in financial and juridical matters, cannot have been lacking in Rome'. There is some debate, however, as to whether the various synagogues of Rome shared a common central organization, or whether the γερουσιάρχαι that appear in Jewish catacomb inscriptions from Rome represented members of a central Roman γερουσία, or only of a local institution within each synagogue. LaPiana (*ibid.*, pp. 361-64) considers an inscription referring to an '*archon alti ordinis*' and two referring to archons πάσης τῆς τιμῆς (τειμῆς) evidence of officers of a pan-Roman γερουσία; but this evidence is hardly compelling (against LaPiana's view see

to a secure Jewish identity that must frequently have irritated Gentile observers.[1]
From the beginning, the Jews enjoyed friendly relations with the Caesar. It is a safe conjecture that in the civil war in 49 BCE the Jews of Rome favored Julius Ceasar against Pompey, who after all had subdued Jerusalem.[2] After his victory Caesar rewarded the Jews for their support with decrees guaranteeing them privileges unique in the Roman empire: free assembly for worship and common ritual meals, fredom to collect funds for the Temple in Jerusalem, and the guaranteed sanctity of the Sabbath, which involved exemption from military service and special dispositions for civil cases.[3]

the discussions in Leon, *Jews*, pp. 174-76, and Schürer, *History*, III, pp. 95-107). An inscription for a γραμμ[ατεὺς] Σεκηνῶν has been interpreted as a reference to the scribe for a 'council of elders', the Greek Σεκηνῶν representing the Hebrew *zekanîm*; but this is doubtful (LaPiana, 'Foreign Groups', p. 357 n. 27; Leon, *Jews*, pp. 150-51). Yet another inscription refers to an ἀρχιγερουσιάρχης (Schürer, *History*, III, p. 98). Could this have been the chair of a pan-Roman council of γερουσιάρχαι?

1 Schürer (*History*, III, pp. 131-32) emphasizes the Jews' special privileges as objects of Gentile resentment, a sentiment that probably determined much of the atmosphere in which Diaspora Jews lived. On pagan attitudes toward Judaism in general, see *ibid.*, III, pp. 150-53, 594-616 (on pagan opponents); Gager, *Origins*; M. Stern, *Greek and Latin Authors*; and *idem*, 'The Jews in Greek and Latin Literature', in *The Jewish People*, II, pp. 1101-59.

2 Cicero implies that the Jews supported the 'popular' party in Rome, from which Caesar would draw his power; Caesar also received military aid from the Hasmonean dynasty in Syria and Judea, and from the Jews of Egypt (discussion in Leon, *Jews*, p. 8).

3 Josephus, *Ant.* 14.185-216; 16.160-79; see Schürer, *History*, III, pp. 116-23. Not for nothing did the Jews of Rome mourn Caesar's death (Suetonius, *Iul.* 84); yet their privileges survived him, being renewed by senatorial decree (Josephus, *Ant.* 14.217-67). Augustus and his son-in-law, Marcus Agrippa, affirmed these privileges, and extended the additional privilege of securing for the Jews their portion in free distributions of oil or grain when these happened to fall on the Sabbath. M. Agrippa also supported the Jewish communities of Greece and Egypt against local persecutions; and both men showed honor to the God of the Jews by making sacrifice at the Temple in Jerusalem (Philo, *Leg.* 155-57; Josephus, *Ant.* 16.14-15). The Jews of Rome apparently honored these benefactors by dedicating a synagogue to each: tomb inscriptions refer to synagogues of

During the Augustan age the Jews and their practices, particularly proselytizing and the Sabbath, drew mention in Latin literature.[1] In general these references are derogatory, but not hostile, and John Gager points out that positive remarks in some other pagan authors correlate well with the widespread enthusiasm for Jewish ways in Roman circles, although Jewish proselytizing activity in Rome may have been more significant for the height to which it reached than for its breadth of appeal.[2]

The Jewish community fared less well under Tiberius, largely because of the machinations of Sejanus who, according to Philo, sought to destroy the Jews (*Leg.* 159-60), and whose policies may have been related to sterner measures in Judea. When in a period of Jewish proselytizing activity four Jewish con-men swindled a Roman noblewoman, wife of a Roman senator and a proselyte to Judaism (προσεληλυθυῖαν τοῖς Ἰουδαϊκοῖς), on the pretext of collecting funds for the Temple in Jerusalem, the imperial reaction was to send four thousand young Jewish men under conscription to Sardinia.[3] Mary Smallwood has argued that the decree must have been provoked by a broader range of proselytizing activities.[4] The exiles were presumably allowed to return after Sejanus' death in 31 CE.

We have no information about the response of Jews in Rome to Gaius Caligula's decree that his statue should be set up in the Temple (Philo, *Leg.* 35-42), or to the Jewish embassy

---

the Αὐγουστησίων and of the Ἀγριππησίων (inscriptions in Leon, *Jews*, nos. 365, 425, 503, 284, 301, 338, 368, 416, 496; discussions in *ibid.*, pp. 140-42; LaPiana, 'Foreign Groups', pp. 352-55; Schürer, *History*, III, pp. 95-98).

1 Leon, *Jews*, pp. 12-14, citing Horace, *Sat.* 1.4.140-43; 1.9.67-72; Tibullus, 1.3.18; Ovid, *Rem. Am.* 219-20; *Ars Am.* 1.76, 1.415-16; and Suetonius, *Aug.* 76.2.
2 Gager, *Origins*, pp. 67-88; cf. Leon, *Jews*, pp. 15-16.
3 Leon, *Jews*, 17-20; Schürer, *History*, III, pp. 75-76; compare the accounts in Josephus, *Ant.* 18.81-84, Tacitus, *Ann.* 2.85.4, Dio Cassius, *History*, 57.18.5, and Suetonius, *Tib.* 36.
4 'Jews Under Tiberius', *Latomus* 15 (1956), pp. 314-29; *idem*, *The Jews under Roman Rule* (Leiden: Brill, 1976), pp. 202-10. Smallwood points to Dio Cassius' indication that the Jews 'were converting many of the natives to their ways' (*History*, 57.18.5).

from Alexandria, which Philo himself headed, petitioning redress of grievances from their Greek neighbors (*Leg.* 44-45). The next event of significance for our purposes comes during the reign of Claudius. Claudius succeeded Gaius with the help of Agrippa, whom he immediately installed as king of Judea in a spectacular ceremony in Rome (Josephus, *Ant.* 19.274-75). These auspicious beginnings would have heralded a time of peace for the Roman Jews, but for two aggravating factors: Jewish unrest in Alexandria, which Claudius put down with a stern warning,[1] and the agitation of Christian propagandists within the synagogues of Rome itself. According to Suetonius' report in *Claud.* 25.4, Claudius 'expelled from Rome the Jews who caused a tumult at the instigation of Chrestus' (*Iudaeos impulsore Chresto assidue tumultuantes Roma expulit*). This report is now widely accepted as an indication of Christian agitation within Roman Judaism.[2] We do not know how or when these first Christians came to Rome:[3] we only know that they were Jews, and that

---

1 Leon relates a recently discovered rescript from Claudius to the Alexandrian Jews, warning them not to 'stir up a general plague throughout the world', to disturbances among the Jews in Rome (*Jews*, 26).

2 For discussions see Leon, *Jews*, pp. 23-27; Schürer, *History*, III, pp. 77-78; Stern, 'Jewish Diaspora', pp. 164-65; *idem*, *Greek and Latin Authors*, II, pp. 115-16; G. Lüdemann, *Paul, Apostle to the Gentiles: Studies in Chronology*, trans. F.S. Jones (Philadelphia: Fortress, 1984), pp. 164-70.

3 Brown rightly rejects the suggestion that Peter may have brought Christianity to Rome (*Antioch and Rome*, pp. 102-103). We should then expect Paul at least to mention his fellow apostle when he writes to the Roman congregations. Two other suggestions are equally possible, and equally unprovable. Although it is certainly only a conjecture that some of the 'Jews and proselytes, visitors from Rome' mentioned in Acts 2.10-11 may have believed in Jesus and then found their way back to Rome, Brown brushes this aside as 'sheer imagination' since 'those described in the list... were *resident* at Jerusalem' (*ibid.*, p. 104 n. 215). To be precise, rather, Acts describes many Diaspora 'inhabitants' (κατοικοῦντες) of Jerusalem; the Romans (alone) are described as 'sojourners' (ἐπιδημοῦντες). It is also perfectly conceivable that the Jerusalem church might have sponsored missionaries to Rome (like Andronicus and Iunia, whom Paul names in Rom. 16.7 as 'preeminent among the apostles, before me in Christ'); Brown's

48   *The Rhetoric of Romans*

their message stirred up considerable controversy within the synagogues, perhaps because of its potentially subversive character.[1] Claudius' action was apparently to banish from Rome the chief troublemakers (i.e., the Christians).[2]

> objection, that we should expect to read about such a mission in Acts (pp. 103-104), does not take into account the possibility that the author of Acts is concerned to make Paul appear to be the first Christian preacher in Rome (cf. Acts 28.21-22). Brown also argues for a strong Jewish 'Jerusalem-Rome axis' based on the political liaisons between imperial Rome and the Hasmonean and Herodian dynasties; but this would seem to be beside the point here. Further, the 'confirmation' of a Jerusalem-Rome connection found in Ambrosiaster's statement that the Romans received Christianity *'ritu licet Iudaico'* (pp. 110-11) would easily be explained as a late inference from the text of Romans. Thus, although the Jewish character of earliest Roman Christianity is apparent enough, the *origins* of the movement cannot be pinpointed. We are ultimately left with Romans itself as our primary evidence regarding the character of Christianity in Rome.
>
> 1 LaPiana ('Foreign Groups', pp. 374-75) notes that our sources give no indication that 'the Jews of Rome, though so numerous, embarrassed the government', even during critical periods, including the Judean war. It may be that the Roman synagogues, sensitive to their precarious position beneath the seat of empire (*ibid.*, p. 362), cultivated the sort of deferential decorum toward the emperor that finds expression in Rom. 13.1-7, and that as a rule, currents that might have disturbed that delicate equilibrium were carefully restrained.
>
> 2 A parallel report by Dio Cassius insists that Claudius did *not* banish the Jews, but rather revoked their right to assemble (*History* 60.6.6); Acts for its part says that Claudius banished 'all the Jews' (πάντας τοὺς Ἰουδαίους, 18.2). Attempts to harmonize these conflicting accounts as accurate reports of different stages in a single sequence of events (compare the treatments in n. 95) are less attractive methodologically than a literary-critical approach, the results of which may be summarized as follows. Suetonius' language, specifically the participle *tumultuantes*, can be taken in a broad or a narrow sense; Dio Cassius seems to take pains to refute the broader interpretation, i.e., that Claudius expelled 'the Jews, who were rioting', when he declares 'he did not expel them' (οὐκ ἐξήλασε μεν). Taken in the narrow sense, Suetonius' report would indicate the expulsion of (only) 'those Jews who were making a tumult', presumably the Christian propagandists; and this is probably what happened. Acts 18.2 supports the broader interpretation of Suetonius' report: Claudius had ordered 'all the Jews' out of Rome. But rather than to harmonize these accounts or to hypothesize cor-

After the expulsion of some Christian Jews from the synagogues of Rome, the Christian community there enters a
tunnel, lost to our sight, and reemerges only with Paul's letter
to a *Gentile*-Christian community. We are pretty much in the
dark as to what happened in the interval, and must rely on
reasoned conjecture.

Two of the persons greeted in ch. 16, which has now been
shown to be an integral part of Paul's letter,[1] are Prisca and
Aquila, who appear in Acts 18.2 as exiles under the Claudian
edict; they have apparently returned to Rome after the edict
was rescinded. Paul names other Jewish acquaintances in
Rome,[2] but whether any of them were also among the
Claudian exiles cannot be answered. The Roman congregations[3] apparently include a number of Gentile converts. One
such is Epainetos, identified as 'my beloved, first fruit of Asia in
Christ' (16.5). It is tempting to try to discern other converts
from Paul's choice of epithets; but definite correlations are
elusive.[4] In any case, Paul's explicit address of this letter to

rupted sources, it seems preferable to recognize that the author of
Acts has a vested interest in bringing Paul to Rome before a Jewish
audience that is relatively uninformed, and therefore receptive,
regarding Christianity (28.21-22). To report that *all* the Jews had
been banished from Rome (18.2), even if a complete fabrication, suits
his purposes beter than admitting that *Christian* Jews had been
banished for causing disturbances within synagogues.

1 Gamble, *Textual History*.
2 Maria, 16.6, must be Jewish; Andronicus and Iunia in 16.7 and
Herodion in 16.11 are explicitly identified as such.
3 At least three distinct house churches are indicated in 16.5, 14, and
15.
4 Cranfield suggests only that 'Paul seems to have tried to attach
some expression of kindly commendation to all the individuals he
mentions', having lapsed only at v. 14 (*Romans*, II, pp. 786-87): an
epithet like 'beloved', then, would in no way distinguish persons so
described from others. On the other hand, it may be significant that
Epainetos, the first convert (ἀπαρχή) in Asia, is called Paul's 'own
beloved' (ἀγαπητόν μου, 16.5), while Paul does *not* use this epithet for
people who have worked beside him as equals (Prisca and Aquila,
16.3; Urbanus, 16.9), or have supported him (Phoebe, who has acted
as Paul's patron [προστάτις], 16.2), or are his seniors in Christ
(Andronicus and Iunia, 16.7). In other letters, Paul uses the term
'beloved' to address his own converts as his 'children' (1 Cor. 4.14;
cf. 10.14, 15.58; Phil. 2.12). It is linked with conversion: Onesimus

those 'among the Gentiles, called of Jesus Christ' (1.6) indicates that he can think of his audience collectively as pagan converts.

It is reasonable to suppose that the Christian gospel had attracted Gentile as well as Jewish adherents from the beginning, *within the synagogues.* As we have seen, Gentile interest in Judaism in Rome was considerable, and 'Judaizing' proclivities had penetrated the imperial household.[1] The more than 500 Jewish epitaphs of Rome include seven proselytes[2] and one woman identified as *'theosebes'*; that this Greek word is used in a Latin inscription may indicate its use in a technical sense.[3] The pattern of Christian mission in Acts indicates a broad positive response from Gentile Godfearers within the synagogues.[4] It seems probable that Gentile adherents to

---

has *become* a 'beloved brother' to Philemon (Phlm. 16); Philemon himself, whom Paul addresses as 'beloved' (v. 1), is apparently Paul's convert (v. 19); the Thessalonians *became* Paul's beloved when they responded to his evangelization (1 Thess. 2.8, ἀγαπητοὶ ... ἐγενήθητε). This data hardly justifies the conclusion that Paul uses the word ἀγαπητός as a cipher for 'convert'. But beyond the correlation in Epainetos' case, the fact that others identified as 'Paul's beloved' (Ampliatos, Rom. 16.8; Stachys, 16.9; and Persis, 16.11) are apparently neither his co-workers, nor Jewish believers, is at least negative evidence for such a hypothesis.

1 Augustus himself boasted of observing the Sabbath fast (!) more faithfully than any Jew (Suetonius, *Aug.* 76.2; Leon, *Jews*, 13). The close ties between the Caesars and the Herodian dynasty extended to having the Jewish kings educated in Rome, sometimes within the emperor's household. Josephus suggests that Nero's wife Poppaea was sympathetic to Judaism (in *Ant.* 20.195 he calls her θεοσεβής; cf. *Life* 3; but see E. Mary Smallwood, 'The Alleged Jewish Tendencies of Poppaea Sabina', *JTS* 10 [1959], pp. 329-55).

2 Leon, *Jews*, pp. 253-56.

3 Inscription #228 in Leon, *Jews*: '*hic posita Epar | chia theose | bes que [v]i | xit annos LV | d(ies) VI dorm[i]tio tua in b[onis?].*' The word *metuens* on other Roman epitaphs may (LaPiana, 'Foreign Groups', p. 391) or may not have any connection with Judaism; the connection is clear in Juvenal, *Sat.* 14.96-196. On the question of 'Godfearers' see the literature cited above. The single inscription from a Jewish catacomb is slim evidence of 'Godfearers' in Roman synagogues; but we should be surprised that even one Gentile finds burial within a Jewish catacomb (if that is indeed what the inscription indicates).

4 Cf. Acts 13.43, 48; 16.14-15; 17.4, 12, 17; 18.7.

Judaism were among the first Romans to 'call upon the name Jesus Christ'.

Wolfgang Wiefel's suggested reconstruction of this interim period carries conviction. After the Claudian edict prohibiting assemblies in the synagogues, the Christians left in Rome, the majority of whom probably were Gentiles, would have been able to assemble only in private homes, no longer in the synagogue. It is reasonable to assume that careful observance of the Jewish Law would quickly have become dispensable for these Christians;[1] moreover, Wiefel argues that this predominantly *Gentile* Christianity would have developed within an atmosphere of strong anti-Jewish sentiment in the city.[2] The subsequent return of Jewish Christians like Prisca and Aquila and their efforts to reconstruct a communal life oriented around Torah observance undoubtedly generated tensions.

Wiefel continues: 'From this emerges the possibility of specifying the *Sitz-im-Leben* of Romans: it was written to assist the Gentile Christian majority, who are the primary addressees of the letter, to live together with the Jewish Christians in one congregation, thereby putting an end to their quarrels about status'.[3] Paul's positive statements about Israel in Romans 9–11 are aimed, in part, 'at elevating the stature of Jewish Christians in the eyes of Gentile Christians to work against the formers' low esteem on account of their Jewish heritage'. The apostle avoids 'following the trend of anti-Jewish senti-

---

1 Wiefel's remark that 'the creation of these semi-legal house churches eliminated the Jewish element which previously had been rooted in the synagogue assembly' ('Jewish Community', p. 113) seems too strong.

2 *Ibid.*, pp. 115-19. John Gager (*Origins*, pp. 63-88) makes an impressive case that the literary sources (e.g., Tacitus) usually taken to reveal a perennial Roman anti-Judaism actually reflect the traditionalist and conservative sentiments of senatorial circles in the late first and early second centuries CE, and are politically oriented; and that Judaism nevertheless continued to enjoy a widespread popularity throughout this period. Indications of interest in Judaism notwithstanding, however, we should probably envision a stereotyped portrait of Judaism as a 'barbarous superstition' (Cicero, *pro Flacco*), and a corresponding reservoir of anti-Jewish sentiment in the city that could be tapped by a shrewd public figure like Cicero— or Nero.

3 Wiefel, 'Jewish Community', p. 103.

ment in this city, and thus turning Christianity into an anti-Jewish movement'.[1]

The hypothesis that Romans is addressed, in part, to actual ethnic and religious tensions between Jewish and Gentile Christians within the Roman congregations has received considerable treatment in recent years. Discussion has been focused in particular on the paraenesis in 14.1–15.13 and on Paul's discussion of Israel's place in salvation history in chs. 9–11.

H.W. Bartsch has suggested that the Jewish Christians who returned to Rome after Claudius' expulsion of Jews were unable to find kosher butchers in the city, and for that reason 'ate only vegetables' (cf. 14.2). The controversy between 'strong' and 'weak' in chs. 14–15 is to be understood, then, as a direct result of the return of Jewish Christians ('the weak') to a city and to a Gentile-Christian community ('the strong') that no longer accommodate their observance of *kašrût*.[2] Paul Minear understands various segments of Romans to be addressed to several different parties in Roman Christianity, identifying the 'strong' and 'weak' in chs. 14–15 in particular as Gentile and Jewish Christians, respectively.[3] J. Christiaan Beker concludes from chs. 14–15 that 'in first-century Rome the Gentile majority felt that it was in a superior position over the Jewish Christian section of the church. Therefore, the apostle to the Gentiles (Rom. 1.5) must warn Gentile Christians against pride'. One of Paul's purposes in Romans is to assist 'Jewish Christians who are being oppressed by Gentile Christians'.[4]

Yet other scholars have expressed doubt that the 'weak' and 'strong' in these chapters have actual referents, and that these terms refer specifically to Jewish and Gentile Christians. Objections to the view represented by Bartsch, Minear and Beker can be synthesized as follows:

(a) The 'weak' referred to in Rom. 14.2 'eats only vegetables'. Ernst Käsemann, among others, holds that this

1 *Ibid.*, p. 119.
2 Bartsch, 'Antisemitischen Gegner'; 'Historische Situation'.
3 Minear, *Obedience of Faith*.
4 Beker, *Paul the Apostle*, p. 75.

cannot refer to orthodox Jewish dietary observances, since 'general abstinence from meat and wine is not found there'.[1] To phrase the objection negatively, Jewish observance would require the avoidance only of meat offered to idols and of libation-wine; but the abstinence of 14.2 is not so discriminating.

(b) There is no evidence before chs. 14 and 15 for parties of 'weak' and 'strong' within Roman Christianity, which suggests that this theme is not paramount among Paul's concerns.[2]

(c) The language of 'weak' and 'strong' may be better explained as a paraenetic generalization of the exhortations worked out concretely in Paul's correspondence with Christians in Corinth (1 Cor. 8, 10).[3] But there—so the objection continues—the issue is not Jewish kašrût, but the tender consciences of converts from paganism who still (wrongly) perceive the eating of meat offered to an idol as participation in the power of the god.[4]

(d) The reference to both 'circumcision' and 'Gentiles' in 15.7-9 cannot be made the key to the identities of 'weak' and 'strong' in 14.1–15.6, either because the reference has only a general, exemplary significance (Karris), or because it is part of a later interpolation (Schmithals).[5]

1 Käsemann, Romans, p. 367; cf. Kümmel, Introduction, pp. 310-11.
2 Beker ('Paul's Theology: Consistent or Inconsistent?') declares it 'curious, if not unintelligible' that within the letter, 'concrete problems' surface only at Rom. 14–15, suggesting that Paul had at best limited or indirect knowledge of the Roman situation.
3 Bornkamm, Paul, pp. 93-94; idem, 'The Letter to the Romans as Paul's Last Will and Testament', in The Romans Debate, pp. 22-23.
4 See Max Rauer, Die 'Schwachen' in Korinth und Rom nach den Paulusbriefen, BT 120 (Freiburg: Herder, 1923).
5 Relying on the work of Bornkamm and Rauer (see previous notes), Robert J. Karris ('Romans 14.1–15.13 and the Occasion of Romans', in The Romans Debate, pp. 93-95) contends that the discussion in Romans is abstracted and generalized from that in 1 Cor. 8 and 10, and thus cannot be used to describe actual circumstances in the Roman community. Walter Schmithals (Römerbrief, pp. 95-96) argues that 15.7-9 must be an interpolation, since Rom 14.1–15.6 address actual differences of sensibility and practice between more conservative ('weak') and more liberal ('strong') converted God-fearers; therefore there cannot be any Jewish Christians in Rome.

The first objection is simply inaccurate. Even if 'Jewish orthodoxy' is taken, on dubious grounds, to refer quite narrowly to the confines of *Mishnah 'Aboda Zara*, the *halakot* of that tractate alone make it clear that observant Jews who could not control the foodstuffs available in the marketplace would be restricted to a diet of vegetables, and only a limited selection of these, not out of an extreme asceticism, but as a reasonable response to circumstances.[1] Moreover the picture of Jewish piety offered in the literature of the Hellenistic Diaspora includes the general abstinence from meat and wine.[2]

Bartsch may be right in suggesting that Jews returning from exile under Claudius would have been reduced to vegetarianism because the disruption of Jewish life in the city had made it difficult to procure kosher meats, although Bartsch apparently envisions a disturbance of larger scale than we consider probable.[3] Securing kosher foods in the marketplace was frequently a real concern to Jews throughout the Diaspora.[4] Of particular relevance for Rome at this time is Josephus' report that while Felix was procurator of Judea (52–60 CE), Jewish priests were sent under arrest to Caesar, and were able to observe *kašrût* only by subsisting on figs and nuts (*Life*, 3). It may also be significant that, in his third satire, the Roman Juvenal apparently ridicules Jewish vegetarian-

---

1 The tractate elaborates the requirements of a basic principle: to avoid being 'constructively guilty of joining in a sacrificial meal, an act of "heathenism"' (Moore, *Judaism*, II, p. 75). There is no reason to speak of a superstitious fear of demonic 'infection' (*contra* C.K. Barrett, 'Things Sacrificed to Idols', *Essays on Paul* [Philadelphia: Westminster, 1982], p. 52). Rather the *de facto* vegetarianism of Rom. 14.2 would be the proper Jewish response to a pagan marketplace (cf. Schmithals, *Römerbrief*, p. 102 [on the less rigorous requirements of the Apostolic Decree]; Paul Billerbeck, *Kommentar zum Neuen Testament aus Talmud und Midrasch* [Munich: Beck, 1926], III, p. 307).
2 Cf. Dan. 1.3-16; Esth. 3.28, 14.17; Jud. 12.1-2.
3 See n. 111 above.
4 Against Kümmel (*Introduction*, p. 311, n. 13), who declares Bartsch's suggestion 'picked out of thin air'. On the contrary: Josephus' collection of decrees granting civic rights to Jewish populations (*Ant.* 14.185-267) shows that such rights often included specific provisions for the marketplace (see 14.226; 245; 261; and Schürer, *History*, III, p. 116).

ism.[1] We conclude that the practice described in Rom. 14.2 may readily be understood as scrupulous Jewish observance in an antagonistic environment, such as may have obtained at least in parts of the city.

Nor should we be surprised to find such observance described, from the Gentile (and Gentile-Christian) perspective, as 'weakness': for so Horace describes even Gentile regard for Jewish scruple.[2] Comparison with the pagan scruples behind 1 Cor. 8 and 10 is therefore unnecessary, except insofar as both letters address the problem of eating εἰδωλόθυτον. There is no reason to neutralize other references in Romans to differences between Jew and Gentile (14.14, 20, 15.8), since these are quite germane to the issue in 14.1-2.

It is nevertheless the case that the paraenesis here is less concrete than that in 1 Corinthians. There are no definite indications that Paul is responding on the basis of precise knowledge of circumstances in Rome.[3] A cautious conclusion would be that Paul's warnings need spring from nothing

1 The character Umbricius has been assailed by a 'madman' who apparently takes him for a Jew: '"Where are you from?" shouts he; "whose vinegar, whose beans have blown you out? With what cobbler have you been munching cut leeks and boiled wether's chaps?— What sirrah, no answer? Speak out, or take that upon your shins! Say, where is your [begging] stand? In what prayer-house [*proseucha*] shall I find you?"' (G.G. Ramsay's translation in Loeb; see Stern, *Greek and Latin Authors*, II, pp. 98-99).

2 *Sermones* 1.9. Horace, hoping to escape a bore, tries to engage a passing acquaintance in conversation:

'Surely you said that there was something you wanted to tell me in private'.
'I mind it well, but I'll tell you at a better time. Today is the thirtieth day, a Sabbath. Would you affront the circumcised Jews?'
'I have no scruples'.
'But I have. I am a somewhat weaker brother, one of the many. You will pardon me; I'll talk another day'.

(Text and discussion in Stern, *Greek and Latin Authors*, I, pp. 324-25).

3 Compare the wealth of such indications in 1 Corinthians: ἐδηλώθη... μοι, 1.11; ἀκούεται, 5.1; περὶ... ὧν ἐγράψατε, 7.1, 7.25, 8.1; ἀκούω, 11.18), although Paul's coworkers in Rome (16.1-15) could well have kept him informed of significant developments (cf. Beker, *Paul the Apostle*, p. 74).

more than the presumption that circumstances in the Roman congregation are no better or worse than in other ethnically mixed congregations. His paraenesis is directed not to correct wrongdoers (the commendations in 1.8 and 15.14 suggest the opposite), but to *prevent* the sort of offense that Paul has seen in other Gentile-Christian congregations, and that he might reasonably expect could arise in Rome as well. His fairly irenic tone is an index not of his timidity (*pace* Käsemann), but of his temerity in imposing on the Romans a *prophylaxis* more broadly intended to protect the sanctity of the worldwide 'offering of the Gentiles' (cf. 15.15-16).

Paul's main target in this paraenesis, as in the letter opening (1.6, 13, 14-15), appears to be Gentile Christians. The exhortation in 14.1 is addressed to them; and although in the amplification in 14.2-12, neither party in the dispute is to despise or judge the other (14.2-4), this is especially directed to the strong.[1] The recapitulation in 14.3 contrasts the 'judgment' of another with the 'judgment' not to set a stumbling-block or offense before the brother, clearly an admonition directed to the strong, who have it within their power so to harm the weak by eating suspect food in their presence. Paul agrees with the strong that the distinction κοινός-καθαρός does not apply, *except* in regard to the brother (14.14, 20); it is nevertheless out of concern for the brother that the strong are asked to forfeit their rights. In effect, Paul has asked his Gentile-Christian audience to behave like proselytes to Judaism, at least so long as they are in contact with Jews (or Jewish Christians), although he bases his request not on the requirement of Torah, but on love and regard for the one for whom Christ died (14.15); on the example of Christ who did not please himself (14.18); and on the desiderata of peace and

---

1 Cranfield considers the verbs ἐξουθενεῖν and κρίνειν to serve as flags for distinct parties (the weak judge; the strong despise), and concludes that in 14.2-4 Paul has turned to address the weak alone (*Romans*, II, pp. 701-702; cf. Käsemann, *Romans*, p. 366). But surely this gives too much weight to the use of different verbs, and creates too violent a shift from 14.1 to 14.2-4.

edification of the community, which is the work of God (14.19, 20).[1]

1 Our reading of Paul's exhortation is thus the reverse of Francis Watson's (*Paul, Judaism, and the Gentiles: A Sociological Approach* [Cambridge: Cambridge University Press, 1986], p. 19) who seeks to demonstrate that Paul's theological reflection on Gentiles and the Law 'legitimates the separation of church and synagogue'. Watson (pp. 96-97) argues, rightly in our view, that Rom. 14.15–15.13 indicate Jewish and Gentile components in Roman Christianity; but Watson proposes that these are '*two congregations, separated by mutual hostility and suspicion over the question of the law, which* [Paul] *wishes to bring together into one congregation*'. He concludes (p. 98) that 'Paul's purpose in writing Romans was to defend and explain his view of freedom from the law (i.e. separation from the Jewish community and its way of life), with the aim of converting Jewish Christians to his point of view so as to create a single "Pauline" congregation in Rome'. It becomes evident already that for Watson 'Romans was addressed primarily to Jewish Christians' (p. 103). We will address the question of the identity and cohesiveness of the letter's intended audience below, in Chapter 1. It must suffice here to point out, *pace* Watson, (a) that Rom. 15.7-12 does not require *two* audiences, Jewish and Gentile, whom Paul wishes to unite in common worship. Paul declares that Christ became 'servant of circumcision' in order that *the Gentiles* might glorify God (15.9), and the Scripture citations that follow all refer to Gentile worship—including the quotation of Ps. 18.49 which immediately follows. (It is a weakness of Watson's interpretation [p. 97] that it depends on reading this citation as a *Jewish* statement.) (b) Although Paul personally endorses the view of 'the strong' that 'no food is unclean in itself' (14.14), he nevertheless enjoins the strong to relinquish their rights in any communal situation that may invite conflict (14.14, 20).

Paul's distance from Jewish sensibilities in his missionary activity among Gentiles should not be exaggerated. For example, with regard to 1 Cor. 10.25 ('Eat whatever is sold in the meat market without raising any question on the ground of conscience', RSV), C.K. Barrett ('Things Sacrificed to Idols', p. 49) has drawn the distinction too sharply: 'It is clear that only by careful inquiry (ἀνάκρισις) could a Jew satisfy himself on these points; and a quick reading of *'Aboda Zara* suffices to show the repeated investigations διὰ τὴν συνείδησιν that were incumbent upon the devout Jew. Paul is nowhere more un-Jewish than in this μηδὲν ἀνακρίνοντες. His whole life as a Pharisee has been essentially one of ἀνάκρισις, not at least into foods.' Barrett concludes that Paul's policy diverges sharply from the so-called 'Apostolic Decree' in Acts 15. But in fact *m. 'Aboda Zara* says little about 'inquiry' (ἀνάκρισις), since the Gentile merchant is *presumed* not only to sell unacceptable wares,

The larger section, 12.1–15.13, betrays this same orientation to the Gentile Christian. Käsemann remarks that 'as the problems of 14.1–15.13 are solved in terms of the catchword of mutual acceptance on a christological foundation, it is no accident that the general exhortation is in 12.1-2 put under a general heading corresponding to the summary in 13.8-14'. But this 'general heading' in 12.1-2 also rides the crest of Paul's argumentation from 1.18. The impiety (ἀσέβεια) of the Gentile world (1.18), characterized by darkened conscience, futile reasonings, a base mind (1.21-22, 28) and bodily disgrace (1.23-24, 26-27), has been reversed in baptism, where the παλαιὸς ἄνθρωπος, the 'body of sin', was neutralized so that Christians who once yielded their bodies 'in service to impurity and lawlessness upon lawlessness' now serve righteousness, presenting their bodily members in service to God (6.19). Now, in 12.1-2, Paul introduces his exhortation to mutual regard under the watchwords of holy and spiritual worship, in which σώματα become 'living sacrifices to God', and the ἀδόκιμος νοῦς is renewed to recognize the will of God.[1]

This exhortation therefore requires a reconstellation of the Christian's standing before the 'mercies of God' (12.1). The litany of Gentile immorality in Rom. 1.18-32 was focused in an indictment of the one who, by judging, showed contempt for God's mercy (2.1-4). The amplification of that indictment implicitly contrasted the human being's judgment of another with the impartial and righteous judgment of the sovereign

but to be eager to pass them off as acceptable. The Jew is therefore encouraged to buy only what can be *presumed* to be innocent of idolatrous associations. The concern is simply to avoid making a purchase that might appear to others as complicity in idolatry. Similarly, Paul urges the Corinthian Christians not to eat meat once its association with an idol is explicit, even if they must scandalize the host of a private dinner by refusing what is set before them (1 Cor. 10.28-29; the RSV has used parentheses to present this as a concession). This shows the same basic concern for 'appearances' found in *'Aboda Zara*, despite the Jewish awareness that 'an idol is nothing' (cf. 1 Cor. 10.19-20).

1 Käsemann, *Romans*, pp. 325-31. See also V.P. Furnish, *Theology and Ethics in Paul* (Nashville: Abingdon, 1968), pp. 101-106; and especially Beker, *Paul the Apostle*, pp. 175, 287-89.

Lord (2.3; cf. 3.26-28). The paraenesis that now follows in chs. 12–13 urges a sober consideration of one's place before God and beside one's neighbor; the more concrete exhortations in chs. 14–15 apply that theme to Jew and Gentile, who are not to judge or despise each other, and more specifically enjoins the Gentile Christian from judging the Jewish Christian and thus usurping the prerogative of the Lord (14.4, 6-12).

Here, we suggest, at least one aspect of the rhetorical situation that constrains the apostle in writing *this* letter is evident. Paul apparently cannot resolve possible Gentile-Jewish tensions by direct appeal to scriptural *miṣwôt*; yet (Käsemann) neither is his exhortation based on 'mere friendliness' or 'a recognition of good intentions', or on appeal for the more or less democratic consideration of a minority viewpoint. Contempt and judgment are the correlates of a *misapprehension* of divine mercy (2.3-6); this theme resurfaces in Paul's warning to Gentile Christians not to misunderstand God's mercy towards *them*, by 'boasting' over the Jew or holding them in contempt (11.13-24).

This connection suggests that the paraenesis in chs. 12–15 is not only directed to concrete circumstances in Rome, but is also prepared for by a *theological reorientation toward God's mercy* in the earlier chapters of the letter. It is the overall thesis of this study that Paul's argumentation in chapters 1–11 provides just such a reorientation. This thesis must bear the burden of proof, however, since it is the received view that the 'theological core' of Romans in chs. 1–8 is a theological exposition of the Christian gospel *in opposition to Judaism*, and that this theme has only a tangential relationship to the paraenesis of chs. 12–15 or to the circumstances of Paul's Roman audience. Consequently we will turn in the following chapters to address the question of the rhetorical character of Romans by analyzing Paul's explicit purposes in writing the letter. A word about method is appropriate here.

4. *A Rhetorical-Critical Approach to the 'Historical Problem' of Romans*

We have suggested that the 'double character' of Romans involves more than the thematic tension betwen a 'dialogue with Judaism' and an explicitly Gentile-Christian address; the troublesome connection between theological content and epistolary situation, or, on the level of text, between letter 'body' and the situationally contingent epistolary 'frame', complicate the question. As we have seen, attempts to resolve these tensions generally proceed either by further loosening the rhetorical connection with the Roman audience—so that Paul speaks 'beyond' the Roman Christians, to Jerusalem or to the eavesdropping synagogue—or by collapsing Paul's epistolary intentions toward the Romans into his anxiety regarding Jerusalem, as this comes to expression in 15.30-32. In these reconstructions the question of possible rhetorical integration of Paul's 'dialogue with Judaism', as this emerges first in Rom. 1.18-2.29, with the intentions expressed in 1.1-17 is neglected, and frequently the resulting impression is that Paul turns from direct address in 1.1-15 to theological essay-making in 1.16ff.[1]

That neglect is most glaringly evident in the light of Consigny's essay on the rhetor's creative redisposition of a situation by means of topics.[2] If Romans does not intelligibly modify the constraints of a rhetorical situation by moving *from* a basis of agreement with the (Roman) audience *toward* the adherence to theses or values that Paul intends, proceeding by acceptable means of inference, then the letter must be considered, in Consigny's phrase, 'inneffective and irrelevant' as rhetoric.

A meaningful rhetorical-critical analysis of Romans should go beyond aspects of style and figures of speech and thought to

---

1 The point can be illustrated from the schematic outline of the letter provided by almost any commentary: 1.16-17 is the letter's 'theme', 1.18–3.20 is a preliminary negative exposition (the 'need for the gospel'), 3.21–8.39 is a positive exposition. The lack of rhetorical integration between epistolary address and exposition is most evident in the comments by Jervell and Noack (see p. 28 nn. 1, 2 above).

2 See pp. 16 n. 3, 17 nn. 1, 2.

penetrate the fundamental problem of the letter's value as argumentation. This will involve examining Paul's selection and application of topics in the letter with an eye to discovering how Paul construes a basis of agreement with his audience and sets about transferring that agreement to new propositions or values. Such a rhetorical-critical approach necessarily requires attention to argumentative *progression* and the *modification* of a rhetorical situation, as contrasted with a mirror-reading approach that projects a historical or rhetorical situation rather flatly out of the material themes of the letter.

In a landmark essay, Wilhelm Wuellner has argued that such content criticism is doomed to failure unless the interpreter understands the argumentative character of the *topos*. Discussing research into the Torah-concept in Paul and Jesus, Wuellner declares that the historical-critical comparison of motifs and concepts in Paul's (Jewish) 'background', no less than the theological concern to establish the degree of continuity or discontinuity in Jesus' position regarding the Torah, will inevitably misconstrue particular statements unless the argumentative character of the *topos* itself, of its contextual function, and of the overall purposiveness of the particular discourse (i.e. its relation to a rhetorical situation) are borne in mind.[1] Insight into the rhetor's use of *topoi* is the same as insight into the redisposition of the rhetorical situation.[2]

Wuellner's discussion of *topos*-criticism holds out hope that new insight into the argumentative character of Romans may be won from the field of rhetorical criticism. It is the more striking, therefore, that in his own interpretation of the letter Wuellner seizes on Rom. 1.13 (καὶ ἐκωλύθην) as Paul's cryptic reference to *Jewish* opposition to his mission, and specifically to his embassy to Jerusalem, and finds here the occasion that prompts Paul's use of the Torah-*topos*. It is remarkable, given his discussion of *topos* theory, that without an exegetical re-examination of Romans with the letter's Gentile Christian addressees explicitly in view, Wuellner

1 W. Wuellner, 'Toposforschung und Torahinterpretation bei Paulus und Jesus', *NTS* 24 (1977-1978), pp. 464-65.
2 *Ibid.*, p. 469.

assumes that Paul's use of the Torah-*topos* is developed in fundamental antithesis to *Judaism*.[1] It would appear that the centrepiece of his method, the question how the selection and use of *topoi* redisposes the constraining relationship of *speaker*, *audience*, and *exigence*, has been suppressed at this crucial point. In fact a number of recent studies of the letter's rhetoric have failed to address the problem of *argumentative character* that we have described, choosing instead to align conventional historical-critical perspectives on the letter with the categories of style and genre discussed in the classical handbooks.[2]

To illustrate this further, we may return to Kümmel's view that Romans is the apostle's self-introduction to the Roman church, which implies that Paul is concerned not so much to win adherence for his εὐαγγέλιον as to secure approval for himself as εὐαγγελιστής. This suggests that the letter is a show-piece of epideictic, the rhetoric of display.[3] George Kennedy describes the letter in just this way:

> Romans is a considerably longer epistle than [1 Thessalonians and Galatians], and it resembles them in structure and

---

1 'Es ist diese drohende Verhinderung durch befürchtete Ereignisse, die ihn bei der Übergabe der Heidenkollekte für die Judenchristen in Jerusalem erwarten (15.30-31), die Paulus dazu nötigt, in allen vier Teilen der Torah Thematik explizit oder implizit auseinanderzusetzen' (*ibid.*, p. 477).

2 So for example Johannes Weiss, 'Beiträge zur paulinischen Rhetorik', in *Theologische Studien*, Festschrift for Bernhard Weiss, ed. C.R. Gregory *et al.* (Göttingen: Vandenhoeck & Ruprecht, 1897). See H.D. Betz, 'The Problem of Rhetoric and Theology According to the Apostle Paul', in *L'Apôtre Paul: personnalité, style, et conception du ministère*, ed. A. Vanhoye (Leuven: Leuven University Press, 1986), esp. pp. 16-21, on the history of research.

3 Epideictic, as traditionally understood, addresses 'an audience that is merely enjoying the unfolding of the orator's argument without having to reach a conclusion on the matter in question' (Perelman and Olbrechts-Tyteca, *New Rhetoric*, p. 21). The authors go on to provide a new and more adequate assessment of epideictic: 'The argumentation in epideictic discourse sets out to increase the intensity of adherence to certain values' (p. 51). See also Walter H. Beale, 'Rhetorical Performative Discourse: A New Theory of Epideictic', *PhR* 11 (1978), pp. 221-46; Christine Oravec, '"Observation" in Aristotle's Theory of Epideictic', *PhR* 9 (1976), p. 162-74.

in topics but is to be regarded as more epideictic in intent... In Romans [Paul] is writing to a church which he has never visited and which has therefore never heard his gospel... The fuller exposition of his thought in chapters one to eleven is needed to explain the faith as he understands it. The exigence for the letter is perhaps provided by Paul's feeling that in his mission to the entire world it is important to reach the Christian community of the capital. He hopes to visit them personally, and this letter is a step in opening communications. The two main rhetorical problems he faces are his audience's lack of personal knowledge of him and the probability that there will be among them those clinging to the law and hostile to aspects of his message. *He wishes to show them in advance what his gospel will be* and thus to anticipate problems which might, and in fact did, arise (Acts 28.24-39).[1]

Kennedy describes Romans as 'an example of the kind of preaching or teaching [Paul] will practice when among them'.[2] Evidently the rhetorical approach to Romans has not led Kennedy to reconceive the letter's character; rather, he has simply translated into the categories of rhetorical theory Kümmel's view of Romans as Paul's self-introduction to Rome, and thus he shares the corresponding view that Paul's topics on the Torah and Israel must be directed to a Jewish or Judaizing audience ('those clinging to the law').

It is curious that this same view leads Klaus Berger to discuss Romans as an example of protreptic exhortation, a subcategory of symboleutic (deliberative) rhetoric:

Als Protreptikos Logos bezeichnet man eine Werbeschrift, die in erster Linie für die Beschäftigung mit einer bestimmten Disziplin, insbesondere der Philosophie, Anhänger gewinnen soll. Das geschieht dadurch, dass die Vorteile dieses Weges aufgezeigt und andere Wege verglichen werden. Entsprechend bezeichnen wir als protreptische Mahnrede *alles, was die grundsätzliche Wahl des*

1 Kennedy, *New Testament Interpretation*, p. 152. David Aune (*The New Testament in Its Literary Environment* [Philadelphia: Westminster, 1987], p. 219) reaches the same judgment: 'Since [Paul's] intention was to present his gospel so that [the Roman Christians] will know more about its character and his mode of argumentation, Romans is primarily *epideictic* in intention'.
2 Kennedy, *New Testament Interpretation*, p. 156.

64   *The Rhetoric of Romans*

> *christlichen Weges zum Thema macht.* Mit Ausnahme des
> Corpus des Römerbriefes, das ich als ganzes zu dieser
> Gattung rechne, gehören dazu im Neuen Testament nur
> jeweils kürzere Stücke, freilich in zentraler Position... In
> Röm 1-11 geht es um den christlichen Weg des Glaubens an
> Jesus Christus, in dem trotz der Vorrangstellung des
> Judentums der jüdische Weg 'aufgehoben' ist.[1]

Berger never tells why the Roman audience should need to be
convinced of the 'advantages' of the Christian way; presumably he does not mean that Paul wants to convert the Romans
to Christianity. Berger assigns Romans to the deliberative
genre more probably on the basis of the 'Jewish' topics taken
up in the letter, albeit with no clear explanation of the situation
that evoked Paul's use of those topics.

The discrepancy between Kennedy's and Berger's assess-
ments of Romans arises in part because of the difficulty in cor-
relating Romans with the rhetorical genres discussed in the
ancient handbooks, namely, 'forensic', 'epideictic', and
'symboleutic' or 'deliberative'. This difficulty corresponds to
the more general problem of aligning *paraenesis* with the
classical categories of rhetorical genre—a point to which we
will return in Chapter 1.[2] It also shows a preference for
approaching rhetorical criticism primarily on the basis of
classical categories, rather than by using the classical handbooks as windows into the nature of rhetorical invention.

1 Klaus Berger, *Formgeschichte des Neuen Testaments* (Heidelberg:
Quelle & Meyer, 1984), pp. 217-18. David Aune (*Literary Environment*, p. 203) combines Kennedy's and Bergers's views when he
writes that 'Romans incorporates protreptic discourse into an epideictic letter'.
2 In his review of Hans Dieter Betz's rhetorical-critical commentary
on *Galatians*, David Aune remarks that 'the relationship between
[the philosophical] setting of paraenesis, epistolary paraenesis, and
the paraenetical sections of the Pauline letters remains a subject for
investigation' (*RSR* 7 [1981], pp. 323-26). Stanley K. Stowers (*Letter-
Writing in Greco-Roman Antiquity* [Philadelphia: Westminster,
1986], p. 52) observes that many of the letter types discussed in
ancient epistolary theory 'correspond to kinds of exhortation
(paraenesis), and exhortation was only tangentially related to
rhetorical theory.... Thus in the hortatory tradition the distinction
between epideictic (praise and blame) and deliberative (giving
advice) breaks down.'

Two other essays bear mention in this respect. Although Robin Scroggs' essay on 'Paul as Rhetorician' begins with the declaration that Paul 'is first of all a preacher, a rhetorician',[1] his discussion makes little use of rhetorical-critical insights or techniques. He proposes to solve tensions within the letter with a source and redaction theory, but does not essay to describe the rhetorical character or persuasive purpose of the final result, our letter. He suggests, in fact, that his proposed model of Paul as a rhetorician should lead us 'to ask of Romans, which is not a "real" letter such as is his other extant correspondence... whether or not the letter has been made up out of sermonic material Paul has perhaps honed and refined from his years of experience as a rhetorician'.[2] Scroggs answers that question in the affirmative, distinguishing two homilies on the basis of thematic continuity, reliance on scripture citation, and rhetorical style.[3] Each homily is, by implication, something of a showpiece in Paul's missionary portfolio; the implication is that Paul has sent a copy of his apostolic dossier to potential sponsors in Rome. The rhetorician 'model' has not changed the conception of Romans; it has only allowed the 'exciting' possibility that 'in these chapters we can hear the actual echo of Paul the preacher'.[4]

No more satisfying in this regard is an ostensibly rhetorical-critical essay by Robert Jewett, which seeks to correlate Paul's

1 Scroggs, 'Paul as Rhetorician', p. 271.
2 *Ibid.*, pp. 273-74.
3 A 'homily on the meaning of Israel's history', preserved in chs. 1–4 and chs. 9–11, reflects midrashic practice and is directed to Jewish listeners; a second homily, 'on the new life in Christ', reflects 'Hellenistic' patterns like the diatribe, and must have been directed to 'an audience informed by Greek culture'. The first homily 'must have been a sermon Paul had used and refined many times in his missionary activity and offered here to the Roman church as exemplifying his best rhetorical skills as well as his basic theological perspective' (*ibid.*, p. 281). As for the second, Scroggs (*ibid.*, p. 285) declares, 'The evidence all points to the conclusion that in these chapters Paul has produced for the Romans a self-enclosed and complete homily which could be called a sermon in diatribe style'. The attempt to solve Romans' historical problem by dissection is not unique to Scroggs: see also J. Kinoshita, 'Romans—Two Writings Combined', *NovT* 78 (1965), pp. 258-77; and Schmithals, *Römerbrief*.
4 *Ibid.*, p. 297.

letter and the categories of classical rhetorical theory.[1] Jewett
reproduces Theodore Burgess's catalog of 27 'types' of epideictic speeches[2] and picks three, 'ambassadorial, parenetic, and
hortatory', that he thinks are 'fused' in Romans.[3] Bolstered by
C.J. Bjerkelund's thesis that παρακαλῶ-clauses like that in
Rom. 12.1-2 derive from 'personal, fraternal' epistolary style[4]
and by studies of 'diplomatic style',[5] Jewett proposes that
Romans is 'an ambassadorial letter'. 'Its purpose is to advocate
in behalf of the "power of God" a cooperative mission to evangelize Spain so that the theological argumentation reiterates
the gospel to be therein proclaimed and the ethical admonitions show how that gospel is to be lived out in a manner that
would ensure the success of this mission.'[6] The subjunctive
quality here imputed to Paul's argumentation ('the gospel to
be therein proclaimed') effectively distances the letter from
any constraining rhetorical situation.

In contrast to the studies just reviewed, the position
embodied in this work is that the constraining power of audience and exigence in relation to Paul's persuasive purposes, as
this may be analyzed through Paul's choice and development
of topics, is the proper object of the rhetorical criticism of
Romans.

The exegesis of Romans begins in Chapter 1 with an examination of Paul's initial disposition of a rhetorical relationship
in the letter opening, 1.1-17, and his recapitulation of the letter
in 15.14-32. These parts of the epistolary 'frame', we will
argue, correspond functionally to the rhetorical *exordium* and
peroratio. We will then hazard a tentative hypothesis regarding the letter's overall structure in correspondence with the
rhetorical situation extrapolated from the epistolary frame:

---

1 Robert Jewett, 'Romans as an Ambassadorial Letter', *Int* 36 (1982),
   pp. 5-20.
2 Theodore C. Burgess, 'Epideictic Literature', *Studies in Classical
   Philology* 3 (1902), pp. 89-261.
3 Jewett, 'Romans', pp. 7-8.
4 C.J. Bjerkelund, *Parakalô: Form, Funktion, und Sinn der parakalô-
   Sätze* (Oslo: Universitetsforlaget, 1967).
5 Jewett, 'Romans', pp. 8-9; the works cited (by Schubart and Welles)
   played a significant part in Bjerkelund's work.
6 *Ibid.*, pp. 9-10.

specifically, that the letter's deep structure corresponds to the 'once—but now' scheme of early Christian paraenesis. Initial conclusions about the letter's paraenetic character will then be drawn.

Chapter 2 is in a sense the heart of the work, for here we tackle the problem of integrating the epistolary address (1.1-15), 'theme' (1.16-17), and the beginning of Paul's purported 'dialogue with Judaism' (1.18–4.25). We will argue that 1.18-32 embodies a paraenetic *topos* that had its significance within the context of paraenesis within Gentile-Christian congregations, and is *not* to be interpreted as part of a rhetorical 'ambush' for 'the Jew'. The chapter continues with an examination of the role of the apostrophes in 2.1ff and 2.17ff and of the dialogue with the Jew throughout Romans 2–4.

In close connection with Chapter 2, a subsequent Excursus takes up the widespread view that chs. 1–4 represent a stylized 'ambush' of the Jew, intended to overcome a rhetorical obstacle to be located *within Judaism* contemporary with Paul. The net effect of Chapter 2 and the Excursus is to realign the interpretation of chs. 1–4 with the constraints imposed by dialogue with a Gentile-Christian congregation, by way of suggesting that 'the Jew' plays a *paradigmatic* role in these chapters.

No understanding of the letter can be reached by treating Romans 1–4 in isolation, however, and so the argumentation in chs. 5–11 will be surveyed in Chapter 3 with the question of rhetorical integration paramount. It will be argued that ch. 5 plays a pivotal role within the letter, channeling the *paradigmatic* argumentation of chs. 1–4 into the predominantly ethical argumentation in chs. 6–8. Romans 9–11, recognized here as a climax within the letter's argument, is not to be isolated from what precedes; these chapters balance the ethical argumentation in chs. 6–8 with a *pathos* appeal aimed at modifying Gentile-Christian attitudes. The implications of those renewed attitudes are treated in the paraenesis of chs. 12–15.

Chapter 4 recapitulates the findings of this work in a discussion of the 'macro-structure' of Romans.

Chapter 1

PAUL'S PURPOSE IN WRITING TO THE ROMANS

1. *The Question of Method*
As we have seen in the Introduction, the 'double character' of
Romans is one way of describing the troublesome interrelation
of Paul's address to an audience of Gentile Christians (Rom.
1.1-13), the wider circumstances that attend his writing
(15.14-33), and an apparently self-contained letter body that
includes a diatribe with a Jewish interlocutor (chs. 2–4) and
discussions of 'Jewish' themes (chs. 2–4; 7; 9–11).

The letter opening and closing (1.1-15; 15.14-33) clearly
must bear interpretive weight, since they serve not only
epistolary but also rhetorical functions. The letter opening
corresponds to the *exordium* of an oration, in which the
speaker 'must define himself, and he must define his
problem'.[1] Similarly, the letter closing serves to recapitulate

---

1 Wuellner makes this point in 'Paul's Rhetoric of Argumentation',
  p. 159, citing Brandt, *Rhetoric of Argumentation*, p. 51. Aune (*Literary Environment*, p. 186) similarly observes that the epistolary
  thanksgiving period 'often praises the recipients, functioning as an
  exordium aimed at securing their goodwill'. On the conventional-
  ized introductory formulae used in ancient Greek letters, see John
  L. White, 'New Testament Epistolary Literature in the Framework
  of Ancient Epistolography', *ANRW II*, 25.2 (1984), pp. 1736-38. Paul
  adapted such formulae in the greeting and body opening to introduce the subject matter of his letters (*ibid.*, pp. 1740-44; note especially P. Schubert, *Form and Function of the Pauline Thanksgivings* [Berlin: Alfred Töpelmann, 1939], pp. 35ff; F.O. Francis,
  'The Form and Function of the Opening and Closing Paragraphs of
  James and 1 John', *ZNW* 61 [1970], pp. 110-26; J.T. Sanders, 'The
  Transition from Opening Epistolary Thanksgiving to Body in the
  Pauline Corpus', *JBL* 81 [1962], pp. 348-62). On the rhetorical
  significance of epistolary formulae see Michael Bünker, *Brief-*

preceding argumentation and consolidate its affective force, as does the rhetorical *peroratio*.[1] It is appropriate, therefore, to begin an investigation of the letter's argumentative character by examining the rhetorical relationship established in the first passage and recapitulated in the second.

One of the most evident structural features in the letter is the transition to formal paraenesis at 12.1. The hypothesis will be advanced below that a clue to the letter's argumentative macro-structure can be found by relating that transition to thematic parallels earlier in the letter, specifically in chs. 1 and 6. It will be argued that these units disclose the topical antinomy within which Paul has construed the rhetorical situation,[2] specifically, the paraenetic *topos* identified by Rudolf Bultmann as the 'once—but now' (*'einst–jetzt'*) scheme of early Christian preaching.[3]

2. *Exordium (Rom. 1.1-17)*

The constraining power of a rhetorical situation is manifest in the fact that the rhetor must 'establish credentials that will guarantee that his arguments will fall into the range of what is acceptable to his audience'. The speaker's self-introduction in the *exordium* 'will be rhetorical in the fullest sense of the word because introductions necessarily attempt to create per-

---

formular und rhetorische Disposition im 1. Korintherbrief (Göttingen: Vandenhoeck & Ruprecht, 1987).

1   White ('New Testament Epistolography', p. 1738) states in summary that the conventions concluding the ancient Greek letter 'serve as a bridge to further contact (whether the tone be positive or negative) and/or as a means of finalizing or underscoring the purpose of the communication'. One may compare H.D. Betz's comments (*Galatians*, Hermeneia [Philadelphia: Fortress, 1985], p. 313) on the hermeneutical importance of the *'peroratio'* in Galatians.

2   Consigny writes, 'I construe the topic as a formal opposition of two (or more) terms which can be used to structure the heteronomous matter of a particular situation. I follow Aristotle in his construal of topics, for whom the topic is an opposition of terms.... The two terms of the topic, when applied to the indeterminate matter of a context, structure that context so as to open up and delimit a logical place in which the rhetor can discover and manage new meanings and new relationships' ('Rhetoric and its Situations', pp. 182-83).

3   Rudolf Bultmann, *The Theology of the New Testament* (New York: Charles Scribner's Sons, 1955), I, pp. 72-73, 105-106.

suasive relationships'.[1] That is, the speaker must establish a context of meaning that will predispose the audience to the argumentation to follow, whether or not the exigence that evokes that argumentation is made explicit.[2] This in fact is accomplished in the opening address formula in Rom. 1.1-7, the thanksgiving clause in 1.8-12, and the disclosure formula in 1.13ff that serves as a transition to the letter body itself.

By means of adapting conventional epistolary opening formulae,[3] Paul begins in 1.1-7 to create a rhetorical relationship with his readers by relating himself and them to the call of God. He is 'servant of Jesus Christ, called to be an apostle, set apart for the proclamation of God's news' (1.1).[4] They are 'called to belong to Jesus Christ' (1.6), 'beloved of God', 'called to be holy' (1.7). He is one commissioned by God 'to secure the obedience of faith among the Gentiles': They themselves are 'among the Gentiles' (ἐν οἷς... καὶ ὑμεῖς, 1.6).[5] Their respective

1 Brandt, *Rhetoric of Argumentation*, pp. 51-57.
2 George Kennedy declares that the 'overriding rhetorical problem' is often 'especially visible at the beginning of a discourse and conditions the contents of the proem or the beginning of the proof'. The ancient rhetorical handbooks recommended an indirect approach (*insinuatio*) for the speaker facing an antagonistic audience; but through the *insinuatio* the speaker nonetheless lays 'a foundation for understanding on the part of the audience before bringing up the central problem' (*New Testament Interpretation*, p. 36).
3 The typical Greek formula was 'N. to N., χαίρειν'. E. Lohmeyer ('Probleme paulinischer Theologie I: Die brieflichen Grussüberschriften', *ZNW* 26 [1927], pp. 158ff) suggested that the nearer parallel to Paul's salutation formulae is an 'oriental' and Jewish convention of separating address and greeting, usually *šalôm* or εἰρήνη. See discussions in William Doty, *Letters in Primitive Christianity* (Philadelphia: Fortress, 1973), pp. 22, 27-32, and White, 'New Testament Epistolary Literature', pp. 1733-38.
4 Despite its form as a substantivized adjective, εὐαγγέλιον functions as a *nomen actionis* (G. Friedrich, 'εὐαγγελίζομαι, κτλ', *TDNT*, II, pp. 726, 729). 'Paul knows himself as one who has been separated, consecrated, by God εἰς εὐαγγέλιον θεοῦ—(that is, for the task of proclaiming) God's message of good news' (Cranfield, *Romans*, I, p. 54).
5 There is some debate whether this phrase indicates that the Roman Christians are themselves exclusively or predominantly Gentiles, or whether Paul means only that the Roman Christians live 'among the Gentiles' (so Beker, *Paul the Apostle*, p. 76; Adolf von Schlatter, *Gottes Gerechtigkeit: Ein Kommentar zum Römerbrief*, 2nd edn

identities—Paul's and the Romans'—are determined by the
prior initiative of God, who has already announced the gospel
in Israel's sacred scriptures (1.2-3) and has by raising Jesus
from the dead established him as 'Son of God in power' whom
Paul and the Romans alike are now made to confess as 'our
Lord' (1.4, 7).

This address formula is more densely packed with self-
descriptive titles and phrases than any of Paul's other letters,
including Galatians. While in the apologetic context of
Galatians Paul quickly turns to a fairly expansive *narratio* in
support of his apostolic commission (1.11–2.21), the effect in
Rom. 1.1-6 is rather an accumulation of phrases that set forth
Paul's claim to divine authority. Regardless of whether the
Roman audience would have heard echoes of the ancient
prophetic books in the phrases 'servant', 'called as an apostle',
'set apart to the gospel',[1] or would simply have perceived these

[Stuttgart: Calwer, 1952], p. 59; see Cranfield, *Romans*, I, p. 68). If
the grammar in this sentence is ambiguous (Beker finds it
significant that the text reads ἐν οἷς, not ἐξ ὧν), the deliberate statements in 1.13 and 1.14-15 are not. What is the case regarding
Gentiles within the sphere of his commission holds true for the
Roman Christians as well. So Cranfield (*ibid.*) declares that Paul's
purpose in characterizing the audience in just this way here in 1.6,
before the address formula in 1.7, must be 'to indicate that the
Roman church, though not founded by him, is nevertheless within
the sphere of his apostolic commission, and that he therefore has a
right to address it in the way he is doing'.

1 See Schlier, *Römerbrief*, pp. 19-21. The prophets are the 'servants' of
God; the phrase is stereotyped in early Jewish literature (1QpHab
2.8-9; 7.5; 1QH 1.3; 4 Ezra 1.32; 2.1, 18, etc.). The prophets are 'sent'
(ἀποστέλλειν, ἀπεσταλμένος, Isa. 6.8; Jer. 1.7; Ezek. 2.3; Hag. 1.12;
Zech. 2.15; 4.9; Mal. 3.23; Exod. 3.10). Ἀφωρισμένος should evoke not
discussions of *parûš* ('Pharisee' in Tannaitic literature) but
prophetic vocation: Käsemann compares the expression with Jer.
1.5 (*Romans*, p. 6), to which we may add the Holy Spirit's command
to 'set apart' two from the prophetic band in Acts 13.22; see also Gal.
1.15. All of these observations crystallize around a fundamental
datum. Without benefit of modern inquiry into 'original' prophetic
speech-forms or redactional layers in the prophetic corpus, ancient
listeners would have accepted the prophetic books in their canonical
shape as characteristically prophetic speech (see now Brevard
Childs, 'The Canonical Shape of the Prophetic Literature', *Int* 32
(1978), pp. 46-55; Gene M. Tucker, 'Prophetic Superscriptions and
the Growth of a Canon', in George W. Coats and Burke Long, eds.,

as elements in a specifically Christian vocabulary,[1] the phrases are clearly meant to stand by themselves, without definition or narrative elaboration. That is to say, Paul simply expects his readers to accept his claim to be heard as the divinely authorized 'apostle to the Gentiles'.

But the letter opening clearly does more than present Paul's apostolic credentials. Verses 2-6 specify, first, the basis of Paul's authority as one called to serve a gospel grounded in Israel's scriptures and centered on Israel's Messiah, and second, the purpose of that authority, the 'apostolic "in order that"': 'to secure faithful obedience among the nations, for his name's sake' (1.5).[2] That Paul's apostolate to the *Gentiles* is shown to be based on the promises to *Israel* brings to expression a derivative relationship between Gentile and Jew that will surface again as a relationship of *priority* in 1.16 ('to the Jew *first*, and also to the Greek'), of dependence in 11.17-24 ('You [Gentile Christians] do not support the root, but the root, you'), and of obligation in 15.26-27 (the Gentile Christians in Macedonia and Achaia are 'in debt' to the Jewish Christians). That the Roman Christians are immediately linked with the Gentiles (1.6) indicates that these are not isolated theologoumena, but rather bring to expression that broader relationship between Jews and Gentiles in which the

---

Canon and Authority: Essays in Old Testament Religion and Theology [Philadelphia: Fortress, 1977], pp. 56-70). To the extent that Paul's rhetoric resembles literary features in those books, including an adaptation of the (canonical) prophetic persona, his rhetoric would presumably have been recognized as a claim to the authority enjoyed by the prophets.

1 'Terms that rise to importance with a movement are ordinarily of special significance to it, and it is clear from NT usage that this is true of the term *apostolos*' (Francis H. Agnew, 'The Origin of the NT Apostle-Concept: A Review of Research', *JBL* 105 [1986], p. 75).

2 'Grace' (χάρις) and 'apostolate' are equivalent (Käsemann, *Romans*, 14; see also A. Satake, 'Apostolat und Gnade bei Paulus', *NTS* 15 [1968-69], pp. 96-107). The genitive phrase ὑπακοὴν πίστεως is epexegetical: 'The apostle's specific task is to create 'obedience of faith' among all the Gentiles' (Käsemann, p. 14). Cranfield declares that 'to make the decision of faith is an act of obedience toward God and also that true faith by its very nature includes in itself the sincere desire and will to obey God in all things' (*Romans*, I, p. 67, cf. n. 1).

rhetorical situation of Romans directly inheres.[1] In this light, the 'traditional' elements used in 1.3-4 to describe the gospel are not chosen incidentally, but for their rhetorical value. Käsemann remarks that 'Christ's Lordship is the basis of the task of the apostle according to v. 5 and of his right to address the Roman church according to v. 6'.[2] But more can be said. The christological formulations deal not with soteriology, justification, or so to speak with God's action *for humanity*, but with God's sovereign action in fulfilling the ancient promises spoken to Israel (1.2), through one born 'of the seed of David' (1.3) and established 'in the heavenly sphere of power'[3] as son of God and 'our Lord' (1.4), that is, Lord, not of the Jews alone, but of the Gentiles as well, whose obedience is now required 'for his name's sake' (1.5).[4] It is not enough, then, to say with Käsemann that 'the formula performed the service of showing that [Paul] shared the same basis of faith as the Christians at Rome'.[5] Paul's adaptation of the sender formula also points toward a 'deep exigence',[6] God's action in

1   See Beker, *Paul the Apostle*, pp. 331-36; 'Faithfulness of God', pp. 14-
    16.
2   See Käsemann, *Romans*, pp. 10-14.
3   So Käsemann (*Romans*, p. 12) takes ἐν δυνάμει to modify the noun
    ὁρισθέντος. But the phrases ἐν δυνάμει and κατὰ πνεῦμα ἁγιωσύνης
    are plerophrastic, since as Käsemann (*ibid.*) rightly notes 'the spirit
    of holiness is the power in virtue of which Jesus is appointed the
    Son of God'.
4   The immediate antecedent of ὀνόματος αὐτοῦ is Christ; but from the
    context it is clear that Christ has come as the instrument of *God's*
    purpose. Cranfield (*Romans*, I, p. 67) is therefore quite correct to
    remark that 'the true end of the preaching of the gospel... is not
    just the good of those to whom the preaching is directed, but also—
    and above all—the glorification of Christ, of God'.
5   Käsemann, *Romans*, p. 13.
6   Bitzer's description of exigence is phrased negatively: 'an imperfec-
    tion marked by urgency; it is a defect, an obstacle, something wait-
    ing to be done, a thing which is other than it should be' ('The
    Rhetorical Situation', p. 6). *Webster's Ninth New Collegiate Dic-
    tionary* defines exigence (exigency) as 'a state of affairs that makes
    urgent demands'; 'that which is required in a particular situation'.
    Accordingly, in the following pages we use the term 'exigence' to
    describe *that aspect of a situation that demands or elicits response*.
    We purposely avoid the distinctly negative sense 'obstacle' to avert

establishing Jesus Christ as Lord, that now brings Paul and the Romans into relationship as those whom God has called: him, to be an apostle bound to secure the obedience of Gentiles, and them, 'who are also among the Gentiles', called 'to belong to Jesus Christ', 'to be holy'.[1] We can see, then, that the opening formula (1.1-6) already begins in a preparatory way to forge a link between the elements of the rhetorical situation, namely speaker, audience and ('deep') exigence, as the following diagram illustrates:

Speaker	*Audience*	*Exigence*
Paul, 'called' as an apostle, 'set apart' to proclaim the gospel of God; that is, one commissioned to secure the obedience of 'all the Gentiles'	The Romans, 'called' of Christ, 'called' to be holy; those who are 'also among the Gentiles'	(The effective call of God, experienced by Paul and the Roman Christians alike; an exigence that resides in God's own integrity, the call to Gentiles being 'for his [Christ's] name's sake')

It is evident that Paul does not enjoy the personal, pastoral relationship with the Romans that enabled him in 1 Corinthians or 1 Thessalonians to address and admonish his own congregations, recalling them to what he had preached to them 'at first'. Presumably, of course, Paul could have learned much from his associates in Rome (16.3ff.) about the Roman

the implication that when we discuss the letter's exigences we mean to talk about 'what is wrong in Rome'.

1 See Satake, 'Apostolat und Gnade', on the correspondence of κλητός and κλητοί in Paul's letter openings. Cranfield (*Romans*, I, p. 68) disputes the interpretation of κλητοὶ Ἰησοῦ Χριστοῦ as a possessive genitive, preferring to take the phrase as a subjective genitive ('those whom Jesus Christ has called'), in parallel with ἀγαπητοῖς θεοῦ. But as Cranfield (I, p. 69) himself points out, the divine call is always effectual; similarly K.L. Schmidt ('καλέω, κτλ', *TDNT*, III, p. 489) declares, 'If God or Christ calls a man, this calling or naming is a *verbum efficax*'. We might then properly fill out the phrase, 'those whom Jesus Christ has called to be his own'. As for κλητοῖς ἁγίοις, Schmidt (p. 494) declares the same phrase at the beginning of 1 Corinthians to be 'defined by the preceding ἡγιασμένοις ἐν Χριστῷ Ἰησοῦ'. In Rom. 1.7 as well we may rightly paraphrase, 'called, and thus made to be, holy'.

congregation. The depth and detail of that knowledge remains a point of debate, and our position in the Introduction was a cautious one. Nevertheless the *exordium* already tells us much about what Paul expects from his audience. They, as Gentile Christians, are familiar enough with the Greek Bible to recognize an appeal to the prophets, and to find Paul's language about the 'son of God' intelligible (1.2-4).[1] They presumably know what an apostle is, and will realize what Paul means by a phrase like 'the obedience of Gentiles for the sake of Christ's name'. They are not a new congregation: nowhere in the letter does Paul condescend to them, and, in fact, his argumentation demands considerable sophistication from them, as Schmithals has pointed out; further, their faith is already 'proclaimed in all the world'. Yet Paul addresses them programmatically as Gentiles, converts (κλητοί) from paganism, as is confirmed in Rom. 6.17-21. It is less clear, and finally of little moment, whether they were called into the eschatological Christian community directly, or by way of a more or less extended sojourn in the diaspora synagogue; either way, they would have been brought to accept what Schmithals calls 'die jüdischen Grundlagen', and these also are some of the constraints Paul shares with his audience.

Here in the *exordium*, Paul plays on those points of presumed agreement in order to establish a relationship of apostle and community *before God* (though not before one another) that is analogous to that found in Paul's other pastoral and paraenetic letters.[2] Unable to appeal to a history of personal acquaintance with the Romans, he relies instead upon premises that he expects the Romans to share—the divinely authorized role of apostle, for example, and the divine origin of the gospel. The conventional (topical) character of this appeal is significant. Although Paul greets friends and co-workers in the Roman congregations at the end of this letter (ch. 16), and

1 Whether, and how, Rom. 1.3-4 is to be understood as a 'pre-Pauline liturgical fragment' (Käsemann, *Romans*, pp. 10-11) remains open. Our point is that Paul's terse phrases reflect the expectation that this language will make immediate sense to his audience.

2 On references to conversion and 'the beginning' of a community as a *topos* in Christian paraenesis, see K. Berger, *Formgeschichte*, pp. 130-135.

could therefore have appealed *at its beginning* to what the Romans had certainly heard of this apostolate among the Gentiles from those individuals, he chooses instead to base his relationship to the Romans on what *God* has called him to be and to do. The following paragraphs show that the rhetorical strategy throughout the letter opening is to link topical references to God's will, to which Paul expects his audience's adherence, with his present communication with them.[1] Unless the Romans reject his use of these topics, this strategy should predispose them to respond to his discourse as they would respond to the call of God.[2]

In the thanksgiving clause (1.8-12) Paul builds upon the foundation laid in the address formula by connecting the 'deep exigence' of their respective 'callings' to his long-felt desire to see the Roman Christians. His commendation of the Romans' faith (1.8) is the sort of expression of good will that rhetoricians and epistolary theorists alike recommended at the outset of discourse to predispose one's audience or one's readers favorably. But this friendly or philophronetic aspect[3] does not automatically indicate a 'delicate' situation (Dahl) or the apostle's 'insecure' feelings (Käsemann). The philophronetic aspect per se could be put into service in paraenetic letters, for example, to provide the framework for exhorta-

---

1 'The aim of argumentation is... to transfer to the conclusion the *adherence* accorded [by the audience] to the premises.... This transfer of adherence is accomplished only through the establishment of a bond between the premises and the theses whose acceptance the speaker wants to achieve' (Perelman, *Realm of Rhetoric*, p. 21). See also Perelman and Olbrechts-Tyteca (*New Rhetoric*, pp. 65ff) on the 'objects of agreement', corresponding roughly to the ἴδιοι τόποι ('the real' and 'the preferable') and the κοινοὶ τόποι (*loci*, 'premises of a very general nature') of classical rhetoric.

2 On the audience's rejection of premises, see Perelman, *Realm of Rhetoric*, p. 21; Perelman and Olbrechts-Tyteca, *New Rhetoric*, p. 65.

3 H. Koskenniemi has highlighted the maintenance of contact as an essential, and sometimes the only purpose in ancient Greek letters (*Studien zur Idee und Phraseologie des griechischen Briefes bis 400 n. Chr.* [Helsinki: Akateeminen Kirjakauppa, 1956]); his work is succinctly summarized in White, 'New Testament Epistolary Literature', pp. 1731-32 and *passim*.

tion;[1] an expression of confidence such as this one could also function indirectly to establish an expectation that the Romans will act in accordance with their worldwide reputation, a possibility we will discuss below in connection with the expression of confidence in 15.14.[2] It is with the oath in 1.8-9 that Paul establishes a new aspect of this ethos, his unflagging personal concern for the Romans, and anchors his desire to see them in his divine service (λατρεία) to the gospel (1.9). It is God's will, not Paul's own, that impels him toward Rome (1.10), in order to see the Roman Christians (11a). This purpose is given precision in conventional terms from Jewish and Christian paraenesis: 'I want to see you in order that I might impart some spiritual gift to you, that you might be strengthened, that is, that we might be mutually encouraged'.[3] Paul clearly presents himself as one capable of

---

1 Abraham Malherbe, 'Exhortation in First Thessalonians', *NovT* 25 (1983), pp. 241-42; developed in Leo J. Perdue, 'Paraenesis and the Epistle of James', *ZNW* 72 (1981), pp. 241-56; see also Stowers, *Letter-Writing*, pp. 38-39.

2 Compare Stanley N. Olson's remarks ('Pauline Expressions of Confidence in His Addressees', *CBQ* 47 [1985], p. 289) regarding other Pauline letters: 'The expressions of confidence about the addressees' compliance in Galatians, 2 Thessalonians, and Philemon are seen to function as polite and friendly, if ironic, means for reinforcing the purpose for which the letter was written'. 'Whatever the emotion behind the expression' in Gal. 5.10, 'the function is to undergird the letter's request or admonitions by creating a sense of obligation through praise'. Olson (p. 295) concludes that 'the epistolary expression of confidence is best interpreted as a persuasive technique rather than as a sincere reflection of the way the writer thinks the addressees will respond to his proposals or to himself'. See also Stowers, *Letter-Writing*, pp. 77-80; Malherbe, 'Exhortation in First Thessalonians', p. 240; Furnish, *Theology and Ethics*, p. 94.

3 Παρακαλεῖν and στηρίζειν are paired as the activity of prophets, apostles, or apostolic messengers in Acts 15.32 and 14.22; cf. especially 1 Thess. 3.2, where Paul sends Timothy as his coworker ἐν τῷ εὐαγγελίῳ to 'strengthen and encourage' the Thessalonians (στηρίξαι... καὶ παρακαλέσαι). The pair may derive from Deut 3.28 (LXX: κατίσχυσον... καὶ παρακάλεσον). The underlying Hebrew words, *'mṣ wḥzq*, are linked in the Qumran literature. To 'strengthen the heart' (2 Thess. 2.16-17) is a related Jewish idiom (cf. also 1QM 16.13-14; 1QH 1.32; 2.28; *2 Bar.* 43.2; 4 Ezra 12.8). On the phrase in exhortation, see E. Earle Ellis, *Prophecy and Herme-*

imparting 'some spiritual gift' to the Romans. The qualification in v. 12 (τοῦτο δέ ἐστιν) points to a mutuality grounded in their common life in the Spirit. Paul and the Romans alike are 'called' of God, and their shared faith can be an encouragement to both. But this mutuality does not imply a reversibility of roles, nor does it mitigate what Paul has said about his apostolic calling in 1.1-6. Again talk of 'uncertainty and embarrassment' is out of place (*pace* Käsemann). Friendly, even intimate expressions of mutuality and trust could be used as conventional devices in moral exhortation;[1] the qualification in 1.12 need not diminish the seriousness of Paul's intentions stated in 1.11 or in what follows.

Paul has adapted the conventional liturgical εὐχαριστῶ-formula[2] and epistolary topics[3] in such a way as to connect the relationship established in 1.1-7 with his purposes in being present to the Romans. Those purposes are elaborated in terms that are imprecise by virtue of their conventional and topical quality; again we see the constraint under which the apostle must *create* a relationship by resort to 'commonplaces' that in other circumstances had already been established

---

neutic (Grand Rapids: Eerdmans, 1978), pp. 130-33; Malherbe, 'Exhortation', pp. 240-41.

1 See Malherbe, 'Exhortation in First Thessalonians', pp. 245-46; *idem, Moral Exhortation: A Greco-Roman Sourcebook* (Philadelphia: Westminster, 1986), pp. 48-67; *idem, Paul and the Thessalonians: the Philosophical Tradition of Pastoral Care* (Philadelphia: Fortress, 1987), pp. 52-60. One may compare Philo's description of the Therapeutae as a community of mutual exhortation in *De vita contemplativa*. Norman Peterson discusses Paul's language of mutuality as a 'mask' for underlying relationships of authority; see the section 'Commanding and Appealing, Rhetoric and Reality' in *Rediscovering Paul: Philemon and the Sociology of Paul's Narrative World* (Philadelphia: Fortress, 1985), pp. 131-51.

2 The earlier understanding of the εὐχαριστῶ-clause as an epistolary convention (Bjerkelund, *Parakalô*; Schubert, *Form and Function of the Pauline Thanksgivings*) has been corrected by insight into its liturgical background in the Jewish *hodayah* and *berakah* (James M. Robinson, 'Die Hodajot-Formel in Gebet und Hymnus des Frühchristentums', in *Apophoreta: Festschrift für Ernst Haenchen,* ed. W. Eltester and F.H. Kettler [Berlin: Alfred Töpelmann, 1964], pp. 194-35; Doty, *Letters*, pp. 32-34; and White, 'New Testament Epistolary Literature').

3 On these see Aune, *Literary Environment*, p. 188.

through his prior 'evangelization'. The relation of speaker, audience and exigence is thus modified in the thanksgiving clause, as the following diagram indicates.[1]

Speaker	*Audience*	*Exigence*
Paul, whose priestly service (λατρεύω) to the gospel imposes a prayerful concern to come to the Roman church (1.9), is, by implication, capable of 'imparting some spiritual gift' to them (1.11), i.e., of 'stengthening' and 'encouraging' them.	The Romans, whose faith is known in all the world (1.8), should nevertheless welcome the opportunity to be 'strengthened' and 'encouraged' together with Paul; they are at once objects of his care and members of the domain of his λατρεία to serve God in the gospel.	(God's will is not only that Gentiles be brought to obedience and holiness [1.5, 7], but also that those who have been so called should be 'strengthened and encouraged', by divine power [χάρισμα ... πνευματικόν], to remain faithful to that calling.)

The third element in the letter's *exordium* is the disclosure formula beginning in 1.13. Grammatical markers extend a hypotactic (periodic) construction through 1.18.[2] Continuity of theme (εὐαγγελίσασθαι in 1.15, εὐαγγέλιον in 1.16, 17; 'revela-

---

1 Rhetoric *redisposes* the constraints of a rhetorical situation, so that for example the audience is 'no longer exactly the same at the end of the speech as it was at the beginning' (Perelman, *New Rhetoric*, p. 23); one aspect of rhetorical criticism is therefore the analysis of *modifications* of the rhetorical situation, including the 'conditioning' of the audience (*ibid.*, pp. 490-95; cf. William Wuellner, 'Paul as Pastor: The Function of Rhetorical Questions in First Corinthians', in Vanhoye, ed., *L'Apôtre Paul*, p. 61 and n. 63).

2 On the rhetorical significance of hypotactic (periodic) construction, see Perelman and Olbrechts-Tyteca, *New Rhetoric*, pp. 156-57, after Eric Auerbach, *Mimesis: The Representation of Reality in Western Literature* (trans. Willard Trask; Princeton: Princeton University Press, 1953), p. 92. The period, 'the argumentative construction par excellence', 'controls the reader, forces him to see particular relationships, restricts the interpretation he may consider, and takes its inspiration from well-constructed legal reasoning' (p. 157). These comments suggest that the period marked by subordinating conjunctions (γάρ) in 1.13-18 bears a rhetorical significance that is neglected when 1.16-17 are extracted from their context as the 'theme' of an exposition in the following chapters.

tion' in the gospel in 1.17, 18) likewise suggests that units usually separated (1.13-15, 16-17, 18-32) are integrally related. The rhetorical critical question must be: How do the elements of this extended hypotaxis serve to modify the rhetorical relationship created in 1.1-12?

Epistolographic identifications of 1.13 as a 'disclosure formula', alerting the readers to what follows, or as a 'transition' to the letter body, help to mark the significance of the verse.[1] The shift from present tense in 1.8-12 ('I make mention of you in my prayers', 'I long to see you') to past tense in 1.13 ('many times I have yearned to come to you') points away from the immediacy of the epistolary relationship to a broader and more long-standing exigence: Paul has been prevented from fulfilling his desire to 'have some fruit' among the Romans 'as among the rest of the Gentiles'. In 1.13 Paul at once explains why he has not yet come to Rome, thus reinforcing an ethos of pastoral concern, *and* also indicates why he should want to come to Rome in the first place. It is important to note that both statements cohere in Paul's divine commission as apostle to the Gentiles. He has intended to come to the Romans to realize a benefit that he has obtained elsewhere within the domain of his apostolic ministry; and it is his faithful execution of that ministry that has so occupied him as to postpone his visit to Rome. Against a tendency to read καὶ ἐκωλύθην as an anxious defense against charges of neglect (Knox) or as a cryptic allusion to Jewish antagonists (Wuellner), we observe that the accent in 1.13 does not fall on Paul's having been *hindered*, but on his hitherto postponed *desire* to be present with the Romans. This suggestion is corroborated in the following verses. The hindrance, elaborated in terms of his obligation to 'Greeks and barbarians, wise and uncultured' (1.14) and identified at the end of the letter as preoccupation in other mission areas (15.22), springs from the same motive

---

1 Y.T. Mullins, 'Disclosure: A Literary Form in the New Testament', *NovT* 7 (1964), pp. 44-50; Sanders, pp. 348-62; Pedersen, 'Zur Isagogik', p. 49. 'The body opening is the point at which the principal occasion for the letter is usually indicated.... The body opening lays the foundation, in either case, from which the superstructure may grow' (John White, *Form and Function of the Body of the Greek Letter* [Missoula: Scholars Press, 1972], pp. 18-19).

that continues to drive him toward Rome, and now impels him to write, although he would much rather see the Romans face to face.

The rhetorical situation is again modified as Paul brings his charge as apostle to the Gentiles and his intentions toward the Romans into direct contact:

Speaker	Audience	Exigence
Paul, whose sincere wish to come to the Romans is the consequence of a broader apostolic obligation to the Gentiles, has been prevented from coming to them by other work in service to that same obligation; which now imposes upon him an urgency (κατ' ἐμὲ πρόθυμον) to evangelize them.	The Romans are made objects of Paul's attention and concern, primarily by virtue of their belonging to the domain of his apostolic obligation: 'also among you, as among the rest of the Gentiles' (1.13); 'so also to you who are in Rome' (1.14-15).	Paul's commission to secure the obedience of the Gentiles (1.5), which has prompted his long-felt desire to come to the Romans (1.13), includes them in its domain: He wants to 'reap a harvest' among them (1.13), to 'evangelize' them (1.15).

Severing 1.13-15 from a 'theme' in 1.16-17 ignores syntactical markers and thus neutralizes the rhetorical dimension of the passage as a whole. On such a reading, Paul's statement that 'he is not ashamed of the gospel' (1.15a) is read as the stylistic figure of an epideictic orator preparing his audience for an exposition of a favored theme.[1] This way of understanding the passage in an expository mode focuses on Paul's supposedly innovative theological topics (e.g., 'the righteousness of God'), particularly when the 'faith-works' dichotomy is (prematurely) imported into 1.16-17 from 3.20-21,[2] at the cost of the rhetorical importance of these verses for Paul's approach to

---

1 See the discussion in the Introduction, pp. 62-63 above.
2 Πιστεύειν is not represented in 1.16-17 as one mode of religiousness contrasted with another; rather, it is qualified by the context as the response to God's call as this is made effective in εὐαγγέλιον. 'The response of the man who is called by God can only be πιστεύειν in the sense of ὑπακούειν' (Schmidt, 'καλέω', *TDNT*, III, p. 489).

the Romans. The coherence of the passage 1.13-17 and the emphasis within 1.16-17 are thus obscured.

Paul is 'not ashamed of (preaching) the gospel' *because* (γάρ) it is 'God's power (δύναμις) unto salvation'; it is God who is at work in the event of εὐαγγέλιον, not Paul alone. This *divine* intentionality, which is the powerful manifestation of God's self-integrity in the creation of faith (δικαιοσύνη ... θεοῦ ... εἰς πίστιν), both emboldens and requires Paul to 'evangelize' the Romans as he has 'the rest of the Gentiles'. The apostle's language here has less to do with the content of a distinctive doctrine ('justification by faith') than with the effective action of God which makes itself present in the event of proclamation. The independent clause at the pinnacle of the extensive hypotactic construction in 1.15-18—'so I am eager to evangelize you in Rome as well'—is the syntactical and semantic focus of the passage; that is, its heart is not the content of 'the Pauline gospel', but Paul's intention to 'evangelize' the Romans.

Here at last the 'deep exigence' underlying the letter *exordium* comes to expression. It is 'the God who brings back the fallen world into the sphere of his legitimate claim',[1] who has set apart Paul as the proximate instrument of that claim toward the Gentiles (1.1, 5), and who in calling the Gentiles into the sphere of Christ's lordship both demands and creates holiness (1.6, 7), who has laid upon the apostle the urgency (κατ' ἐμὲ πρόθυμον) to evangelize the Romans, that is, to realize the εὐαγγέλιον among them which is nothing other than God's own saving power. It is arbitrary to isolate 1.16-17 from their functional roles within the letter *exordium*, for this is to break apart the rhetorical exigence of the letter and the divine κλῆσις that claims apostle and believers alike. Such an interpretative move subtly transforms Paul's statements of intention in 1.11-15 into a subjunctive mode and, contrary to the clear tendency of the language here, removes *this* letter from the domain of Paul's divine obligation (1.14). We suggest, to the contrary, that the proper interpretation of Romans is impossible apart from the insight that in the lengthy disclosure period (1.13-17), the 'deep exigence', God's redemptive

1 Käsemann, *Romans*, p. 29.

purpose as this has claimed Paul *and* the Romans, is fused
with the immediate epistolary exigence that now brings them
together. The letter is directed to perform the very function
that Paul would have performed in person had he not been
'hindered', namely, the 'evangelization' of the Romans.[1] To
break the connection between εὐαγγελίσασθαι in 1.15 and
εὐαγγέλιον in 1.16 is to insulate the epistolary situation from
the δύναμις... θεοῦ.[2]

These observations lead to the hypothesis that Paul intends
this letter to Rome to serve as the medium of his 'evangelization' of the Romans. But in what does this εὐαγγελίσασθαι
consist? Against Günter Klein's proposal, it does not mean the
presentation of a 'genuine' Pauline gospel as the requisite
means of founding an ἐκκλησία,[3] for this implies that εὐαγ-

---

1 This has already been suggested by Dahl ('Missionary Theology',
   p. 77) and Pedersen ('Zur Isagogik', pp. 63-67), but the insight has
   not been carried through. Our position here has much in common
   with Robert Funk's discussion ('Apostolic *Parousia*', p. 258) of
   Paul's letters as a surrogate for his personal presence, except that
   Funk (p. 268), following Knox, considers Romans to be an encyclical
   modified for dispatch to Rome by the addition of 15.14ff.
2 Numerous commentators follow text editions (e.g., Nestle-Aland[26])
   in isolating 1.16-17 as the letter's 'theme', almost as if the super-
   scription περὶ τοῦ εὐαγγελίου or περὶ τῆς δικαιοσύνης θεοῦ stood in the
   text at this point. Indeed, the supposition that the letter body constitutes a thematic essay has enjoyed wide acceptance, but has
   received almost no *critical* examination. K. Donfried has included
   M.L. Stirewalt's study of 'The Form and Function of the Greek
   Letter-Essay' in *The Romans Debate* (pp. 175-206), but, despite
   Donfried's discussion ('False Presuppositions in the Study of
   Romans', *ibid.*, pp. 145-48), Stirewalt's essay cannot provide an
   answer to the question of the letter's genre. Far from being analogous to Rom. 1.16-17, the treatise introductions that Stirewalt discusses have a distinct and stereotyped form in which the author
   states his purpose (for example, 'I have prepared this essay on
   such-and-such a topic'), indicates a reason (a request from a corre-
   spondent or student, the supposed usefulness of the essay to a wider
   audience, etc.), and often identifies the process of composition ('I
   have gone through my notes', 'I have summarized my larger
   treatment on this same subject', etc.). The treatise proper begins
   with an obvious marker such as 'first, then...' All this is without
   analogy in Romans, suggesting that if Paul intended to write a
   'letter-essay', he went about it in a wholly unconventional way.
3 See above, pp. 23, 28.

γελίσασθαι (1.15) means merely 'to set forth a description of the εὐαγγέλιον', particularly in its 'universal' aspect (cf. Ἰουδαίῳ τε πρῶτον καὶ "Ελληνι). Paul's other statements in the context confirm the effective character of εὐαγγελίσασθαι: it includes 'strengthening' and 'encouragement' (1.11-12). The letter is not *protrepsis*, i.e., rhetoric inviting the audience to adopt a *new* way of life (*contra* Berger). The apparent incongruity that Klein perceives in Paul's desire to 'evangelize' those who have already responded to the gospel is resolved in the realization that, for Paul, the Christian life as the continuing answer to God's call is only a possibility because of the power of God (δύναμις... θεοῦ, 1.16) made available to the Christian congregation in the gifts of the Spirit (cf. χάρισμα, 1.11).

If we are not simply to empty the word εὐαγγελίσασθαι of any meaning in the context,[1] we must coordinate it with εὐαγγέλιον, which always brings the power of salvation (1.16),[2] which manifests God's righteousness (1.17) and the revelation of divine wrath against human wickedness and impiety (1.18). To act as the instrument of this gospel—εὐαγγελίσασθαι—is to announce God's claim upon the creature: it is to require obedience, *within* the assembly of believers no less than without. If we are not to sunder the connection at 1.15-16, we must consider the possibility that Paul intends this letter to function as the bearer of that divine claim.

It remains to be seen how Rom. 1.18-32 functions to build upon what we have identified as the *exordium* in 1.1-17. That discussion must be delayed, however, until Chapter 2, where the interrelation of 1.18-32 with 1.1-17 and 2.1-16 can receive sustained treatment. At present it is necessary to test the hypothesis that the letter's *exordium* serves broadly paraenetic purposes—that is, the *exordium* prepares the

---

1 Käsemann (*Romans*, pp. 20-21) reduces εὐαγγελίσασθαι to a transitional cipher before the thematic description of the εὐαγγέλιον in 1.16-17.

2 'Wherever it is proclaimed... this gospel is charged with power. It creates faith (Rom. 1.16f; Phil. 1.27), brings salvation, life (Rom. 1.16; 1 Cor. 15.2)' (U. Becker, 'Gospel', in Colin Brown, ed., *New International Dictionary of New Testament Theology* [Grand Rapids: Zondervan, 1976], II, p. 111).

audience for a letter that will 'demand something of them' by comparing the *exordium* with Paul's recapitulation of his purposes.[1]

3. Peroratio (Rom. 15.14-32)

The paraenetic character of Romans is confirmed by the correspondence of letter opening and closing, or, to identify their oratorical analogues, of *exordium* and *peroratio* (1.1-17, 15.14-32). The recapitulative function of 15.14-15 is obvious (ἔγραψα ὑμῖν... ἵνα). In this *peroratio*, Paul reiterates his obligation to serve the gospel (15.16; cf. 1.13-14) and the Spirit's power that has propelled that ministry throughout the world, that is, what 'Christ' has done, which is his only 'ground for boasting' (15.17-20; cf. 1.16), toward the end of Gentile obedience (15.18; cf. 1.5). Here, as in the *exordium*, that divine ministry is related to Paul's orientation toward the Roman Christians. But there are two differences. First, now the direction of thought is reversed. Whereas in the *exordium* Paul 'zoomed in' from a wide view of his apostolic responsibility to *all* Gentiles (1.1-5) toward a sharp focus on his intention and desire to be *among the Romans*, in ch. 15 the view moves *outward* from his writing to the Romans in fulfillment of his 'commission' (χάρις, 15.15; cf. 1.5) and 'divine service' (λειτουργόν, ἱερουργοῦντα, 15.16; cf. ὁ θεὸς ᾧ λατρεύω, 1.9) to his boast in what Christ has done through him in other parts of the world (15.19-23) and his plans to go on to Spain (15.24, 28). Second, just as there is no reference to Spain in ch. 1, so here in ch. 15 there is no talk of 'evangelizing' the Romans. That language is reserved now for points to the west of Rome (15.20-24).

This last fact has led some interpreters to conclude that here, and *not* in Rom. 1.11-15, are the clues to Paul's purpose

---

1 This choice of phrase derives from Epictetus' remarks contrasting the 'style of exhortation' (ὁ προτρεπτικὸς χαρακτήρ) with epideictic display-speeches (*Diss.* 3.33.33-38): 'There is nothing more effective in the style for exhortation than when the speaker makes clear to the audience that he requires something of them' (ὅτι χρείαν αὐτῶν ἔχει). (The last phrase is obscured in W.A. Oldfather's translation [Loeb], 'that he has need of them': see the Liddell-Scott *Lexicon*, s.v. χρεία, #3.)

in writing Romans: the congregation in Rome is not the final target, but serves only an intermediary role as the means to another, more remote end. But that conclusion is unnecessary, and is refuted by the observation that Paul's declaration about his apostolic obligation (15.15b-16) is related, not only to the following remarks about his previous work in the east (15.17-21) and about his prospective work in the west (15.22-24), but to 15.15a, to which it is immediately subordinate (διά plus accusative, 1.15b). In the connection of these two verses, as in 1.1-15, Paul's divine ministry is tied to his intentions *toward the Roman Christians*. But now his orientation is not forward, to some hypothetical projected visit, but *backward*, to the letter itself (ἔγραψα).

The simplest explanation of the discrepancy between Paul's much desired visit to evangelize the Romans (1.15) and the anticipated stopover for 'refreshment' in 15.24 is that they are not references to the same trip; that is, Rom. 1.15 describes the visit Paul would like to have made, *but cannot*; Rom. 15.24 refers to the visit he *will* be able to make after delivering the collection to Jerusalem (15.25-29). 'Evangelizing' the Romans is absent from Paul's future plans, not because that was never really his intention, but because that intention *has been achieved* between chs. 1 and 15, that is, *by the letter itself*. Romans is written as a surrogate for the visit Paul has long desired to make (1.10-15) under the constraint of his obligation as apostle to *all* the Gentiles, including the Roman Christians. The letter *is* Paul's εὐαγγελίσασθαι. The *resolution* of an exigence described in our discussion of the *exordium* may be represented in the following diagram:

Speaker	Audience	Exigence
Paul has written 'on account of' (διά) the apostolic χάρις given him to perform priestly service (λειτουργῶν) to Christ before the Gentiles; thus doing 'sacred service' (ἱερουργῶν) for the gospel.	(The Romans, in receiving his letter, participate in his divine liturgy toward 'the Gentiles'.)	Paul's divine liturgy remains a binding obligation (15.17-21): it has prevented him from coming to Rome (διό, 15.22); and it impels him toward other work (15.23-24). But this obligation no longer lays upon him an 'urgency' toward the Romans (cf. 1.15).

The clear statement of purpose in 15.14-16 (ἔγραψα ὑμῖν... ἵνα) bears attention. Paul's 'boldness' in writing (15.15) consists precisely in addressing this letter to those who Paul is confident can 'instruct' each other (15.14, RSV). The Greek verb is νουθετεῖν, which might better be translated 'admonish', 'exhort', 'instill sense in', etc. It bears noting that ancient epistolary theorists discussed a variety of what we should call paraenetic letters, one among these being the 'admonishing type' of letter, νουθετητικὸς τύπος:

> The admonishing type is one which indicates through its name what its character is. For admonition [νουθετεῖν] is the instilling of sense [νοῦν ἐντιθῆναι] in the person who is being admonished, and teaching him what should and should not be done... [1]

That Paul can speak of 'admonition' in describing the letter's purpose suggests that Romans was conceived as a paraenetic or admonitory letter. Neither Paul's statement of confidence in the Romans in 15.14, nor his characterization of the letter as written 'by way of reminder' (ὡς ἐπαναμιμνῄσκων) in 15.15 precludes this possibility: In fact they corroborate it. Expressions of confidence in the reader's ability or willingness to comply represented a stereotyped *topos* in epistolary paraene-

---

1 Pseudo-Demetrius, *Typoi Epistolikoi*; translation and discussion in Abraham Malherbe, 'Ancient Epistolary Theorists', *OJRS* 5 (1977), pp. 3-77.

sis,[1] as did references to 'reminding' readers of what they already knew was the proper way of life.[2] 'Boldness' itself is a characteristic of the true friend's beneficient admonition.[3] Consequently, to speak of a polite ecclesiastical diplomacy, of timidity or defensiveness, or to construe Paul's 'boldness' as a self-conscious reflection on the uniqueness of his personal theology,[4] is to miss the point.

As we have seen, a number of attempts to resolve the letter's 'double character' have aligned the 'debate with Judaism' within the letter with references to the proposed trip to Spain, possibly to be underwritten by the Roman church (15.24), or with the collection and Paul's anxieties about 'unbelievers in Judea' (15.25-32).[5] These hypotheses depend on references late in ch. 15 for clues to the letter's exigence, to the detriment of what we have seen to be direct statements of purpose in 1.8-15 and the recapitulation of the letter in 15.14-16. Our discussion of the resulting character of Romans as the medium for Paul's 'evangelization' of Christians in Rome casts doubt on those hypotheses that read the letter as Paul's theological self-introduction, calculated to gain Roman political or financial support with regard to Jerusalem. Once Romans is conceived as a theological dossier, then its rhetorical purpose is seen to lie in persuading the Romans of *Paul's* legitimacy; Rom. 1.1-15

---

1 See the references in n. 2 on p. 78 above. Olson's essay on 'Pauline Expressions of Confidence' is particularly helpful, but unfortunately he does not apply his insights into the persuasive function of the epistolary expression of confidence to Rom. 15.14-15, presumably because he does not see the letter's overall purpose as paraenetic (as in Galatians). Rather, he considers these verses 'a transition to an apology for Paul's intended way of relating to the addressees' (p. 293). This surrenders the expression's rhetorical function for a fragmentive reading of Rom. 15.

2 See Dahl, 'Anamnesis'; Perdue; Perdue, 'Paraenesis', pp. 244-45; Malherbe, 'Exhortation in First Thessalonians', p. 240. Seneca's discussion (*Epistle* 94) of 'the value of advice' (*monitio*) is devoted to the importance of rehearsing 'precepts' although they are well known.

3 Malherbe, 'Exhortation in First Thessalonians', pp. 247-49.

4 Käsemann, *Romans*, pp. 390-92; Pedersen, 'Zur Isagogik', pp. 64, 65.

5 See pp. 25-28 above.

has then appeared, by contrast, as a reserved, calculated proem in which Paul holds back his true purposes.

Käsemann only puts into precise terms a more widely held view when he contrasts Paul's timidity in ch. 1 with the directness of ch. 15:

> The advance as compared with the obscurities, reservations, and retractions of the proem is not only expressed in the fact that Paul now sets forth his purposes much more concretely, explicitly, and definitely. An apologetic tendency now emerges undisguised, which compelled him to write what from this perspective is in some respects at least a kind of account of his preaching... So long as the theology had not been sketched and focused, the proem could offer only relatively vague indications, but now these are replaced by precise statements and conceptions.[1]

The picture of Paul that results from Käsemann's reading of ch. 15 is something of a shrewd salesman:

> Usually the high diplomacy which has gone into the construction of our epistle is not perceived. Paul carefully guards against falling into the house as soon as the door opens. For various reasons he needed Rome's help in his work, and he thus thought it good even without some pressing occasion to acquaint this unknown congregation with his preaching and work before giving his concern a clear contour. To that extent the whole epistle prepares the way for this 'epilogue'.[2]

To be sure, Käsemann here has rightly recognized the importance of Paul's anxiety regarding Jerusalem (15.30-32) for a construal of the letter's occasion. But he has also neutralized the purpose expressed in 1.10-15 and thus collapsed the tension between Rom. 1 and Rom. 15 by way of a one-sided emphasis on the latter. The letter is thus taken to serve 'to acquaint this unknown congregation with his preaching and work', rather than to bring the members of the congregation themselves into the sphere of that work, as 1.13-15 suggests.

We have argued, on the contrary, that the tension between Rom. 1 and Rom. 15 is more satisfactorily interpreted in part

---

1 Käsemann, *Romans*, p. 390.
2 *Ibid.*

on the theory that Paul accomplished *in this letter* the purposes expressed in the *exordium*. The *peroratio* clearly has a recapitulative function; Paul's 'bold' writing, 'by way of reminder', applies not just to the 'paraenetic section' of Romans 12–15, but to the whole letter. Now, at the end of the letter, having accomplished the purposes set out in the *exordium*, Paul is free to discuss their broader context in his missionary concerns.

But this does not mean that Paul's anxiety regarding Jerusalem (15.30-32) is a mere afterthought, tangential to the letter's purpose. On the contrary, we mean only to interpret the relation between the letter and the Jerusalem campaign in such a way as to balance his intentions toward the Romans themselves (1.10-15, 15.14f.) in the equation. The precise relationship between Jerusalem and Rome in the letter's purpose remains to be determined.

We contend that the letter is not simply a tool for securing Paul's goals *in Jerusalem*. Rather, Jerusalem is a powerful tractive force affecting his interaction with the Roman Christians. The solution is to be found in the 'hinge' at 15.15-16 which connects the epistolary act with Paul's apostolic χάρις before the Gentiles (including, but not limited to, the Romans). It is widely recognized now that the 'offering of the Gentiles' represents not only a financial contribution but the symbolic self-giving of Gentile converts, in material community with their Jewish fellows in Jerusalem as well as in expression of 'indebtedness' to them (15.27), and in holiness to God (cf. 15.16; 15.13). In Paul's view, the offering is evidence for the Jerusalem saints that in the mission among the Gentiles the ancient promises of Scripture are being fulfilled (15.7-12).[1]

The simplest reading of the causal links in 15.14-16 (διά, εἰς τὸ εἶναί, ἵνα) implies that in Paul's view, the sanctity of the 'Gentiles' offering', the προσφορὰ τῶν ἐθνῶν, depends on the Romans' response to this letter. Paul has directed an admonitory letter (νουθετεῖν, 15.14) to the Romans, on the basis of the 'grace' or 'commission' (χάρις; cf. 1.5) given to him to be a minister of Christ Jesus to (all of) the Gentiles, '*in order that*

---

1 Dieter Georgi, *Die Geschichte der Kollekte des Paulus für Jerusalem* (Hamburg-Bergstet: Reich, 1965).

the offering of the Gentiles may be acceptable, sanctified by the Holy Spirit'.

Paul does not so much want the Romans' money—he is already en route to Jerusalem (15.25)—nor does he say anything about their possible political influence on his behalf; he has not yet asked for their prayers (cf. 15.30-32). How, then, are they to participate in the 'offering of the Gentiles'?[1] First and foremost, we suggest, Paul desires their faithful obedience and holiness. The paraenesis in chs. 12–15 is brought to a close in a prayer that God will bless the Roman readers 'with all joy and peace in believing' (15.13). As it stands now, following 15.7-12, that prayer asks that God secure their place among the Gentiles who, in fulfillment of Israel's Scriptures, have turned to God in faith and thanksgiving. The paraenetic section of the letter was introduced with an appeal to the Romans to present themselves 'living sacrifices, holy and acceptable to God', their 'spiritual worship' (12.1-2; RSV), that is, by undergoing the 'transformation by the renewal of your minds' that is manifested in mutual consideration and love (12.3ff), even to the point of indulging the 'weaker' brother's conscience (14.1-15.3). This paraenesis culminated in praise of God's effective purposes in turning the Gentiles to himself in thanksgiving (15.9-12). In 15.14-16, where the letter is recapitulated, the paraenetic orientation is linked with Paul's priestly service in presenting an offering (the προσφορὰ τῶν ἐθνῶν) to God. This parallel suggests strongly that Paul conceives the sanctity of the worldwide offering of which he is minister to require the holy living of the Gentiles in Rome whom God had called. The paraenetic exigence of the immediate epistolary situation and the 'deep' exigence of Paul's divine service (λατρεία) are thus fused.

---

1 A.J.M. Wedderburn ('Purpose and Occasion', pp. 137-41) puts his finger on this question as the key to the letter's purpose, but focuses on 15.30-32 to the neglect of 15.14-16, and relies on the conjecture of antagonistic Jewish sentiments in the Roman congregation (p. 140).

Speaker	Audience	Exigence
Paul, writer of an admonitory letter, and (thereby) λειτουργῶν of Christ to the Gentiles.	The Romans, who by performing their own spiritual λατρεία (12.1-2) participate in the προσφορὰ τῶν ἐθνῶν foretold in Scripture (15.9-12, 16).	(God's purpose, foretold in Israel's Scriptures, to be honored by the Gentiles as well as by Israel [15.9-12]; which is *now* fulfilled through Paul's priestly service [15.16].)

The relationship between the letter's paraenetic aspect and Paul's anxiety concerning Jerusalem correlates with the exhortation to the Christians of Rome to have regard for the scruples of their brothers and sisters, exhortation which means, at least in part, that Gentile Christians are to defer to Jewish scruples in matters of common life. The explanation consists in recognizing a fundamental 'spiritual' premise in the apostle's thought: the acceptability of the 'offering of the Gentiles' is the first of all a matter of the holiness of the Gentiles whom God has called (cf. 15.16, 31).

When Paul expresses trepidation about his trip to Jerusalem, *he says nothing at all about Jewish opposition to his theological views.* He does consider the reception of his 'service' (διακονία) to Jerusalem, that is, the collection, to be in jeopardy. It is, in particular, the collection's 'acceptability' and 'sanctity' that is at risk (15.16, 31), and in 15.16-22 the sanctity of the offering is related immediately to 'what Christ has done' through Paul *'unto the obedience of Gentiles'* (15.18). These correlations lead us to conclude that what Paul wants from the Romans is not first of all their approval or endorsement of 'his gospel', but *their holy living*, for *this* will guarantee the sanctity of the offering of the Gentiles. He writes to secure that obedience.[1]

---

1 Note in this regard that in 15.17-20, 'what Christ has done' through Paul in securing the obedience of the Gentiles, 'through signs and wonders', can also be described as 'fulfilling the gospel of Christ' (πεπληρωκέναι τὸ εὐαγγέλιον τοῦ Χριστοῦ) and as 'evangelizing' (εὐαγγελίζεσθαι). This suggests the content of the same verb in 1.15: Paul wants to be the instrument through which Christ works to create obedient faith *among the Romans.*

4. *The Letter's Macro-Structure: A Clue*

We may recapitulate the results of our examination of *'exordium'* and *'peroratio'* in Romans.[1] Paul writes to the Romans to 'strengthen', 'encourage', and 'evangelize' them; that is, to realize the 'power of God' among them (1.13-17). The 'depth dimension' of the letter's exigence is God's call to obedience and holiness, which constrains Paul to address the Romans (1.13-15, 15.14-15); its 'proximate dimension' in the epistolary situation is a plea for the Romans to conduct themselves in mutual regard and consideration, despite *possible* tensions over Jewish observance within the congregation, and thus to accept a cooperative role in the eschatological 'offering of the Gentiles' (15.9-12; 16).

So far as chs. 1 and 15 give us indication, the rhetorical situation has little or nothing to do with convincing the Romans of Paul's theological acceptability, and—to put our

---

1 Our restriction of the 'recapitulative' function of a *peroratio* to Rom. 15.14-32 has for the most part neglected the question of the role played by Rom. 16, primarily because the recapitulative and argumentative function of 15.14-32 is clear, and is at most reinforced (but not further developed) in ch. 16. It is probably significant that in the list of greetings concluding a letter that, on the hypothesis presented above, may address ethnic and religious tensions within the Roman congregations, Paul gives a weighty endorsement to Prisca and Aquila (16.3-5), co-workers and friends who were among the Jews expelled from Rome (Acts 18.2), and commends other members of the Roman congregations who were certainly Jewish (see the Introduction, above). To emphasize the contributions of Jewish Christians among the Romans serves to give 'presence' to Paul's discussion of the 'remnant' of Israel in Rom. 11 (on techniques of presence, see Perelman and Olbrechts-Tyteca, *The New Rhetoric*, pp. 144-48). Further, in contrast to a disposition widespread especially among Protestant commentators to emphasize the innovative aspects of Paul's theology and mission, it may also be significant that Paul emphatically commends Phoebe, the deacon of the Cenchrean congregation who has benefitted Paul as a patron (16.1-2), Prisca and Aquila, who have 'risked their necks' for him (16.3-4), and Andronicus and Junia, two (most probably Jewish-Christian) apostles 'before me in Christ' (16.7)—that is, persons who enjoy authoritative status in Christ and in the gospel *independently* of Paul, to whom in fact Paul is indebted. Here the dependence of the Gentile mission on the continuing heritage of Israel (cf. Rom. 11) is given very personal expression.

position most sharply over against, for example, Käsemann's—nothing to do with encountering the objections of an
antagonistic Jewish or Judaizing sentiment in Rome.

It bears emphasis that our approach to the 'rhetorical situation' of the letter is based on explicit statements in those parts
of the letter that should be expected to bear most directly on
the letter's purposes, namely the opening and closing sections
that serve argumentative functions corresponding to the
rhetorical *exordium* and *peroratio*. A comparison of this
approach with 'ways not taken' seems worthwhile. That our
procedure has been fruitful, and in a way unanticipated in
previous secondary literature, may be in part the result of a
deliberate decision *not* to approach the rhetorical situation by
way of a 'mirror-reading' of the supposed 'debate with
Judaism' in chs. 1–8, but to hold the function of those chapters
in temporary suspension. It is, in our judgment, the opposite
decision in the history of interpretation that has generated the
problem of the letter's 'double character'. But neither will it be
sufficient to rest with the examination of the letter opening
and recapitulation, for as we emphasized in the Introduction,
the rhetorical character of Romans depends upon the
function of the *whole* letter to provide a fitting redisposition of
the constraints that constitute a rhetorical situation.
'Rhetorical situation' is not an aspect of isolated pericopes,[1] but
of the whole unit of discourse (in this case, the letter itself).

We have proposed a coherent situation within Roman
Christianity, based on the conjecture that Christian Jews
returning to Rome after being expelled by Claudius occasioned ethnic tensions within the (predominantly Gentile-)
Christian congregations established there, a conjecture which
we find corroborated in Rom. 14.1–15.13 (see the

---

1 George Kennedy (*New Testament Interpretation*, pp. 34-35) gives the
misleading impression that a 'rhetorical situation' can be identified
for segments of a text, declaring that the rhetorical situation
'roughly corresponds to the *Sitz im Leben* of form criticism'. This is
incorrect; the form-critical *Sitz im Leben* is a typical, *routine* setting
in life, *not* the specific contingent situation that invites a *particular*
discourse. The resulting misunderstanding is evident, for example,
in A.H. Snyman's attempt to correlate 'Style and the Rhetorical Situation of Romans 8.31-39' (*NTS* 34 [1988], pp. 218-31).

Introduction). Our examination of the letter opening and recapitulation (1.1-17; 15.14-33) suggests that Paul wrote this letter with definite persuasive purposes in mind, and we have proposed that these purposes bear directly on the situation described.

The next task should properly be to substantiate this proposal by examining the argumentative content of the letter as a unit of discourse. For unless the comprehensive progression of the letter would reasonably serve to 'transfer to the conclusion the adherence accorded to the premises',[1] that is, to move the Roman Christians whom he addresses as *Gentiles* (1.6, 13, 14-15) to an attitude of consideration and deference to the religious sentiments of their Jewish brothers and sisters (14.1-15.13),[2] the letter body cannot be considered appropriately 'rhetorical'. It should, in that case, be seen as what Perelman and Olbrechts-Tyteca describe as 'mere essay-making, without concern for real life', rhetoric 'addressed to conventional audiences, of which such rhetoric can afford to have stereotyped conceptions'.[3] If Paul in the letter body does not 'work through what Aristotle calls the *pragmata* of the situation in such a way that an issue emerges from his interactions with the situation', if he fails to take the constraints of the rhetorical situation into account, 'spinning issues from his imagination', he 'may rightly be dismissed as ineffective and irrelevant'.[4]

A full-scale rhetorical-critical exegesis of the whole letter cannot be attempted here. We must be content instead in Chapters 2 and 3 with a compressed treatment of several

---

1 Perelman, *Realm of Rhetoric*, p. 21.
2 Perelman and Olbrechts-Tyteca (*The New Rhetoric*, p. 45) further specify that the goal of rhetoric is 'to set in motion the intended action... or at least [to create] in the hearers a willingness to act which will appear at the right moment'. The distance of the communicative situation from 'the precise circumstances in which this communion will be put to the test' is the measure of epideictic rhetoric (*ibid.*, p. 53). By limiting our discussion to a *rhetorical* situation evoking Romans we deliberately focus upon Paul's efforts to intensify adherence to certain values, without relying on one or another view of the particular historical circumstances in Rome (or elsewhere) that may have prompted those efforts.
3 Perelman and Olbrechts-Tyteca, *The New Rhetoric*, p. 20.
4 Consigny, 'Rhetoric and its Situations', p. 178.

large segments of Paul's argument that merit much fuller examination. The purposes of this book would not be served by neglecting those segments, especially the argumentation in chs. 6–11, altogether.

We have seen that the paraenesis in Rom. 12.1-15.13 is not simply a random accumulation of general, conventional precepts,[1] but shows particular relevance for a situation wherein ethnic and religious differences between Jewish and Gentile Christians have provoked criticism and contempt.[2] Moreover, as V.P. Furnish has shown, the heading that stands over this paraenesis (12.1-2) echoes themes dominant in previous chapters. He notes parallels between 1.16-32 and 12.1-2:

> In 1.18ff, with the Gentiles particularly in mind, the apostle is anxious to show that knowing God (vs. 21) does not necessarily mean that one honors him as God or gives thanks to him.... God's righteousness demands the surrender of all those human pretensions and 'claims' which constitute, in Paul's view, man's bondage to sin. The consequences of sin are vividly presented in vss. 24ff. God 'gives up' the sinners to the dishonoring (ἀτιμάζειν) of their bodies (σώματα, vs. 24); though they seek to become wise (σοφοί), they become fools (vs. 22); their 'knowledge' becomes a lie, and they end up worshipping (σεβάζεσθαι) and serving (λατρεύειν) the creature rather than the creator (vs. 25). They are given up to a reprobate mind (ἀδόκιμος νοῦς) and to 'improper conduct' (ποιεῖν τὰ μὴ καθήκοντα, vs. 28).
>
> The correspondence in vocabulary and concern between Romans 1 and 12 is striking. In 12.1-2 Paul is calling the brethren to a new life exactly opposite that which he has previously described. They are to 'present' their σώματα to God, not 'dishonor' them; they are no longer to serve (λατρεύειν) the creature, but are to offer 'spiritual worship' (λογικὴ λατρεία) to God. The ἀδόκιμος νοῦς has been transformed;

---

1 See especially Furnish, *Theology and Ethics*, pp. 99-106; Käsemann, *Romans*, p. 325.

2 Käsemann similarly finds a purposeful sequence of 'general exhortation' in chs. 12–13 and 'special exhortation' in chs. 14–15. He is appropriately cautious, however, about ascribing *precise* knowledge of conditions in Rome to the apostle: 'As a postulate we might venture the thesis that Paul presupposes or suspects the existence of contending groups at Rome and that this is important for his concerns in writing' (*Romans*, pp. 364-65).

hence Paul in 12.2 can speak of the ἀνακαίνωσις τοῦ νοός. And 'improper conduct' (ποιεῖν τὰ μὴ καθήκοντα) must now yield before the exhortation to 'find out what God's will is' (δοκιμάζειν τί τὸ θέλημα τοῦ θεοῦ) and do it. Rom. 12.1-2 is but the restatement, now to be sure, in a hortatory mode and context, of the theme which had already been emphasized in 1.16-17.[1]

Furnish draws particular attention to parallels between Rom. 6 and 12:

Of special significance are the relationships between chap. 6 and the appeal of 12.1-2... [Paul] reiterates the proposition that the Christian is 'under grace' and no longer 'under law' (vs. 14), but emphasizes that freedom from the law also means freedom from the power of sin (vss. 6ff) and freedom for obedience (vss. 16ff). In developing this theme special use is made of the concept of 'presentation', the verb (παριστάναι) occurring five times in this chapter (vss. 13 [twice], 16, 19 [twice]). The Christian is called upon to present himself to God for obedience, righteousness and sanctification....

When the Pauline exhortations of Romans 12-15 are introduced by the solemn appeal to 'present [παραστῆσαι] your whole beings as a living sacrifice, holy and acceptable to God, your spiritual worship', the appeals made already in chap. 6 are simply being recapitulated and reemphasized.[2]

Furnish's observations point to a fundamental antinomy that gives structure to the letter: the contrast between human depravity and immorality pictured in 1.18-32, and reflected as the former existence of Paul's audience in Rom. 6, and the new life of holiness and sobriety for which Paul pleads in 12.1-2—a new life possible within the sphere of Christ's lordship (Rom. 6). We have suggested above that this antinomy resembles the characteristic 'once—but now' schema of early Christian paraenesis identified by Rudolf Bultmann. If that suggestion can be borne out exegetically, it would imply that Romans should be conceived fundamentally as a paraenetic letter. We will turn to an exegesis of the opening chapters of Romans in Chapter 2, immediately below; but it is appropriate here to clarify our recourse to the category 'paraenesis'.

1 Furnish, *Theology and Ethics*, p. 103.
2 *Ibid.*, pp. 105-106.

In speaking of the 'paraenetic character' of Romans we mean to draw attention to the letter's functional value as an instrument for the reinforcement or modification of values, rather than to presumed *formal* models of 'paraenesis'. This distinction arises from the observation that paraenesis was discussed in antiquity as an *activity* rather than as a form or genre of literature.[1] In fact, the classical rhetorical handbooks refer to this activity only glancingly, and deliberately avoid discussing it, since their object is the study of *civic* discourse.[2] Epistolary theorists discussed different kinds of paraenetic letter, but only briefly, and provided only skeletal models.[3] Nevertheless, we are convinced that the category of paraenesis, understood functionally, is valuable for understanding the character of Romans.

1 See Theodore C. Burgess, 'Epideictic Literature', pp. 229-33; Abraham Malherbe, 'Exhortation in First Thessalonians', pp. 238-39; Leo J. Perdue, 'Paraenesis and the Epistle of James', pp. 241-43.
2 Aristotle associates both private exhortation (ἰδίᾳ συμβουλεύειν) and legislative proposal (κοινῇ δημηγορεῖν) with the deliberative genre, since in both cases 'those who speak... either exhort or dissuade' (*Rhetoric* 1358b); but the first subject is completely neglected in favor of the second. The *Rhetorica ad Alexandrum* similarly distinguishes ἰδίαι ὁμιλίαι from κοιναὶ δημηγορίαι (1421b), but beyond a brief paragraph on 'things expedient to the individual' (14.22a), pursues the oratory of legislative assemblies exclusively (1423aff.). Cicero admits that his discussion of rhetoric has neglected 'many other duties of the orator, those of encouraging, comforting, teaching, and warning, all worthy of the most eloquent treatment, yet having no place of their own in those systems hitherto expounded' (*De Oratore* 2.64). In his *De officiis* he assigns 'the power of speech in the attainment of propriety' to two headings, *contentio* (adversarial speech in the lawcourts) and *sermo* (conversation), and notes that although 'there are rules for oratory laid down by rhetoricians, there are none for conversation' (1.37), a lack he does not trouble himself to remedy.
3 David Aune (review of Betz, *Galatians*, pp. 323-26) notes that paraenesis, especially epistolary paraenesis, plays no role in the classical rhetorical handbooks. Stanley K. Stowers (*Letter-Writing in Greco-Roman Antiquity*, p. 52) observes that the epistolographic tradition was independent of rhetoric, and that a number of letter 'types' embody exhortation, which has characteristics of both deliberative and epideictic rhetoric: 'Thus in the hortatory tradition the distinction between epideictic (praise and blame) and deliberative (giving advice) breaks down'.

Abraham Malherbe and Leo G. Perdue have argued that Martin Dibelius' *formal* approach to paraenesis[1] must be supplemented by a more functional understanding of paraenesis as the activity of moral exhortation. Malherbe describes 1 Thessalonians (and not the formally 'paraenetic' material in chaps. 4–5 alone) as a 'paraenetic letter',[2] and identifies typical characteristics of epistolary paraenesis: it consists primarily of traditional or unoriginal material, usually precepts of general applicability that are often addressed to one who knows them or has heard them before; it relies on examples of virtue or vice, and it involves the representation of a close personal relationship between the sender and the recipient of exhortation. Focusing attention on social function, Perdue incorporates Dibelius' and Malherbe's observations on the traditional, generally applicable, and redundant character of paraenetic sayings in his understanding of paraenesis as secondary socialization:

> Paraenesis... is a means by which an individual is introduced to the group's or role's social knowledge, including especially norms and values pertaining to group or role behavior, internalizes this knowledge, and makes it the basis for both behavior and the meaning system by which he interprets and orders his world.[3]

1 Dibelius (*James*, rev. Heinrich Greven, trans. Michael A. Williams, Hermeneia [Philadelphia: Fortress, 1976] p. 3.) defined paraenesis as 'a text which strings together admonitions of general ethical content. Paraenetic sayings ordinarily address themselves to a specific (though perhaps fictional) audience'.

2 Abraham J. Malherbe, 'Exhortation in First Thessalonians', pp. 238-56. In a similar way, David Aune (*Literary Environment*, p. 191) distinguishes '*epistolary* paraenesis, which is found in defined concluding sections of some Christian letters, and *paraenetic styles*, which permeate letters (e.g., 1 Thessalonians, Galatians, Colossians)'.

3 Perdue, 'Paraenesis', p. 251. Wayne A. Meeks (*The Moral World of the First Christians* [Philadelphia: Westminster, 1986], p. 126) speaks similarly of 'a process of resocialization which undertakes to substitute a new identity, new social relations, and a new set of values for those which each person had absorbed in growing up'. The essentially conservative and traditional nature of paraenesis is highlighted in Meeks' presidential address to the Society of Biblical Literature: 'Understanding Early Christian Ethics', *JBL* 105 (1986),

1. *Paul's Purpose in Writing to the Romans* 101

Attention is thus shifted from formal characteristics of text segments, treated in isolation, to the rhetorical function of argumentative parts, style conventions, etc. within a purposeful whole. This new perspective on rhetorical and social aspects of paraenesis alerts us to the importance of the social world in which the paraenetic activity makes cognitive and affective sense. It is within this understanding of the nature of paraenesis that we believe Furnish's observations may have their greatest significance for interpreting Romans.

To the extent that early Christian communities shared and fostered an ethos distinct from their environment,[1] paraenesis served to establish social boundaries,[2] and to maintain them in the life of the group.[3] In his letters Paul explicitly and implic-

---

pp. 3-11. Of course socialization can also mean *resocialization* into a group with values at variance with those of the larger society. On resocialization as 'alternation', i.e., conversion, see P. Berger and T. Luckmann, *The Social Construction of Reality* (New York: Doubleday, 1967), pp. 157-63.

1 On ethos see B. Gerhardsson, *The Ethos of the Bible*, trans. Stephen Westerholm (Philadelphia: Fortress, 1981); J.H. Schütz, 'Ethos of Early Christianity', *IDB* Sup., pp. 289-93; L.E. Keck, 'On the Ethos of Early Christians', *JAAR* 42 (1971), pp. 435-72; Allen Verhey, *The Great Reversal: Ethics and the New Testament* (Grand Rapids: Eerdmans, 1984); Meeks, *Moral World*, and *idem*, 'Understanding Early Christian Ethics'; K.H. Schelkle, *Theologie des Neuen Testaments*, vol. III: *Ethos* (Düsseldorf: Patmos, 1970), pp. 31-38. On the mutually reinforcing cognitive and affective aspects ('wordview' and 'ethos') of religious symbolism see Clifford Geertz, *The Interpretation of Cultures* (New York: Basic Books, 1973), chapters 2 and 3.

2 Perdue ('Paraenesis', p. 255) remarks that 'in cases of entrance into a group, paraenesis plays an important part in the establishment of group identity and cohesion during the process of socialization. In the general social setting in which paraenesis is often given, the individual is about to enter or recently has entered a new social group. In order for any group to exist, definite boundaries must be constructed which demarcate the group and its distinctive social world from other groups with differing social worlds'. Paraenesis, then, 'presents a group ethic designed to maintain a clear differentiation between in-group and out-group'.

3 After their initial incorporation into the new community, individuals are called 'to a serious reflection upon [their] initial entrance into [their] present group or position' (*ibid.*, p. 249). The establishment and maintenance of social boundaries has received emphasis

itly invokes his apostolic authority as a spokesman for God in order to exhort Christian congregations to live out their calling in Christ (cf. 2 Cor. 5.20-21). His own self-characterization as one 'sent' by God, his appeal to the power and presence of the Spirit in his own ministry and in the life of the congregation, and his exhortations to holiness, grounded in the 'calling' of his hearers out of 'the present evil age' into the realm of God's rule, the consummation of which is to be eagerly awaited,[1] constitute the eschatological-paraenetic orientation of his apostolic rhetoric.

It is just this eschatological-paraenetic aspect of Paul's apostolate which Nils Dahl has emphasized in an essay on Paul's missionary theology *in Romans*: 'In several letters Paul states the goal of his intercession and whole endeavor in terms like these: "so that you... may be pure and blameless for the day of Christ", or "guiltless in the day of our Lord Jesus Christ".' The broad exigence for Paul's missionary efforts, which included his letters to particular congregations, was 'to be able to present them to Christ at his coming, which Paul expected in the near future'.[2] In another essay, Dahl brought out the post-conversional character of paraenesis as distinct from the kerygma, whose content it nonetheless echoed:

in other recent treatments of early Christian paraenesis: see Wolfgang Schrage, *Ethik des Neuen Testaments* (Göttingen: Vandenhoeck & Ruprecht, 1982), p. 190; Berger, *Formgeschichte*, pp. 130-35 (on 'postconversionale Mahnrede'); *idem*, 'Hellenistische Gattungen im Neuen Testament', *ANRW* II.25.2, pp. 1340-42 (on 'Abgrenzung'); Meeks, *Moral World*, 125-130; *idem*, *The First Urban Christians* (New Haven: Yale University Press, 1983); Peterson, *Rediscovering Paul*; Gerd Theissen, *The Social Setting of Pauline Christianity: Essays on Corinth*, trans. John Schütz (Philadelphia: Fortress, 1982); and O. Larry Yarbrough, *Not Like the Gentiles: Marriage Rules in the Letters of Paul* (Atlanta: Scholars Press, 1985).

1   On the apocalyptic context of Pauline exhortation, see Furnish, *Theology and Ethics in Paul*, pp. 115-62, 214-16; Schrage, *Ethik*, pp. 170-76; Meeks, *First Urban Christians*, pp. 171-79; John Gager, 'Functional Diversity in Paul's Use of End-Time Language', *JBL* 89 (1970), pp. 325-37; and Beker, *Paul the Apostle*, pp. 272-94.

2   Nils Dahl, 'The Missionary Theology in the Epistle to the Romans', in *Studies in Paul* (Minneapolis: Augsburg, 1977), p. 73. Dahl makes the same point in an unpublished paper on Galatians, discussed briefly in White, 'Epistolary Literature', p. 1745.

In the epistles of the New Testament, the writers call to memory the life, words, and deeds of the apostles, and possibly also the religious fervor of the communities at the time of their foundation—their 'first love'. More often they stress their very initiation into Christianity... As Paul puts it in a famous passage, it is the very content of the gospel of salvation that is recalled: 'I would remind you, brethren, in what terms I preached to you the gospel which you received'... By these and other similar citations we see that for Paul, as well as for the first apostles the gospel, the preaching of salvation, was the message of a past event: the act of God in Christ... The central content of the epistles and of the preaching to the communities was certainly the same as that of the missionary preaching. But the faithful already knew the message; they had been made participants, they had been made part of the divine work of which the kerygma was a proclamation. That is why, precisely when it is a question of the very core of the gospel, the preaching to the communities was more recollection than proclamation. Thus what we understand generally by 'to preach', namely, to deliver a sermon in the church, no longer corresponds to the *kēryssein* of the New Testament, but rather closely to *hypomimnēskein*, to restore to memory.[1]

The question raised by the present chapter is whether Romans is an exception to this broad characterization of Paul's letters, or to Beker's description of 'words on target'. Dahl makes a number of observations that would lead one to set Romans alongside the other Pauline letters as a paraenetic letter. He points out, for example, that 'Paul himself says to the Roman church that he has written his letter to revive memories' (Rom. 15.15).[2] He also enjoins serious attention to the explicitly stated purpose of Romans: 'Paul wrote to the Christians in Rome in order to exhort and strengthen them without intruding upon them and without doubting the genuineness of their Christian faith. What Paul does in his letter is what he had for a long time hoped to do in person: he preached the gospel to those in Rome'.

---

1 Nils Dahl, 'Anamnesis: Memory and Commemoration in the Early Church', *Jesus in the Memory of the Early Church*, pp. 18-19. See also Berger, *Formgeschichte*, pp. 130-34, on 'postconversionale Mahnrede'.
2 Dahl, 'Anamnesis', p. 17.

These remarks suggest that one could with confidence assign Romans to the broader category of paraenetic letters. Yet Dahl immediately continues: 'The Christians in Rome needed to know what Paul taught and how he understood his own mission if they were going to ally themselves with other Pauline churches and intercede for a favorable reception of the collection'.[1] The last remark retreats from understanding Romans as a paraenetic letter and adopts a more conventional reading of the letter as a sample sermon or a précis of Pauline theology.

Our hypothesis regarding a clue to the letter's macro-structure in the correspondences in chs. 1, 6, and 12, and, correspondingly, regarding the letter's paraenetic character, must be tested exegetically in the rest of the letter.[2] We turn next to examine the opening chapters of Romans; argumentation in Rom. 5–11 is our concern in Chapter 3.

1 Dahl, 'Missionary Theology', p. 77.
2 The title of this section makes deliberate allusion to Hendrikus Boers' valuable article, 'The Problem of Jews and Gentiles in the Macro-Structure of Romans' (pp. 184-96). It may be helpful to point out just where our presentation will diverge from his. Boers looks to rhetorical questions throughout Romans as clues to the letter's macro-structure, convinced that they 'may have been breathers, to see if [Paul] he has made any progress. In his reasoning, Paul knew where he wanted to come out, but he did not know how to get there' (p. 185). Our approach is more intentionally diachronic (but cf. Boers, p. 186!); our use of the term 'macro-structure' refers to an overarching governing pattern that emerges in the course of the argument's progress, rather than to the repetition of questions that get Paul 'back on track' in the midst of an unwieldly argument. We shall have occasion to return to Boers' insights in Chapter 4, below.

Chapter 2

PAUL'S USE OF TOPICS ON THE LAW
IN ROM. 1.13–4.25:
THE 'DEBATE WITH JUDAISM' REEXAMINED

1. *Introduction*
In the Introduction we discussed the prevalent view that
Paul's letter to the Romans has a 'double character', a view
derived from the perception of a 'debate with Judaism' in a
letter explicitly addressed to a Gentile-Christian audience. We
held in Chapter 1 that the letter's epistolary 'frame' (1.1-17;
15.14-32) indicated a *paraenetic* intention: Paul wanted the
Romans to preserve the sanctity of the 'offering of the
Gentiles' by heeding his admonitions for mutual respect
between Jewish and Gentile Christians. Moreover, we found
reason tentatively to relate the 'macro-structure' of the letter
with the *'einst–jetzt'* scheme of early Christian paraenesis.
   Our task in the present chapter and in Chapter 3 is to test
this preliminary understanding of the letter's character
against the argumentative flow within the letter 'body'. If our
hypotheses regarding the letter's paraenetic character are
correct, we should expect to find the argumentation *from the
beginning* oriented toward establishing a common basis of
agreement with the (Roman Gentile-Christian) audience,
and proceeding to modify that basis so as to win the audience's
disposition to act in accordance with the paraenesis in chs. 12–
15.
   In fact, the earlier chapters of Romans threaten to disap-
point such expectations, for here, a host of interpreters agree,
the heart of the letter is shown to be a 'debate with Judaism'.[1]
In this widely accepted view, Rom. 1.18–3.20 serves as a sort

---

1 Kümmel, *Introduction*, p. 309; Beker, *Paul the Apostle*, p. 75.

of digression from Paul's main 'theme', the 'righteousness of God' now revealed in Christ (1.16-17; 3.20-21), the purpose of which is to show the need for God's righteousness[1] by proving that 'all people, Jews and Gentiles alike, are under sin' (3.9).

This reading of 1.18–3.20 has been enormously successful, and has a couple of observations to commend it. First, the positive theme of the 'gospel of God's righteousness' sounded in 1.16-17 seems to be left hanging until 3.21; further, the theme of 'God's wrath' seems to intrude at 1.18 (if indeed 1.16-17 announce a 'theme'). It seems logical enough, then, to treat 1.18–3.20 as something of a digression, albeit an important digression, that serves to support the main theme.[2] Furthermore, the declarations in 3.9 ('I have already charged that all, both Jews and Greeks, are under the power of sin') and 3.19b ('so that every mouth may be stopped, and all the world may be held accountable to God') seem to sum up what precedes as a two-part indictment of human sinfulness; and as 3.19b is punctuated in all modern editions ('whatever the Law says, it speaks to those under the Law', RSV), the weight of that indictment falls upon the Jew.

This view, however, presents two problems for a *rhetorical-critical* understanding of the letter. As we have seen, rhetoricians insist that the essential purpose of argumentation is to 'bring the audience along' as the speaker moves from shared premises to the argumentative destination. But, in fact, the view that Rom. 1.18–3.20 is an 'indictment' of sinful humanity, designed to show the need for Paul's gospel of God's righteousness, finds textual support only at the end of this section (3.9, 20), not at its beginning, for in fact Paul gives his audience no clue *at the start* (1.16-18) that such is his purpose.

---

1 'St. Paul has just stated what the Gospel is; he now goes on to show the necessity for such a Gospel. The world is lost without it' (Sanday and Headlam, *The Epistle to the Romans*, p. 40). Cranfield (*Romans*, I, p. 103) declares the purpose of 1.18–3.20 to be 'to make it clear that there can be no question of any other righteousness of men before God than that which is "from faith to faith"'.

2 'Indeed, the view that [all] are sinners, which [Paul] develops at length in Rom. 1.18–3.20, is a basic one for his doctrine of salvation' (Bultmann, *Theology*, I, p. 227). Käsemann (*Romans*, p. 34) declares that 'in fact the presupposition of all that is to come is given here'.

How are the Roman Christians listening to this letter to understand Paul's talk about God's wrath coming upon human immorality and iniquity (1.18-32)? They must wait, on this view, for the retrospective summary in 3.9 (προητιασάμεθα γάρ).

Furthermore, the view that 3.9 is an *outline* of the preceding—Gentile immorality having been sketched quickly and in conventional terms in 1.18-32 before Paul turns his attention to 'the Jew', either at 2.1 or 2.17—immediately raises the rhetorical-critical question: How does this prolonged dialogue *with the Jew* relate to the letter's *Gentile-Christian* audience? That the letter's rhetorical integrity is at stake in this question[1] is obvious from the comments of interpreters who perceive *no* relation between Paul's 'digression' and the letter recipients: The letter's address to an actual audience has simply dropped out of sight in the letter body![2] The problem is

1 It is for this reason astonishing that Wilhelm Wuellner ('Paul's Rhetoric of Argumentation', pp. 168-69) does not address the question at all. By extending the *exordium* through 1.15 and cutting 1.16-17 loose as a *'transitus'*, he neutralizes the rhetorical significance of what in the text is a sustained thought, and thus severs the *'confirmatio'* of 1.18–15.13 from its rhetorical context.
2 Bent Noack ('Current and Backwater', p. 155) declares that 'it really is a problem why Paul, just in Romans, inserts a discussion of the fate and experience of Israel... Why should the disobedience of Israel be discussed exactly in a letter to a congregation, or congregations, of Gentile extraction?' He goes on to focus what we have called the 'double character problem' on the 'hinge' passage, 1.13-18, asking rhetorically: 'What is there in the address to the Romans in 1.14-15 to open the sluices through which the stream of argument in the following chapters pours forth?' (pp. 161-62). Finding the 'current' of the letter to be Paul's defense of his trip to Jerusalem against presumed Roman sentiments that Paul should concern himself instead with the most important of the Gentile congregations, Noack is compelled to consider the passage 1.18–3.8 (which evidently contributes nothing to that purpose) to be 'backwater'. Jacob Jervell ('The Letter to Jerusalem', p. 70), who also considers Paul's central concern in the letter to be gaining the Romans' support for his trip to Jerusalem, has similar difficulty integrating the letter body with the epistolary frame: 'Actual letter style can only be found in the introduction and conclusion of the letter. Only from these elements can it be determined that the letter has concrete recipients to whom Paul is writing. However, between 1.18–11.36 the recipients are no longer in focus'. Jervell goes on to point out

obviously sensed by those interpreters who advance theories of 'other' audiences (e.g., the eavesdropping synagogue; Jewish antagonists from other Pauline mission areas; the church in Jerusalem; etc.) behind the Gentile-Christian addressees.[1]

2. The Starting Point of Argumentation in Romans (1.16-32)

In light of Scott Consigny's essay on the crucial role played by topics in establishing and redisposing the constraints of a rhetorical situation,[2] we might well be surprised that interpreters have not suggested integrating the epistolary address in 1.1-15 more directly with the indictment of pagan immorality in 1.18-32. After all, the latter passage is universally recognized—despite its apparent Jewish provenance[3]—as a stock *topos* in the early church's evangelization of *the Gentiles*.[4] Form critics routinely identify the pericope as an example of the 'vice lists' that served in evangelization

that the letter functions very poorly as an 'introduction' to Paul's gospel: 'On the whole, this document is neither consistently written in letter style nor as a didactic monolog serving as an introduction to Paul's preaching.... This is obviously not the way one writes a letter or a didactic treatise'. Jervell concludes that Romans is actually written over the heads of the Roman congregation, so to speak, to the Jewish-Christian community in Jerusalem.

1 See the discussion in the Introduction above.
2 'Rhetoric and its Situations'; see pp. 16-17 above.
3 Apparent through comparison with Wisdom of Solomon 11–15 and Philo (*Decal.* 61-63, *Spec.* 1.13-27, *Vita* 5-10), for example: see the studies by Bornkamm ('The Revelation of God's Wrath', in *Early Christian Experience*, trans. P.L. Hamner [New York: Harper & Row, 1969], pp. 1-70), A. Daxer ('Römer 1.18–2.10 im Verhältnis zur spätjüdischen Lehrauffassung', diss. Rostock, 1914), S. Schulz ('Die Anklage in Röm 1.18–3.20', *TZ* 14 [1958], pp. 161-73), P. Dalbert (*Die Theologie der hellenistisch-jüdischen Missionsliteratur unter Ausschluss von Philo und Josephus* [Hamburg: Herbert Reich, 1954]), and C. Bussmann (*Themen der paulinischen Missionspredigt auf dem Hintergrund des spätjüdisch-hellenistischen Missionsliteratur* [Bern: Herbert Lang, 1971]). In the Jewish *topos*, idolatry is the root of 'specifically Gentile sins', sexual perversions and particularly homosexuality (Käsemann, *Romans*, p. 44). 'The making of idols was the beginning of πορνεία' (Wis. 14.12).
4 Bultmann's summary ('The Preaching of God', *Theology*, I, pp. 65-92) of 'Christian missionary preaching in the Gentile world' is fundamental.

(*protrepsis*) and paraenesis.[1] The proclamation of God's wrath
upon those who do such things was directed at securing
repentance and conversion,[2] and was probably used for just
that purpose by Paul himself.[3] The Gattung could also be
employed in paraenesis addressed to converts to reinforce
their commitment to the new life.[4] Abraham Malherbe
observes that philosophical speeches 'frequently began by
listing vices, which revealed the true condition of the listeners,
before setting about to correct them'.[5]

Yet the passage in Romans is usually not associated with
any *paraenetic* intent:[6] Käsemann specifically insists that 'the
epistle is clearly addressed to a community whose firm status
as Christians is not in doubt.... The accusations made by the
apostle [in 1.18–3.20] are not directed against them and are
not meant to stir them to repentance'.[7] Phrased in this way, of
course, Käsemann's statement poses a false dilemma, since

1 A. Vögtle's seminal work *Die Tugend- und Lasterkataloge im Neuen Testament* (Münster: Ascendorff, 1936) is now supplemented, with reference to the Qumran discoveries, by S. Wibbing, *Die Tugend- und Lasterkataloge im Neuen Testament* (Berlin: A. Töpelmann, 1959).
2 Bultmann, *Theology*, I, pp. 72-73. Berger (*Formgeschichte*, p. 199) recognizes in the larger section Rom. 1.18–2.29 the Gattung of 'Scheltrede mit dem Zweck der Bekehrung'.
3 'Paul's argument in Romans 1 and 2 ... enables us to determine the method of approach Paul likely had used in Thessalonica ... The argument is vehement, as Paul's sermon would have been, in its thrust to convict rather than to inform' (Malherbe, *Paul and the Thessalonians*, pp. 31-32).
4 'Die Kataloge [haben] die Funktion einer Grenzabsteckung. Ziel ist vor allem, vor einem Rückfall in das Stadium vor der Bekehrung ('Heidentum') zu bewahren' (Berger, *Formgeschichte*, pp. 148-49). Vice lists were used in *protrepsis* as well as in paraenesis, where they could 'remind the reader of an earlier worse condition' (Malherbe, *Moral Exhortation*, p. 138) On the distinction of *protrepsis* from *paraenesis* see also Stowers, *Letter Writing*, p. 92.
5 Malherbe, *Paul and the Thessalonians*, p. 24.
6 Rudolf Schnackenburg (*Moral Teaching of the New Testament*, pp. 302-303) recognizes the topical nature of Rom. 1.21-31, but asserts that 'this description does not, of course, come in the paraenetic section [of Romans], but is intended to show the perdition of unredeemed mankind'.
7 Käsemann, *Romans*, p. 34.

paraenesis aims precisely at reinforcing values already held by a community.[1] Its traditional, 'abstract' or hypothetical character was part of its rhetorical value.[2] The vice list in particular was intended not to characterize specific *individuals* but to warn, in a general and stylized way, against behaviors inconsistent with those values.[3]

Admittedly, there is a problem with interpreting Rom. 1.18-32 as a straightforward paraenetic application of the *topos* on idolatry or of the vice list. The paraenetic use of such *topoi* in early Christian preaching is usually embedded in what Bultmann called the 'once—but now' scheme: 'Once' you did such things (as are enumerated in the vice list), 'but now' you have been delivered from that way of life.[4] Paul used the scheme with reference to the change effected in baptism: '—And such were some of you. But you were washed, you were sanctified, you were justified' (1 Cor. 6.9-11); 'Thanks be to God that you who were once slaves of sin have become obedient to the standard of teaching to which you were committed' (Rom. 6.17-18, baptism in context). Further, his use of the 'once—but now' scheme could involve *reminding* his congregations of his first preaching among them, wherein he presumably used the same *topoi* in evangelization or *protrepsis*: 'I warn you, as I warned you before, that those who do such things will not inherit the kingdom of God' (Gal. 5.21); 'Finally, brothers and sisters, we beseech and exhort you in the Lord Jesus that as

---

1 Malherbe, *Moral Exhortation*, p. 125. Seneca's famous 94th Epistle is devoted to the value of exhortations (*praecepta*) even when moral duty is recognized.

2 'Paraenesis is really an indirect way of addressing a behavioral problem. Since the content of paraenesis is generally approved by society, it provides a basis of agreement in situations that are potentially divisive' (Aune, *Literary Environment*, p. 191; see the discussion above, pp. 81-82).

3 'Die Kataloge beschreiben Taten, nicht Personen im ganzen, sondern bestenfalls "Täter" und sind damit sehr stark typenhaft ausgerichtet. Gerade darin aber wird ihr paränetischer Sinn erkennbar: Sie wollen vor Einzeltaten warnen (und nicht Aussentehende im einzelnen charakterisieren)' (Berger, *Formgeschichte*, p. 148).

4 Bultmann, *Theology I*, pp. 72-73; Dahl, 'Early Christian Preaching', pp. 30-36; Berger, *Formgeschichte*, pp. 130-31.

you learned from us how you ought to live and to please God...' (1 Thess. 4.1-8). Just these features, which in other places mark the *paraenetic* use of the vice list, are absent in Rom. 1.18-32 (although Paul uses the 'once–but now' scheme elsewhere in Romans: 6.17-18; 11.30-31).

In response to this objection we note that the lack of any more direct cue at 1.16 or 1.18 indicating to the reader the onset of a theological or didactic treatise[1] encourages us to ask whether the *topical* character of 1.18-32 in fact points to the passage's function at the beginning of the letter. Is Paul's description of immorality in the pagan world supposed to remind the former pagans of Rome of the terms of their own conversion, upon which basis he may now address them as 'the called of Jesus Christ' (1.6)?

It bears noting that the thematic statement in 1.18, 'God's wrath is being revealed upon all human impiety and injustice', is hypotactically subordinated to Paul's reason for wanting to visit the Romans, 'to evangelize you in Rome as well' (γάρ, 1.16, 17, 18). Further, the word order in 1.16b emphasizes that the gospel is the δύναμις... θεοῦ... εἰς σωτηρίαν; this element of power seems to be the gospel's dominant aspect here, not so much its restriction to 'all who *believe*'. Of course this statement goes against a long tradition of reading 1.16-17 as the announcement of Paul's theme in Romans, the gospel of justification by *faith* (rather than by works); but that particular contrast is not made until 3.20-21.

Moreover, focusing on the gospel's character as the power of God allows us to make better sense of the continuity between vv. 15-18. Paul is eager to evangelize the Romans (1.15) *because* the gospel does not put him to shame (1.16a); that is, it is always God's effective power at work through him (so that he can 'boast' of what Christ has done through him 'to win obedience from the Gentiles, by word and deed, by the power of signs and wonders, by the power of the Holy Spirit' [15.17-19]). Paul has no reason to be put to shame, because it is *God's* integrity that is revealed through the preaching of the gospel (1.17), an effectual revelation 'from faith'—that is, proceeding from God's faithfulness—'to faith'—creating

1 Jervell, 'Letter to Jerusalem'; see above, pp. 81-82.

faithfulness where there was none, life where there was death, so that 'out of faithfulness the righteous shall live'. The verses tell what happens when Paul does what he says he wants to do among the Romans: in the gospel the power of God is at work, faith is created, God's righteousness is thus revealed. Here a 'prophetic' aspect of Paul's rhetoric comes to expression as his apostolic presence is made the medium of *God's* saving power.

When we bear in mind that Romans was written to a congregation which the apostle had neither founded nor visited, the rhetorical function of these verses may be clarified. In other letters Paul resumes his personal contact with his congregations by referring, however briefly or extensively, to earlier stages of their relationship, and especially to the beginning of the community, which may be evoked at great length (cf. 1 Cor. 1–4; Gal. 1.6-11; 3.1-5; 1 Thess. 1–3—note that even the paraenesis in ch. 4 is still phrased in terms of 'what you learned from us'). There may be particular emphasis on Paul's personal conduct, his preaching and baptizing activity, specifics of instruction given, and so on, so that one of Paul's sources for rhetorical 'topics' becomes his own history with a particular congregation.[1] The convergence of topics under discussion—the 'post-conversion hortatory'

---

1 John White ('New Testament Epistolary Literature', pp. 1746-47) extends Robert Funk's discussion of Paul's past contact with his congregations as a dimension of the 'apostolic *parousia*'. 'The appeal to the past is sometimes joined concretely to the recitation of paraenetic materials, which are similar in kind to those identified by M. Dibelius in his study of James or to the other forms of stereotyped teaching identified, subsequently, by numerous scholars. On other occasions, Paul reminds his readers of the former instruction, without citing the actual examples, or he recounts the nature of his conduct when he was present. This, then, constitutes a fourth medium by means of which Paul is present to his recipients.' White asserts that 'the paraenesis/appeal to the past tends to follow the appeal to the letter, the dispatch of a courier, and the announcement of a visit', a pattern he discerns in 1 Thess. and Gal; he considers 1 and 2 Cor. exceptions to the rule. On the contrary, the appeal to the past plays a decisive role at the *beginning* of Paul's letters: note the first three chapters of 1 Thess. alone, or the first four chapters of 1 Cor.

topic that invokes the 'time of the beginning',[1] Paul's epistolary topic of past contact with his congregations, and the con-
ventionalized protreptic-paraenetic vice list–is a routine
strategy in Paul's pastoral letters.[2] Just this strategy is of
course impossible in Romans. And yet, we suggest, the apostle
sets out to establish the corresponding background of 'earlier
stages of the discussion' (Perelman) by invoking for his audience, by means of topics, the same powerful reality that he has
shared personally with his own congregations.

This suggestion can be clarified by reference to recent work
on the 'liminal' dimension of paraenesis. Drawing on Victor
Turner's study of liminality in rituals of initiation[3] and on
Peter Berger's essay on religion as world-construction,[4] Leo
Perdue observes that 'some paraenetic texts are an important
part of a rite of passage often involving inexperienced novices
who are going through either status elevation or initiation into

1 'Postconversionale Mahnrede', Berger (*Formgeschichte*, p. 130)
   declares, 'ist... noch immer ganz am Zeitpunkt des Wechsels
   orientiert, ist also ein echter *reditus ad baptismum*'.
2 'The philophronetic sections of the letters are elaborate and often
   very long: the relationship between writer and readers is fundamental to the attempt to persuade. This relationship is described in
   a way that stresses the common experience, the shared biography,
   so to speak, of apostle and congregation. Reminders of the beginning—the first preaching, the early instruction, the conversion, the
   baptism—become the basis for appeals for appropriate behavior'
   (Meeks, *First Urban Christians*, p. 136).
3 'Van Gennep has shown that all rites of passage or 'transition' are
   marked by three phases: separation, margin (or *limen*, signifying
   "threshold" in Latin), and aggregation' (Victor Turner, *The Ritual
   Process: Structure and Anti-Structure* [Ithaca: Cornell University
   Press, 1969], p. 94). It is in the intervening 'liminal' period, when
   'the characteristics of the ritual subject (the "passenger") are
   ambiguous; he passes through a cultural realm that has few or
   none of the attributes of the past or coming state', that instruction,
   or the inculcation of values, is most powerful: 'It is as though [the
   initiates] are being reduced or ground down to a uniform condition
   to be fashioned anew and endowed with additional powers to enable
   them to cope with their new station in life' (p. 95). Turner's work
   has played an important role in Norman Peterson's study of 'the
   sociology of Paul's narrative world' as well (*Rediscovering Paul*).
4 Peter Berger, *The Sacred Canopy: Elements of a Sociological Theory
   of Religion* (New York: Doubleday, 1967); see also Berger and Luckmann, *Social Construction of Reality*.

a social group'. In other instances, paraenetic texts 'occasionally are given at a time after incorporation and tend to call the
recipient to a serious reflection upon his initial entrance into
his present group or position'.[1] We want to focus on what
Perdue writes about the liminal dimension of paraenesis:

> The ontological refashioning [that takes place] by means of
> paraenesis is made possible by anomy which accompanies
> the liminal individual who has been separated temporarily
> from his former social structure. The individual's tempo-
> rary loss of structure leads to loss of meaning, disintegration
> of character, displacement of moral bearings, and increas-
> ing uncertainty about cognitive affirmations. Thus, the
> instruction provides a nomos of meaning, a structure,
> which allows the individual to interpret his world and to find
> a meaningful place within its order (p. 253).

In his discussion of paraenesis in the Epistle of James, Perdue
attempts to correlate the liminal situation of 'anomie' with
historical circumstances.[2] Those hypotheses may be right, but
they are not *necessary* as explanations for anomic features in
paraenesis.[3] The rhetor can *generate* anomie as a strategy for
approaching an indeterminate situation (Consigny).[4] The
constructive aspect of paraenesis—'*nomos*'—involves 'the
establishment of group identity and cohesion' which in turn

---

1 Perdue, 'Paraenesis', pp. 248-49.
2 Perdue ('Paraenesis', p. 250) writes that the letter was written 'by a
  teacher at a time when he is either separated from his audience (a
  paraenetic letter) or is about to leave them because of increasing age
  and approaching death...'. The more affluent members of the
  community are 'experiencing major problems that tempt them to
  leave and return to the world'.
3 A distinction should perhaps be made between the 'sociological
  function' of paraenesis (in generating and transforming social
  anomie) and 'social setting' (which is much more elusive in ancient
  texts).
4 Along these lines, Steve Kraftchick has emphasized Paul's creative
  redispostion of the situation faced in the Galatian churches: Paul's
  'anti-Law position' in Gal. 3–4 functioned as an attack on the world-
  ordering *nomos* of his audience, generating an anomie that could be
  alleviated by the Spirit-oriented paraenesis of chs. 5–6 ('Ethos and
  Pathos Appeals in Galatians 5 and 6: A Rhetorical Analysis' [diss.
  Emory University, 1985], pp. 265-72); *idem*, 'Some Functions of the
  Paraenetic Section of Galatians', unpublished paper.

requires the construction and maintenance of social boundaries.[1]

Perdue remarks that 'conflict in a verbal form is occasionally used to obtain these results', and cites a rhetorical indictment of the wealthy from the Cynic epistles.[2]

As Berger and Lukmann point out, generating such tension
within an alternative social world is not optional. 'The old
reality as the collectivities and significant others that previously mediated it to the individual, must be reinterpreted
within the legitimating apparatus of the new reality. This
reinterpretation brings about a rupture in the subjective biography of the individuals'.[3]

The rhetorical significance of the 'once—but now' scheme
in early Christian preaching resides therefore in its persuasive *redefinition* of the converts' previous lives as 'immorality'
and 'idolatry'. In paraenesis, the vice list can evoke for the
convert the reality left behind. Apocalyptic language of divine
judgment and the 'wrath of God' provides the symbolic context within which such paraenetic appeals makes sense.[4] On
this basis we suggest that in Rom. 1.15-18 Paul not only
announces his *intention* to evangelize the Romans, but *begins
to do so*, invoking through the opposition of 'God's power unto
salvation' and 'the wrath of God' the eschatological context of
their conversion.[5] In these phrases Paul places his listeners in

1 *Ibid.*, p. 255; Berger, *Formgeschichte*, pp. 130-35; *idem*, 'Hellenistische Gattungen, pp. 1340-42 ('Abgrenzung').
2 Perdue, 'Paraenesis', p. 255.
3 Berger and Luckmann, *Social Construction of Reality*, pp. 159-60.
'Pre-alternation biography is typically nihilated *in toto* by subsum-
ing it under a negative category occupying a strategic position in the
new legitimating apparatus: "When I was still living a life of sin",
"When I was still caught in bourgeois consciousness", "When I was
still motivated by these unconscious neurotic needs". The biographi-
cal rupture is thus identified with a cognitive separation of darkness and light' (*ibid.*). The most illuminating of the parallels in
Paul's letters comes in Rom. 6.20-21: 'when you were slaves to
sin... [doing] things of which you are now ashamed'.
4 Meeks, *First Urban Christians*, pp. 170-75.
5 Consigny ('Rhetoric and its Situations', pp. 182-83) construes the
topic as 'a formal opposition of two (or more) terms which can be
used to structure the heteronomous matter of a particular situation.... The two terms of the topic, when applied to the indetermi-

the liminal crucible of 'ontological refashioning' (Turner, Perdue) in which protreptic and paraenesis are potent.[1]

The dominant 'affective charge' (Berger and Luckmann) of protreptic, *shame*,[2] is also the motif that gives structure to Paul's litany against Gentile wickedness. In contrast to Paul's service to the gospel (λατρεία, 1.9), in which he is not put to shame because in it is revealed the righteousness of God (1.16-17), the Gentile world is characterized by impiety (ἀσέβεια); by

---

nate matter of a context, structure that context so as to open up and delimit a logical place in which the rhetor can discover and manage new relationships'.

1 The focus of Turner's work is *ritual*, a subject Perdue has no occasion to treat. It would seem that paraenesis can have the effect of what Turner calls 'ontological refashioning' once the old status has been symbolically suspended, as the dramatic nature of ritual makes possible (cf. Walter Burkert, *Homo Necans: The Anthropology of Ancient Greek Sacrificial Ritual and Myth*, trans. Peter Bing [Berkeley: University of California Press, 1983], pp. 1-34). Paraenesis must in this case perform the invocative and representational functions of ritual. In this light the liturgical context of Paul's letters and his solemn doxological style in the letter openings is especially noteworthy.

2 We use the word here in the positive sense it has both in English (compare the negative term 'shameless') and in ancient Greek culture (Bultmann, 'αἰδώς', *TDNT*, I, pp. 169-71). 'Shame', writes Bruce Malina (*The New Testament World: Insights from Cultural Anthropology* [Atlanta: John Knox, 1981], p. 44), 'is a positive symbol, meaning sensitivity for one's own reputation, sensitivity to the opinion of others. To have shame in this sense is an eminently positive value.... On the other hand, a shameless person is one who does not recognize the rules of human interaction, who does not recognize social boundaries'. The evocation of 'shame' was one of the salutary effects of philosophical protreptic: see texts and discussion in Malherbe, *Moral Exhortation*, pp. 48-67. Dio Chrysostom says that the philosopher seeks to lead others to virtue 'partly by persuading and exhorting, partly by abusing and reproaching', thus 'expelling insatiate greed and shamelessness and moral weakness' (*ibid.*, p. 51). Lucian gives two vivid reports of shame experienced at the application of philosophical reproach (*ibid.*, pp. 56-59). Plutarch goes so far as to say that to listen to admonition without 'burning with shame' shows that one is 'dead to all modesty' (*ibid.*, p. 60). The affective valence of the vice list in early Christian paraenesis is apparent when Paul refers to the sins of the former life as 'those things of which you are now ashamed' (ἐφ' οἷς νῦν ἐπαισχύνεσθε, 6.21).

the worship (ἐσεβάσθησαν, ἐλάτρευσαν) of the creature rather than of the Creator, whom the Gentiles did not honor (οὐχ ὡς θεὸν ἐδόξασαν ἢ ηὐχαρίστησαν); and by wickedness (ἀδικία). The impious are delivered over to impurity (ἀκαθαρσία) that they may be dishonored in their bodies (ἀτιμάζεσθαι), and to dishonorable lusts (πάθη ἀτιμίας), so that they work 'what is not fitting' (τὴν ἀσχημοσύνην, τὰ μὴ καθήκοντα). They are filled with all ἀδικία. Correlates of honor (δικαιοσύνη; οὐκ ἐπαισχύνομαι) are opposed to correlates of dishonor (note the privative forms: ἀσέβεια, ἀδικία, ἀκαθαρσία, ἀτιμάζεσθαι, ἀτιμία, ἀσχημοσύνη). The contrast between what should have been appropriate and honorable reverence for the divine benefactor, on the one hand, and the actual spiral of rebellion and depravity, on the other, is construed primarily as an offense against God's honor and as a corresponding attitude of shamelessness (ἐματαιώθησαν ἐν τοῖς διαλογισμοῖς αὐτῶν καὶ ἐσκοτίσθη ἡ ἀσύνετος αὐτῶν καρδία, 1.21).

The contrast between 'then' and 'now' that made the vice list effective in paraenesis is absent here, or rather it is displaced. As we have seen, the positive force of the *topos*[1] comes into play later in the letter's rhetoric when Paul calls for 'a living and holy sacrifice, pleasing to God, your rational (or spiritual, or reasonable) worship' (12.1-2). More immediately Paul continues the rhetoric of reproach (2.1ff.

The apostle's approach is properly 'topical', then, in that it allows him to be *receptive* to the constraints of a novel situation, and at the same time manifests a rhetorical *integrity* that invites the readers to perceive the situation *as Paul construes*

---

1 Aristotle discusses the *topos* of the shameful (ποῖα δ'αἰσχύνονται, *Rhetoric* 1383b-1385a), an auxiliary topic in deliberative rhetoric (1358b). The topic plays a minor role in his discussion because Aristotle does not conceive of the necessity to encourage people to do what is honorable (*Rhetoric*, 1369b): the only relevant issues for him are which of several honorable options is more honorable or more possible (1363b). By contrast, reproach—the evocation of shame— was an important component of protreptic in those philosophies that set up 'a standard of values different from those of the world outside and could serve as the stimulus to a stern life' (A.D. Nock, *Conversion: The Old and the New in Religion from Alexander to Augustine of Hippo* [Oxford: Clarendon, 1933], p. 173).

it, without leaving the apostle at a loss for words or bound to a predetermined theological agenda as he approaches the Roman congregation.[1] That is, he responds to the necessity of establishing a foothold without the usual appeal to his own earlier work among the recipients, and therefore he construes 'the earlier stages of the discussion' by evoking themes that he presumes his audience will recognize from their own 'beginning'; at the same time he sets the terms of the discussion to follow by evoking the 'deep exigence' that determines the epistolary situation, the 'righteousness of God'.

The last point concerning Paul's disclosure of a 'deep exigence' bears confirmation from the juxtaposition of 'God's saving power in the gospel' (1.16) and 'God's wrath upon all human impiety' (1.18). The narrative that follows (1.19-32) makes it clear that God has, with perfect right, abandoned sinners to pursue the lusts of their hearts (1.24-32), since they, to whom 'what can be known of God' was plainly manifest (1.19-20), refused to honor God (1.21-23) and are therefore 'without excuse' (1.20; 1.32–2.1). The wrath of God and the righteousness of God are not opposed to each other as the divine verdicts on succeeding salvation-historical epochs, God's wrath being limited to 'the situation prior to the gospel'[2]—the 'time before the gospel' was instead 'the time of patience' (3.25)—but rather the 'revelation of God's righteousness' and the 'revelation of God's wrath' are a single eschatological event.[3] The salvation brought when the gospel is preached cannot be merely a merciful 'rescue' from divine wrath, as the rhetorical indictment of 2.1-6 makes forcefully clear: 'Do you suppose, O mortal, that when you judge those

---

1 See Consigny, 'Rhetoric and Its Situations', pp. 180-81. Consigny's essay and Wuellner's discussion of 'Toposforschung' are important theoretical contributions to the discussion of *topoi*. Other work in the New Testament discipline has been devoted to the adequacy of a formal (form-critical) approach (see D.G. Bradley, 'The *Topos* as a Form in the Pauline Paraenesis', *JBL* 72 [1953], pp. 238-46; recent criticisms in J. Brunt, 'More on the *Topos* as a New Testament Form', *JBL* 104 [1985], pp. 495-500).

2 Lietzmann, *An die Römer*, ad loc.

3 Bornkamm, 'The Revelation of God's Wrath', in *Early Christian Experience*, trans. P.L. Hammer (New York: Harper & Row, 1969), pp. 62-64.

who do such things and yet do them yourself, that you will escape the judgment of God? Or do you contemptuously presume upon the riches of God's kindness and forbearance and patience?' The salvation offered in the gospel is God's power at work, the effectual proclamation of God's sovereign claim upon creation. Rom. 1.18-32 and 2.1-16 are integrated in a topical approach that shows itself to be more than Paul's presentation of a central theological theme: It is his strategic redisposition of a rhetorical situation.

But our next question must be: Given the topical *potentiality* of this description of pagan ungodliness in a letter addressed to *converts* from paganism, how is that potentiality *actualized* in the letter? The answer to that question depends on the relation of 1.18-32 to its context, particularly to 2.1-6.

3. *The Rhetoric of Apostrophe (Rom. 2.1-16)*

The logic connecting Rom. 1.32 and 2.1 is a difficult problem, complicated by the proximity of the apostrophe to the Jew in 2.17ff. Is the Jew already addressed in 2.1? How does the *Gentile* shamelessness described with such exasperation in 1.32[1] relate to the attitude of judgment assailed in 2.1; and what is the force of δίο there? Is the individual addressed in the second person singular in 2.1 to be identified with the people accused in 1.18-32, or distinguished from them?[2]

---

1 There are voices claiming that the indictment in 1.18-32 is too broad to be restricted to Gentiles alone. Cranfield (*Romans*, I, p. 105) notes in particular the accounts of *Israel's* idolatry in the wilderness (Ps. 105.20, LXX; Jer. 2.11) as background for Rom. 1.23, 'they exchanged the glory of the immortal God for images resembling mortal humans or birds or animals or reptiles'. Actually the parallel includes only the phrase 'exchange (or forfeit) the glory', which in the LXX passages is specifically Israel's (τὴν δόξαν αὐτῶν; in Jeremiah, αὐτοῦ, that is τοῦ λαοῦ), not God's (as in Romans). Further, the idolaters in Rom. 1 worship human images, which is never said of Israel. The language here is also reminiscent of Deut. 4.15-18, where Gentile idolatry is in view ('things which the LORD your God has allotted to all the peoples under the whole heaven... but the Lord has taken you [Israel]... to be a people of his own possession', RSV).

2 Bultmann ('Glossen im Röm', *ThLZ* 72 [1947], pp. 197-202) declared 2.1 a gloss, thus eliminating the problem; C.K. Barrett (*Romans*, p. 43) proposed that 1.32 be considered a parenthesis; F. Flückiger

The interpretation of the apostrophes in Rom. 2 should proceed from exegetical observations of the integrity of 1.18-32 and 2.1-11 (or 2.1-16),[1] and from a nuanced understanding of the diatribal mode of rhetoric.[2] There are other significant hermeneutical questions involved once it is determined that Paul's purpose in Rom. 2 is an 'indictment' of the Jew, or a 'demolition of Jewish privilege' (Käsemann), but that determination should await exegetical confirmation. Our consideration of those issues is consequently best left for an excursus, which will follow below.

The logical connective διό in 2.1 continues the rhythm of similar constructions in 1.21, 24, 26, and 28, inviting the expectation that Paul will follow the statement in 1.32 in the same way: 'therefore [διό, διὰ τοῦτο] God has given them up...' or perhaps 'therefore they are without excuse' (cf. 1.20). Indeed the verdict in 2.1 echoes the theme of human inexcusability that stands over 1.21-32, showing that an argument by analogy is at work.[3] The person indicted is culpable (ἀναπολόγητος) on the same grounds (διό) that condemn the sinners in 1.29-32: just as they are 'fully aware

('Zur Unterscheidung von Heiden und Juden in Röm 1.18–2.3', *TZ* 8 [1952], pp. 154-58) pushed the address to the Jew back from 2.1 to 1.32, thus explaining the force of διό in 2.1, but failings to explain what it might mean for the Jew to 'approve those who do such things' in 1.32.

1   The argumentative unity of Rom. 1.18–2.11 has been argued effectively by Jouette Bassler (*Divine Impartiality: Paul and a Theological Axiom* [Chico: Scholars Press, 1982], pp. 123-37).

2   Rudolf Bultmann's work on the diatribe and Paul (*Der Stil der paulinischen Predigt und die kynisch-stoische Diatribe* [Göttingen: Vandenhoeck & Ruprecht, 1910]) is now surpassed by Stanley Stowers' study, *Diatribe*. Other important studies include Schmeller, *Paulus und die 'Diatribe'*; and *The Diatribe in Ancient Rhetorical Theory*, ed. Wilhelm Wuellner (Berkeley: Graduate Theological Union, 1976).

3   Stanley Stowers ('Text as Interpretation: Paul and Ancient Readings of Paul', in *New Perspectives on Ancient Judaism*, vol. III, ed. J. Neusner and E. Frerichs [University Press of America, 1986], p. 21) adduces Nathan's parabolic indictment of David in 2 Samuel 12.1-7 as a functional parallel. Argument by comparison with others' offenses was a standard *topos* of prosecution rhetoric when the defendant pleaded for mercy (cf. *Rhetorica ad Herennium*, 2.25; *Rhetorica ad Alexandrum*, p. 36; Cicero, *De Inventione* 2.107).

of God's verdict, that those who do such things are worthy of death' (1.32), so the individual who judges another shows, in the very act of judging (ἐν ᾧ γὰρ κρίνεις), knowledge and consent with the moral standard which that same individual violates (τὰ γὰρ αὐτὰ πράσσεις).[1] 'Judging' is not the offense which Paul rebukes; hypocrisy, which reveals itself as knowingly violating the divine command, is.[2] The arrogance of the hypocrite, however, extends beyond contempt for the neighbor. It is also contempt for God's judgment: 'Do you think... that you will escape the judgment of God? Or do you despise the riches of the divine kindness and patience and mercy?' (2.3-4).

The amplification in 2.5-16 elaborates the basis for the indictment in 2.1. There is no exception to God's wrath against human impiety (1.18, 2.5), for human beings are without excuse, their knowledge of God's righteous requirement (1.19-20) condemning them when they willfuly violate it (1.32–2.1): for God's judgment is 'according to works' (2.6-10). In light of the sustained insistence that God judges impiety and wicked-

---

1 The juxtaposition of those who 'approve' evildoers (1.32) and the one who 'judges' evildoers (2.1), who would otherwise seem to be incomparable, is thus made clear: the point is that in either case the will of God, though recognized, is flouted. Bassler (*Divine Impartiality*, p. 134) brings this logic out by showing that 2.2 repeats the principle ıf culpability stated in 1.32: God rightly judges 'those who do such ıings'. Rom. 2.1 is evidently a specific application of that principle. ſ ıe paraphrases 1.32–2.2: 'Knowing God's righteous decree that those who do such things are worthy of death, they not only do these things but also approve others doing them. Therefore (they are without excuse, and) you have no excuse, O man who judges, for in passing judgment on your fellow man (you demonstrate that you know God's decree, and thus) you condemn yourself, for you who judge do the same things. For we know that God's judgment falls rightly on those doing such things.' The rhetorical handbooks discuss prosecuting someone who pleads ignorance of the law: 'The first question will be, "Could he or could he not have been informed?"' (*Rhetorica ad Herennium*, 2.24).

2 Stowers (*The Diatribe*, p. 111) points out that arrogance already comes in for attack in Rom. 1.29-31 (ὑβριστής, ὑπερήφανος, ἀλαζών). 'Above all, the ἄνθρωπος in 2.1-5 is pretentious (ἀλαζών) because he sets himself up as a judge of others while he does the same things for which he condemns them. He is someone who pretends to be better than others'.

ness and evil works throughout 1.18–2.12, it is inadmissible to reject this principle as 'unpauline'.[1] Neither can we be satisfied with the discovery of 'divine impartiality' as a theological axiom in Rom. 2.11-16, for the argumentative flow is not from other premises toward 'impartiality', but *from* God's impartiality *as* an axiom ('for [γάρ] there is no impartiality with God', 2.11; 'for' [γάρ] Jew and Gentile are judged alike on the principle, 'the doers of the Law are justified', 2.12-16), *toward* the main thesis, 'there is no excuse before God's judgment' (cf. 1.20, 2.1), since God judges 'what is hidden in human hearts' (2.16).[2]

This observation will be important for our interpretation of the rhetorical macrostructure in Romans 1–5, and so bears emphasis here. Paul clearly declares that Jew and Gentile stand on the same footing before God: the criterion for divine judgment is, to paraphrase, 'the doing of what the Law requires'. So, in Rom. 2.12-16, Paul argues that those who sin are judged, whether they sin 'apart from the Law' or 'within the Law' (2.12). Not those who have heard the Law (or, by implication, those who have not), but those who have *done* the Law (οἱ ποιηταὶ νόμου) are justified before God (2.13). But Paul is not so concerned as he was in 2.9-11 to sustain a careful balance between Jew and Gentile; he seems more concerned in 2.12-16 to argue that Gentiles who, although they do

1 This has been effectively argued, quite against the tide, by Klyne Snodgrass ('Justification by Grace—To the Doers: An Analysis of the Place of Romans 2 in the Theology of Paul', *NTS* 32 [1986], pp. 72-73).

2 Bassler's summary (*Divine Impartiality*, p. 137) of Rom. 1.18–2.11 is accurate: 'What is underscored in this unit, for all of its apparent diversity, seems to be the impartial consistency of God in exacting retribution. From the beginning, with Jews and Gentiles, and in the final assize God recompenses all [people] impartially according to a strict but neutral standard of merit.' By making a major division between 2.11 and 2.12, however, Bassler (*ibid.*, pp. 137-54) raises the principle of 'impartiality' to the preeminent position, and casts 2.12-29 as an argumentative unit in which the paramount question is whether the Law provides a basis for discrimination. The grammatical subordination of 2.12-16 to what precedes (γάρ, 2.12) and the adversative construction in 2.17 (εἰ δὲ σύ) suggest, however, that 2.12-16 reiterate the principle of inevitable accountability to God's judgment on the basis of works (2.6-11), of which 'divine impartiality' is a supporting argument.

not 'have' the Law, nevertheless do what the Law requires (τὰ τοῦ νόμου ποιῶσιν), are 'a law unto themselves' (2.14), the point being that they are no less accountable before God's righteousness for not 'having the Law' (2.15-16).

Paul apparently expects this argument to be intelligible to his audience. He does not explain how, or whether, Gentiles may be found who 'do the things of the Law', nor does he justify the claim that Gentiles who 'by nature' do the things of the Law show that they have the 'work of the Law written in their hearts'. He does not treat any of these propositions as if they were controversial. Rather he *relies* upon them, and on the axiom in 2.11, to support the principle embodied in his indictment (2.1-6): No one is exempt from God's judgment. Even God's mercy is not to be interpreted as indulgence which releases one from accountability before God, for this is to 'despise' that mercy which is intended 'to lead you to repentance' (2.4). To pursue a complacent course of sinning 'in spite of God' is to store up wrath on the day of judgment (2.5-6).

The course of argument in 1.18–2.16 is subtle. It proceeds from what the audience will presumably grant, the inexcusability of the pagan world whose immorality is portrayed at some length, to establish a principle of accountability to God that allows no exception; which is then applied, by way of analogy, to any individual who presumes to stand in a different situation before God than others, presuming on divine mercy to provide exemption from judgment. Paul's answer, in effect, is that God is not merciful in that way. God's patience is intended to lead to repentance: it never qualifies God's righteousness, which is manifest as wrath against human impiety (2.8–9). The argument is essentially a syllogism which determines how God's mercy is to be understood: God's wrath is justly revealed against *all* impiety, since impiety is always witting and willful (1.18-32); there are *no* exceptions, since God treats Jew and Gentile exactly the same way ('impartially'), whether or not they 'have' the Torah (2.7-12); therefore whatever else is true of God's mercy, it does not provide an exemption from absolute accountability to God's judgment 'according to works' (2.1-6). The offense at the center of Paul's apostrophic indictment is nothing other than considering oneself 'excused' from God's righteous demand.

Insight into the nature of the diatribal mode of rhetoric helps us to understand how this apostrophe (which includes within its logic the depiction of human immorality in 1.18-32 as well as 2.1-16) manages the constraints of a rhetorical situation that includes Paul and the Roman audience. 'Diatribe' is a strategic mode of rhetoric,[1] characterized by the simulation of dialogue,[2] which functions to manipulate the 'real' constraints of a rhetorical situation by inviting the audience into a set of 'hypothetical' constraints and premises of the speaker's design.[3] Diatribe resembles drama in that it portrays characters—really only embodiments of attitudes or emotions, roles—that the audience is invited to 'try on'.[4] In

1 Malherbe (*Moral Exhortation*, p. 129) defines diatribe as a form of exhortation that 'may more usefully, if not precisely, be described as a mode rather than a genre'; George Kustas ('Diatribe in Ancient Rhetorical Theory', p. 14; cf. p. 5 for specific reference to Romans) remarks that 'we would be helped toward an appreciation of diatribe if we thought of it less as literary type and rather as literary mode'. In light of the original oral setting of 'diatribal' discourse we should prefer to speak of 'rhetorical' rather than 'literary mode'. These proposals are substantiated by Stowers' history of research in *Diatribe* (pp. 7-78). Stowers (*ibid.*, p. 57) relies heavily on Epictetus' description of a philosophical rhetoric, modeled on Socrates' use of 'socratic method', that combines προτρεπτικὸς λόγος and ἐλεγτικὸς λόγος (*Diss.* 2.26), and thus arrives at a definition of diatribe as 'discourses and discussions in the school where the teacher employed the "Socratic" method of censure and protreptic' (*ibid.*, p. 76).
2 Stowers' review of sources (*Diatribe*, p. 76) convinces him that 'the dialogical element of the diatribe was an important part of this pedagogical approach'.
3 The *Rhetorica ad Herennium* brings out the deliberative quality of 'Hypothetical Dialogues' (*sermocinationes consequentes*), a figure of amplification (4.65): 'There are likewise Hypothetical Dialogues, as follows: "Indeed what do we think those people will say if you have passed this judgment? Will not every one say as follows:—?" And then one must add what they will say.'
4 Kustas ('Diatribe in Ancient Rhetorical Theory', p. 12) characterizes diatribe as 'the practical theater in which ethical prescription could be put to effective and popular use.... Hypothetical Dialogue provides a kind of philosophical stichomythy which seeks to convince us of the truth of its message by inviting us into its own inner tensions. The frankness disarms and captures merely by the display of an emotional process.'

doing so, diatribe implicitly imposes a set of values and premises. By controlling the 'objections' that an imaginary interlocutor raises, the speaker can manipulate the range of possibilities perceived by the audience, and thus set the bounds for the ensuing argument.[1] In this sense the interlocutor can be seen to reflect the speaker's construal of a particular audience, 'the ensemble of those whom the speaker wishes to influence by argumentation',[2] whether or not the interlocutor actually comes to speech. To be effective, the interlocutor's characterization must be intelligible and meaningful: if that characterization can be challenged by a member of the audience as being unrealistic or one-sided, the technique is defeated.

Several aspects of the apostrophe in Rom. 2.1 bear notice in this light. First, the person addressed is characterized, very generally, as someone who 'judges another' for practicing the sins enumerated in 1.18-32 'and yet doing the same things'. No more precise identification (i.e., as Jew, Gentile, etc.) is possible, nor, we suggest, is such restrictive precision intended. The characterization is *hypothetical*, corresponding semantically to a general condition protasis ('if you judge others and do the same things...'), but given greater presence in the imagination by use of the second person. Otherwise the interlocutor's identity remains indeterminate, by intention.

Members of Paul's audience are here offered a personification of the willful disobedience of God's command (cf. 2.2), cast as presumption on God's mercy (2.3-4), and are thus invited, by indwelling that persona, to contemplate what God's mercy

1 According to Paul Wendland (*Philo und die kynisch-stoische Diatribe* [Berlin: Gerog Reimer, 1895], pp. 4-5; cited by Stowers, *Diatribe*, p. 14), in the 'later diatribe' of the Latin philosophers 'the course of the discussion is rigidly circumscribed beforehand and is seldom determined by an external cause such as the objections of an opponent'. This argumentative circumscription of options is not limited to the 'rigidity' of later writers, however; it is the inherent strategic value of the diatribal mode itself. Perelman and Olbrechts-Tyteca's comments (*The New Rhetoric*, pp. 35-40) on the rhetorical preeminence of dialogue are relevant here. Texts related to *sermocinatio* are collected in Lausberg, *Handbuch der literarischen Rhetorik*, pp. 407-11.

2 Perelman and Olbrechts-Tyteca, *The New Rhetoric*, p. 19.

means *for them* on 'safe' or 'neutral' ground. Paul does not address them directly: he will not apply any of his arguments to their own lives until ch. 12. They are nonetheless addressed implicitly.[1] The indictment functions 'to bring home, to concretize and to sharpen the indictment in 1.18-32 (especially vv. 28-32) for Paul's audience. It takes the indictment of "them" in 1.18-32 and makes it into a personal indictment of any of the audience to whom it might apply.'[2] The subjunctive mood in this statement captures the force of the apostrophe.

This is its point: no one in the audience should expect to be exempt from God's righteous requirement by virtue of an appeal to divine mercy that is not accompanied by true repentance (2.5) and good works (2.6-11). Paul wants the Christians in Rome to take that message seriously. There is no good reason, *on rhetorical grounds*, to insulate the letter's intended audience from the persuasive force of the apostrophe or its implicit call for repentance. Yet this is the price of an interpretation that reads 1.18-32 as the beginning of a purely didactic essay on the need for redemption.[3] In particular it appears arbitrary to restrict the apostrophe's force to 'the Jew'.[4]

We will return to this last issue in the excursus below. At present we want to emphasize the two aspects of the rhetor's strategic use of topics that are evident here. The rhetor must

1 Plutarch preferred this 'technique of indirection' to direct rebuke, especially when circumstances did not permit private admonition ('How to Tell a Flatterer from a Friend', 70d-71c: Malherbe, *Moral Exhortation*, pp. 48-50).

2 Stowers, *Diatribe*, p. 110.

3 Käsemann (*Romans*, pp. 35-36) writes that Rom. 1.18-32 'are not pedagogical preparation for the message of salvation... but characterize its cosmic breadth and depth. Its reality and necessity coincide. To bring out its world-embracing reality, the apostle first proclaims its necessity.' Yet it is apparent from what follows that in Käsemann's view, this 'necessity' does not involve the Roman Christians directly: 'He does this for Christians who no longer need propaedeutics or a missionary point of contact... Here, then, the Gentiles are not addressed directly on the subject of the reality which determines them.'

4 Stowers' conclusion (*Diatribe*, p. 112) is put more strongly: 'It is anachronistic and completely unwarranted to think that Paul has only the Jew in mind in 2.1-5 or that he characterizes the typical Jew'.

be receptive to the rhetorical situation (Paul presumes the audience's acceptance of his depiction of Gentile immorality in 1.18-32), and yet maintain rhetorical integrity in redisposing that situation (Paul applies the audience's adherence to the principles of human accountability and impartial divine judgment to the specific 'case' of presumption on God's mercy). To insist that *either* Paul is addressing what he knows to be actual circumstances in Rome *or* that he turns away from his audience, so to speak, to address his gospel's inherent opposition to Judaism[1] is to pose the false dilemma between the rhetorical situation's absolute determinacy and the rhetor's absolute creative freedom.[2]

4. *The Second Apostrophe: To the Jew (Rom. 2.17-29)*

The second apostrophe, in 2.17-29, differs markedly from the first. There is an obvious shift to a new conversation partner: 'But you, for your part—' (εἰ δὲ σύ). The person now addressed is specifically a Jew; and this characterization is developed much more fully than in the first apostrophe. Whereas the 'one who judges' was addressed suddenly, 'caught out' in the act of judging (2.1), the Jew's characterization is a matter of deliberate choice and a source of pride ('if you call yourself a Jew'). The Jew is further characterized in terms that stand in sharp contrast to the idolatrous Gentiles in 1.18-32. The Jew 'rests upon the Law and boasts in God': the Gentiles refuse to honor God (1.21, 23, 25—contrast Paul's pious *berakah*!), and defy the divine commandment (1.32). The Jew 'knows God's will and approves what is excellent, instructed from the Law' (2.18): the Gentiles suppress the truth (1.18); their 'thinking has been brought to naught and their senseless minds darkened' (1.21) so that they spurn their Creator, turn instead to idols, and violate their own bodies, being consumed with passion; they break God's Law. The clauses that follow

---

1 These are respectively the views of Karl P. Donfried ('False Presuppositions') and Günther Bornkamm ('Paul's Last Will and Testament'); cf. Stowers, *Diatribe*, p. 2.
2 These are the opposite views of the rhetor's response to the rhetorical situation (of Lloyd Bitzer and Richard Vatz, respectively) rejected by Scott Consigny in his article on 'Rhetoric and its Situations', pp. 175-76, 183.

develop the characterization of the Jew in explicit contrast to the Gentiles: '—being convinced that you are a guide to the blind, a light to those in darkness, a teacher of the foolish, an instructor of babes, holding in the Law the very embodiment of knowledge and of truth' (2.19-20). That Paul here portrays the real self-estimation of his contemporary Jews can be documented from ancient Jewish literature, and need not be contested. But this characterization arises more directly from the mention of Jews in 2.9-10, 12-13, who are described solely in terms of their relation to Torah ('those who sin in the Law', who 'are judged by the Law', who 'hear the Law' and who 'do the Law').

Paul turns immediately to questions that challenge the consistency of the individual who holds so high a view of his or her possession of the Torah. 'You who teach others, do you fail to teach yourself? Preaching against stealing, do you steal? Saying "Do not commit adultery", do you yourself commit adultery? Expressing your abhorrence of idols, do you rob temples?' Here resemblance to the philosophical diatribe is most obvious, for as Stowers has shown, 'one of the most common themes, especially in Epictetus, in texts which address the fictitious opponent, is the attack on inconsistency and hypocrisy'. Exposing the discrepancy between someone's noble profession and actual conduct is a regular part of the *topos*.[1]

As Stowers also points out, diatribal indictments generally functioned to 'describe a certain vice or type of ignorant and wretched person... One of the functions of addressing the interlocutor is to produce an embodiment of the evils which the indictment is intended to bring to light'.[2] It is noteworthy in this regard that several of the passages Stowers adduces as parallels to Rom. 2.17-24 share either the conditional construction (εἰ δὲ σύ) or the interrogative mode evident here.[3]

---

1 *Diatribe*, p. 101, cf. pp. 79-118; cf. Malherbe, *Paul and the Thessalonians*, pp. 52-60; *idem, Moral Exhortation*, pp. 38-40.
2 *Ibid.*, p. 107.
3 Note Epictetus, *Diss.* 2.9.17, 19-21; 2.17.26-27; 3.2.8-10; Seneca, *De Vita beata* 27.4. A passage from Seneca's 95th Epistle indicates the semantic equivalence of apostrophic characterization and paraenesis in the conditional mode (cited by Stowers, *Diatribe*, pp. 106-107).

The diatribal apostrophe must remain conditional and hypothetical since it does not address an actual member of the audience who can respond, negatively or positively, to the questions asked. It is appropriate, then, that Paul continues by drawing conclusions about the significance of circumcision and what it means to be a Jew (2.25-29) without first getting any answer to his questions.[1] His purpose is not to pronounce a verdict, but to establish by the vivid illustrative technique of diatribe a legal principle: not *possession* of the Law (or circumcision, or the heritage of the covenant) but *obedience* characterizes the true Jew who is 'justified' (2.13) and rewarded from heaven (2.29).

This suggests that just as the first apostrophe in 2.1-5 serves to give rhetorical presence to a principle—unconditional accountability to God's righteous demand—rather than to castigate individuals within the Roman congregation, so the second apostrophe in 2.17-24 is intended not so much to disqualify the claims of actual Jews as to bring home the points made in 2.12-13: those who sin 'in the Law' will be judged by the Law. It is those who do the Law (not those who only hear it) who will be justified. The conclusions reached in 2.25-29 are of similar import: 'circumcision is indeed of value if you keep the Law'. 'Being a Jew is not a matter of what is (outwardly) evident, nor is circumcision a matter of what is evident in the flesh; but the Jew is (one who is a Jew) in what is hidden, and (true) circumcision is (circumcision) of the heart, in spirit not in letter'.

---

1 The Nestle-Aland text (26th edn) sets question marks in 2.21 (twice) and 2.22 (twice). A colon at the end of 2.23 draws a conclusion that indicts the Jew: '(You) who boast in the Law, through the transgression of the Law you dishonor God!' In general such punctuation is a subsequent addition to the text; sometimes, as here, it constitutes an interpretation of the text. It cannot be insignificant that the earliest manuscript to provide extensive punctuation in Rom. 2—Codex Sinaiticus—clearly places question marks at the ends of all five clauses, including 2.23 ('You who boast in the Law, do you dishonor God by transgressing the Law?'). This reading is of course no less an interpretation. It has on its side the parallel construction in four preceding sentences, however, and may reflect the way this text was read and heard in the fourth century.

Attention to the illustrative potential of the diatribal apostrophe may help us to understand how this address to a *Jewish* interlocutor relates to the audience in Rome, whom Paul has explicitly addressed as *Gentiles*. It should not be necessary to posit a Gentile-Christian audience with 'Judaizing' sentiments (Schmithals); evidence elsewhere in Romans (11.13-36) in fact suggests the opposite.[1] Yet neither are we bound to understand this pericope as addressed 'over the heads' of the Roman congregation to the eavesdropping synagogue, or to Jewish-Christians in Jerusalem or elsewhere. In particular, the observation that this part of Romans 2 could have served as a synagogue exhortation to greater observance of Torah[2] must cast in doubt the view that Paul's purpose here is a 'radical demolition of Jewish privileges'.[3] What does the apostrophe communicate to the epistolary audience?

Stowers finds here 'the picture not just of the pretentious person but of the pretentious moral and religious leader and teacher':

> The 'Jew' here pretends to have a special relationship with God. He boasts (καυχᾶσθαι) of his relation to God (2.17). Bragging about what one does not truly possess is the chief mark of the pretentious person. He also boasts in the law while breaking it. This person pretends to have great ethical knowledge, knowledge of the law and of God's will. Finally, he pretends to be a teacher and moral guide to others, although he does not embody what he teaches (19-22).[4]

Yet even this statement reads the apostrophe too flatly, too *indicatively*. Paul is not setting 'the Jew' up as the paradigmatic braggart: in particular he is not attacking someone who

1 See the discussion in Chapter 3.
2 Sanders, *Paul, the Law, and the Jewish People*, p. 129.
3 Käsemann, *Romans*, p. 78. It is one of the weak points of Käsemann's commentary that the important issue of the *accuracy* of the indictment perceived here—an issue that has come to the fore in E.P. Sanders' *Paul and Palestinian Judaism*, but before that in G.F. Moore's *Judaism* as well—finds no place. Käsemann insists, to the contrary, that Paul's argument throughout Rom. 2–3 is meant as an actual indictment of his contemporary Jews. These issues will bear examination in the excursus.
4 Stowers, *Diatribe*, pp. 112-13.

'pretends' to possess 'what one does not truly possess'. The Jew's privileges are real (cf. 3.1-2, 9.4-5); nor does Paul ever deny that the Law really is the 'embodiment of knowledge and truth'. Here he does not accuse, but asks—penetrating questions, but not presumptive of the answer. Here is evident a different tone from that in 2.1-5, where guilt was presumed: 'Did you really think you could get away with this?' is the gist of the questions there. Here the questions are more simply interrogative: 'Are you trying to get away with anything?'

In light of the Jew's real privileges, this interrogation of the Jew appears to provide not only an illustration of Paul's principle that no human being is 'excused' from accountability to God, but its conclusive proof. The apostrophe substantiates, in a dramatic way, the second half of the legal principle in 2.12-13. 'As many [ὅσοι] as have sinned in the Law'—Paul asks his Jewish interlocutor: Have *you* sinned 'in the Law'? (2.21-24)—'will be judged by the Law'—Will *your* circumcision not be counted as uncircumcision? (2.25b); 'for it is not those who hear the Law'—so the interlocutor is characterized (2.17-20)—'but those who do the Law who will be justified': 'Circumcision will benefit *you*, if you keep the Law' (2.25a). By 'proving' one half of the proposition in 2.12-13, the half relating to the Jews, the apostrophe by implication substantiates the whole: just so surely will those 'who have sinned apart from Law also perish apart from Law'.

The apostrophe functions, then, as the protasis for an argument *a fortiori*. If anyone enjoyed the privilege of exemption from God's wrath, surely it must be the Jew, who 'boasts in God' and 'relies upon Torah': but for Paul this possession is itself the medium of the Jew's accountability to God, for it is the very revelation of God's will, the 'embodiment of all knowledge and truth'. The Jew, above all others, cannot plead ignorance. If the Jew, who possesses such privileges as are described in 2.17-20, is not exempt from God's judgment when he or she violates the very Torah that constitutes those privileges (2.12b), then how can Gentiles who have never shared those privileges lay any claim to God's indulgence (2.12a; cf. 2.3-5)? Of course such an argument *a fortiori* is undermined *logically* by the very principle that God treats everyone alike (2.11). But the argument could be rhetorically persuasive for

those who (rightly or wrongly) perceived in Judaism a
peculiar realm of divine benevolence.[1]

5. *The Nature of Israel's 'Privilege' and the Accountability of the Jew (Rom. 3.1-9)*

That the interpretation just advanced is on the right track is
confirmed by what immediately follows in 3.1-9, for here Paul
is eager to specify the exact nature of the Jew's covenantal
advantage. 'What, then, is the advantage of being a Jew? Or
what is the benefit of circumcision?' The questions arise naturally from the preceding, not because Paul has denied that the
Jew has any real advantage—that interpretation, frequently
voiced, imputes duplicity to Paul's answer in 3.2—but because
Paul has shown that the Jew has no advantage that constitutes an exemption from God's righteous claim. The syntax
and logic here are difficult, not least because of Paul's terse
expression and the asyndetic style of the diatribal interchange.
The basic thrust of the passage is clear enough, however: at
issue is the relation of the Jew's 'advantage' (3.1) to God's
faithfulness (3.3) and righteousness (3.5). The summary
questions (οὖν) in 3.1 and 3.9 are particularly important, and
it is unfortunate that the second question (προεχόμεθα?) has
been so troublesome for translators. It seems preferable to take
προεχόμεθα as a genuine middle, meaning 'do we have a
defense?'[2] or, 'do we raise a counterplea against God?' This

---

1 Brandt (*Rhetoric of Argumentation*, ch. 1) shows that what is
  rhetorically persuasive is rarely compelling by the strict codes of
  logic. Even the 'deductive syllogism' is a 'study in futility' (p. 30).
2 Cranfield (*Romans*, I, p. 187-89) rejected the middle translation
  because he doubted that προέχεσθαι could be used intransitively to
  mean 'raise a defense for oneself'; and because with the transitive
  middle, 'hold before oneself (as an excuse)', he properly expected the
  question τίνα, not τί, and the answer οὐδέν, not οὔ. But the preva-
  lence of the legal metaphor in Rom. 1–3, and the lack of attestation
  for the middle προέχεσθαι with active sense, lend weight to the suggestion that here, indeed, we have a (unique) intransitive occur-
  rence of the middle. We now also have Nils Dahl's helpful text-criti-
  cal and exegetical discussion ('Romans 3.9: Text and Meaning', in
  Paul and Paulinism, p. 194) of this verse, which calls our attention
  to an analogous (though transitive) use of προέχεσθαι in the context
  of the eschatological divine lawsuit in 1 Enoch. Dahl quotes from the
  Greek text of 1 Enoch 9.3-4: 'Prepare yourselves, you righteous, and

translation not only avoids more serious philological difficulties by taking the verb in its most natural sense, but also illuminates Paul's argument. Yes, the Jew has real privileges (3.1-2), but No, these privileges—which are founded upon the righteousness of God—do not undermine God's righteousness when Jews are disobedient (3.3-8): this suggestion is in fact blasphemous! For God is proved right even when all human beings, including God's chosen people Israel (cf. ἡ ἀδικία ἡμῶν, 3.5) are proved false. That means that 'we Jews have no defense', we raise no excuse, against God (3.9).

The dialogue presents from yet another angle the basic truth outlined in 2.1-13, except that now Paul is eager to distinguish between two things that may be confused in the minds of his audience: Israel's privileges remain real and valid (3.1-2), but these privileges do not constitute a 'boast' or 'defense' that might insulate the Jew from God's judgment (3.9). If this were the meaning of the covenant, God's integrity would be compromised (3.3): but this is impossible (3.4: the Psalm quotation is axiomatic for Paul).

This reading of 3.1-9 differs from the most common interpretation. The statement made in 3.9 goes beyond the principle in 2.12-13, for there Paul says that 'the doers of the Law'—Jew and Gentile alike—will be justified; here he says that 'we have already charged that all people, both Jews and Gentiles, are under sin' (3.9). When this statement is read as a summary of 1.18-3.8, the missing premise that must be supplied between 2.12-13 and 3.9—namely, that no one, in fact, keeps the Law, and so no one is justified on those terms—is taken to be the point of 2.17-29 (or 2.1-29). Of course the Gentile does not keep the Law (cf. 1.18-32), Paul supposedly argues: but neither, O Jew, do you (cf. 2.21-24). There are problems with this interpretation. First, if Rom. 1.18-32 is supposed to function as the proof of one half of the verdict in 3.9, namely that Gentiles are 'under sin', then Paul's refer-

hold your supplications before you, that they may be remembered' (προέχεσθε τὰς ἐντεύξεις ὑμῶν εἰς μνημοσύνον: for the Greek text see M. Black, *Apocalypsis Henochi Graeci in Pseudepigrapha Veteris Testamenti* [Leiden: Brill, 1970]). Dahl notes an amenable translation by J.C. O'Neill (*Romans* [London: Penguin, 1975], p. 68): 'What, then, do we put up as a defense?'

134   *The Rhetoric of Romans*

ence to Gentiles 'doing the things of the Law' in 2.14-15 is
voided of meaning. Further, as we have seen, the interrogation of the Jewish interlocutor in 2.21-24 does not result in a
conclusive indictment, and thus can hardly serve as a
demonstration that 'all Jews are under sin'. Finally, the
statement in 3.9 is not phrased as a conclusion to the argumentation going back to 2.1 or 1.18, but as a supporting argument (γάρ) for the immediately preceding insistence that 'we
Jews have no defense' or excuse before God. Its function is not
to summarize everything between 1.17 and 3.8 (or 3.20), but to
provide another argument, parallel to that in 3.1-8, showing
that Israel's covenant provides the Jew no exemption from
God's righteous judgment.

It cannot be denied, of course, that Paul has come to the
conclusion in 3.9b by way of the 'hidden premise' that no one is
put right with God through 'doing the Law'. But this conclusion is prior (προ-ητιασάμεθα!) to the argument that appears
here. Paul apparently expects his audience to assent that 'all
people are under sin' without requiring that he 'prove' it. It is
not argued in Rom. 2.17–3.8. What that unit *does* argue is
that there is no excuse from accountability to God. The Jew
who sins against Torah cannot expect his circumcision or the
mere possession of the Law to cancel that accountability (2.17-
29); the covenant with Israel has never meant anything else
(3.1-8). Instead of a syllogism that runs,

> God justifies only those who keep   (major premise)
> the Law (2.13):
>
> But neither the Gentiles (1.18-32)   (minor premise)
> nor the Jews (2.17-29) in fact
> keep the Law;
>
> Therefore we have established   (conclusion)
> that all people, Jews and
> Gentiles, are under sin (3.9),

Paul's argument here runs as follows:

God is always righteous, judging   (major premise)
with wrath *all* human impiety
(1.18-32), but justifying *all* who
keep the Law and do good works
(2.6-10, 13):

And since   (minor premises)

God judges all people impartially
(2.6, 11);

the Jew, who might be expected
to enjoy such exemption from
judgment, is in fact no less
accountable to God through
Torah (2.17-29)—(That this is
true has always been the nature
of Israel's covenant, since it
depends not on human righteousness but on God's own
integrity [3.1-8], and since as we
already know 'all people' —Jews
included—'are under sin'
[3.9b]);

and since God's mercy is
intended to lead 'you' to repentance, not to exempt 'you' from
God's judgment (2.3-5):

'You' are without excuse when   (conclusion)
you judge another and yet do
things that you know are an
affront to God (2.1-2).

This outline depends in part on the above discussion of argumentation in 1.15–2.29 and in part on features of diatribe style in 3.1-9 to which Stowers has called attention. Stowers contends that the 'dialogical character' of the passage is frequently misconstrued; in particular, he says, the conventional rendering of pronouns throughout the passage 'shows how really incoherent is the accepted reading of the text':

This approach, as reflected in the RSV, has Paul using a collective 'we' referring to humanity in v. 5, an exemplary or generalizing first person singular in v. 7, a first person plural referring to Paul himself and his fellow workers in v. 8, a first person plural in v. 9a meaning 'we Jews' and another first person plural in v. 9b, which is read as an 'authorial we' and translated as 'I'. How readers cou'd understand so many shifts in the reference of the first person in such a short space of text has never been explained. In fact, the necessary contextual indicators for those shifts are not present, and it is solely on the basis of a priori assumptions that certain types of statements could only be made by or about certain groups of people ('Paul', 'Jews', 'Christians', 'libertines') that the traditional reading is possible.

Stowers proposes that 'a more natural and coherent interpretation of 3.1-9 and its context is possible if one employs models of dialogue from the diatribe to suggest how one might read the text'.[1] In his view, the interpretative problems disappear when this passage is read as a continuous dialogue between two people: Paul and his imaginary dialogue partner, the Jew.

Considerations of typical dialogical patterns in the diatribe lead Stowers to advance an alternative reading of 3.1-9. He shows, for example, that in an interchange in Epictetus, *Diss.* 2.23, 'Epictetus states the questions which represent false reasoning or unthinkable alternatives so sharply that the interlocutor is forced to reject the questions and, in fact, state the logical alternative toward which Epictetus is leading him. Thus, the interlocutor himself provides the evidence or conclusion'. Even when an interlocutor begins an interchange with an objection, as the interchange continues 'the teacher usually but not always leads the questioning. No matter who asks the questions, however, the teacher is in control and guides the discussion to a point or points of agreement and realization on the parts of the interlocutor'.[2]

Turning to Rom. 3.1-8, Stowers agrees with Käsemann, for example, that 3.1 is the 'objection' of a Jewish interlocutor, and that Paul's response begins in 3.2. But while Käsemann extends Paul's response through 3.4 and then takes 3.5 as a second objection from the Jewish interlocutor, Stowers assigns 3.4 to the interlocutor, thus reading 3.3 as the sort of 'leading

---

1 Stowers, 'Paul's Dialogue', pp. 709-10.
2 *Ibid.*, pp. 712-14.

question' used by a teacher to guide the conversation.[1]
Throughout the interchange, Paul 'will lead the interlocutor
not only to answer his own objection, but also to an admission
of the apostle's basic theological claims'. Stowers attributes 3.4
to the interlocutor, who 'can only deny in the strongest terms'
Paul's rhetorical suggestion by quoting Psalm 5.14: 'As in the
diatribe, Paul has led his discussion partner to be the witness,
to provide the evidence'.[2] On the same pattern, 3.5 and 3.7-8
are made into Paul's pressing questions; 3.6 and 3.9 are the
Jewish interlocutor's response, the final verse (3.9) being
something of a last protest before the interlocutor must
capitulate to Paul's logic.[3] Stowers contends that his outline
not only conforms to the pattern of the diatribe, but also allows
3.1-9 to retain an argumentative cohesion. The passage
makes sense, he suggests, in the context of an intra-Jewish
discussion of the grace of God: the interchange in 3.5-8 in
particular makes sense 'when they are understood to imply a
belief on the part of the interlocutor in a kind of cheap grace
for Israel'.

This study makes important contributions to our interpretation of Romans 3, not least by focusing attention on the
routine patterns of dialogue into which diatribal discourse
almost naturally fell. Stowers also allows the *character* of the
Jewish interlocutor to retain a certain consistency or integrity:
The Jew quotes Scripture to defend the honor of God (3.4),
rather than (as in Käsemann's treatment) fighting to retain
the last scraps of covenantal privilege. Stowers rightly points
out that the interlocutor's 'plausibility' is an important persuasive aspect of the diatribal mode.[4] Further, attention to the
pedagogic and protreptic intention of the diatribal mode is
properly distinguished from the polemical tone of invective.
This insight leads Stowers to protest, 'the interlocutor is not an
enemy but a student or partner in discussion. The idea of E.
Käsemann and others that Paul polemicizes against Judaism
as representative of pathological religion in 2.17-24 and 3.1-9

1 *Ibid.*, pp. 715-16.
2 *Ibid.*, p. 716.
3 *Ibid.*, pp. 717-18.
4 *Ibid.*, p. 713.

does not even fit the style.'[1] Much the same point is brought
out in *The Diatribe*: 'The objections in 3.1-9 and elsewhere
should not be thought of as aimed at Jews as opponents, but
rather as addressed to the Roman church in the mode of
indictment or censure. Their intent is not polemical but pedagogical.'[2] Finally, Stowers interprets the question and answer
in 3.9 in such a way that the verse does not simply cancel out
3.2.

There is nevertheless room for improvement in Stowers'
outline of the passage—on the grounds of his own observations
about diatribal style. Why, for example, is Rom. 3.1 necessarily
an 'objection' raised by an interlocutor? According to Stowers'
own evidence, such objections, when they 'interrupt' the
speaker, are normally expressed in direct discourse, and are
normally (and necessarily?) marked either by an explicit
formula such as τίς ἐρεῖ or ἐρεῖς, or by an adversative construction that makes a break with the discourse, such as ναὶ
ἀλλά. The interruptive objection is to be distinguished, then,
from the recapitulative 'leading question' by which the
teacher guides the student to the appropriate conclusion by
the Socratic procedure of question and answer. Here the
routine marker is τί οὖν; or equivalent. Not all questions in the
diatribe are 'indicting' (as Stowers labels the questions in Rom.
2.21-24), nor do all 'leading questions' put forward obviously
false conclusions to be rejected (as is the case at Rom. 6.1 and
6.15). Yet Stowers does not systematically distinguish these
patterns.[3]

---

1 *Ibid.*, p. 722.
2 *Diatribe*, p. 153. These remarks, based on Stowers' comparative
   study of the diatribe, are better grounded than his subsequent conclusion, which seems to derive from a prior assumption about the
   character of Romans: 'In using these objections from various
   groups it is as if Paul were instructing a classroom of Jews and
   various sorts of Christians *in the gospel and its implications*' (*ibid.*,
   emphasis mine).
3 This is the most serious drawback to the otherwise thorough treatment in Stowers' chapter (*Diatribe*, pp. 119-54) on 'Objections and
   False Conclusions'. Compare Richard Hays' comment ('Abraham',
   p. 79 n. 13): Objection 'is an appropriate term if one thinks of the text
   as a dialogue between Paul and an imaginary interlocutor. In the
   absence of specific indicators in the text (as in a Platonic dialogue),

Nothing in 3.1 marks an 'interruption' or 'objection'. It would be reasonable to conclude, on purely formal grounds, that the recapitulative question that begins τί οὖν is (within the fiction of the diatribe) Paul's own; more, that Paul is steering the discussion in a direction he considers important. The same is true at 3.9, which begins with the identical phrase τί οὖν. The syntactical and stylistic markers themselves point us away from polemic and apologetic and toward collaboration and pedagogy: Paul calls upon the Jewish interlocutor to help him make a point.

Following Stowers' observations, it is possible to reorganize Rom. 3.1-9 along the lines of a diatribal interchange. Following the apostrophic 'proof' that the Jew has no privileged exemption from God's judgment (2.17-29), Paul 'interrogates' his Jewish interlocutor about the nature of the covenant:

(Paul asks)	What, then, is the advantage of being a Jew? Or what is the benefit of circumcision?
(The interlocutor's response)	Much in every way! First, they were entrusted with the oracles of God.
(Paul again)	What now: If some were disobedient, their unfaithfulness does not nullify God's integrity, does it?[1]
(The Jew)	May it never be! Let God be proven true, though every human being be false, as it is written...

however, it would seem preferable not to posit an actual change of speakers'.

1 Here, πίστις θεοῦ is used to set off ἐπιστεύθησαν (3.2), ἠπίστησάν τινες;... ἡ ἀπιστία αὐτῶν. The 'faithfulness of God' meant here, however, is God's self-faithfulness, integrity, as the following verse (the interlocutor's response) makes clear (πίστις θεοῦ = ἀλήθεια θεοῦ).

(Paul again)

But if our wickedness, [my Jewish friend,] serves to show the justice of God [that is, if our transgressions provide God an opportunity to be 'merciful' to us], what shall you and I conclude? Surely not that God is unjust who bears wrath? [For why should God be merciful one moment and wrathful the next?] You recognize that I am speaking in [unenlightened] human terms!

(The Jew)

May it never be! How, in that case [if God were indeed unjust to bear wrath—if God's 'justice' consisted in mercy alone] could God judge the whole world [as we know God will do]?

(Paul again)

But if God's truth abounds all the more in my falsehood unto divine glory [as the Psalm verse might suggest], why do I still stand under a verdict as 'sinner', and [why is the case] not just as we [Jews] are blasphemed, and some accuse us [Jews] of saying—'Let us do evil in order that good may come'? [Are others correct to interpret Israel's covenant as a matter of privilege against God's judgment?]

(The Jew's proper answer)

The condemnation of such [slanderers] is just!

(A final leading question)

What then [have we discovered]: Do we [as Jews] hold up anything as a defense? [Is the covenant, or the possession of Torah, a shield against God's judgment?]

(Conclusion) Not at all! (Basis:) For we
already know that all people,
Jews and Greeks alike, are
under a verdict of sin, just as
Scripture says...

We have identified the 'we' indicated in 3.5, 8, and 9 as 'Jews', reflecting the belief that Paul maintains the diatribal fiction throughout this pericope. That his point applies to Gentiles as well, however, may be implied by his reference to God 'judging the world' (3.6), and it is at any rate the purpose of including this apostrophe to the Jew *here* in the first place. The conclusion in 3.9a may, within the fiction of the diatribe, indicate first that 'we Jews' have no defense against God's claim. But that conclusion is meant to have immediate implications for *all people*. That the Jewish interlocutor represents a *paradigm, not the target* of Paul's rhetoric should also be evident from the construction in 3.9a. The verb προεχόμεθα (which is admittedly enigmatic) stands without any construction expressing comparison ('Are we better off than—?'), in an 'absolute' sense ('Do any of us have any advantage at all?').[1] Consequently we take the fundamental point of argumentation in Rom. 1.18–3.9 to be an insistence upon God's unqualified righteousness, and *not simply* the proof of divine 'impartiality'. The argument in 2.17–3.9 is not nakedly that 'Not even the Jews have an excuse', but that '*Since* not even the Jews have an excuse, no one does'.

---

1 See above, n. 2 on pp. 132-33. The Bauer-Arndt-Gingrich-Danker *Lexicon* notes that the middle form with active meaning ('jut out, excel, be first') is 'not found elsewhere'. If the verb is given 'its customary sense [i.e.,] hold something before oneself for protection (see also 1 Enoch 99.3)', and 'if the "we" in προεχόμεθα refers to the Jews, then the οὐ πάντως that follows vigorously rejects the idea that they possess anything that might shield them from God's wrath'. The *Lexicon* also suggests that the verb might be taken as a passive, 'meaning "are we excelled?" then "are we in a worse position (than they)?"': but the instances of either the active or the passive being used in the comparative sense that are supplied by the Liddell-Scott *Lexicon* involve either a genitive of comparison or a prepositional construction, neither of which is present in Rom. 3.9.

6. *Proof from Scripture (Rom. 3.10-20)*

It would seem to follow, then, that the ensuing proof from
Scripture (καθὼς γέγρατραι) is meant to support the verdict in
3.9 as it stands ('all people, Jews and Greeks, are under sin'),
and is not directed only to Jews or only to Greeks. That sins of
speech figure prominently in the catena[1] is further confirmation that the proof offered refers *not only* to the Jews: for
although the immediately preceding context does address a
Jewish interlocutor (2.17–3.9) and does raise the possibility
that the Jew's actions do not match what the Jew claims
(2.21-24), the catena more clearly echoes 1.18 ('the
wickedness of human beings who in wickedness suppress the
truth'). Paul has argued by means of analogy (1.21–2.2),
axioms (God's mercy is meant to lead to repentance; God
returns to everyone according to works; there is no partiality
with God), and an *a fortiori* argument by way of apostrophe
(2.17–3.8); now he appeals to the witness of Scripture to show
that no human voice can be raised in protest against God's
judgment.

Many commentators nevertheless consider the catena to be
directed primarily at demonstrating the culpability of the *Jew
specifically*.[2] This interpretation is based on the usual translation of 3.19, as Beker shows. He finds the 'argumentative point
of Rom. 1.18–3.20' to be directed against *Jewish* superiority
and pride. 'What is argued is the equal status of Jew and
Gentile under sin; what is presupposed is the self-evident
character of the Gentile under sin'. He finds this logic confirmed in 3.19:

> If the law speaks only to 'those under the law', why does it
> apply to 'the whole world'?... Paul addresses his Jewish
> target. For if it can be shown that the catena of Scripture of
> 3.11-18 applies to the Jews, then it is self-evident that the

---

1 Cranfield, *Romans*, I, p. 194.
2 The citations of Scripture 'apply primarily to the Jews'; the Jew as a
  representative of the pious person is the real opponent in the discussion' (Käsemann, *Romans*, pp. 85, 87).

whole world (i.e. the Gentiles) is accountable to God as well, for Gentiles are by nature sinners.... [1]

In this view one of the most extraordinary aspects of the catena is its appropriation of Scriptures that in general refer to *Israel's enemies* in order to indict *the Jew*.[2] This attributes to the apostle a harshly polemical reapplication of Scripture.[3]

1 Beker, *Paul and the Apostle*, p. 80. Käsemann (*Romans*, p. 85) similarly rephrases the argument: 'All the world can really be pronounced guilty if even the righteous is'.
2 Rom. 3.10b-12 are loosely adapted from Ps. 13.1-3 LXX, excerpted from a community lament that represents the enemies of the righteous in the person of 'the fool' (ἄφρων) who considers that 'there is no God'. The psalm goes on to describe the workers of lawlessness (οἱ ἐργαζόμενοι τὴν ἀνομίαν) who 'eat up' God's people 'as bread, and do not call upon the Lord' (13.4). Similarly, Rom. 3.13 quotes Ps. 5.10 (LXX), a verse from a lament psalm that makes the same contrast between the righteous plaintiff and his wicked enemies. The righteous one appeals to God as to one 'who does not delight in lawlessness' (οὐ θέλων ἀνομίαν), before whose eyes 'the lawless [παράνομοι] may not stand', who hates 'the doers of lawlessness' (ἐργαζομένους τὴν ἀνομίαν). Those imprecated in v. 11 (LXX: κρῖνον αὐτούς!) are described in v. 10 in sharp contrast to the righteous one and his confederates. The reference to slanderous tongues (Rom. 3.13a) links the phrases from Ps. 5.10 to a fragmentary quote (concerning lips, Rom. 3.13b) from Ps. 139.4 (LXX). That psalm is an appeal from the righteous to be delivered from evil people (ἐξ ἀνθρώπου πονηροῦ, v. 1). In 3.14, again, the mouth as an organ of wickedness is the pivot to a new quotation, this time from Ps. 10.7. This psalm, another community lament, invokes judgment against the impious (ἀσεβής), the sinner (ἁμαρτωλός) who renounces the Lord, the wrongdoer (ὁ ἀδικῶν) who does not seek God, in whose eyes 'there is no God' (Ps. 9.2-25, LXX). At Rom. 3.15 the catena moves from the psalter to the book of Isaiah, but the source context is similar. Instead of a lament psalm with imprecations against the wicked, Isa. 59 begins with an indictment of the wicked in the second person, then shifts (at v. 4) to the third person. Paul quotes the description of violence from Isa. 59.7-8 in Rom. 3.15-17. He then returns to the psalter to quote Ps. 35.2 (LXX), 'There is no fear of God before their eyes'. In the psalm, that phrase describes the lawless sinner (ὁ παράνομος), whose sin is repeatedly called ἀνομία. In short, as Lloyd Gaston (*Paul and the Torah*, p. 121) points out, 'the catena is not evenhanded but excoriates Gentile sinners'.
3 In H. Räisänen's opinion (*Paul and the Law*, p. 99) the general bad fit of Paul's arguments in Rom. 2–3 to the purposes to which Paul supposedly puts them is 'rounded off by the in itself trivial observa-

Of course the original contexts are not necessarily determinative of the meaning imputed to these excerpts in Paul's letter. Nevertheless, this observation, combined with the preceding understanding of Paul's argumentation in 1.18-3.9, casts doubt over the assumption that Paul's primary target in 3.10-18 is the Jew.

The catena has been crafted (either by Paul or by someone else) to convey the message expressed in its first verse: 'there is no one righteous, not even one'. This theme makes the catena suitably adapted to confirm the verdict announced as 'already established' in 3.9. That this 'universal' indictment is pointed especially at the Jew (Käsemann, Beker) is a straightforward interpretation of Rom. 3.19 as the verse is punctuated in the RSV (and every other English translation I have consulted): 'Now we know that whatever the Law says it speaks to those who are under the Law, so that every mouth may be stopped, and the whole world may be held accountable to God'. This translation accurately reflects the punctuation in the Nestle-Aland[26], which renders the phrase ὅσα ὁ νόμος λέγει as the subject of the sentence, and the phrase τοῖς ἐν τῷ νόμῳ λαλεῖ as the verb clause. The rhetorical weight of the indictment thus falls upon the Jews (τοῖς ἐν τῷ νόμῳ λαλεῖ). But of course this punctuation is secondary. Does the punctuation obscure Paul's intent? Cranfield worries what Paul can mean 'when he claims that all the things which Scripture says are spoken to the Jews', and concludes, 'perhaps we should take Paul's meaning to be that everything that the OT says (including the things which are said about Gentiles) is indeed addressed in the first instance to the Jews, and is intended for their instruction, so that, so far from imagining themselves excepted from its condemnations of human sinfulness, they ought to accept them as applying first and foremost to themselves'.[1] We have already noted Beker's parallel question: 'If the law speaks only

tion that Paul's concluding argument, the appeal to Scripture (3.10-18), badly twists the original meaning of the Biblical sayings. Paul makes use of a catena of citations which originally described the nature of the impious (as opposed to the pious). That this should demonstrate that *all* are "under sin" is another *petitio principii.*'

1 Cranfield, *Romans*, I, p. 196.

to "those under the law", why does it apply to "the whole world"?'

Those questions are resolved, and the catena comes to fit its rhetorical context with a good deal more sense, when the comma inserted into 3.19 is displaced by one word. If we allow the indicative verb forms (λέγει, λαλεῖ) to structure the sentence, the phrase τοῖς ἐν τῷ νόμῳ falls into place more naturally modifying the preceding λέγει than the following λαλεῖ. The result is a declaration that explains the pastiche of verses from Israel's Scripture about Gentile wickedness, and is in keeping with Paul's preceding argument (as we have interpreted it): 'We know that whatever the Law says to those in the Law, it speaks in order that every mouth may be stopped, and all the world be brought to account before God'.[1] The ἵνα clause of v. 19 takes up references to slanderous and wicked speech in the catena (3.13-14) and directs them against 'every mouth', 'all the world'. If this suggestion bears any weight, the catena and its recapitulation in 3.19 may be heard as a declaration that although the Law is given to the Jews (cf. 2.17-20), not to the Gentiles (cf. 2.14, ἔθνη τὰ μὴ νόμον ἔχοντα), it nevertheless announces God's righteous verdict upon all human sinfulness, a verdict that is specifically *not* limited to the Jews. Far from being an indictment directed primarily at the Jews, the catena thus becomes another proof that God's judgment falls equally upon all sinners, Jews and Gentiles alike; accountability is not limited to those who 'possess' the Torah.

That this is the Law's purpose is the intent of 3.20. The Law does not provide anyone with the means to secure a claim against God, *not* because doing the works of the Law is impossible—this at least is never Paul's explicit argument[2]—but

---

1 οἴδαμεν δὲ ὅτι ὅσα ὁ νόμος λέγει τοῖς ἐν τῷ νόμῳ, λαλεῖ ἵνα πᾶν στόμα φραγῇ.

2 *Pace* Cranfield (*Romans*, I, p. 198): 'The reason why this is so is that ἔργα νόμου in the sense of such a perfect obedience as would merit justification are not forthcoming'. It is closer to Paul's logic to say, as Cranfield does in the same place (n. 2), that even 'the ἔργα νόμου which *are* forthcoming where the promise of Jer 31.31 is being fulfilled..., that is, ἔργα νόμου in the sense of faith and the true, though imperfect, works of obedience in which it expresses itself— these, of course, while accepted by God, constitute no claim to justification'. We have argued above that in 2.17-29 Paul does not charge

because the Law instead voices God's claim against humanity (διὰ γὰρ νόμου ἐπίγνωσις ἁμαρτίας). Of course these statements would constitute a powerful refutation of a form of Judaism that was devoted to fulfilling the 'works of the Law' as a means of attaining God's favor; but, as several scholars have pointed out, this understanding of Judaism is not reflected by ancient Jewish literature in general[1] (a point to be taken up in the excursus below). In any case, we should expect Paul to make a more forceful defense of this proposition if it were in fact the point of his argument, a point he expected Jewish hearers to controvert. But the statement is presented—here as well as in Gal. 2.16[2]—as something he expects his audience to accept: it supports his contention (διότι)[3] that the Law speaks in order to bring 'all the world' to account before God.

7. *The Revelation of God's Righteousness and the Exclusion of Human Boasting (Rom. 3.21-31)*
Rom. 3.21-26 take up the theme raised in 1.16-17, the revelation of God's righteousness. Yet these verses also echo themes

that Jews have *actually failed* to observe the commandments of the Law.
1   See, for example, the sermon against presuming on one's own 'righteousness' or 'righteous actions' in Deut. 9. Sanders' extended treatment of purported 'Jewish works-righteousness' in *Paul and Palestinian Judaism* should be regarded as a definitive statement of the problem.
2   See Hays, 'Abraham', p. 85; Douglas J. Moo, '"Law", "Works of the Law", and "Legalism in Paul"', *WJT* 45 (1983), p. 97; James D.G. Dunn, 'The New Perspective on Paul', *BJRL* 65 (1983), pp. 104-22. Dunn (p. 111) emphasizes (rightly, in our opinion) that Jewish Christianity shared Paul's beliefs expressed in Gal. 2.16—that 'justification' came not from 'covenant works,' but through 'faith'. In his view, Sanders' discussion of Palestininan Judaism suggests that the declaration would not have been unacceptable to non-Christian Jews either: 'In the light of Sanders' findings, as we have already noted, it is much less obvious than once appeared that the typical first-century Jew would have denied justification by faith'.
3   The particle διότι is a krasis of διὰ τοῦτο, ὅτι (Liddell and Scott, *Lexicon*, p. 435; Blass–Debrunner–Funk, *Grammar*, p. 154); its use in Rom. 3.20 is causal, equivalent to ὅτι (Bauer–Arndt–Gingrich–Danker, *Lexicon*, p. 199b; Blass–Debrunner–Funk, *Grammar*, p. 238).

from the intervening chapters: the relation of God's righteousness to the Law (3.21; cf. 2.12-29; 3.10-20), the impartiality of God's dealings with humanity (3.22; cf. 2.6-11; 3.19), the
universality of human sin (3.23; cf. 3.9, 19), and the underlying exigence of the vindication of God, which came directly
into focus in 3.1-9 and becomes explicit again in 3.25-26. This
continuity casts doubt on the view that the paragraphs
between 1.17 and 3.21 are only a digression laying the 'theological presuppositions' for Paul's exposition of his gospel in
3.21ff and Rom. 5-8.[1] The 'righteousness of God' is at the
center of attention on both sides of 3.20-21, so a major division
between those verses is less appropriate than an interpretation
of the whole of Rom. 3 as a vindication of God in the face of
human impiety.[2]

In fact what Paul now says about the redemption offered in
Christ capitalizes upon the cumulative effect of Paul's argumentation through 3.20. The diatribal 'indictment' in 1.18–2.5
and its amplification and corroboration in 2.6–3.20 have
served to qualify the theme of God's righteousness, as this
comes upon the scene as 'salvation-creating power' when the
gospel is preached (1.16-17), in such a way that the justification bestowed in Christ (3.21-24) can now be understood not
only as the vindication of God's integrity (3.25-26) but as the
corresponding exclusion of human boasting (3.27-31).[3] In the
gospel, 'it is in reality God himself who enters the earthly

---

1 Having concluded that the dialogical elements in Rom. 1–2 have no
  direct contact with the epistolary audience, Schmeller (*Paulus und
  die 'Diatribe'*, p. 285) declares that the apostrophe to the Jew simply
  provides 'die notwendigen theologischen Voraussetzungen für ein
  Verständnis des folgenden'.
2 See Richard Hays, 'Psalm 143 and the Logic of Romans 3', *JBL* 99
  (1980), pp. 107-15.
3 There is a wealth of literature on Paul's phrase 'the righteousness
  of God'; the survey by Manfred Brauch in Sanders' *Paul and Palestinian Judaism* (pp. 523-42) is quite helpful. The phrase is appropriately interpreted as 'salvation-creating power' (Käsemann, 'The
  Righteousness of God in Paul'), but this should not be taken to
  exclude the meaning 'the loyalty of God to his own name', God's
  'inviolable allegiance to act always for his own name's sake—to
  maintain and display his own divine glory', especially in 3.5 and in
  3.25-26 (John Piper, 'The Demonstration of the Righteousness of
  God in Romans 3.25-26', *JSNT* 7 [1980], pp. 2-32).

sphere in what he grants' to those who believe, God 'who brings back the fallen world into the sphere of his legitimate claim'.[1] A 'mercy' that tolerates continuing rebellion against God (2.1-5) can be no part of that righteousness, for God's wrath rightly comes against all human impiety (1.18-32). No counterplea can be raised against God's claim, for even the Law, in which the Jew possesses the very revelation of God's will, cannot be wielded against God, but remains the expression of that claim (2.17–3.20). In this extended argument, as we have shown, the Jew's accountability to God through Torah has been made paradigmatic for *universal* human accountability to God (3.19-20). The argument as a whole has served to 'clear the ground' of any cover behind which *any* human beings could take shelter from God's righteous demand. Only on this basis can the sovereignty and integrity of divine grace be made evident.

We can see, then, that Paul's concern up to this point is less with soteriology per se than with vindicating the righteousness of the saving God. That concern remains preeminent in 3.21-31. 'Apart from the Law', Paul now says—that is, in the clearing made when even that (falsely presumed) defense against God has been removed—God's righteousness has been revealed 'now' (3.21). This 'apart from the Law' (χωρὶς νόμου) does not constitute an absolute dichotomy between Law and gospel, as if the gospel nullified the Creator's claim on the world spoken through Torah. On the contrary, the Law and the prophets are valid 'witnesses' to God's righteousness, now revealed in the gospel (3.21b); and as Paul will insist at the end of this rhetorical unit, the faith of which he speaks does not cancel out the Law, but establishes and confirms its validity (3.31). Above all, the contrast of 'Law' and 'gospel' must not be hardened into opposed soteriological categories or epochs, as if having reached a dead end in the Law, which thus becomes obsolete, God's saving purposes must now be rerouted through 'faith'. Rather the fact that God's righteousness is now revealed 'apart from Law' reveals God's purpose, not only to redeem human beings, but by redeeming them through the costly blood of Christ 'to prove divine righteousness at the

1 Käsemann, *Romans*, p. 29.

present time—that the very One who justifies those who have faith in Jesus is righteous' (3.25, 26).[1] The righteousness of God has made its appearance 'outside' of the Law, that is, where there cannot be even the *illusion* of a human claim or 'boast' against God, in order that the sovereign and gracious initiative of God should be unavoidably evident. That statement necessarily implies that within the realm of the Law, where God's revealed will is known and can be obeyed (cf. 2.17-20), there is a risk that the Law could be misunderstood as the means to achieving righteousness before God. Within that realm, God's integrity and the sovereignty of divine grace therefore remain necessarily ambiguous.[2] But now, through the redemption offered in Christ to those who cannot make any pretense to merit, God's righteousness has been decisively revealed as sovereign grace (δωρεὰν τῇ αὐτοῦ χάριτι), for all those who are justified through this redemption are without exception sinners, who have fallen short of God's glory (πάντες γὰρ ἥμαρτον... δικαιούμενοι).[3] Only through the costly expiation won through Christ's blood is the 'forbearance' of past sins shown to be consistent with God's integrity, God's 'inviolable allegiance to act always for his own name's sake' (3.25-26).[4] The divine 'patience' (ἀνοχῇ) does not

---

1 The profusion of purpose clauses (εἰς ἔνδειξιν τῆς δικαιοσύνης αὐτοῦ, 3.25; πρὸς τὴν ἔνδειξιν τῆς δικαιοσύνης αὐτοῦ ἐν τῷ νῦν καιρῷ, εἰς τὸ εἶναι αὐτὸν δίκαιον καὶ δικαιοῦντα, 3.26) shows just how central the vindication of God is in this section.
2 This is, after all, the implication that Paul has taken pains to dispel in 2.17-29. We shall contend in the excursus that follows that this argument is not with Judaism as such, but with a misunderstanding of Judaism that in his view threatens the righteousness of God.
3 The participle δικαιούμενοι in 3.24 is significant not because it does not fit syntactically into its context (one of Käsemann's reasons for considering these verses to contain pre-Pauline liturgical materials), but precisely because it does. δικαιούμενοι modifies πάντες, the subject of 3.23, as a circumstantial participle with concessive sense: 'For all sinned and fall short of the glory of God, (that is, precisely those who are now) justified freely by his grace....'
4 Käsemann (*Romans*, pp. 98-99; 'Zum Verständnis von Römer 3.25-26', in *Exegetische Versuche und Besinnungen*, I [Göttingen: Vandenhoeck & Ruprecht, 1960], pp. 96-100) and Kümmel ('πάρεσις und ἔνδειξις, ein Beitrag zum Verständnis der paulinischen Rechtfertigungslehre', *ZTK* 49 [1952], pp. 154-67) argue that Paul could not

stand alone as a timeless attribute of deity upon which the
sinner may depend; rather it is the temporary abeyance of
wrath on the part of One who has always intended to deal
finally and decisively with sin through the cross.[1]

Paul says more here than that God has offered in Christ
what was not possible through the Law. That bare statement,
after all, could be taken to mean that the redemption in
Christ's blood provided just the sort of reliance on divine
mercy to exempt one from judgment that Paul attacks in the
apostrophe at 2.1ff, and that he has been at pains to argue (for
the sake of the argument's paradigmatic significance) was

have used the phrase πάρεσιν τῶν προγεγονότων ἁμαρτημάτων to
mean 'passing over' or 'overlooking former sins', since Paul does
not know of a former period of leniency, but characterizes the time
before Christ as a time of wrath (Rom. 1.18, 24; 2.4). For Kümmel
this must mean that the πάρεσις is the 'forgiveness' of sins, and that
3.25-26 simply repeat 3.21-22; for Käsemann, that Paul has taken
over a traditional formulation without correcting this aspect of its
theology. John Piper ('Righteousness of God', pp. 15-16) has shown
that these arguments are based on an 'over-simplification' of Paul's
theology, since the apostle himself can speak of the 'kindness' of
God (2.4) toward the sinner as God's patience; one might also compare 9.22 (God's 'patient endurance' of the vessels of wrath). Piper
('Demonstration', p. 28) places 3.25-26 directly against the background of Paul's indictment of Gentile immorality in 1.18-32: 'For
God to condone or ignore the dishonor heaped upon him by the sins
of men would be tantamount to giving credence to the value judgment men have made in esteeming God more lowly than his creation'. See also Cranfield, *Romans*, I, pp. 211-12; Barrett, *Romans*,
pp. 79-82.

1 'But for God simply to pass over sins would be altogether incompatible with His righteousness.... God has in fact been able to hold His
hand and pass over sins, without compromising His goodness and
mercy, because His intention has all along been to deal with them
once and for all, decisively and finally, through the Cross'
(Cranfield, *loc. cit.*). Cranfield doubts that διὰ τὴν πάρεσιν should
mean 'for the purpose of forgiveness of sins', since this is redundant folowing ἱλαστήριον; further, the specification of προγεγονότων
ἁμαρτημάτων suggests that the ἱλαστήριον in Christ has *now* dealt
(νυνὶ δέ) with sins that previously were 'left standing', so to speak.
He defines προγεγονότων ἁμαρτημάτων as 'the sins... committed
before the time of Christ's becoming ἱλαστήριον. Up to that time sins
were neither punished as they deserved to be nor atoned for as they
were going to be' (p. 212 n. 1).

not possible through Torah (2.17–3.9). Even when he comes back to the theme of the salvation offered in Christ, it is the integrity of God that remains the paramount issue for Paul. Not soteriology but theodicy is at stake here, the vindication of God against the implication that the forgiveness of sins in Christ might somehow compromise divine righteousness.

The point of this passage can be missed when the premises which Paul *shares* with his Christian audience in Rome— that God has offered Christ as an expiation for sins, *that* this is God's gracious and unilateral act on behalf of sinners, *that* justification is offered apart from the performance of 'works of the Law' (3.21, 28)[1]—are seized upon as Paul's theological innovations, the core of his gospel in its inherent opposition to Judaism (Käsemann, Bornkamm), and the sum of his message to Rome (as the exposition of that gospel).[2] When we focus instead on how Paul adapts, modifies, redisposes and reconstellates those premises, the thematic continuity and argumentative progression throughout 1.16–3.31 over-shadow the perceived breaks at 1.17/1.18 and 3.20/3.21. Rom. 3.21-31 are illumined as Paul's application to the Christian κήρυγμα of the implicit admonition that has run through the previous chapters of the letter.

The whole argument may now be summarized: no one may presume on God's mercy (2.1-5); there is no exception to God's

---

1 Two recent essays on Paul's doctrine of justification emphasize that 'Hellenistic Christianity' before Paul had already developed a doctrine of justification by faith alone, yet proceed to discuss Paul's theology in terms of antithesis to *Jewish* thought alone: Georg Strecker, 'Befreiung und Rechtfertigung', in *Rechtfertigung: Festschrift für Ernst Käsemann*, ed. J. Friedrich, W. Pöhlmann, P. Stuhlmacher (Tübingen: J.C.B. Mohr [Paul Siebeck], Göttingen: Vandenhoeck & Ruprecht, 1976), pp. 479-508; Dieter Lührmann, 'Christologie und Rechtfertigung', in the same volume, pp. 351-63.

2 The net effect of Käsemann's tradition-critical hypotheses concerning this pericope (*Romans*, pp. 95-101; *idem*, 'Zum Verständnis von Römer 3.24-26') is to cast the 'traditions' supposedly taken over here as expressions of *Jewish*-Christian covenantal theology: Thus Paul's 'correction' of those traditions becomes another aspect of his gospel's inherent antithesis to *Judaism*. Cranfield (*Romans*, I, p. 200 n. 1) considers it simply incredible that Paul should have proceeded to craft so subtle an argument for something as vitally important to him (cf. Schlier, *Römerbrief*, p. 107 n. 8).

righteous judgment (2.6-16); the Jew's accountability to God
(2.17-29) is paradigmatic of the accountability of *all* people
before the Creator's rightful claim (3.10-20); the redemption
in Christ, precisely because it is the revelation of God's
righteousness outside the sphere of Law (3.21-22) and the
justification of those who have sinned and forfeited God's glory
(3.23-24), shows itself to be the final and decisive
demonstration (ἔνδειξις) of God's integrity (3.25-26).

'Where therefore is boasting?' (3.27), where, that is, in light
of the sheer, unmerited, and unilateral initiative of God in
Christ? Cranfield rightly emphasizes that the exclusion of
boasting in 3.27-31 is, by implication (οὖν), 'a conclusion
which must be drawn from what precedes (whether vv. 21-26
or the whole of 1.18–3.26)', and that on the basis of that
preceding argument 'there can be no question of any man's
putting God in his debt'.[1] These statements must, however, be
given a forceful precision. Boasting is excluded *not simply*
because God's righteousness is revealed 'apart from Law', as if
the Jewish boast 'in God' and 'in the Law' (2.17-20) were the
sole target of Paul's argument. To equate the καύχησις in 3.27
with καυχᾶσθαι in 2.17-20 in such a way as to restrict the
exclusion of boasting in 3.27 to an assault on a false *Jewish*
boasting *in the Law* ignores the fact, observed above, that the
Jew's 'boast' in Romans 2 is grounded in real privileges—the
interrogation in 2.21-24 ponders the betrayal of those
privileges, but not their unreality—and suppresses the
'christological theodicy' in 3.21-26 upon which 3.27-31 are
grounded. A 'polemical sharpening' of an anti-Jewish thesis
(Käsemann) is not Paul's point. What was 'excluded' in 2.20-
28, and in 3.9, was any notion that the Jew's legitimate
privileges constitute a moral indemnity before God. This
argument did not stand by itself, however, but rather
supported the overarching theme of *universal* inexcusability
(1.20, 2.1-16, 3.19-20). Just as the Jew's boast *in God*
(καυχᾶσθαι ἐν νόμῳ), though in itself legitimate, could not
constitute a boast *against* God (καύχησις or καύχημα πρὸς
θεόν: cf. 2.17–3.9, 4.2), neither was any human being left room
to boast against God's verdict that all are under sin, a verdict

1 Cranfield, *Romans*, I, pp. 218-19.

spoken in Torah but universally valid (3.9-20). Nor did the expiation of sins in Christ's blood allow for human boasting, for *precisely* therein has boasting been excluded, definitively and forever. Just this was God's sovereign purpose, so to deal with sin, precisely where no pretense of merit could be made, as to manifest the integrity of divine grace.

The terse comments that follow (3.27b-31) center on the relationship of 'boasting' to Law. Paul has said that the Law proclaims the absolute inexcusability of all humanity before God (3.19-20); yet the righteousness of God is revealed 'apart from Law' (3.21), so that God's integrity can be made manifest (3.25-26). If, as we suggested above, God's integrity is left in question within the realm where the Law can be misunderstood as a shield against God's judgment, then just how does the Law relate to God's integrity?

The questions 'how is boasting excluded? By what kind of Law?' ask about the relation of the Law to God's action for the sake of divine integrity. If the verb ἐξεκλείσθη in fact refers to an exclusion 'effected by God Himself (the passive concealing a reference to a divine action),'[1] then Paul is asking very pointedly, 'By what sort of Law has God excluded boasting?'[2] The question does not conceive of a simple opposition of 'faith and Law', as if 'faith ends the operation of the Torah'.[3] The question wrests the Law out of human hands, where the

---

1 Cranfield, *Romans*, I, p. 219.
2 Cranfield (*ibid.*) cites with approval G. Friedrich's interpretation ('Das Gesetz des Glaubens Röm. 3.27', *TZ* 10 [1954], p. 415): 'Demnach fragt Paulus nicht, welches von verschiedenen Gesetzen das Rühmen ausschliesst, sondern nach der Beschaffenheit des Gesetzes. Wie muss der *nomos* aussehen, der das Rühmen ausschliesst?'
3 Käsemann, *Romans*, p. 103; he must then insist that the phrase νόμου πίστεως is 'paradoxical', and is used simply to establish a stylistic contrast with νόμος ἔργων. Similarly Bultmann (*Theology*, I, p. 259) translates the first phrase with 'principle of faith'. Käsemann's citation of W. Gutbrod ('νόμος, κτλ', *TDNT*, IV, p. 1071) is less corroborative of his position, however, for although Gutbrod uses the word 'rule', what he says in particular about 3.27 points more clearly to the Law as God's instrument: νόμος means law 'in the broader sense of the divine ordinance which describes faith, not works, as the right conduct of man, to the exclusion of self-boasting before God' (*ibid.*).

declaration of 3.21 might otherwise have left it, and shows that it remains God's holy instrument through which the divine claim upon creation is raised (and all human boasting thereby excluded).

Here Paul's thought must be carefully and forcefully distinguished from an interpretation that has him wielding the Law *only* as a device for exploding the presumed 'boast' of the Jew. On this view, Paul's object in 2.17–3.20 has been to show that the Jew in fact cannot fulfill the commandments of the Law, which is understood as a system of works-righteousness; thus 'a law of works' does indeed 'exclude boasting', though this now means exclusively *Jewish* boasting.[1] Paul then goes on to say that *another* 'law', the rule of faith, has been established *in the place of* the 'law of works' of Judaism, and this new rule of faith *also* excludes boasting but on different grounds, i.e., no longer because sufficient works are not evident, but because God has in Christ provided an alternative route to justification ('faith'). There are then *two* 'laws' that exclude boasting (corresponding to 2.17–3.20 and 3.21-26), both directed primarily at the Jew.[2]

This distorts Paul's meaning. He does not say that there is a law of works that excludes (the Jew's) boasting *in addition* to the 'rule of faith' established through faith in Christ;[3] in fact

---

1 Note the interpolation in FG Vulgate, ἡ καύχησις σου. The pronoun ('your' boasting—'the Jew's') is sometimes supplied in interpretation even when the variant reading is rejected: Michel declares, 'Vielleicht ist sogar zu lesen: "wo bleibt dein Rühmen?"' (*Römer*, p. 155).

2 This interpretation is given precise exposition by Richard W. Thompson, 'Paul's Double Critique of Jewish Boasting', *Bib* 67 (1986), pp. 520-31; see also J. Lambrecht, 'Why is Boasting Excluded? A Note on Rom. 3.27 and 4.2', *ETL* 61 (1985), pp. 365-69. Thompson speaks throughout of 'Paul's double critique' of 'the boasting of the Jews'.

3 Thompson ('Paul's Double Critique') observes that the construction οὐχί, ἀλλά can be used to 'reverse an expectation that is reasonable or understandable, but is nonetheless incorrect', then argues on this basis that in Rom. 3.27 Paul means not that the first possibility (τῶν ἔργων?) is incorrect, but that it has been superseded in his argument. He paraphrases the question, 'Is boasting *still* excluded by a law of works? Certainly not: *Now* it is excluded by a law of faith'; and again, 'Through a law of works (as in fact we had

there is no such law of works, for this (he says in 9.32) is how those of Israel have *misunderstood* the Torah, albeit tacitly, when they fail to see that it leads to faith in Christ (cf. 10.4); and at any rate (he says in 3.28) 'we know that people are not justified out of works of the Law'. The Torah, rightly understood as a Law that requires trust in the righteousness of God (νόμος πίστεως), necessarily excludes *all* human boasting as a rejection or rebellion against that righteousness. The purpose of his question 'by what sort of Law is boasting rejected?' is to point out that despite the possible misunderstanding of the commandments of the Law as a means to attaining righteousness—a misunderstanding, it is important to reiterate, which Paul has not explicitly ascribed to the Jews, or to anyone else for that matter, in what precedes; and a misundestanding, we have suggested, that is implied by the χωρὶς νόμου of 3.21—the Law *in fact* points to God's righteousness in Christ (μαρτυρουμένη ὑπὸ τοῦ νόμου καὶ τῶν προφητῶν, 3.21) and thus serves God's purpose by excluding all human boasting. To call for trust in God's righteousness *cannot* undermine the Torah but in fact confirms and complements it (3.31).

Far from spiralling 'inward' to indict *the Jew*, Paul's rhetoric in Rom. 2.17–3.31 moves *outward*, from his Jewish interlocutor's witness to the Jew's accountability under the Law (the principle in 2.12b thus being amplified through the device of apostrophe in 2.17–3.9) to the confirmation of *universal* accountability and inexcusability before God's judgment, even of those who stand outside of the Law (the principle in 2.12a thus being confirmed through the catena in 3.10-18, as we have argued is the point of 3.19). Yet his argument does not leave the Law behind. The Law may speak to those 'in the Law', but its message is the accountability of all human beings (3.19); it testifies to God's decisive revelation of divine integrity 'now', in Christ, in providing expiation for previous sins (3.21); it is in fact 'the Law that requires trust [in

---

argued in 2.17–3.20)? No, now, because of the new revelation (in 3.21-26), boasting is eliminated by a law of faith'. This is not only exegetically dubious; it in fact misses the point of the pericope.

God]' (νόμου πίστεως, 3.27),[1] and consequently finds its confirmation in the gospel (νόμον ἱστάνομεν, 3.31).

Once we recognize, with Cranfield, that 'justification by faith, not by works' (3.28) is not Paul's innovation here, rather (as the γάρ shows) 'Paul appeals to the fact that believers know that men are justified by faith, apart from works of the law',[2] then it appears that the burden of Paul's argument throughout 3.27b-31 is to affirm the validity of the Law *rightly understood*. He seems less directly concerned to check the abuse of the Law as a means of erecting a boast against God— he does not attack 'boasting' in the works of the Law as such,[3] nor does he directly argue that the 'works of the Law' cannot be performed[4]—than he is to insist that the exclusion of boasting of which he speaks is *not* restricted to the putative realm of a 'law of works'. A 'law of works', after all, would *not* exclude boasting (3.27b); yet boasting *is* absolutely excluded by the Law (which is a law of faith). The point is not, as it is in Galatians, to argue that a system of works-righteousness falls under a 'curse' (Gal. 3.10)—or to adapt the language used in Romans 3, that a 'law of works' excludes boasting—but that the *'law of faith'* itself excludes boasting. His argument inheres in the unity of God (3.29-30): God is not the God of the Jews alone. That means not only that God is concerned to

---

1 Cranfield (*Romans*, I, p. 220) translates the phrase 'God's law... properly understood as summoning men to faith'.
2 Cranfield, *Romans*, I, p. 218.
3 As we have argued above, Rom. 2.21-24 is aimed not at exposing self-righteousness at the core of Torah observance, but at establishing the radical accountability to God even of the Jew who holds the Torah; in 3.1-9, where the nature of the Jew's covenantal 'advantage' or 'benefit' or 'privilege' is explicitly at issue, Paul's use of diatribal rhetoric is not accusatory but didactic, and his Jewish interlocutor is not a defendant but a witness for Paul's argument.
4 Here is one of the more significant differences between the argumentation in Romans and that in Galatians. In the latter situation Paul counters a Gentile-Christian movement to adapt some of the 'works of the Law' as emblems of identity with the heritage of Abraham; he 'solemnly declares' to such individuals that 'they must keep all of the Law' (Gal. 5.3), which he apparently assumes they have no interest in doing. *That* argument finds no place in Romans, because, we may reasonably assume, Paul is not concerned to counter a 'Judaizing' tendency through the letter.

'justify' both Jews and Gentiles, but that God justifies Jews and Gentiles *in the same way*, namely on the basis of faith (3.30), for just this shows God's integrity. There are not two standards—'works' for the Jews (working to disqualify them), 'faith' for the Gentiles (working to qualify them before God)— but one standard, now as always; and this standard, faith, coheres with the Law itself (3.31).

Rom. 3.27b-31 recapitulates the whole argument as it has unfolded since 1.18. The apostrophe to the Jew has allowed Paul to corroborate his principle that all are 'without excuse' before God (1.20; 2.1), that both within the realm of Torah and apart from that realm human beings are accountable to God, who judges impartially (2.12-16; cf. 3.29-30); and that this is nothing else than the message of Torah itself, which speaks (albeit to the Jews) in order to render all the world answerable to God (3.19). Paul's argumentation has shown that standing outside of the Law (2.12, 14-16) does not negate one's culpability as that is proclaimed by the Law (3.10-20). The 'faith' that is the proper response to the gospel of Jesus Christ cannot 'nullify' the Law, then (3.31), but rather confirms its validity insofar as the Law reveals sin (3.20).

As the continuing stream of monographs on 'Paul and the Law' confirms, there are other questions about the Law's significance that are not answered here. Paul is content to establish the principle of accountability to God's righteous requirement, which is brought to expression in Torah (2.26; cf. 8.4) and which extends to those who are not 'in Torah' (2.12) or 'under Torah' (cf. 6.14-15). That this first part of his argument can be summarized in terms of vindication of the Torah (3.31) indicates that one important element of the epistolary exigence as Paul conceives it is to resolve the issue of Torah, specifically its precise relation to the divine righteousness, in such a way that neither possessing the Law nor standing outside of the Law can be raised as a counterclaim against God's righteousness. That this is a message directed to the Christians of Rome becomes evident in what follows.

8. *The Heritage of Abraham's Children (Romans 4)*
Paul's interpretation of Abraham in Romans 4 does more than bring forward a Scriptural example to corroborate his

proposition that the faith of which he speaks 'establishes the Law'. The chapter both depends on what has preceded (τί οὖν ἐροῦμεν, 'what shall we say in light of what has been established to this point') and introduces a new theme: What does it mean to be Abraham's children, or (in the words of v. 1) to have Abraham as ancestor? The discussion is phrased in the deliberative first person plural, but we are not to think of a reappearance of the Jewish interlocutor of 2.17–3.9.[1] Rather, the Roman audience, who up to this point have been drawn into Paul's deliberations only implicitly,[2] are now more directly involved, as both the subject matter[3] and the closing summation show: 'This was not written for his sake alone, namely that "it was reckoned to him", but for us as well, to whom it will be reckoned, to those who believe on the One who raised Jesus our Lord from the dead, who was delivered for our transgressions and raised for the purpose of our justification' (4.23-25).

Paul asks what it means to participate in the heritage of Abraham's 'children' (4.1). 'What shall we say we have found: Is it in terms of the flesh that we should consider Abraham our forefather?'[4] As we shall see in Chapter 3, a similar question is

1 Cranfield (*Romans*, I, p. 227) declares that 'there is no need to think of any imaginary Jewish objector' in 4.1 or 2. As we argued concerning 3.1-9, the diatribal style more likely reflects Paul's 'leading questions'. But it is improbable that the fictitious persona of the *Jewish* interlocutor is here resumed after 3.9 (note especially 3.21-26).

2 The first person plural forms appearing in diatribal sections (οἴδαμεν, 2.2; προεχόμεθα, προῃτιασάμεθα, 3.9; οἴδαμεν, 3.19; λογιζόμεθα, 3.28; καταργοῦμεν, ἱστάνομεν, 3.31) function as figures of presence, involving the audience in deliberation with Paul (through the persona of his interlocutor) but not addressing them directly.

3 Once the syntax of the question in 4.1 has been elucidated, it is evident that the subject is not 'what Abraham, our forefather according to the flesh, has found', but 'what we have found: Is Abraham our forefather according to the flesh?' (see Hays, 'Abraham'). There are no grounds for restricting the address of this discussion to Jews. That Gentile Christians were absorbed with the issue of their identity as Abraham's children should be expected on the basis of the promises in Gen. 17 and 18 alone, and is given ample confirmation in Paul's letter to the Gentiles in Galatia.

4 Hays ('Abraham', pp. 77-83) makes a convincing case, first that the question τί... ἐροῦμεν should stand alone as an introduction to

raised in Romans 8–9, where the sure foundation of those who in Christ have been incorporated as 'children of God' (8.14-39) stands in sharp contrast to the poignant failure of Israel, to whom 'the sonship belongs', to believe (9.1–10.21). The emphasis in Paul's discussion of the promise to Abraham in 9.6-9 is on the absolute sovereignty of God's mercy. That theme contributes to Paul's warning to Gentile Christians not to 'boast' against their Jewish brothers and sisters, for the temporary 'hardening' that has come upon Israel is a part of God's hidden plan, now revealed through Paul, to 'consign all to disobedience in order to have mercy upon all' (11.32). Here, the heritage of Abraham is discussed in the more abstract terms of exegesis, for Paul sets out to establish the basis on which 'righteousness' was reckoned to Abraham (cf. 4.10). He clearly expects his audience to grant him several premises: that the figure of Abraham is both *representative* of those who, as his 'children', 'inherit' the promise made to him and to 'his seed'; that he also provides a *paradigm* of living within that heritage; and that the nature of both roles can be determined by exegesis of Scripture.

Paul sets about to answer the question in 4.1 by way of another question that gets at the heart of what follows: Was Abraham justified on the basis of works (of the Law)? That is, did Abraham—and by extension, do his children—exercise any constraint upon God's grace? It is significant that Paul does not begin to answer this second question by looking at the story of Abraham to discover whether Abraham 'did works'. He does contrast 'the one who works' and thus lays an obligation upon another for what is 'due' (ὁ μισθὸς... κατὰ ὀφείλημα) and the one who does *not* work but instead 'believes on the One who justifies the impious', to whom that trust is reckoned as

another rhetorical question (as elsewhere in the Pauline corpus), then that εὑρηκέναι corresponds to a technical term in Jewish (rabbinic and Philonic) exegesis (esp. pp. 81-83). He translates strictly: 'What then shall we say? Have we found Abraham (to be) our forefather according to the flesh?' (p. 81); in light of the fact that Abraham has not been mentioned previously but seems to be called in to illustrate a point about Israel's covenant, Hays subsequently paraphrases, 'Look, do you think that we Jews have considered Abraham our forefather only according to the flesh?' (p. 87).

righteousness. But that contrast is established *not* so that Paul can determine how Abraham approached God, whether, that is, through works or through faith—the answer to that question is already given, for Paul's purposes, in the Genesis text (15.6, cited in Rom. 4.3: ἐπίστευσεν... τῷ θεῷ)—but to establish how God 'reckoned righteousness' to Abraham, whether, that is, it was under constraint (κατὰ ὀφείλημα). The verses constitute a complex argument from correlatives and from contraries:[1]

Abraham believed God and it was reckoned to him as righteousness;	(premise)
'Working' correlates with receiving a wage according to obligation; 'believing' correlates with receiving a gift freely;	(principle of correlation)
since believing is not working, and therefore cannot receive a reward on the same principle (4.4-5);	(argument from contraries)
Therefore Abraham was reckoned righteous out of God's grace.	(conclusion)

It seems unlikely that Paul is setting out to refute a system of 'justification from works',[2] since his conclusions would then be given already in the way he has laid out the question. Rather Paul wants to show that from the very beginning, the promises to Abraham and the righteousness reckoned to Abraham have been acts of sheer grace (cf. 9.6ff).

That argument consequently concludes with a 'proof' from Ps. 31.1-2 in which David 'blesses' those whose sins (ἀνομίαι,

---

1 Aristotle describes the argument 'from relative terms', ἐκ τῶν πρὸς ἄλληλα (*Rhetoric*, 1397a): for example, 'if rightly or justly can be predicated of the sufferer, it can equally be predicated of the one who inflicts suffering'. The premise for such an argument (the principle of correlation) is established in Romans 4.4-5, relying in part on an argument from contraries (ἐκ τῶν ἐναντίων, *ibid.*; Aristotle's example: 'self-control is good, for lack of self-control is harmful').
2 Bultmann, *Theology*, I, pp. 279-80; Käsemann, *Romans*, p. 105, among others.

ἁμαρτίαι) have been forgiven. By labelling the citation a blessing of 'the one who has been justified apart from works', thus using language that does not appear in the Psalm, he assimilates forgiveness of ἀνομίαι with justification χωρὶς ἔργων. This hardly advances an argument about how Abraham came to be reckoned righteous; but it does emphasize the graciousness of God's unmerited favor.

Paul turns next (4.9-12) to determine whether 'the blessing' of God's grace comes 'upon circumcision' or 'upon uncircumcision'. Since Abraham received the 'sign' of circumcision *after* the promise was given (4.10-11), the promise is 'on (his state of) uncircumcision', and extends to 'all those who (are characterized by) uncircumcision' as well as to all those of the circumcision who follow in Abraham's faith (4.12). The point is that justification by faith is valid for Jews and Gentiles alike.

There are two aspects to Paul's argument in Romans 4 that have led interpreters to two different readings of the chapter, readings often conceived to be mutually exclusive. On one view, Paul opposes justification by faith (which has been revealed in the Christian gospel) to justification by works (which is the 'doctrine of redemption' of Judaism). The point of the chapter is here understood to be a Scriptural proof for the 'proposition' in 3.28: God does not justify (and in fact never has justified) human beings on the basis of works.[1] The opposed view insists that Paul's concern is not to exclude Jews but to include Gentiles; Romans 4 is a proof not of 3.27-28 but of 3.29-30, that 'God justifies Jews and Gentiles on the same basis'. 'The fundamental problem with which Paul is wrestling in Romans is not how a person may find acceptance with God; the problem is to work out an understanding of the relationship in Christ between Jews and Gentiles'.[2]

But neither argument carries the weight of Romans 4. That Abraham was justified by works, not by faith, on the one hand (4.3-5), and that Abraham is 'our father', 'father of us all', Jew and Gentile together (4.1, 11-12), appear rather as premises

---

1 See previous note.
2 Hays, 'Abraham', p. 84; cf. Lloyd Gaston, 'Abraham and the Righteousness of God', 39-68 (reprinted in *Paul and the Torah*, pp. 45-63); Gager, *Origins*, pp. 217-18.

than as conclusions reached through argument. We suggest that these two components in Romans 4—the question of how Abraham came to be reckoned righteous before God, and the question about the scope of his 'posterity'—correspond to two components in the argumentation in Romans 1–3 that have provoked a similar division among interpreters. Paul has been concerned on the one hand to show that the Law has never provided the Jew the basis for a boast against God (2.17-29, 3.9a); on the other, that Jews and Gentiles stand on an equal footing before God (2.9-16; 3.9b, 19, 29-30). Yet the interpretation advanced above suggests that these two components are integrated within the argumentative cohesion of the letter. That the Jew has no boast in Torah is advanced, we have suggested, as a paradigm of *universal* accountability to God, a theme that Paul wishes to apply paraenetically with the Christian congregation in Rome.

In this light we can see that Paul sets out to determine the meaning of being 'Abraham's children' by showing first of all that Abraham did not raise a boast against God but trusted in divine grace and power (4.3-8), and next showing that the 'blessing' Abraham consequently received as the gift of God's unmerited grace applies to Jew and Gentile alike (4.9-12). Here again, as in 3.21-31, Paul's purpose is not simply soteriology but is first of all theodicy, the vindication of God. For Paul continues (4.13ff.) by declaring that what he has just described as God's gracious justification of the impious, the only way in which God justifies Jews and Gentiles, is also the only way in which God could have preserved the divine promises to Abraham intact: 'for if the heirs were to be such out of the Law, the faithfulness (of God) has been made futile and the promise has been forfeited' (4.14). This is so because the Law works wrath, i.e., by appropriately exposing and condemning transgression; therefore, Paul implies, God's promise must be fulfilled outside the realm of the Law, 'where there is no transgression' (4.14). What Paul says here about Torah is reminiscent of 3.19-20, where the Law speaks to render 'all the world' accountable to God, and of 3.9, where 'Jew and Greek' are both declared to be 'under sin'. But the more immediate context focuses upon the Gentiles: the promise to Abraham that he should become 'the father of us all', that is, 'father of many nations' (4.16-17, cf.

Gen 17.5), had to be fulfilled 'outside of Law', in order that the promise be secured 'for all Abraham's seed, not those from the Law alone' (4.16). This echoes the χωρὶς νόμου of 3.21.

The theme of Romans 4 is God's unswerving perseverance in fulfilling the divine will, especially with regard to the promise given to Abraham that he should become the father of a magnificent posterity. This promise could be fulfilled only outside the realm of Torah, for on the basis of Torah the Gentiles could not have been included (since Gentiles *in general*—that is, despite the 'exceptional case' described in 2.14-15—do not perform the Law).[1] This does not mean, however, that God has established two 'parallel tracks' for the fulfillment of the promise—Torah for the Jews, Christ for the Gentiles.[2] Rather God's promise has *always* been founded only upon God's grace and human trust in it.

1 To be sure, Paul qualifies the Jewish claim to Abraham as well by insisting that Abraham became the father 'not of those of the circumcision as such [μόνον], but of those [of the circumcision] who also follow in the footsteps of the faith he showed while he was uncircumcised' (4.12). But Paul is not absorbed by that issue; he does not ask here whether Israel has shown that faith, etc. He is concerned to anchor the heritage now enjoyed 'through faith' by God's grace in God's unconditioned integrity (εἰς τὸ εἶναι βεβαίαν τὴν ἐπαγγελίαν, 4.16).

2 Lloyd Gaston (*Paul and the Torah*, p. 32) rightly argues that in Paul's thought, Gentiles 'exist in a covenant and commandment relationship to God which is different from but parallel to that of Sinai'; Paul neither requires Gentiles to submit to Torah observance nor requires Jews to abandon it. But this should *not* be taken to mean a conception of 'two religions, two chosen people', as Gaston suggests when he writes (regarding Romans) that 'Israel has always had cultic means of expiation, but now God has presented Christ Jesus as such a means for the Gentiles, apart from or along-side his covenant with Israel' (*ibid.*, p. 122); or again, that 'for Paul, Jesus is neither a new Moses nor the Messiah, he is not the climax of the history of God's dealing with Israel, but he is the fulfillment of God's promises concerning the Gentiles, and this is what he accuses the Jews of not recognizing' (*ibid.*, p. 33; cf. Gager, *Origins*, pp. 217-18, 263-64). To the contrary, Paul's letters give us every reason to infer that he shared with his Jewish-Christian colleagues the conviction that Jesus *was* Israel's Messiah, and as such was *both* 'the climax of the history of God's dealing with Israel'—Paul's own phrase is 'the goal of the Torah' (Rom. 10.4)—*and* 'the fulfillment of God's promises concerning the Gentiles', made, one notes,

That this message is of significance *for the audience in Rome* becomes explicit in 4.23-25. That significance resided in the analogy of Abraham's faith in God's competence to fulfill the divine promise, despite the complete inadequacy of circumstances ('his dead body and the deadness of Sarah's womb', 4.18-20), to the Christian's faith 'in the One who raised Jesus our Lord from the dead' (4.24). Both Abraham and his Gentile-Christian descendants are called upon to trust in the power of God to 'bring the dead to life and to call into being things that are not' (4.17); and the power of God to justify the impious (4.5) is nothing else.

Romans 4 thus serves as a crucially important bridge to the explicit discussion of the Christian's 'boast' in Romans 5 and beyond. In 1.18–3.31, the thematic concern—demonstrating that precisely in God's justification of human beings God's own righteousness or integrity is made manifest—corresponds to the predominant use of diatribal apostrophe that serves to contain and control the range of possible interpretations. Paul will move from the more 'hypothetical' or 'conditional' deliberations of these early chapters to a very concentrated ethical argument aimed more directly at his Christian audience and based on explicitly Christian premises in Rom 6.1–8.13.[1] The transition between these two sections of the letter is achieved in chapters 4 and 5. But the argument in Romans 5 is definitely *christological*; Romans 4, by contrast, alludes only at the end to Christ (4.24-25), leading some interpreters to address the problem how Abraham can be presented as a 'proto-Christian', being 'justified by faith' before the revelation of the δικαιοσύνη... θεοῦ διὰ πίστεως in Christ (3.21-22).[2]

The juxtaposition of the two chapters is crucial. Romans 4 sets the ground rules for Romans 5, so that (to state the matter

---

to Israel. Gaston is on far safer ground when he concedes that we have no conclusive evidence regarding what Paul might have said to a *Jewish*-Christian audience regarding Christ and Torah: 'Paul says nothing against the Torah and Israel but simply bypasses them as not directly relevant to his gospel' (i.e., as he proclaims it among Gentiles; *ibid.*, p. 33; cf. Gager, *Origins*, p. 262).

1 See Chapter 3, below.
2 Ernst Käsemann, 'The Faith of Abraham in Romans 4', in *Perspectives on Paul*, pp. 79-101.

sharply) nothing can be determined about the salvation offered in Christ that is not consonant with the absolute integrity of God as it has been established in Romans 1–4. In this light Romans 1–4 appear to include something of a lengthy theological preamble to the christology of Romans 5, expounding the gospel's rootedness in God's fidelity to the promises made to Abraham and recorded in Israel's Scriptures (cf. 1.2-3; 4.16-17). Rom. 1.17–3.31 shaped a polarity of God's righteousness and human boasting: Romans 4 distills that polarity into its prototypical expression, the story of the promise given to Abraham, which becomes the paradigm for all that follows. In one sense, the subsequent argumentation in chs. 6–11 is only an explication of Romans 4: the interweaving of soteriology and paraenetic themes in chs. 5–8 reflect the insistence in 4.1-8 that Abraham's justification (Gen. 15.6) in no way qualified God's sovereignty; through the disclosure of a 'mystery', Romans 9–11 show how the purpose described in 4.9-17 (or more properly, in Gen. 15.5 and 17.5) will be fulfilled.

Before continuing this line of examination, however, we must pause to defend some of the findings of this chapter. In several places, the exegesis of Romans 1–4 presented here deviates significantly from areas of broad consensus in contemporary Pauline studies. We have chosen first to put forward a sequential exegesis of Romans 1–4 with a minimum of interaction with alternate interpretations so that a coherent picture of the rhetoric in this section of the letter may emerge. It would however be irresponsible to ignore those interpretive alternatives completely, especially in light of the wide acceptance which they have won and of the importance accorded to issues that emerge within that consensus. The following excursus is therefore devoted to examining the merits of reading Romans 1–4 as part of Paul's 'debate with Judaism'.

EXCURSUS

ROMANS 1–4 AS A 'DEBATE WITH JUDAISM'

1. *Introduction: The Rhetorical Problem*

The interpretation of Romans advanced in the preceding chapters challenges the prevalent view that the letter is in large part a 'debate with Judaism'. Our reading has depended on attention to cues within the text that link the letter 'body' (1.16–15.13) to the epistolary 'frame' (1.1-15; 15.14–16.27), and to how sections within the letter 'body' are related to each other. Perhaps more important than any particular exegetical decision, however, is the conception of the problem that this work is written to address. The reading presented above arises from suspicion of the common assessment that Romans is a theological essay in epistolary form, for which the circumstances that brought Paul and the Romans together provide only a bare point of contact. In contrast, we are in pursuit of an interpretation that satisfactorily integrates the apparently diverse elements in the letter into one coherent response to a rhetorical situation.

One important test of any interpretation of Romans is how adequately it relates the 'Jewish' topics discussed in the letter, e.g., Torah, the 'righteousness of God', Abraham, Israel, to a comprehensive view of Paul's purpose in writing. When the letter's explicit address to a *Gentile-Christian* audience (1.6, 13, 14-15) has been taken seriously, that relationship has generated a critical interpretive problem, the 'double character' problem discussed in the Introduction. That problem, as we have already suggested, is an acute rhetorical-critical problem in which the integrity of the letter as a contingent response to rhetorical constraints is at stake. This is nowhere more evident than with regard to those sections of the letter that have seemed most clearly to constitute a 'debate with

Judaism', i.e., chs. 2–4, and it is no coincidence that these chapters have figured prominently in recent controversy over Paul's theology.[1]

Our present concern is to examine the rhetorical-critical adequacy of the view that Romans 1–4 include a 'confrontation' with Judaism.

Admittedly there is current a range of interpretations as to just what this 'dialogue with Judaism' is intended to accomplish. The range is evident in the choice of phrases used, i.e., whether the mode of discourse perceived in Romans 1–4 is described as 'attack', 'indictment', 'polemic', 'confrontation', or somewhat more moderately 'debate'[2] or 'dialogue'.[3] Whether under the name 'boasting' Paul attacks the human effort 'to achieve... salvation by keeping the Law',[4] or only 'a

---

1 Bultmann (*Theology*, I, p. 227) justified his treatment of Pauline theology by way of antithesis ('Man Prior to Faith' and 'Man Under Faith') by implicit appeal to the letter's division at 3.20/3.21; a similar appeal to 'the arrangement of Romans' grounds his treatment of Paul's gospel in antithesis to Judaism (I, p. 279). As a result, Sanders' reversal (*Paul and Palestinian Judaism*, pp. 442, 474-511). of the approach shared by Bultmann, Conzelmann, and Bornkamm under the rubric 'solution precedes plight' is necessarily involved with just these chapters of Romans. Our perception of a broad consensus on the character of Rom. 1–4 as a 'dialogue with Judaism' finds some support in the fact that while the *theology* expressed in these chapters is today the subject of lively dispute, their *rhetorical* function within the letter is generally assumed. Sanders provides the most striking example, for although he considers Rom. 2 completely inadequate as a proof that 'Jews are culpable', he nevertheless believes that this is what Paul intended to communicate in the chapter (*Paul, the Law, and the Jewish People*, pp. 123-35).

2 Kümmel, *Introduction*, pp. 309-10.

3 J. Jeremias, 'Zur Gedankenführung in den paulinischen Briefen', in *Studia Paulina in honorem Johannes de Zwaan, septuagenarii* (Haarlem: Bohn, 1953), pp. 146-54; Beker, *Paul the Apostle*, pp. 74-93. Of course this more moderate language does not exclude the perception of polemic in Rom. 1–4: Beker, for example, describes Romans as a 'dialogue with Judaism' in which 'Paul... is forced by the exigencies of the time and the problem in Rome to contemplate the proper role of Judaism in salvation history' (p. 77), but nevertheless holds that in 1.18–3.20 'Paul's aim... is the demolition of Jewish pride in the Torah and the destruction of Jewish narcissistic self-elevation over the Gentiles' (p. 80).

4 Bultmann, *Theology*, I, p. 264.

narrowly ethnocentric form of Judaism'.[1] is the subject of a lively controversy today which at its heart is the dilemma whether Paul's message in Romans is primarily an answer to the question 'how may I be saved?' or to the question 'how are Jews and Gentiles to be related to each other in Christ?'[2] Furthermore, while serious efforts have been made to anchor the 'Jewish' argument of the letter in a situation within the Roman congregation,[3] it is more widely held that the confrontation with Judaism is aimed *not* at actual Jewish individuals or sentiments in Rome, but at Jewish adversaries elsewhere—either in previous mission situations,[4] or in Jerusalem[5]—or else reflects an antithesis that was inherently and inevitably a dimension of Paul's gospel wherever he preached it.[6] On this line Bornkamm writes:

> The observation is important that Romans, too, also remains a polemical letter. But who is the opponent? The answer must be, not this or that group in any specific congregation in the East or in Rome, but rather the Jew and his understanding of salvation. What does this mean? Does Paul in this letter addressed to Christians shout out of the window as it were to Jews, to non-Christians? Most certainly not! For Paul, the Jew represents man in general, and indeed man in his highest potential: the pious man who knows God's demands in the Law but who has yet failed to meet God's claim and is lost in sin and death. Exactly as antithesis to this man, who exults in his piety before God, Paul develops his doctrine of the Law and the message of grace which is now offered to all believers in Christ.[7]

1 Hays, 'Abraham'; Gager, *Origins*, pp. 248-40 and *passim*.
2 Stendahl, 'Paul and the Introspective Conscience of the West', *HTR* 56 (1963), pp. 199-215.
3 So the hypotheses of G. Klein, W. Schmithals, and J.C. Beker, discussed in the Introduction above.
4 So the frequently repeated view that Romans contains material from Paul's controversies with his Jewish opponents (cf. Jeremias, 'Gedankenführung'; Scroggs, 'Paul as Rhetorician', among others).
5 Jervell, 'The Letter to Jerusalem'.
6 Schlier, *Römerbrief*, p. 4 n. 12.
7 Bornkamm, 'Paul's Last Will', pp. 28-29.

There is finally a tension between various interpretations of the rhetorical purpose and effectiveness of this 'dialogue with the Jew', even when its representative or paradigmatic character is recognized (that is, even when the argument is not seen to address actual Jews). Bornkamm, for example, provides for one possible way of integrating Paul's indictment of 'the pious person' (in the guise of the Jew) and the epistolary situation reflected in 11.13-36, although to be sure he does not develop the suggestion at all, when he remarks that the pious person who is Paul's target

> is not somewhere outside among the unbelievers; he is, in disguise, a Jewish Christian too, of Jerusalem and elsewhere, and equally, as Romans 11 shows, a Gentile Christian who now boasts to the Jews that he is saved, and not they.[1]

On the other hand, Stowers, who argues at length that the diatribal elements in Romans reflect pedagogy, not polemic, and thus 'censure Jews, Gentiles, and Gentile Christians alike',[2] finally settles for a view of Romans as a showpiece of Paul's pedagogical style designed to prepare the Romans to welcome him as a teacher:

> The dialogical element in Romans is not just a marginal stylistic phenomenon, but is central to the expression of the letter's message. In the letter Paul presents himself to the Romans as a teacher. The dialogical style of the diatribe is central to this self-presentation....
> ... In Romans, then, Paul uses the style of indictment and protreptic and presents himself to the Roman Christians not as a spiritual father and guide, but as a (philosophical) or... religious-ethical teacher....
> ... The reason, then, for Paul's choice of the dialogical style of the letter was to serve as a kind of protreptic to his teaching in Rome. It is the self-introduction of Paul as a teacher and preacher of the gospel. The body of Romans is written in the style he would use in teaching a group of Christians. In the letter Paul surveys the central concern and emphases of his particular message. By doing this he is creating interest

---

1 Bornkamm, *Paul*, pp. 95-96.
2 Stowers, *The Diatribe*, p. 177.

and receptivity at Rome and preparing them for his intended
tenure with them as the teacher of the Gentiles.[1]

We cannot review the variety of interpretations in greater
detail here. Our purpose is simply to assess a couple of
assumptions that characterize a number of them, specifically:
that 'the weight' of the argument in 1.18-3.20 'falls upon the
Jew', and that 'the Jew' somehow personifies a particular
obstacle to Paul's gospel that must be overcome before his
argument may continue.

To serve that purpose it will not be necessary to take up the
questions, worthy in their own right, of Paul's contribution to
the history of Christian anti-Judaism and, consequently, of
how his theology should be evaluated today.[2] We limit ourselves to a prior question: What is Paul trying to say in
Romans? The scope of this excursus is consequently restricted
to two related subjects: (a) the *intelligibility* of Paul's
argument in 1.18-3.20 as a 'debate with Judaism', and (b) its
rhetorical plausibility. That is, we want to ask on the one hand
(a) whether this argument really presents itself, through
recognizable cues, as a 'polemic' against the Jew or against
Judaism—how clear is it that the Jew is addressed in the
rhetorical indictment at 2.1, or that the Jew addressed in 2.17-
29 is really being 'indicted'?—and on the other hand, (b) on the
assumption that these chapters *do* in fact involve such a
polemic, whether that argument would carry any conviction
with a Jewish audience, or would instead constitute only a
massive *petitio principii*.

These two questions are interrelated, and are of greater
importance to an adequate interpretation of Romans than is
generally realized (to judge from their rarity in the secondary
literature). To take the last question (b) first: If Paul's argument in 1.18-3.20 (or 4.25) proceeds from different premises

1 *Ibid.*, pp. 179, 180, 182.
2 These are questions raised and discussed by Rosemary Radford
   Ruether, *Faith and Fratricide* (New York: Seabury, 1974), and
   (partially in response to her book), by Gager, *Origins*, and the con-
   tributors to Alan Davies, ed., *Antisemitism and the Foundations of
   Christianity* (New York: Paulist, 1979), and Granskou and Richardson, eds., *Anti-Judaism in Early Christianity, Vol. 1: Paul and the
   Gospels*.

than his Jewish contemporaries were likely to have granted—
a proposition that has received ample substantiation in the
past, especially recently, albeit with various explanations[1]—
then it is not properly 'argumentative', but instead *postulates*
what Paul wishes to *prove* to the Jew.[2] Language about Paul's
'radicalized' or 'apocalyptic' perspective on the Law frequently means simply that Paul's assumptions about the Law are
no longer congruous with Judaism (so, frequently, Käsemann
in his commentary). But this implies that Paul's gospel is,
from the Jewish perspective, beside the point; and if these
arguments are (either in Romans, or in a previous missionary
setting from which they have been imported into Romans)
intended to be cogent and convincing to Jews, then they are
very poorly thought out.

In other words, if it is probable that an intelligent and devout
Jew could have parried one or another of Paul's thrusts
(again, under the presumption that Paul wants to 'indict' the
Jew) with a simple qualification, a gentle correction, or an
honest denial, then however a purported indictment of the
Jew is to be construed from Romans 2–3, that indictment can
hardly be considered an informed or fair confrontation with a
typically Jewish perspective. If the supposed debate with the
Jew does not develop out of a real awareness of and sensitivity
to Jewish premises, in such a way as to reflect 'the influence of
the earlier stages of the discussion on the argumentative
possibilities' available,[3] then that debate—presuming, again,
that these chapters are intended as a debate—is bad rhetoric,
and Paul is 'ineffective and irrelevant' as a speaker.[4]

If, on the other hand, Paul here relies on a rhetorical arti-
fice, the apostrophe to the Jewish interlocutor, not because of

1 The problem has been set out with admirable clarity and with a history of its treatment by E.P. Sanders, *Paul and Palestinian
   Judaism*, pp. 1-24. In addition to Sanders' amplification of his
   treatment of Paul in *Paul, the Law, and the Jewish People*, see also
   the recent works by Räisänen, *Paul and the Law*, and Hübner, *The
   Law in Paul's Thought*.
2 On the *petitio principii* as an error of rhetoric, see Perelman and
   Olbrechts-Tyteca, *The New Rhetoric*, pp. 112-14.
3 Perelman and Olbrechts-Tyteca, *The New Rhetoric*, p. 491.
4 Consigny, 'Rhetoric and its Situations', p. 179.

its plausibility on Jewish terms but, so to speak, *despite its lack* of the same, for the sake of its intended effect on a (Gentile) Christian audience, then Romans should be regarded as 'mere essay-making, without concern for real life', rhetoric 'addressed to conventional audiences, of which such rhetoric can afford to have stereotyped conceptions'.[1]

On these terms, the alternatives left before the interpreter would be either that Paul has misunderstood Judaism,[2] or misrepresented it as a result either of his new views as a convert to Christianity[3] or of the overwhelming success of the Gentile mission and antipathy toward Jewish opponents,[4] or else—the view that has prevailed in 'theological' commentaries—has by extraordinary means come to understand the Jews better than they could have understood themselves.[5]

To be clear, however, our purpose here is not to choose between these alternatives, but to assess the view of Romans that is at their basis—*if* these chapters are oriented against Judaism. The considered judgment that the argument in Romans 1–4 would *not* be effective in 'undermining the Jewish position', i.e., a negative answer to question (b) above, should lead us, not immediately to hypotheses about how Paul came to apply this supposed polemic, but to question (a) above: Is it really evident that Paul is trying to 'get' the Jew in Romans 1–4? Here we are simply suggesting that a number of theological, psychological and historical hypotheses should be held in suspense pending a reconsideration of the *exegetical* question.

1. The Indictment in Rom. 1.18–2.16; A 'Trap' for the Jew?

There is little doubt that the indictment of human impiety and immorality in Rom. 1.18-32 is aimed particularly at the Gentile world in terms developed in the propaganda literature of the Hellenistic synagogue. In literature like the Wisdom of Solomon (13–14) or Philo's hortatory exegesis of the Law

1 Perelman and Olbrechts-Tyteca, *The New Rhetoric*, p. 20.
2 See Montefiore, *Judaism and Saint Paul*, pp. 92-112; Schoeps, *Paul*, pp. 24-36; Sanders, *Paul and Palestinian Judaism*, pp. 1-12.
3 Sanders, *Paul and Palestinian Judaism*, pp. 496-97, 550-52.
4 Räisänen, *Paul and the Law*, pp. 256-63.
5 Barth, *Romans*; Käsemann, *Romans*.

(*Decal.* 61-63; *Spec.* 1.13-27; *Vita* 5-10), the Gentiles, in contrast to the faithful Jews, are presented as ignoring the Creator's manifestation in creation, either in a vain philosophical materialism or in (what is more objectionable for the Jews) idolatry, thus showing themselves to be not only foolish but also ungrateful to their supreme benefactor. Idolatry is the root of 'specifically Gentile sins',[1] sexual perversions and particularly homosexuality. The coercive aspect of pagan Hellenism played an important part in Jewish martyrology (1, 2 Maccabees), and the shamelessness of those who encourage others to do evil (cf. Rom 1.32) was a commonplace.[2]

As we have seen, the *topos* on Gentile immorality also played an important role in early Christian evangelism and protreptic, and we have suggested that it is this background that provides the clue to the rhetorical potentialities of Rom. 1.18-32. That suggestion must stand or fall with the interpretation of 2.1 and the consequent understanding of how 1.18-32 and 2.1-16 are related.

Hans Lietzmann provided in his exegesis of Rom. 2.1 what Anders Nygren would later champion as 'the key to the second chapter of Romans'.[3] The person addressed in 2.1 is not the 'wrongdoer' of 1.32, but is instead 'der selbstgerechte Jude'. The 'key' to this interpretation is the perceived similarity of themes and arguments in Romans to those in Wisdom 13–15. In this view, although 'the Jew' is explicitly addressed only at 2.17, Paul has set a skillful 'trap' for the Jewish auditor already in 1.18-32, where he 'invites Jewish agreement with his description of [the Gentile] world'; the trap is sprung at 2.1.

---

1 Käsemann, *Romans*, p. 44.
2 The aggressively seductive or contagious quality of Gentile impiety is particularly repellent in Hellenistic Jewish literature, especially in Philo's *De Ebrietate*, where the one complicit in evildoing is condemned: 'for he purposes not only to do wrong, but to join with others in doing wrong. He consents to initiate evil himself, and also to comply with what others initiate, that thus he may leave himself no ray of hope that may serve for his redemption' (25). For similar descriptions of coercive evil, often with the structure οὐ μόνον ἀλλὰ καί, see Philo, *Decal.* 123; *Conf.* 91, 116, 117 (note ἀναισχύνται); *TJud* 4.8; *TAsh* 6.2; *1 Enoch* 94.5; 98.15.
3 Lietzmann, *An die Römer*, pp. 38-39; Nygren, *Romans*, p. 114.

In contrast to Lietzmann's view that διό in 2.1 is 'eine farblose Übergangspartikel', however, Nygren insists that the διό retains its logically conjunctive force *precisely* as it serves to indict the Jewish judgmentalism portrayed in 1.18-32.[1]

This view is widely accepted,[2] but its most pointed presentation may be that of J. Christiaan Beker:

> The argumentative point of Rom. 1.18–3.20 is not an equal and separate indictment of Gentile and Jew. Although Paul does not spare the religious and moral bankruptcy of the Gentile world, his specific aim is directed against Jewish superiority and pride. After all, both Paul and the Jew already know from their heritage the self-evident sinful condition of the Gentile; it is a point that does not need to be argued. What is argued is the equal status of Jew and Gentile under sin; what is presupposed is the self-evident character of the Gentile under sin.[3]

If the Law's indictment can be applied to the Jew, Beker argues, 'then it is self-evident that the whole world (i.e. the Gentiles) is accountable to God as well, for Gentiles are by

---

1 Anders Nygren, *Commentary on Romans* (Philadelphia: Fortress, 1949), pp. 116-17.

2 Käsemann (*Romans*, I, pp. 79-80) declares that Rom. 2.1-11 'can be understood only as a polemic against the Jewish tradition' evident in Wis. 15.1-2, where 'Gentile idolatry is judged. The pious person, freed from this basic sin, can appeal to his knowledge of God as his righteousness and thus deal lightly with his own guilt' (*Romans*, pp. 53-54). Bornkamm ('Revelation of God's Wrath', p. 59) follows Lietzmann's interpretation, insisting that 'it should not be contested that in 2.1ff the Apostle, in fact, has the Jews especially in mind' (p. 69, n. 54). Barrett does not cite Lietzmann or Nygren, but concurs nevertheless that 'the full force' of 2.1ff. 'will be felt if we set beside it words from Wisdom', and then quotes Wisdom 15.1-2 (*Romans*, pp. 44-45). Cranfield (*Romans*, I, p. 138) goes to some length to prove that 'Paul had the Jews in mind right from 2.1'; but beyond a reference to Wis. 11–15, the 'weighty arguments' he claims to adduce consist in the generalizations that 'an attitude of moral superiority toward the Gentiles was so characteristic of the Jews (as vv. 18ff. themselves indicate), that in the absence of any indication to the contrary, it is natural to assume that Paul is apostrophizing the typical Jew in 2.1ff.', and that 'a confident expectation of special indulgence (see v. 3) was equally characteristic of them' (*Romans*, I, p. 138).

3 Beker, *Paul the Apostle*, pp. 79-80.

nature sinners (cf. the Wisdom of Solomon)'.[1] Paul's argument through Rom. 3.19 is seen, then, to be aimed primarily at a Jewish target.

That this interpretation of Rom. 2.1 depends heavily on a perceived parallel in the Wisdom of Solomon is evident. Nygren demurs from suggesting any literary relationship between Romans and Wisdom, but contends nevertheless that 'Paul's view does stand in very special relation' to Wisdom:

> It is not against an imaginary opponent that Paul contends. He is not putting his own words into the mouth of the Jews. He merely presents what they had themselves said. When he says, 'O man, you who judge', he addresses himself to the Jew's manner of life, as we see it in the Book of Wisdom.[2]

By this connection, Nygren believes he has explained the troublesome conjunction of Rom. 1.32 and 2.1. διό is neither a 'colorless transition particle' (Lietzmann), nor a causative particle restricting 2.1-16 to the scope of Gentile disobedience in 1.18-32 (that is, τὰ γὰρ αὐτὰ πράσσεις ὁ κρίνων is not to be taken literally). Rather, διό now makes sense as a causative particle precisely because the Jew's presumption on divine grace (cf. 2.3) is based on moral distance from Gentile immorality.

Nygren's interpretation is vulnerable on three counts. First, his appeal to supposed parallels in Wisdom is selective and to a degree artificial; second, nothing else in Rom. 2.1-5 makes a *Jewish* characterization obvious; and finally, Nygren's understanding of the passage must supply a missing middle term in an implied syllogism, namely, the reader's judgmental response intuited between 1.32 and 2.1.

To take up the first problem, we may observe that Nygren's attempt to corroborate his exegesis of Romans 2 from Wisdom 15 depends on the assumption that both the author of Wisdom and the reader who responds with horror between Rom 1.32 and 2.1 represent a characteristically Jewish attitude of moral superiority and privilege before God. We quote Nygren at some length to illustrate the importance supposed parallels in Wisdom have for his exposition of Romans 2.

1 *Ibid.*
2 Nygren, *Romans*, p. 115.

> *Precisely 'therefore',* because that which has been said about
> the Gentiles is also true as to the Jews, 'therefore' the Jew is
> himself without excuse, when he judges. In passing judg-
> ment on others he condemns himself. For, as we read in the
> Book of Wisdom, the Jew confesses that he too sins. But he
> expects God to judge him and the Gentile in different ways.
> 'For even if we sin we are thine, knowing thy dominion'
> (Wisd. 15.2). With biting irony Paul says, 'Do you suppose, O
> man, that when you judge those who do such things and yet
> do them yourself, you will escape the judgment of God?'
> (vs. 3). No, God's is a true judgment, corresponding with
> reality (κατὰ ἀλήθειαν, vs. 2). For 'God shows no partiality'
> (vs. 11).
>
> The Jew says, 'Thou, our God, art good (χρηστός) and
> true, patient (μακρόθυμος) and directing all with mercy.' To
> this he adds the citation from the Book of Wisdom, 'For even
> if we sin, we are thine, knowing thy dominion' (15.1-2). Paul
> answers, 'Do you presume upon the riches of his kindness
> and forbearance and patience?' (vs. 4).
>
> The Jew says, 'God is merciful and forbearing in judg-
> ment, giving his foes opportunity for repentance', εἰς
> μετανοίαν (Wisd. 11.23). Paul replies, 'Do you not know that
> God'd kindness is meant to lead you to repentance?'
> (μετανοίαν, vs. 4).
>
> The Jew says, 'God judges the heathen in his wrath; but it
> is different with us. We are saved from his wrath. When he
> chastises us, he does so in gentleness' (Wisd. 11.9f.; cf.
> 12.22). Paul replies, 'By your hard and impenitent heart you
> are storing up wrath for yourself on the day of wrath when
> God's righteous judgment will be revealed' (vs. 5).[1]

Nygren relies on Wisdom of Solomon because there—and
more narrowly, in Wis. 15.2a, quoted twice in the paragraphs
excerpted above—he perceives evidence that the target of
Paul's indictment in Romans 2 is a *characteristically* Jewish
presumption (Paul 'addresses himself to the Jew's manner of
life, as we see it in the Book of Wisdom'): the Jew admits sin,
but also expects the covenantal relationship to offer protection
from divine judgment. The Jew says, in Nygren's paraphrase,
'we are saved from [divine] wrath'.[2]

---

1 *Ibid*, pp. 116-17.
2 It would not be fair to imply that Nygren believed he could general-
  ize about ancient Judaism on the basis of this verse fragment, or

But Wis. 15.2 hardly supports the weight that Nygren's interpretation imposes. The moral presumption Nygren perceives in the first part of the verse, 'even if we [Jews] sin, we are thine', is qualified by what immediately follows (which finds no place in Nygren's commentary): 'But we shall not sin, since we know that we are yours; for to know you is complete righteousness, and to know your dominion is the source of immortality'. Rather than a presumption on God's grace, the whole verse speaks of God's faithfulness in sustaining the covenant with Israel *despite* Israel's sin (cf. Rom. 3.1-8!).[1] Wisdom knows a divine 'double standard' regarding Israel and the Gentiles, to be sure; this is evident (as Nygren and others have frequently pointed out) in 12.22, for example: 'While chastening us, you scourge our enemies ten thousand times more'. But the point of this verse in its broader context (ch. 12) is not that Israel can presume upon God's grace when they sin, but to the contrary, that God has been amazingly lenient with sinners, and (by comparison) harsh with the faithful of Israel, in order to bring both to repentance. What may appear to human eyes a moral disparity is nonetheless God's sovereign and righteous will 'to spare all' (12.16, cf. Rom. 11.32-36!). It is not a proprietary claim established by membership in the covenant, but the repentance of sins that is Israel's hope (12.19); its opposite is the willful refusal to learn from God's chastisements (12.26, 27—a closer parallel to Rom. 2.4!).

Nygren's other references to Wisdom appear similarly arbitrary. He puts into the Jew's mouth the statement (adapted from Wisdom 11.23) that God 'gives his foes opportunity for repentance' in order to provide a Jewish target for Rom. 2.4: 'Do you not know that God's kindness is meant to lead *you* to repentance?' Beyond the obvious addition of emphasis, Nygren has also rewritten the Wisdom quote (the

that those who follow Nygren would concede that the characterization of Jewish presumption rests on so slender a textual basis. It is accurate, however, to state that Nygren and most scholars who follow his interpretation on this point are satisfied to bring forward this evidence alone—even the Strack–Billerbeck *Kommentar*.

1 Schlier (*Römerbrief*, p. 68, n. 2) misses this point when he writes that 'Niemand kann nach Paulus wie Weish. 15,2 sprechen'.

Greek text at 11.23 has ἁμαρτήματα ἀνθρώπων; Gentiles are
not indicated). He has overlooked Wisdom's insistence that
God also chastens Israel in order to bring Israel to repentance;
and when he does mention Wis. 11.9 and 12.22, it is not to
illustrate Rom. 2.4 (which would suggest that the Jew already
knew that God wills the repentance of sins),[1] but to serve as
the foil to Rom. 2.5. Yet neither these nor any other verses in
Wisdom give the reader an impression of a 'hard and impenitent heart'.

This cursory review of Nygren's references to the Wisdom
of Solomon suggests that *precisely* on the basis of the Jewish
point of view expressed in Wisdom, when Paul (in Nygren's
view) asks the Jew, 'Do you presume upon the riches of [God's]
kindness and forbearance and patience?' the Jew should be
expected to answer, 'Certainly not! Knowing God's dominion,
we shall *not* sin' (15.2). When (to pursue Nygren's interpretation) Paul asks the Jew, 'Do you not know that God's kindness
is meant to lead you to repentance?' the Jew would answer,
'Of course we Jews know this: precisely the history of God's
forbearance of Gentile sins teaches us that God's rule is
absolutely righteous, and demands our repentance as well!'
Just those passages in Wisdom that Nygren adduced as
expressions of the Jewish duplicity that Paul attacks in
Romans 2 actually work against his interpretation.

This problem should not be minimized as Nygren's poor
choice of prooftext, as if the characteristically Jewish combination of judgmentalism and moral complacency (precisely
the combination Nygren needs for his explanation of the logic
in 2.1) could be read out of any number of other Jewish texts.[2]

---

1 We should be given pause by the frequency with which interpreters
  acknowledge that what Paul says in Rom. 2.1-5 was 'already known
  in Judaism'—so Schlier (*Römerbrief*, p. 69) admits that the οἴδαμεν
  of 2.2 'ist das Wissen des Juden', with reference to *Abot* 3.16, 4 Ezra
  7.34, *2 Bar.* 85.9, 1QS 4.19f; about the 'knowledge' that God's mercy
  leads to repentance (Rom. 2.4), he writes 'das hat auch das Judentum gelegentlich [!] schon erkannt, wie z.B. Sir 5.4ff. zeigt' (p. 71)—
  yet insists that it is *precisely* the Jew who must be told these truths!
2 For example, Ps. Sol. 15.8 and 9.5, cited as parallels in the margin
  of Nestle-Aland[26], readily distinguish those who will receive mercy
  in judgment from those who will be condemned, 'and will not
  escape the judgment of the Lord' (οὐκ ἐκφεύξονται... τὸ κρίμα

180   *The Rhetoric of Romans*

In light of Paul's evident 'dependence on Jewish tradition' in this indictment of the person who hypocritically judges others, presuming to be immune from God's righteous judgment,[1] it is surprising that so many commentators should consider his *target* here to be specifically a characteristically and recognizably *Jewish* attitude.[2] Of course parallels can be adduced to

κυρίου, 15.8). Yet this distinction cannot be construed as the presumption that Jews who 'do the same things' as their immoral pagan neighbors can expect to 'escape God's wrath' (Rom. 2.3). The suggestion is in fact absurd in the context of the Psalms' enormous preoccupation with 'proving God right' in all his judgments (9.2 and elsewhere). Schlier (*Römerbrief*, p. 68) adduces 4 Ezra 3.32f. as an example of 'die Naivität des an sich verhafteten Frommen' in support of his reading of Rom. 2.1. The verses read, in part, 'Has another nation known you besides Israel?... They abound in wealth, though they are unmindful of your commandments. Now therefore weigh in a balance our iniquities and those of the inhabitants of the world; and so it will be found which way the turn of the scale will incline'. Schlier concedes, 'und wer sollte dem Juden nicht recht geben?'; but immediately qualifies this concession, supplying a premise that makes this Jewish attitude a fitting object for Paul's indictment: namely, 'dass solches Urteil nur möglich ist, weil er, der Jude, unkritisch in bezug auf sich selbst ist und seiner eigenen Sünden vergisst und diese Vergesslichkeit das Verurteilen des anderen ermöglicht'. This imposes on 4 Ezra an attitude not evident in the text itself, in order to establish some external corroboration for what is taken to be the object of Paul's attack. The widespread reliance on Nygren's exegesis at Rom. 2.1-6 may betray an intuition that other corroborative evidence will be scarce. To be sure, a wealth of Jewish literature attests that 'an attitude of moral superiority toward the Gentiles was characteristic of the Jews' (Cranfield, *Romans*, I, p. 138): but this attitude cannot self-evidently be construed as moral presumption against God's judgment. Barrett's declaration that 'the moral purity of the Jews was their legitimate boast' (*Romans*, p. 43) is as remarkable for being uncommon as it is for being a straightforward historical assessment of ancient Judaism. One may also find in Israel's prayers abundant expressions of confidence that the Lord will be merciful to forgive the penitent; but it would be tendentious, to say the least, to construe these prayers as expressions of moral complacency (see J.H. Charlesworth, 'Jewish Hymns, Odes, and Prayers', in *Early Judaism and its Modern Interpreters*, pp. 423, 425).

1 Käsemann, *Romans*, p. 55; see previous note.
2 Käsemann (*Romans*, p. 53) states: 'What follows can only be understood as a polemic against the Jewish tradition'. How can Paul's

show that within Judaism the temptation to presume on God's covenantal grace was recognized as a perennial problem, and was combatted.[1] But this hardly allows us to view the rhetoric in 2.1-5 as a criticism of what is essentially or endemically Jewish.[2]

More pointedly: nothing in the text suggests that Paul intended to 'mark' the hypocritical judge as a Jew. The use of vocabulary similar to that found in Wisdom or Sirach might have given these phrases a solemn tone—it is even conceivable that it might have constituted something of a literary allusion—but at most this would have shown that

thoroughly *Jewish* assault on the hypocrite reflect an assault on the *Jew* specifically? Käsemann answers: 'It is plain how strongly the apostle identifies himself with the opponent [the Jew] and his premises in order to lay hold of him from that perspective' (p. 55).

1 On the question of Jewish 'arrogance' regarding the covenant, E.P. Sanders (*Paul and Palestinian Judaism*, p. 87) summarizes his findings concerning the Tannaitic literature: 'The rabbis were no more plagued by arrogance than any other people who have held a doctrine of election.... The idea of being privileged as children of Abraham may have been abused, but abuses were criticized by the rabbis themselves. Smugness was resisted'. G.F. Moore (*Judaism*, I, p. 508) cites *m. Yoma* 8.8-9, 'If anyone says to himself, "I will sin, and repent, and I will sin and repent", no opportunity is given him to repent', to demonstrate that throughout Judaism, anyone 'who so presumes on the remission of sins through the goodness of God does not know the meaning of repentance, and annuls [in oneself] the very potentiality of it' (*Judaism*, I, p. 508). The apostrophe in Sir. 5.4-7 is perhaps the most striking example of a Jewish admonition against presuming upon God's grace, remarkable for both its verbal and its stylistic similarity to Rom. 2.1-6 (quoted from RSV):

4   Do not say, 'I sinned, and what happened to me?' for the Lord is slow to anger.
5   Do not be so confident of atonement that you add sin to sin.
6   Do not say, 'His mercy is great, he will forgive the multitude of my sins', for both mercy and wrath are with him, and his anger rests on sinners.
7   Do not delay to turn to the Lord, nor postpone it from day to day; for suddenly the wrath of the Lord will go forth, and at the time of punishment you will perish.

2 Käsemann (*Romans*, p. 56) declares that the person determined by a 'hard and impenitent heart' is 'represented typically by the Jew'. Cranfield (*Romans*, I, p. 138) says that 'a confident expectation of special indulgence... was equally characteristic of [the Jews]'.

Paul's indictment had 'authentic' precedent: it hardly constitutes a cue to the reader that a distinctively *Jewish* attitude is being described.

Thomas Schmeller has advanced an argument for reading 2.1-5 as an indictment of the Jew that is based first on internal, rhetorical clues rather than on perceived external corroboration (Nygren).[1] He shows that the logical connection between 1.18-32 and 2.1ff. is the principle of culpability through recognition of God's righteous demand, evident especially in the verbal links between 1.32 and 2.1-2 (ἐπιγνόντες—οἴδαμεν; τὸ δικαίωμα τοῦ θεοῦ—τὸ κρίμα τοῦ θεοῦ; οἱ τὰ τοιαῦτα πράσσοντες—τοὺς τὰ τοιαῦτα πράσσοντας), but that the person addressed in 2.1 who 'judges' evildoers is to be distinguished from the persons described in 1.32 who 'approve' of evildoers. The connective link διό is only intelligible with regard to the principle of culpability.[2] This part of his analysis carries conviction.[3] Schmeller goes on, however, to identify the target of Paul's indictment in 2.1-5 as the person who endorses the critique of Gentile immorality in 1.18-32: the 'hearer' in 2.1ff. is the 'speaker' in 1.18-32.[4] And

---

1 Schmeller, *Paulus und die 'Diatribe'*, pp. 225-86.
2 ' "Unentschuldbar' ist der κρίνων "deshalb", weil er wie die Subjekte von 1,32 das Gebot Gottes in dessen offenbarender Schöpfung (vgl. ἀναπολογήτους in 1,20) erkennen kann und es dennoch übertritt; in dieser Hinsicht gehört er zu den 'Menschen' von 1,18-32. Andererseits setzt er sich durch sein Richten von ihnen ab; in dieser Hinsicht ist 2,1 von 1,32 deutlich geschieden und das διό nicht mehr als Folgerung verständlich' (*ibid.*, p. 274).
3 *Judging* as such is not the point (so Käsemann, *Romans*, p. 54). 'Judging' (κρίνων) is not to be assimilated to 'doing the same things' (τὰ τοιαῦτα πράσσων), as if 'in the very act of judging the judge is involved in the same conduct as the man he condemns' (*pace* Barrett, *Romans*, p. 44).
4 'Da ein solches Richten in 1,18-32 stattfindet und im Zusammenhang damit die Subjekte von 1,32 in 1,20 für unentschuldbar erklärt werden, ist die Deutung unausweichlich, dass 1,18-32 eine Schilderung der richtenden Aktivität des in 2,1ff. Angesprochenen ist, die ihm selbst den Vorwurf der Unentschuldbarkeit einträgt. Das Verhältnis zwischen beiden Gruppen ist also eindeutig so gedacht, dass sie in 1,18-32 als Angeklagte und Ankläger auftreten, während in 2,1ff. der bisherige Ankläger selbst zum Angeklagten wird und von einem neuen Ankläger Vorwürfe erfährt. Oder anders ausgedrückt: das als "Hörer" gedachte Gegenüber in 2,1-5

that person—Schmeller concludes from the opposition of Jew and Gentile in 2.6-11—is the Jew.[1]

Against Schmeller's conclusion that the 'hearer' in 2.1-5 is the 'speaker' in 1.18-32, we may observe that 1.18-32 clearly stands under the rubric of the revelation of God's wrath (1.18), which is justified by human defiance and rebellion (1.20). The 'speaker' in 1.18-32—that is the author of the judgment that comes to expression there—is God, not any human being (as in 2.1ff.). Further, nothing within that pericope suggests that the perspective represented is false: the litany in 1.18-32 is florid, but not ironic. The theme that God's righteous judgment inevitably and invariably brings wrath upon human impiety is announced in 1.17-18, amplified in 1.18-2.5, and recapitulated in 2.5-6; it seems unlikely therefore that '1,18-32 ist von vorneherein auf 2,1-11 hin konzipiert',[2] or that from 1.18 on Paul is driving at an 'ambush' of the Jew.[3]

Furthermore, not only does Rom. 2.1-5 provide no more explicit cues to the identity of the person indicted as a hypocritical judge;[4] neither is there any dialogical reflection of a supposed interlocutor's 'response' to 1.18-32. The equation Schmeller establishes between the 'accused' in 2.1ff. and the 'accuser' in 1.18-32 requires the retrojection of a (Jewish)

ist identisch mit dem gedachten "Sprecher" von 1,18-32' (Schmeller, *Paulus und die 'Diatribe'*, pp. 279-80).

1 *Ibid.*, p. 280. Schmeller's argument is that the distinction between the parties involved in 1.32 and 2.1 is that one reckons on judgment (1.32) and the other does not (2.3-4); but Paul goes on to insist that God's judgment is impartial, meaning specifically that Jew and Greek are put on the same level (2.9-11); therefore the 'distinction' between 1.32 and 2.1 must be that between Jew and Gentile. Other observations (the link between κρίνων in in 2.1 and κριθήσονται in 2.12; and the Jewish background of 1.18-32) are taken as *corroboration* that the prevalent view of 2.1-5 as an indictment of the Jew is correct.

2 *Ibid.*, p. 282.

3 Schmeller (*ibid.*, p. 274) cites Wilckens' assertion (U. Wilckens, *Der Brief an die Römer* [Neukirchen-Vluyn: Neukirchener Verlag, 1978], I, p. 123); that 'seit 1,18 [Paulus] auf diese Wendung an den Juden als Überraschungseffekt hinauswill'; Schmeller's qualification notwithstanding, his own view is quite close to Wilckens'.

4 Schlier's comment (*Römerbrief*, p. 68) that 'in 2,3ff wird der Jude unzweideutig charakterisiert' is groundless.

interlocutor back into 1.18-32 as the *real* 'accuser', instead of God (1.18, 24, 26, 28). That is, his declaration that in 2.1ff. 'der bisherige Ankläger selbst zum Angeklagten wird und von einem neuen Ankläger Vorwürfe erfährt'[1] only makes sense if the 'accuser' in 1.18-32 is not really God, but is the Jewish hearer who is about to be 'ambushed' in 2.1. This retrojection would be plausible if there were any indication of a rhetorical 'displacement' of personae at 2.1, where according to Schmeller, Nygren, and a host of others, a Jewish interlocutor appropriates and approves the judgment voiced in 1.18-32. Stanley Stowers has paraphrased the transition so as to make this displacement explicit:

> Paul graphically describes the decline of the Gentile nations into sin (1.18-32). Just as the audience is at the point of saying, 'Amen, the world is sinful, brother Paul', he says, 'when you judge another, mister, you judge yourself'...[2]

But this is only an exegetical expedient. Precisely this implied response of the audience as interlocutor is missing in 2.1;[3] and it is just this lack that makes the transition between 1.32 and 2.1 so problematic.[4]

Further, it is not the interlocutor's presumption of *moral superiority* over 'those who do such things' that comes under Paul's attack in 2.1-5 (for then the attack should focus on proving that the accused in fact 'does the same things'); it is rather the interlocutor's presumption of *escaping judgment*

---

1 Schmeller, *Paulus und die 'Diatribe'*, pp. 279-80.
2 Stowers, 'Text as Interpretation', p. 21. It is one of the virtues of Stowers' earlier work, *Diatribe*, pp. 129-34, that in it he carefully avoids this troublesome interpretation; (for a judicious treatment of the transition, see Bassler, *Divine Impartiality*, pp. 129-34).
3 We should expect at least an adversative conjunction to introduce a shift of character, as in fact happens at 2.17 (εἰ δὲ σὺ Ἰουδαῖος ἐπονομάζῃ).
4 In fact by retrojecting the 'hearer' of 2.1ff. into the role of 'speaker' in 1.18-32, Schmeller (*Paulus und 'Diatribe'*, p. 281) only moves the rhetorical problem back one place; for he must subsequently ask who is the 'hearer' in 1.18-32. 'Übertragen auf Röm 1,18-32 heisst das, dass hier nicht nur, wie wir feststellten, ein Jude als Sprecher, sondern auch ein Jude als Hörer gedacht ist'. How an audience is to follow this unexpressed shifting of identities is not explained.

for doing the same things (2.3-4).[1] Paul's rhetoric is abusive:[2] his target is a hypocrite, *not* 'the pious person'. Despite the popularity of Karl Barth's indictment of human religiosity, and its undeniable legitimacy on its own terms, that is not the point of Rom. 2.1-5. (Rom. 2.17ff. is another matter, as we shall see.) It is not the presumption on one's moral merit, but the presumption on God's grace—precisely in its undeserved-ness!—that Paul attacks here.

It is a curious paradox that the effect of interpreting this first apostrophe as an indictment of *the Jew* (as a cipher for 'the pious person') is often to deflect the apostrophe's rhetori-cal impact away from Paul's audience. While some commen-tators discuss the indictment of *homo religiosus* in a way general enough to include the Christian on principle (Barth, Käsemann, Bornkamm), the Christians to whom Paul has written play little or no part in this exposition. Especially when the letter 'body' in 1.16ff. is taken as an exposition of Paul's theology and 1.18–3.20 becomes a 'propaedeutic to the gospel', the response expected of the Roman Christians is by implica-tion not repentance, but appreciation of the apostle's theologi-cal insight or didactic technique.[3] But this ignores the rhetori-

1 The target of the indictment is hypocrisy, not 'judging' as moral discrimination. In this light a textual variant at 2.3 is at least provocative: Codex Porphyrianus (ninth century) reads, instead of 'Do you suppose, you who judge those who do such things and do the same things', simply, 'Do you suppose, then, you who do these things...?' In this reading, 'judging' is no longer in view: hypocrisy is clearly the target. It is hardly probable that this reading is authentic; but it seems to be an attempt to streamline the text around what actually is Paul's central concern. (Note the reverse movement when the tension between κρίνων and τὰ... αὐτὰ πράσσεις in 2.1 and the overfull replication at 2.3 led Bultmann ['Glossen'] and Käsemann [*Romans*, p. 54] to speak of a gloss at 2.1, retrojected from 2.3.)

2 'Typically Pauline are the absurd motives ascribed to the adversary' (Käsemann, *Romans*, p. 54, after Bultmann, *Stil*, p. 67); Schmeller (*Paulus und die 'Diatribe'*,, p. 279) points out that the opponent in 2.2-4 is not allowed to speak independently, but is only addressed polemically.

3 Käsemann (*Romans*, pp. 35-36) specifies that in 1.18–3.20 Paul 'proclaims the necessity' of the gospel 'for Christians who no longer need propaedeutics or a missionary point of contact'. 'The accusa-tions made by the apostle are not directed against them and are not

cal potentiality of the diatribal mode, namely, its usefulness in discriminating undesirable attitudes or sentiments through a fictive device, without directly confronting (and possibly alienating) the real audience.

Neither does anything in the amplification of this indictment (2.7-16) indicate that Paul's aim is to challenge or dispute Jewish convictions. Particularly Paul's assertions that God judges everyone according to works (2.6), either positively or negatively, and that this judgment applies first to the Jew (2.9-10), cast doubt on the view that Romans 2 is part of the apostle's attack on Judaism as a religion of 'justification by works' (and for that reason are generally discarded as not reflecting Paul's own viewpoint).[1] To be sure, Paul sets Jew and Gentile on the same footing before God's judgment, an equivalence that implicitly denies any special privilege to the Jew. But if that implicit denial is Paul's point, it is strangely suppressed in the text, where attention is rather focused on the Gentiles' accountability to God. What is said explicitly about Jews—that they are 'justified' or 'judged' on the basis of whether they do what the Law requires (2.12b-13)—is indis-

---

meant to stir them to repentance' (p. 34). The two recent studies of Paul's diatribal rhetoric similarly consider the applicability of the apostophe in 2.1ff. to the Roman Christians in hypothetical and general terms. Schmeller (*Paulus und die 'Diatribe'*, p. 285) concedes that on one hand 'wird *indirekt* auch jedes einzelne Gemeindemitglied persönlich angesprochen, insofern ihm die negative Darstellung der Unheilssituation die eigene Heilssituation bewusst macht und die richtige Einschätzung, Aneignung und Bewahrung dieses Heils nahebringt. Zum anderen ist der Abschnitt Teil der Darlegung des paulinischen Evangeliums und dient als solcher *direkt* dazu, die notwendigen theologischen Voraussetzungen für ein Verständnis des folgenden zu bieten'. Stowers (*Diatribe*, p. 110) declares at one point that 'the function of 2.1-5 is to bring home, to concretize and to sharpen the indictment in 1.18-32 (especially vv. 28-32) for Paul's audience. It takes the indictment of "them" in 1.18-32 and makes it into a personal indictment of any of the audience to whom it might apply'. This proposition is not developed, however, and the diatribal elements in Romans are at least interpreted as the means Paul has chosen to present himself to potential supporters as a philosophical teacher. (See above, pp. 170, 171).

1 See the important treatment by Snodgrass, 'Justification by Grace'.

tinguishable from what E.P. Sanders has called 'covenantal nomism'.[1]

That fact presents a tremendous problem to interpreters bound to find an 'anti-Judaistic thrust' in these verses.[2] A 'sharpening' of Paul's 'attack on the Jews' can only be perceived here if words are put in the apostle's mouth: 'The law is not [the Jews'] inviolable possession'.[3] This is in fact the approach taken by interpreters who find Paul's polemic to be directed not to supposed Jewish works–righteousness but to Jewish exclusivism. So John Gager, who points out that the principles set out in 2.12-13 were 'presumably taken for granted by most of Paul's Jewish contemporaries, certainly by those whose background was similar to his own', finds the argumentative burden throughout Romans 2—3 to focus on 'Israel's claim to exclusive access to God's righteousness and thus to the privileges that flow from it', 'the issue of collective exclusivity for Israel'.[4] But that message is read out of 2.17-29 and 3.1-20; it remains invisible in 2.1-16.

It cannot be denied that what Paul says here *varies* from the understanding of the Gentiles' relation to Torah evident, for example, in some of the Tannaitic literature or pseudepigrapha. Judaism held to the universal validity of Torah itself,[5] even over Gentiles who had not accepted its yoke, by projecting into the future God's final judgment of the Gentiles for not observing Torah,[6] and by projecting into the past an

1 Sanders, *Paul and Palestinian Judaism*, pp. 75, 236, 426-28.
2 Käsemann, *Romans*, p. 62.
3 *Ibid.*
4 Gager, *Origins*, pp. 214-17, 248-49.
5 'In content and intention the Law is universal' (Moore, *Judaism*, I, p. 279).
6 'A rather different result of the equation of Law and wisdom is the idea that strictly all men equally are to keep the Law. This arises mainly in the form of an eschatological hope, and as such it is a favorite notion of Hellenistic Judaism' (G. Bertram, 'νόμος', *TDNT*, II, p. 1048). See also John Collins' discussion (*Between Athens and Jerusalem*, pp. 137-74) of a 'common ethic' in Diaspora Judaism; cf. Gaston, *Paul and the Torah*, pp. 15-44; 85-86. One of the most provocative aspects of Lloyd Gaston's work is his thesis that Paul inherited from ancient Judaism the 'apocalyptic conception of the angels of the nations', who mediate the Gentiles' subjection to the Law which Israel alone obeys (*Paul and the Law*, pp. 9-11, 23-25, 35-

aboriginal refusal of the Torah,[1] a refusal evident even in the
Gentile inability to keep the so-called Noachian

44). The most direct evidence for the notion that the Gentiles are
answerable to God in terms of the Torah are later Tannaitic aggadot
(see the following note); in order to trace this conception back into
the Judaism of Paul's time, Gaston appeals to the identification of
Torah with Wisdom in, for example, the Wisdom of ben Sira. 'As
soon as the Torah is identified with *wisdom*, then all nations are
under the Torah as they are under the laws of creation, but as soon
as wisdom is identified with *Torah*, then the nations must keep all
the laws given to Israel without being part of the covenant God
made with Israel' (*ibid.*, p. 27). The relevant passage from ben Sira
reads, '[God] established with men an eternal covenant, and
showed them his judgments... and said to them, "Beware of all
unrighteousness". And he gave commandment to each of them
concerning his neighbor.... He appointed a ruler for every nation,
but Israel is the Lord's own portion' (17.1, 14, 17, RSV). Similarly the
Liber antiquitatum biblicarum of pseudo-Philo has God say to
Moses, 'I have given an everlasting Law into your hands and by this
I will judge the whole world. For this will be a testimony. For even if
men say, "We have not known you, and so we have not served you",
therefore I will make a claim upon them because they have not
learned my law' (11.2-3; *OTP*, II, p. 318). In 4 Ezra as well, the angel
of the Lord tells Ezra, 'Those who dwell on the earth will incur
torment because though they possessed reason, they committed
iniquity, and though they received the commandments, they did not
observe them, and though the Law was imposed on them, they
rejected what was imposed' (7.70-73; cf. 3.32-36; 5.27; 7.11, 20-24).
Finally, the third Sibyl denounces the nation for 'trangressing the
holy law of immortal God, which they transgressed' (599-600). The
disparity between the small number of these references and their
fairly incidental role in their respective literary contexts, on the one
hand, and the importance Gaston gives them in his reconstruction
of Paul's Jewish background, on the other, is probably to be
explained by observing that ancient Judaism was not so concerned
to specify the status of Gentiles before Torah as it was simply to
assert the Torah's universal validity. It is Paul himself, who *was*
vitally concerned with the Gentiles' relation to Torah, who has
provided in his letters the best evidence—albeit indirect—for the
conception that Gaston posits for Paul's Jewish *background*.

1 Relevant here are the aggadot about God's offering the Torah to the
nations, and their refusing it, 'so that they are without excuse'
when judged by God (*Mekilta, Bahodesh* 1-5; *Targum Pseudo-
Jonathan* at Deut 33.1-2 (the source for the following midrashim as
well); *Sifrê on Deuteronomy* 343; *Pesikta de Rab Kahana* 5.2, Sup.
1.15, Sup. 2.1; *Pesikta Rabbati* 30.4, 15, 21.3; *Pirkê de Rabbi Eleazar*
41; *Midrash Tanḥuma, Berakah* 3). Note in particular *Mekilta,*

commandments.[1] Paul, on the other hand, does not dispute that Gentiles are outside the realm of Torah (Gentile sinners sin ἀνόμως, 2.12), that they are those who 'do not possess the Torah' (2.14); or for that matter that Gentile Christians 'are not under the Law but under grace' (6.15). He nevertheless

Baḥodesh 5: 'And it was for the following reason that the nations of the world were asked to accept the Torah: in order that they should have no excuse for saying, "Had we been asked we would have accepted it". For behold, they were asked and they refused to accept it.' Also note *Pesikta de Rab Kahana*, Sup. 1.15: 'Rab Abbahu said, "It was revealed and known to Him who had only to speak to have the world come into being that the peoples of the world would not accept the Torah... Why, then, did He offer it? Because if He did not, they would have cause to reproach Him".' Moore (*Judaism*, I, p. 277) insists that the aggadah is 'not... a scholastic conceit or a play of homiletical subtlety; it was the teaching of both the great schools of the second century, the schools of Ishmael and Akiba, and is therefore presumably part of the earlier common tradition from which they drew'. Gaston ('Israel's Enemies in Pauline Theology', *NTS* 28 [1982], p. 405 = *Paul and the Torah*, p. 86) declares the point of such aggadot to be 'to alleviate the tension between the concepts of the election of Israel and God's rule over creation'. We should emphasize the vital role played by such aggadot in constructing and maintaining the symbolic world of Judaism in the Hellenistic and Roman periods (see the next note).

1 Any discussion of the 'Noachian commandments' in rabbinic literature must distinguish between Maimonides' discussion of the righteous among the Gentiles, Tannaitic halakot regarding resident aliens within Palestine, and midrashic aggadot. On the subject see Moore, *Judaism*, I, p. 340; Gaston, 'Paul and the Torah', pp. 56-57; E. Urbach, 'Self-Isolation or Self-Affirmation in the First Three Centuries: Theory and Practice', in *Jewish and Christian Self-Definition*, II, pp. 275-77. (The confusion in Sanders' treatment [*Paul and Palestinian Judaism*, pp. 208-12] results from a failure to make just these distinctions.) As Urbach ('Self-Isolation', p. 277) points out, the Noachian commandments serve in aggadic midrashim to respond to a particular set of problems. 'The Jewish claim to election based upon the willingness of the people of Israel to accept the yoke of the Torah was queried by the nations of the world, who could easily argue: "Had we been asked we should certainly have accepted it".' The aggadic response attributed to R. Simon b. Eleazar (cited above from the *Mekilta*) argued that if the Gentiles 'are not able to keep the seven commandments which were given to the descendants of Noah, and which were accepted by them, how much more would they be unable to keep the commandments if they had been given all the Torah'.

insists that Gentiles are just as accountable to the righteousness that Torah requires as are Jews to Torah itself.[1] This argument is more nearly an extension of Torah than a curtailment of it: the 'work of the law', the manifestation of the divine will before which all human beings are accountable, is a reality outside the realm of Torah (2.15), just as it is made present to the Jew through Torah. This does not curtail the applicability of Torah (the Jew must still 'do Torah' to be justified); rather it shows that the divine demand embodied in Torah—'the good' (2.10), 'the things of the Law' (2.14), 'the work of the Law' (2.15), 'the righteous requirements of the Law' (2.26)—is absolutely and universally valid, i.e., even outside the sphere of those who 'have' the Law.

Paul develops out of this first apostrophe (2.1-5) the principle of universal accountability to God on the basis of doing 'the things the Law requires' (τὰ τοῦ νόμου). This argument is brought to completion (2.6-16) without any explicit qualification or refutation of Jewish claims. This must be considered a serious challenge to the assumption that Paul's intention in these verses is to mount an attack on Jewish privilege—that this is an *assumption* should be evident from the difficulty with which interpreters must wring it from the text—and should nudge us toward considering other possible interpretations of the apostrophe (such as is presented in Chapter 2, above).

---

1 Paul's phrase for this requirement *as it applies specifically to Gentiles* is τὸ δικαίωμα τοῦ νόμου (cf. Rom. 2.26; 8.4). It is an important insight that this 'requirement' is inextricably related with the Torah given to Moses, and is not a cipher that Paul can fill with content rather arbitrarily. 'For the law of the Jews and the law of the Gentiles is one, although it is manifested to them in different ways' (Bornkamm, 'The Revelation of God's Wrath', p. 60). Bultmann writes that 'under God's demand stand the Gentiles as do the Jews, except that for the former this demand has not taken shape in the Law of the Old Testament'; he translates the phrase ἔργον τοῦ νόμου (2.15) with 'the deed demanded by the Law', in line with the phrase δικαίωμα τοῦ νόμου (*Theology*, p. 261).

3. *The Apostrophe to the Jew in Rom. 2.17–3.20:*
An Indictment?
In contrast to the apostrophe in 2.1ff. , where the character of
indictment was obvious but the specific identity of the accused
could not be determined, in 2.17-29 the Jew is unquestionably
addressed, but the intent of the apostrophe requires investigation. Clearly the questions put to the Jew, invoking the Deca-
logue and the glorious privileges entrusted to the Jew as a
member of the covenant people, strike at the heart of Jewish
identity. But what is the point of these challenging questions?
Commentators generally agree that here Paul indicts the
typical Jew, but the substance of his charge is disputed.

Stanley Stowers finds in 2.17-24 'the picture not just of the
pretentious person but of the pretentious moral and religious
leader and teacher'.

> The 'Jew' here pretends to have a special relationship with
> God. He boasts (καυχᾶσθαι) of his relation to God (2.17).
> Bragging about what one does not truly possess is the chief
> mark of the pretentious person. He also boasts in the law
> while breaking it. This person pretends to have great ethical
> knowledge, knowledge of the law and of God's will. Finally,
> he pretends to be a teacher and moral guide to others,
> although he does not embody what he teaches (19-22).[1]

This describes the rhetorical indictment of the ἀλαζών, the
boastful person, as it appears in the ancient diatribe: but is the
apostrophe in Rom. 2.17-24 such an indictment? Several considerations suggest not. First, none of the privileges enumerated in 2.17-20 are refuted elsewhere in Romans. Indeed, 'the
Jew was summoned to all this by the Old Testament'.[2] Strictly
speaking, then, the Jew cannot rightly be described as
'bragging about what one does not truly possess', for as Paul
affirms, 'to them were entrusted the oracles of God' (τὰ λόγια
τοῦ θεοῦ, 3.2). Nor is Paul's point that the Jew only 'pretends
to have a special relationship with God': for he will go on to
declare that the disobedience of some Jews does not cancel
God's faithfulness to Israel (Rom. 3.3), and that 'to them
belong the sonship, the glory, the covenants, the giving of the

1 Stowers, *Diatribe*, pp. 112-13.
2 Käsemann, *Romans*, p. 69.

Law, the worship, and the promises; to them belong the patriarchs, and of their race, according to the flesh, is the Christ' (9.4-5).

If Paul's recital of the privileges of the Jew (2.17-20) is not clearly ironic, then the burden of any supposed indictment cannot be that the Jew makes false pretenses about God, or the Law, or the privileges accruing to the covenant people, but rather that the Jew betrays God's trust and 'does not fulfill the religious and ethical expectations which the name is supposed to imply'.[1] Indeed, this is the view proposed by most commentators, for whom Käsemann may be quoted as representative: 'The new section passes over to a concrete attack on the Jews. The phrase in 2.3, ὁ κρίνων... καὶ ποιῶν αὐτά, is now established. The claim of the pious Pharisee and his rabbinic leaders is not acknowledged from the Christian standpoint, although it is not treated ironically. Jewish practice is advanced against it'.[2] Paul's indictment is based, then, on pointing out the fact that Jews transgress the Law.[3]

Paul's supposed argument is vulnerable, however, since it relies on what may be recognized as the 'exceptional' case (the Jew who steals, commits adultery, robs temples). Käsemann tacitly admits the problem when he declares that 'an apocalyptic approach is again presenting what may be empirically an exception as representative of the community'; but instead of addressing that problem, he is content to offer the corroboration of the Strack–Billerbeck *Kommentar* for the veracity of the 'exceptional' case,[4] and to affirm that 'the Jew is in truth

1 Stowers, *Diatribe*, p. 113.
2 Käsemann, *Romans*, pp. 68-69.
3 The Jew's 'boasting in God (2.17) and in the law (2.23) is empirically contradicted by his immoral behavior and the public transgression of the law (2.23-24)' (Beker, *Paul the Apostle*, p. 82). Similarly Bultmann (*Theology*, I, p. 263) summarizes the argument of Rom. 1.18–2.29: 'The reason why man under the Law does not achieve "rightwising" and life is that he is a transgressor of the Law, that he is guilty before God'.
4 *Romans*, p. 71. To illustrate Jewish thievery, Billerbeck adduces the Talmudic discussion of 'die Beraubung eines Goi' (*b. Baba Kamma* 113). In contrast, Urbach ('Self-Isolation', pp. 283-84) shows that the passage illustrates a sustained effort on the part of Yavnean sages to go beyond Pentateuchal halakah 'towards a more open and

a transgressor of the law to which he appeals, and dishonors the divine name thereby'.

Other interpreters are more troubled by the wholesale generalization implied here. E.P. Sanders declares that Paul's argument here 'is not convincing: it is internally inconsistent and it rests on gross exaggeration'.[1] Charles Cosgrove concurs that 'if the apostle endeavors here to establish the liability of Jews universally to divine judgment, his argument falls short of conviction'.[2] Heikki Räisänen considers the leap from the questions in Rom. 2.17-24 to the verdict of 3.9 'a blatant non-sequitur': 'Far from being a "sober and absolutely realistic judgment of the world" [Mussner]', Paul's argument is here simply a piece of propagandist denigration. It is somewhat embarrassing to note that it is given pride of place in Paul's argument in Rom. 1-3'.[3] C.K. Barrett similarly poses the question as a crisis regarding the apostle's credibility:

> It is certainly possible to adduce instances of all three [sins], but such instances are beside the point. Paul's argument is lost if he is compelled to rely on comparatively unusual events, and it is simply not true that the average Jewish missionary acted in this way. It was the purity of Jewish ethics (and of Jewish ethical practice as well as Jewish ethical theory) which (together with Jewish monotheism) made the deepest impression on the Gentile world.[4]

It is not evident, however, that Barrett has resolved the question in such a way as to reaffirm the apostle's rhetorical integrity. He writes:

equitable attitude to outsiders', in order to avoid Gentile profanation of the divine Name. Similarly, Billerbeck (*Kommentar*, III, pp. 108-15) illustrates Paul's question about ἱεροσυλεῖν with halakic discussions concerning property from pagan sacred precincts, taken out of context; and tales of individual Jewish peccadillos, or of a sage's distress at sexual desire, are adduced to illustrate, despite the clear restriction of the Sixth Commandment, 'dass aber das Leben auch angesehener Leiter und Lehrer des Volks dieser Strenge vielfach nicht entsprochen hat'.

1 *Paul, the Law, and the Jewish People*, p. 125.
2 'What If Some Have Not Believed? The Occasion and Thrust of Romans 3.1-8', *ZNW* 78 (1987), p. 91.
3 Räisänen, *Paul and the Law*, pp. 100-101.
4 Barrett, *Romans*, p. 56.

> The fact that the actual crimes were occasionally committed
> adds of course some vividness to the argument, and the
> criminals in some sense involved the nation in their guilt;
> but the nation was inwardly guilty already. When theft,
> adultery, and sacrilege are strictly and radically understood,
> there is no man who is not guilty of all three.[1]

Similarly, Cranfield who goes to some length to declare that
'the fact that isolated instances of all these things were to be
found among Jews was, as far as Paul's argument was concerned, beside the point',[2] echoes Barrett's judgment that
'Paul is thinking in terms of a radical understanding of the
law.... Where the full seriousness of the law's requirement is
understood, there it is recognized that all are transgressors'.[3]
But how are the questions in Rom. 2.21-23 phrased in such a
way as to make such a 'radical understanding' obvious to the
hearer? And how could the questions function as an indictment if they require to be taken so 'radically' that they are
meaningless as questions?

The problem is that the apostrophe in 2.17-29 *does not work*
to establish the verdict declared in 3.9. In fact the apostrophe is
better suited to an exhortation to keep the Law. 'Logically
Paul's argument proves no more than that circumcision is of
no avail to a Jew who is guilty of serious transgressions of the
law, and that a true Jew is one who behaves like one (whether
circumcised or not)'.[4] Sanders goes further:

> Paul's conclusion [in 3.9], in fact, comes as something of a
> surprise after reading chapter 2. The conclusion which
> would naturally follow from chapter 2 is 'repent and obey the
> law from the bottom of your heart, so that you will be a true
> Jew'. If God's forbearance is intended to lead to repentance

1 *Ibid.*
2 'Even the extremely dark picture of the state of Jewish morals in the
  decades preceding the destruction of Jerusalem' assembled in
  Billerbeck's *Kommentar* 'scarcely imples, as Paul does, that all contemporary Jews are guilty of the evils which are described. It is
  anyway of course quite certain that there were many Jews in Paul's
  day who were not guilty' of these sins (*Romans*, I, p. 168).
3 *Ibid*, p. 169. Curiously Cranfield proceeds to interpret the question
  'Do you rob temples?' by reference to Billerbeck's discussion of
  halakot relating to pagan temples.
4 Räisänen, *Paul and the Law*, p. 99.

(2.4), and if even some Gentiles are better observers of the law than you Jews (2.14, 27), and if all will be judged on the same basis, heartfelt observance of the Mosaic law (2.13, 28), surely what one should do is to examine one's motives to make sure they are pure, to be sure that observance of the law is not merely external, and to act in such a way as not to bring disgrace on the synagogue... in short to repent and to mend one's ways.

I think that the best way to read 1.18–2.29 is as a synagogue sermon. It is slashing and exaggerated, as many sermons are, but its own natural point is to have its hearers become better Jews on strictly non-Christian Jewish terms, not to lead them to becoming true descendants of Abraham by faith in Christ.[1]

For Sanders and Räisänen alike, this credibility gap—the 'non sequitur' between 2.17-29 and 3.9—stands as evidence that Paul thinks 'backwards' here: he already knows the conclusion he wants to reach in 3.9, and has rashly mustered in its support an argument that cannot do what he wants it to do.[2]

Cosgrove attempts to exonerate Paul of the apparent non sequitur. He rightly shows that Paul's supposed 'trap' laid for the Jew in Romans 2 is an inadequate basis for the verdict of 3.9, since Paul has apparently neglected to close off his intended quarry's most obvious route of escape: to the rhetorical questions of 2.20-23 the Jew of antiquity might easily, and

---

1 Sanders, *Paul, the Law, and the Jewish People*, p. 129.
2 'The rhetorical point, to be sure, is to lend force to the condemnation of the Jews (2.14: even Gentiles are better than you Jews!); nevertheless 2.12-15 and 2.26 do not square well with the conclusion that all are under the power of sin (3.9, 20)... Paul knows what conclusion he wants to draw, and it is the conclusion which is important to him, since universal sinfulness is necessary if Christ is to be the universal savior. This only points out, to be sure, what can be discovered in other ways: Paul did not come to his view of sin and salvation by beginning with an analysis of the human plight' (Sanders, *Paul, the Law, and the Jewish People*, pp. 124-25; this is of course dependent on his much fuller treatment in *Paul and Palestinian Judaism*, pp. 474-511). Similarly Räisänen (*Paul and the Law*, p. 108) declares, 'The explanation must be that Paul is *pushed to develop his argument into a preordained direction*. It can only be the firmness of a preconceived conviction that has prevented Paul from seeing the weakness of his reasoning. He simply *had* to come to the conclusion that the law cannot be fulfilled.'

honestly (if we assume that the ancient Jews believed and practiced what they prayed and wrote), have answered 'No'.[1] Cosgrove insists that 'Paul does not share that interpretation of his thought which imagines that no one can be blameless in the law, as if Torah-faithfulness meant perfection in the ethical sphere, both in deed and thought;'.[2] He goes on to argue that the verdict in 3.9 does not depend solely on an indictment of Jews who *transgress* Torah in 2.17-29; rather that first indictment is supplemented by a second indictment of Jews who *obey* Torah, but without believing in Christ, in 3.1-8.[3] This relieves 2.17-29 of the argumentative burden that Cosgrove, like Sanders and Räisänen, have rightly shown it cannot bear.[4] But Cosgrove's solution is exegetically infeasible, since there is simply nothing in the text in 3.1-8 or before it to justify equating 'the unbelief of some (Jews)' in 3.3 with rejection of the Christian gospel, and rhetorically implausible as well, for as Cosgrove himself admits, 'no Jew unreceptive to the gospel will have granted such a premise'.[5] Where, then, is the persuasive force of the dialogue?

We should pause to clarify the exact nature of the problem under discussion. It is clear enough that in Rom. 2.17ff. Paul turns in an apostrophe to 'the Jew', that is, to the Jew *specifically* and *as such*, and asks penetrating questions about the congruence of the Jew's actions with the Jew's boast in God and in the Law. It is equally clear that in 3.9 Paul comes to declare 'all people, both Jews and Greeks, to be under sin'. The problem is how these two sections of Romans are related to each other. If Paul intends the interrogation in 2.21-24 to demonstrate the verdict in 3.9, then his argument must rest

---

1 If the questions in 2.21-23 are really intended to prepare for the 'verdict' in 3.9, Cosgrove ('What If Some Have Not Believed', p. 91) asks, 'Shall not the Jewish (Christian) objector retort: Do all Jews commit adultery and rob temples? Are all Jews liable to the law's judgment, hence divine wrath (see 1.18; 3.5) on empirical grounds?'
2 Cosgrove, 'What If Some Have Not Believed?', p. 97.
3 'Paul preaches that God's sentence of wrath rests upon the Torah-faithful who spurn his gospel' (*ibid.*).
4 That is, it 'relieves 2.17-24 of having to supply the sole and sufficient preparation for the statement of 3.9 in its focus on the Jews' (*ibid.*, p. 103).
5 *Ibid.*, p. 97.

on the presumption that the Jewish interlocutor would have to answer 'Yes' to his questions; that is, that the Jew, *specifically and as such*, is a transgressor of the Law.[1] It is striking that Paul never makes this implied premise explicit by supplying the Jew interlocutor's answers.[2] Further, subjecting the verdict of 3.9 to empirical verification would seem to be a very vulnerable procedure.[3] Rather than attempting to defend what appears to be strained logic on Paul's part (Barrett) or simply attributing to him a certain enthusiastic short-sightedness (Sanders), it is preferable, in our opinion, to question the *interpreter's* premise that 2.17-24 is posed as the 'proof' of 3.9.

That suggestion frees us to ask whether Paul has had recourse to his apostrophe to 'the Jew' for reasons other than the Jew's supposed self-evident guilt as a transgressor of Torah. In fact the characterization of the Jew (which is so important for understanding the diatribe's argumentative function)[4] centers on the Jew's knowledge of the will of God revealed in Torah (2.17-20); on the Jew's *accountability*, that is (cf. 1.20, 1.32, 2.2), rather than on the Jew's presumed *culpability*. This suggestion explains why Paul does not need to secure a confession from his Jewish 'witness'. His aim is to establish the principle of accountability to God to which the Jew, *as one who knows the Torah*, must unavoidably assent;

---

1 'But the problem remains: it is not Paul's point that some Jews sometimes do such things; he pretends to be speaking of things that are characteristic of "Judaism *as a whole* and of *every* individual Jew without exception in view of the coming judgment" (Räisänen, *Paul and the Law*, p. 100; citing Kuss).

2 Paul knows the technique of *subiectio*, of putting words into the interlocutor's mouth so as to answer one's own questions (see Lausberg, *Handbuch*, I, pp. 381-82), as is evident in Rom. 3.1-9; the technique is not used in 2.21-24, however, where it would (on the reading under examination) be particularly useful.

3 'The syllogism suggested in v. 9 (Jews and Greeks are all under sin) would only follow, if the description given of Jews and Gentiles were empirically and globally true—that is, on the impossible condition that Gentiles and Jews were, without exception, guilty of the vices described' (Räisänen, *Paul and the Law*, p. 99). Our point is not that Paul does not believe what he says in 3.9, but that he has not come to that conclusion 'empirically'.

4 See Stowers, *The Diatribe*, pp. 106-107.

for that purpose it is not necessary to argue that the Jew, *as a Jew*, cannot do what the Torah requires (cf. 2.13).

4. *Circumcision and the Covenant in Rom. 2.25–3.20: The 'Demolition of Jewish Privilege?'*

The relation of 2.17-24 to 3.9 may be clarified by observing the coherence of the intervening verses, 2.25–3.8. Both sections 2.25-29 and 3.1-8 begin with the same question, the 'benefit of circumcision' (περιτομὴ ... ὠφελεῖ ἐὰν νόμον πράσσῃς, 2.25; τίς ἡ ὠφέλεια τῆς περιτομῆς;, 3.1), indicating that they are two parts of one argument aimed at defining and qualifying the benefit of the Jew's covenantal standing. That argument may be summarized: circumcision is of real benefit so long as it is an external sign of 'genuine' circumcision, the 'circumcision of the heart' (2.29); but that real benefit does not compromise God's integrity when the Jew sins (3.3-4), because God remains the righteous judge of the whole world (3.5-6). The covenant signified by circumcision was never a guarantee of divine indulgence of sin.

We have argued in Chapter 2 that this coherent argument makes sense within the context of Romans 1–3, where Paul discusses the *Jew's* accountability within Torah as a paradigm of *universal* accountability to God. Here we wish to show that that interpretation is preferable to breaking 2.25–3.8 into a disqualification of Jewish privilege in 2.25-29 which must then be defended against supposed Jewish objections in 3.1-8.

The view that in Romans 2–3 Paul is out to 'get' the Jew is on no surer footing in 2.25-29, where the preceding interrogation of the Jew yields fruit. Paul's declaration that 'circumcision is of value if you keep the Law' can hardly be read as a denial of circumcision's value: Paul writes περιτομὴ ... ὠφελεῖ ἐὰν νόμον πράσσῃς, not περιτομὴ οὐκ ὠφελεῖ καὶ ἐὰν νόμον πράσσῃς.[1] The 'circumcision of the heart' of which Paul speaks (2.29)—itself a biblical image (Deut. 30.6-8; Jer. 4.4; 9.25-26)—would come to be wielded in later Christian debates with Judaism in a polemic against physical circumcision (see,

---

1 'There is here no renunciation of circumcision, nor any indication that "true" circumcision is optional' (Sanders, *Paul, the Law, and the Jewish People*, p. 117 n. 24).

for example, Justin, *Dialogue* 12.3), but here in Romans 2 Paul
has not gone so far as to say that what is of value is 'spiritual',
not physical circumcision. It is not at all clear that Paul can be
said to 'dismiss circumcision as irrelevant because of circumcision of the heart'.[1] It is in fact just such an interpretation
that Paul refutes in 3.1ff ('What is the advantage of circumcision? Much in every way!').

Fabricating a Jewish *Gegenthese* in which 'circumcision as
such has saving force'[2] is neither fair to the Jewish sources
nor the most natural way to get at Paul's purpose here. It is
entirely correct to say that the Diaspora synagogue never
abandoned the physical rite in favor of its ethical or 'spiritual'
meaning.[3] On the other hand, even when in the Hellenistic
period the Greek contempt for the rite pushed it to the fore-
front of Jewish consciousness,[4] and when Jews like Philo were
compelled to defend the integrity of the physical act against
'allegorists' who would spiritualize it away (cf. *Spec.* 1.304-
306; *Migr.* 92),[5] the significance of circumcision as a symbol of
the whole individual's obedience was not obscured.[6]

---

1 Käsemann, *Romans*, p. 73.
2 *Ibid.*, p. 72, citing Strack–Billerbeck, *Kommentar*, II, pp. 32-40.
3 The exceptional cases, the 'conversion' of Izates and Philo's
   'allegorists', should be taken as just that. John Nolland
   ('Uncircumcised Proselytes?', pp. 173-79) has provided a remarkably
   clear-headed perspective on the whole question.
4 R. Meyer, 'περιτέμνω', *TDNT*, II, pp. 77-79.
5 Peder Borgen ('The Early Church and the Hellenistic Synagogue',
   ST 57 [1983], p. 68) takes pains to exonerate Philo of the implication
   that 'physical circumcision is not necessary'; see also his essay,
   'Paul Preaches Circumcision and Pleases Men', in Hooker and
   Wilson, eds., *Paul and Paulinism*, pp. 37-46. The relevant passage is
   Questions on Exodus 2.2, προσήλυτός ἐστιν οὐχ ὁ [περιτμηθεὶς, under-
   stood] τὰς ἡδονὰς καὶ τὰς ἐπιθυμίας καὶ τὰ ἄλλα πάθη τῆς ψυχῆς. The
   qualification is obviously not meant to be exclusive: Philo does not
   mean 'the proselyte is one who does *not* circumcise his flesh', but
   rather, 'the proselyte is a proselyte not because of external circumcision but because of the metaphorical circumcision of the passions
   of which the external act is a sign'.
6 It is simply a tendentious reading of the sources (though alas not an
   uncommon one) to conclude that in the Tannaitic period 'the purely
   physical understanding of circumcision was exclusively asserted'
   (Meyer, 'περιτέμνω', p. 79).

Paul's introduction of the Torah-observant Gentile as a foil
to the Jew who violates the Law (2.26-27) is certainly harsh
from the Jewish perspective, but does not step definitely outside the bounds of Jewish rhetoric.[1] Paul says that being a Jew
is a matter of 'what is hidden', not what is evident; the same is
true of circumcision; but this does not imply that the
(externally) circumcised Jew is not 'really' a Jew. His concern
is to define exactly what it means to be a Jew; to qualify, rather
than to disqualify, the Jew's privilege.

If the statements in Rom. 2.25-29 do not scandalize the Jew,
it is hard to understand how 3.1-8 would have arisen necessarily as the 'objections' or 'protests' of Jews anxious to protect
their salvation-historical privilege against Paul's assault.
There is correspondingly little room to speak of Paul's over-
compensating 'exuberance' in describing the covenantal
privileges;[2] even less to speak of Paul's self-contradictory
'Pharisaism' or 'patriotism'.[3] Cosgrove points out that the
questions in 3.1-8 do not ring true as Jewish 'objections':

> What motivates these questions? Here we encounter perhaps
> the most puzzling feature of the passage. *Prima facie* the
> entire line of argument in 3.1-8 is entirely *unobjectionable*.
> One can scarcely imagine Jewish or Jewish-Christian
> detractors disagreeing with what Paul says here. Everything
> follows as a matter of course, as the use of μὴ in v. 3 and v. 5
> itself suggests. That is to say, given the premises stated,
> none of the 'objections' is *plausible* from 'a Jewish perspec-
> tive'. What Jew will dispute that the ἀπιστία of some, even
> the majority, of God's people calls into question God's own
> faithfulness (v. 3)? What Jew will contest God's justice in
> bringing down wrath upon the unrighteous (v. 5)? What Jew
> will take issue with Paul's own dismissal of the *non sequitur*
> in v. 7 and the antinomian inference in v. 8?

1 Sanders (*Paul, the Law, and the Jewish People*, pp. 129-30) finds 'no
  evidence that at any point in Romans 2 does Paul step outside the
  Jewish perspective', although he acknowledges that some of Paul's
  statements are without strong parallels in Jewish literature.
2 'In view of the radical demolition of Jewish privileges in what
  precedes, the exuberance [of the phrase πολὺ κατὰ πάντα τρόπον] is
  astounding unless one sees that the problem of chs. 9-11 is already
  in view' (Käsemann, *Romans*, p. 78).
3 Dodd, *Romans*, p. 43.

> It comes as no surprise, then, that interpreters have read into the passage the idea of 'justification by faith' in order to lend it a certain *offensiveness*... [But] Paul inquires in v. 5 not whether God is unjust to justify the unrighteous, but, assuming an obvious negative answer, whether God is unjust to inflict wrath upon them.[1]

Cosgrove concludes that the objections raised in 3.1-8 do not make sense as *Jewish* objections. To question whether God is right to exercise wrath against unrighteousness (3.5, 7) makes no sense from the Jewish perspective: '*that* God has the right to try and sentence his people when they are disobedient Paul's Jewish (Christian) detractor will not have disputed'.[2]

We hasten to add that the same incongruity applies with regard to Rom. 2: if the apostrophe to the Jew can do no more *intrinsically* than to exhort the Jew to greater faithfulness to the Torah, then it seems incongruous that Paul should have to face immediately the protest of the Jew that God is unjust to condemn human rebellion against the divine will revealed therein.

Cosgrove resolves the implausibility by reading the 'disobedience of some Jews' (ἀπιστία αὐτῶν, 3.3) as the failure of some Jews to believe *in Jesus*. This is hardly more credible, since that equation is nowhere explicit in Rom. 1-3, and certainly is not natural following 3.1-2.[3] But how then are we to understand the incongruity of these questions as 'Jewish objections'?

John Piper and Stanley Stowers have each sought to make the questions in 3.3, 5, 7, and 8 plausible from the Jewish perspective by postulating a Jewish opposition that champions a theology of 'cheap grace for Israel'.[4] It is evident that Paul

---

1 Cosgrove, 'What If Some Have Not Believed?', pp. 94-95.
2 *Ibid.*, p. 96.
3 It is ironic that Cosgrove's solution does just what he protests in Käsemann's commentary. That is, he makes the questions plausible as Jewish 'objections' by supplying an 'objectionable' content that is invisible in the preceding discussion: 'the justification of the impious' for Käsemann, 'salvation by faith in Christ alone' for Cosgrove.
4 Stowers, 'Paul's Dialogue with a Fellow Jew', p. 717; Piper ('The Righteousness of God in Romans 3.1-8', p. 10) concludes that 'Paul's opponents construed the righteousness of God in Rom. 3.5 as saving

wants to combat the supposition that God's righteousness could be collapsed into God's mercy, so that God would be 'unjust' or 'unfaithful'—or, to paraphrase, 'acting out of character'—to punish sin or to condemn the sinner (3.6-7). Against Piper and Stowers, however, Jewish parallels for the 'antinomianism' or 'cheap grace' theologies that they discern behind Romans 3 are scarce.[1] Further, the suggestion that Romans 2 should evoke from these supposed Jewish opponents the objection that Paul has not indulged their pseudo-theology remains inexplicable.

These considerations of inherent plausibility and our earlier discussion of formal features in diatribal dialogues flow together toward a new hypothesis: Rom. 3.1-8 is not a digression in which Paul faces Jewish 'objections' to his argument in Romans 2. These verses are rather a continuation of Paul's attempt to circumscribe the real privileges of the Jew in light of the nonnegotiable axiom of God's righteousness. The Jewish interlocutor appears in 3.1-8 not as a heckler who tries to preserve some scrap of exclusive access to God, but as a collaborator and witness who furthers Paul's argument by endorsing the verdict derived from the psalm: 'May God be acknowledged true, though every human being be proved false!' (3.4).

This reading, which has been put forward in greater depth in Chapter 2, not only alleviates the question of plausibility as this has developed out of comparative studies but also clarifies the logic in Romans 2–3. The verdict of universal sinfulness in 3.9 is no longer a summary of Paul's preceding argument,[2] so

and gracious not retributive'. Piper has combatted an interpretation of 'the righteousness of God' as God's saving power alone by transposing that proposition onto the lips of Paul's 'Jewish opponents' in Rom. 3.

1 See Cosgrove, 'What If Some Have Not Believed?', pp. 96-97, nn. 22, 23.

2 The verb προητιασάμεθα itself militates against that judgment, for the compound with προ- and the aorist form alike suggest a pre-established verdict, a 'foregone conclusion', consonant with the testimony already set down in Scripture (καθὼς γέγραπται, 3.9): 'We have known from the outset that all people, Jews and Greeks alike, are under sin'. We should have expected a summarizing statement to be phrased with the perfect (cf. 4.1); and we should have expected it to use a recapitulative marker such as οὖν rather than γάρ.

Romans 2 is relieved of a burden it could not bear. The point of all that precedes is not to establish the empirical *fact* that all are under sin; that is assumed. It is rather to insist that everyone is *accountable* to God for their complicity in sin. No one is exempt from God's righteous judgment. Once we allow the recognition that Paul makes his case from *Israel's* Scriptures (Rom. 3.4, 10-18), and admit the possibility that his Jewish contemporaries might have taken those Scriptures as seriously as he did, the conclusion lies close at hand that Romans 2–3 are written not *against* the Jew but *with* with the Jew, so to speak.

Some of the exegetical decisions made in Chapter 2 enhance this reading of Romans 2–3. By taking προεχόμεθα in 3.9 in its most natural sense as a middle, meaning 'Do we hold up anything as a defense?',[1] we dissolve the tension that otherwise is perceived between 3.1 ('much in every way!') and 3.9 ('not at all!'), since the two verses answer two different questions. Yes, the Jew has a real 'advantage' in the covenant (3.1); No, the Jew does not thereby gain a preemptive claim against God (3.9). By moving a mark of punctuation in 3.19, or rather by *removing* a mark that was inserted as an interpretative aid, we neutralize the incongruity between a catena of Scriptures that originally focused on the sins of Israel's enemies (3.10-18) and a summary statement that appeared to bear especially against the Jew (3.19). What the Law (Scripture) says to those who are 'in the Law' it says, not only with regard to them, but in order to shut *every* mouth and make *all* the word accountable to God. These exegetical decisions have several considerations in their favor. First, they are perfectly natural and unforced readings; there is no attempt, for example, to force an improbable sense out of προεχόμεθα in order to arrive at 'what Paul must have meant'. Second, they clarify the argumentative coherence throughout Romans 1–3: The Jew's standing in Torah (2.17–3.9) is put forward as a paradigm of universal accountability to God (1.18–2.16; 3.10-19). The logical 'grammar' of the larger section is encapsulated in the syntax of 3.19: what is true for the Jew (ὅσα ὁ νόμος λέγει τοῖς ἐν τῷ νόμῳ) is true for the whole world (λαλεῖ, ἵνα πᾶν στόμα

---

1 Bauer, Dahl (see Chapter 2, pp. 132-33 n. 2, 141 n. 1, above).

φραγῇ), that is, that the whole world is under sin (cf. 3.9), for 'through the Law comes the recognition of sin' (3.30). Third, these decisions allow Paul to 'make sense'. He is exonerated of having pressed into service an 'empirical' argument (in 2.17-24) that on any account was tendentious and did not logically support his 'conclusion' in 3.9). Fourth, and of paramount importance for the issue raised in this excursus, these exegetical decisions, and the innovative reading of which they are a part, free the first part of Romans from the onerous implication that Paul's supposed argument against Judaism constitutes a tremendous *petitio principii*. He can declare axiomatically that 'there is none righteous' and that 'all are under sin' before God,[1] *without* having to 'prove' that sinfulness through a contrived calculus of transgression:[2] in this way he can argue on the basis of premises intelligible to the Jew, rather than flouting them.

---

1 The biblical conviction that 'there is no one who has not sinned' (Eccl. 7.20; 1 Kgs 8.46; Ps. 51.5; etc.) was developed in striking form in the piety of the Qumran covenanters: 'There was no righteousness in humanity' (לא אנוש צדקה, 1QH 4.30; cf. 7.17-18; 9.14-15), and more broadly in postbiblical Judaism, where it is in particular *the pious* who cry, 'Righteousness belongs to the Lord our God, but confusion of face to us' (Bar. 1.15, 2.6); 'To whom will you show mercy, O God, if not to those who call upon the Lord? You will cleanse from sins the soul in confessing, in redemption, because shame [αἰσχύνη] is upon us and in our faces concerning all [our sins].... And your mercy is upon those who sin, when they repent' (Ps. Sol. 9.6-7).

2 E.P. Sanders (*Paul and Palestinian Judaism*, pp. 271-312) observes that the Qumran covenanters could acknowledge in prayer the human incapability to please God, the 'weakness' or lack of 'righteousness' that was theirs by reason of their belonging to 'flesh', without compromising the urgency of exhortations to maintain 'rightness of way' by observing the commandments. His point is that 'salvation' within the community did not mean being transferred 'from' the situation of human weakness and inadequacy before God, but meant the forgiveness of transgressions of which the sinner has repented. We wish to emphasize a corollary conclusion: the lack of righteousness before God that is endemic to human beings as creatures in contrast to God is, for Paul as well as for the Qumran covenanters, a theological axiom prior to any calculation of particular violations.

5. The 'Righteousness of God' and 'Boasting in Works' in Rom. 3.20–4.25: Against the Jew?

It would not be unreasonable to describe Rom. 3.20-31 as the fulcrum on which the reading of Romans 1–4 as a 'dialogue' or 'debate with Judaism' pivots. Here Paul contrasts the 'righteousness of God' which is 'now revealed... through Jesus Christ unto all who believe' (3.21-22) to the false possibility of being 'justified out of works of Law' (3.20), an opposition which excludes the possibility of human 'boasting' (3.27), that is, boasting 'before God' (or 'against God', πρὸς θεόν, 4.2). It has appeared self-evident to generations of interpreters that the 'boasting' to which Paul opposes God's righteousness in Christ is none other than the false boast of *the Jew* who hopes to secure a righteousness of his or her own through the performance of 'works of the Law'. We cite Rudolf Bultmann:

> The contrast between Paul and Judaism consists not merely in his assertion of the present reality of righteousness [Rom. 3.21], but also in a much more decisive thesis—the one which concerns the condition to which God's acquitting decision is tied. The Jew takes it for granted that this condition is keeping the Law, the accomplishing of 'works' prescribed by the Law. In direct contrast to this view Paul's thesis runs—to consider its negative aspect first: *'without works of the Law'* ....
>
> What does this antithesis of Paul's to the Jewish view signify?... For the time being one thing is clear about it: *'faith' is the absolute contrary of 'boasting'*. The announcement of the thesis 'by faith, apart from the Law', Rom. 3.21-26, is followed by a question addressed to Paul's Jewish opponent: 'Then what becomes of boasting? It is excluded. On what principle? On the principle of works? No, but on the principle of faith? (Rom. 3.27). 'Boasting (in the Law)' is the fundamental attitude of the Jew, the essence of his sin (Rom. 2.17, 23), and the radical giving up of boasting is faith's attitude.[1]

It can be noticed immediately that Bultmann's interpretation of this passage as Paul's 'antithesis to the Jewish view' relies on some important 'supplements' to the text. First, the 'boasting' that is excluded in 3.27 is taken to be specifically the

1 Bultmann, *Theology*, I, pp. 279, 281.

'boasting (in the Law)' of Paul's 'Jewish opponent'. Second, Bultmann accepts the opposition he has perceived as a realistic assessment of Judaism: 'The Jew takes it for granted that [the condition to which God's acquitting decision is tied] is keeping the Law, the accomplishing of "works"'; boasting 'is the fundamental attitude of the Jew, the essence of his sin'.[1] To ask at this point the questions that are at the heart of this excursus—Is Paul's argument here intelligibly and plausibly a dispute with the Jew, who is to be construed as representative of some *obstacle* to Paul's gospel—requires the determination whether these 'supplements' are necessary for interpretation, or in fact prejudice the interpretation of the passage.

At the risk of distortion that inevitably accompanies broad generalizations, we may summarize recent discussion on these questions under three heads.

(a) Some scholars have continued Bultmann's line of interpretation, locating the antithesis between Paul and Judaism in the opposition of faith to (Jewish) boasting in observance of the Law. Romans 2–3 is seen to set forth a penetrating Christian analysis of life under the Law (Bornkamm, Käsemann, Beker). (The question whether Paul's 'penetrating insight' into Judaism aligns with the evidence of contemporary Jewish literature is usually not a paramount concern.)

(b) Other scholars, agreeing that the point at issue in Romans is the opposition of righteousness through faith to a futile pursuit of righteousness through the Law, have acknowledged that Judaism in Paul's day probably was not accurately or fairly represented in the present language about boasting and righteous

---

1 In the German original: 'Diese Bedingung ist für den Juden selbstverständlich die Erfüllung des Gesetzes, die Leistung von "Werken", die das Gesetz vorschreibt... Das καυχᾶσθαι (ἐν νόμῳ) ist ja die sündige Grundhaltung des Juden... und ihre radikale Preisgabe ist die Haltung des πίστις' (*Theologie des Neuen Testaments*, ed. Otto Merk [9th edn, Tübingen: J.C.B. Mohr (Paul Siebeck), 1984], pp. 280, 281). One searches in vain for the use of the subjunctive in descriptions of 'the Jew'.

ness through the achievement of works. Paul therefore would not have come to this antithesis through
an objective assessment of the Jew's religious attitude,
but only retrospectively, on the basis of what he has
come to believe about the justification offered in
Christ. The relation Bultmann described between the
'analysis of the human plight' and the 'solution' in
Christ are logically reversed in Paul's thought; that
is, Paul proceeds from the *prior* conviction that salvation is available only in Christ to the conclusion that
any other 'soteriology', including in particular salvation through the observance of Law, is unfounded.
The question-begging argumentation of Romans 2–3
hardly shows us Paul's acumen in theological
anthropology; rather it gives us a glimpse of the
apostle's passion as a missionary propagandist eager
to defend the Gentile church (Sanders, Räisänen).

(c)   A third line of interpretation repudiates the view that
Paul's target in Romans is a false Jewish striving to
achieve righteousness. Rather Paul attacks Jewish
exclusivity. The 'boasting' that Paul says is excluded
(Rom. 3.27) is boasting in the privileges that Israel
alone enjoys, as the rhetorical question in 3.29 shows:
'Or is God the God of the Jews alone?' The contrast of
'faith' and 'works of the Law' is not so much aimed as
a polemic against Judaism as it furthers an apology
for the inclusion of Gentiles within God's favor
('righteousness') apart from the Law (Gager, Gaston,
Hays; at some points, Sanders and Räisänen as well).

This range of interpretations is possible in part because Paul
does not give his language more specificity: we do not learn
exactly what *he* thinks constitutes 'justification by works of
the Law', for example; and in part because we cannot with
any degree of certainty supply the content of his terms from
external sources, that is, by discovering what Judaism meant
by 'justification by works of the Law', since Jewish literature
does not use the phrase. As a consequence, it is in this passage
in particular that the problems of intelligibility and plausibility
are acute and interrelated. We cannot determine whether

Paul means to dispute a *Jewish* conviction when he declares that 'no flesh shall be justified through works of the Law' without some indication within the text that Paul intends the phrase to serve as a shorthand reference to Judaism, or without external evidence sufficient to confirm that the phrase would have been recognized by Paul's audience as such a reference even without Paul's explicit cues. If we look to the text for unambiguous cues that Paul is talking about Judaism, i.e., for evidence that his 'debate with Judaism' is *intelligible* at this point, we will be disappointed. If on the other hand we *assume* that this is his purpose, we are nevertheless left with the problem of *plausibility*, or perhaps better, *credibility*: would this characterization *of Judaism* be fair, or is the argument strained because of forces external to it?

We may begin with the phrase in 3.20: 'no flesh shall be justified out of works of the Law'. No one questions that νόμος here means the Mosaic Law, Torah; but what exactly 'works of the Law' are is a more difficult question. 'The commandments which the Law requires' seems a straightforward equivalent, and Jewish parallels can be adduced for understanding the phrase in this way.[1] Since Paul does not polemicize against observing the commandments of Torah except in passages relating directly to how one is 'justified' before God, it seems natural on this view to conclude that in Rom. 3.20 Paul means to repudiate '"works" … considered to be good actions which could be regarded as meritorious', which '*could* be expected to establish a situation of merit' if they could be fulfilled.[2] What is wrong with 'works of the Law' is that they

---

1   See Douglas J. Moo, 'Law', pp. 82-84. Moo identifies only a single exact equivalent to ἔργα νόμου in the מעשי תורה of 4QFlor 1.7 (91); 'Other close linguistic equivalents are מעשיו בתורה, "his works in the law" (1QS 5.21; 6.18), מעשי הצדקה, "works of righteousness" (1QH 1.26; 4.31), "works of the commandments" [*2 Bar.* 57.2: *opera praeceptorum*] and the rabbinic terms מעשים ("works"), which usually implies works of the law, and מצוות ("commandments"), which often designates the concrete results of the fulfilling of the demands of the תורה' (*ibid.*).

2   Moo, *ibid.*, pp. 96, 98, in 'support of the use made of this phrase by the Reformers'.

are (human) *works*.[1] There is nothing wrong with 'works of the Law' in themselves; but one cannot be justified through them, either because they cannot be performed in adequate number to accomplish 'justification', owing to human inability to perform them, or that they are not performed in the proper attitude, but are appropriated by a self-righteous legalism.

On the other hand, the observation that the commandments of the Mosaic Law were never presented as the means by which one may 'justify' oneself (the equivalent phrase 'to be justified from works of the Law' is completely unattested in Jewish literature)[2] has led some interpreters to insist that Paul cannot mean by this phrase to reject obedience to Torah as such. Rather, as Ernst Lohmeyer and (following him) Joseph Tyson have argued, Paul uses the phrase ἔργα νόμου to refer to a 'context of existence', 'the conditions out of which deeds may be accomplished': they are works done 'in service to the Law' (*in Dienst des Gesetzes*).[3] By opposing the right eousness now granted in Jesus Christ to δικαιοῦσθαι ἐξ ἔργων νόμου, then, Paul means to 'repudiate the system [of Judaism], not on account of a human impossibility, but because he believes God has repudiated it'. What is wrong with 'works of the Law' is that they are works *of the Law*, and the 'religious system' centered upon the Law has now been decisively supplanted by the economy of salvation in Christ.

Along this line, J. Christiaan Beker writes:

> Paul does not oppose motivation or intent to doing; he does not blame Judaism for adhering to an alleged externality of 'doing works' rather than researching the inner impulses of the heart, and he does not psychoanalyze the mistaken

1 Calvin (*Romans*, p. 69) appears to endorse this view, writing that 'in order, therefore, to remove more explicitly the power of justification from all works, Paul has used the term [ἔργων νόμου] of those works which have the greatest ability to justify, if any such exist'.

2 So Markus Barth, *Ephesians* (Garden City: Doubleday, 1974), I, p. 245; Snodgrass, 'Justification by Grace', p. 84; Moo, "'Law'". Hebrew parallels sometimes adduced from *1 Enoch* or the Qumran literature are parallel to ποιεῖν νόμου or ἔργα νόμου, but never to δικαιοῦσθαι ἐξ ἔργων νόμου.

3 E. Lohmeyer, *Probleme paulinischer Theologie* (Stuttgart: Kohlhammer, 1954); Joseph Tyson, '"Works of Law" in Galatians', *JBL* 92 (1973), pp. 423-31.

intent of the Jew (cf. Bultmann). Rather, he opposes 'the works of the law' primarily because the system of Judaism has come to an end in the new lordship of Christ. Paul's new allegiance to Christ is the primary reason for his stance toward the law, and it is this new posture that makes him say that works of the law condemn before God. Works of the law are not inherently wrong because they are works; they are primarily wrong because in the new dispensation of Christ they are clearly shown not to have been fulfilled by the Jews.[1]

For Beker, this means not only that 'works of the Law' become an index of one's transgressions or failures to obey the Law; rather the fact that the Jew *tries* to obey the Law shows that the Law's function as 'sin's deceptive instrument' has not been perceived. It is then precisely the Jew's standing under the Law, expressed in the effort to obey God through the Law and in the Jewish 'boasting in the Law' (Rom. 3.27), that blinds the Jew to the hopeless plight of being 'slave to sin'. The 'works of the Law' serve in two opposite roles in Romans 2–3: they are first of all an indication of the Jew's 'nomistic service', that is, the zeal to obey Torah (Lohmeyer), and *also* an index of the Jew's *transgressions* of Torah.[2] On this view, Paul opposes δικαιοῦσθαι ἐξ ἔργων νόμου both because it is attempted obedience to Torah and because it is actual disobedience of Torah.

Still other interpretations of the phrase have been advanced. J.G.D. Dunn approves of Sanders' demonstration that Judaism contemporary with Paul was not marked by 'works-

---

1 Beker, *Paul the Apostle*, p. 246.
2 Beker's treatment (*Paul the Apostle*, pp. 246-47) shows some ambivalence at this point, for he perceives the Jew (in Paul's view) to be at once zealous for keeping the Law *and* a transgressor of the Law: 'Indeed, the law deceives me, for when I hear the imperative and act on it, I discover myself either as a transgressor of the law or as deluded by the law. In other words, the law informs me about my imperative, "Do this and you shall live" (Lev. 18.15; Rom. 10.5), but not about my indicative, "I am carnal, sold under sin" (Rom. 7.14), so that even prior to my attempt at obedience I am already in a state of sin' (p. 246). In this dialectical reading, Rom. 3.20 and 27 are interpreted in terms supplied from Rom. 7. Whether the resulting ambivalence is originally that of the apostle himself remains to be seen.

righteousness', as well as his description of that Judaism under the rubric 'covenantal nomism'. Dunn goes on to argue that it is just this 'covenantal nomism' that Paul attacks under the title 'works of the Law'. According to Dunn, it is just those observances which 'were widely regarded as character-istically and distinctively Jewish', and which the Jews themselves regarded as 'identity markers', 'badges of covenant membership', namely, circumcision, the Sabbath, and *kašrût*, that Paul refers to with the phrase 'works of the Law'.

> The conclusion follows very strongly that when Paul denied the possibility of 'being justified by works of the law' it is precisely this basic Jewish self-understanding which Paul is attacking—the idea that God's acknowledgement of covenant status is bound up with, even dependent upon, observance of these particular regulations—the idea that God's verdict of acquittal hangs to any extent on the individual's having declared his membership of the covenant people by embracing these distinctively Jewish rites.[1]

What Paul opposes, then, is 'covenantal nomism': '... what he denies is that God's justification depends on "covenantal nomism", that God's grace extends only to those who wear the badge of the covenant'. Dunn concludes that Paul is concerned to exclude 'the *racial* not the *ritual* expression of faith; it is *nationalism* which he denies not *activism*'.[2] This interpreta-tion parallels John Gager's view that the phrase ἐξ ἔργων νόμου is 'thus to be seen as a compressed reference to Paul's underlying rejection of the Jewish insistence that Gentiles must still enter the covenant community through obedience to the commandments of Moses'.[3] At issue in 3.20 and 3.27 is 'Jewish boasting', but this does not mean 'that individual Jews sought to establish their own righteousness'; rather it is 'the issue of collective exclusivity for Israel'.[4]

As the above discussion already shows, the interpretation of 3.27, 'boasting is excluded', goes hand in hand with the inter-

---

1 Dunn, 'The New Perspective on Paul', p. 110.
2 *Ibid.*, p. 115.
3 Gager, *Origins*, pp. 250-51.
4 *Ibid.*, pp. 248-49.

pretation of 'works of Law' in 3.20. The 'boasting' of which the
Jew is supposed to be guilty is either the individual's 'sinful
self-reliance', manifested in the desire to secure one's standing
before God through achieving 'works' (Bultmann), or else the
arrogant conviction that salvation is available only within the
confines of the Mosaic covenant (Gager; Dunn). On any
reading, the boasting Paul opposes here is, if not *exclusively*
Jewish, at least *especially* Jewish. That it is related in the
immediate context to 'works of Law', and that Paul's previous
use of the verb καυχᾶσθαι was in his apostrophe to the Jew
(2.17-20), is taken as sufficient proof that Paul here repudiates
a *distinctively* and *characteristically Jewish* failing.

We will not address the important issue of the *plausibility* of
Paul's characterizing Judaism as a 'system of works-righteousness': that task has been performed for us, comprehensively and definitively, in E.P. Sanders' demonstration that
'the kind of religion best characterized as legalistic works-
righteousness' is not predominant in early Jewish literature.[1]
In fact, in our opinion none of the interpretations discussed
above can be properly evaluated before it can be established
exegetically that it is Paul's purpose in Rom. 3.20 and 3.27 to
dispute a *Jewish* conviction. But just that supposition is in
doubt on exegetical grounds, as the following considerations
should show.

It is not clear how readily Paul's audience could have picked
up his supposed intention to repudiate *Jewish* convictions by
declaring that 'through works of the Law shall no flesh be
justified'. To be sure, the reference to the 'Law' would almost
certainly suggest the *Mosaic* Law. But the fuller phrase,
δικαιωθήσεται ἐξ ἔργων νόμου, is not attested outside Paul's

---

1 Sanders, *Paul and Palestinian Judaism*. As Räisänen (*Paul and
   the Law*, p. 168) points out, 'whereas Sanders has been criticized by
   other experts in rabbinics for imposing the pattern of Paul's religious expression on Tannaitic sources, even the harshest critic has
   admitted that the thesis of "covenantal nomism" is a "wholly sound"
   and "self-evident" proposition and in this regard the work is "a complete success"' [J. Neusner, 'Comparing Judaisms', pp. 177, 180].
   That is: regardless of how other aspects of Sanders' work will stand
   the test, with respect to the topics relevant to Paul's treatment of the
   law he has made his point'.

letters as a Jewish formulation. Why should we suppose that it would be understood as one by Paul's readers?

To pursue this question: in 3.20 Paul uses language very similar to that found in Ps. 143.2. Even if his audience did not recognize the partial citation, the 'biblical' language in his statement (πᾶσα σάρξ, δικαιωθήσεται), as well as its similarity to the theme struck through the immediately preceding catena of Scriptures (3.10-18: οὐκ ἔστιν δίκαιος), could well have led an audience to suppose that Paul was again appealing to the witness of Scripture—that is, the Scripture of *Israel*, of the synagogue—to make a point. Especially if we imagine that the 'biblically literate' among the congregations in Rome might have thought of other places in the Scriptures where human beings are urged not to presume upon their own merits before God (e.g., Deuteronomy 9, Psalm 143), we must consider the possibility that Paul's declaration here, ἐξ ἔργων νόμου οὐ δικαιωθήσεται πᾶσα σάρξ ἐνώπιον αὐτοῦ, might have sounded positively consonant with Jewish convictions, might even (to stretch the point) have been heard as a *summary* of Judaism, not as its antithesis.[1]

The breadth of 3.19 ('to shut every mouth, and make all the world accountable to God') belies a restriction of 3.20 to *the*

---

1 Morna Hooker asks whether Sanders' description of Judaism as a religion of 'covenantal nomism' is not much closer to Paul's theology than the contrast at the end of Sanders' *Paul and Palestinian Judaism* implies ('Paul and "Covenantal Nomism"', in Hooker and Wilson, eds., *Paul and Paulinism*, pp. 47-56). She notes that '... just as Palestinian Judaism understood obedience to the Law to be the proper response of Israel to the covenant on Sinai, so Paul assumes that there is an appropriate response for Christians who have experienced God's saving activity in Christ... The demands... are not *the Law*, but they are *the law of Christ* (Gal. 6.2), and they can even be described as a fulfilling of the Law (Rom. 13.8-10)... In many ways, the pattern which Sanders insists is the basis of Palestinian Judaism fits exactly the Pauline pattern of Christian experience: God's saving grace evokes man's answering obedience' (p. 48). On these terms, it appears that what Paul says in Rom 3.20, that 'no flesh shall be justified out of works of the Law', points to the *similarity* between Paul's theology and Palestinian Judaism: neither can be described as a religion of works-righteousness. It is hard to se therefore how the slogan in 3.20 can be taken as a self-evident *repudiation* of Judaism.

Jew: 'all flesh' is excluded from appropriating the 'works of the Law' against God. The close connection between the two clauses in this sentence (διὰ γάρ) suggests that the second clause, 'for through the Law comes the knowledge of sin', is true for 'all flesh' as well (not just for the Jew).[1] This would give external support for the reading of 3.19 advanced above; 'What the Law says to those in the Law, it speaks in order to shut *every* mouth...'

The reasons for considering καύχησις in 3.27 to mean specifically and exclusively *Jewish* boasting are similarly inadequate. To be sure, the Jew was characterized as 'boasting in God' and 'boasting in the Law' in 2.17-20, but while that boast was *qualified* (it provides no exemption from judgment for the transgressor: 2.21-29), it was not *rejected* (3.1: circumcision is of 'much benefit in every way'). To suggest that the Jew's 'boast' can be excluded in 3.27 because the Jew has been accused of violating the Law in 2.21-24 implies that the Jew's 'boast in God' (2.17) was nothing of the sort, but was instead a boast in *one's own ability to keep the Law*; but this interpretation now requires rewriting Paul's letter for him. Further, to tie the 'exclusion of boasting' (3.27) to the Jew by reason of the proximity of 3.29 ('Or is God the God of the Jews alone?'), so as to make 'boasting' equivalent with Jewish exclusivism, implies that 'boasting' is excluded *for the Jew alone*, for only the Jews have lost the presumed privilege of holding the Torah to themselves. The context does not unambiguously exclude this interpretation, but it flies in the face of Paul's theme of divine *impartiality* and *universal* accountability to God's judgment.

The logic of 3.21-26 *between* 3.20 and 3.27 is crucial. If the 'boasting' excluded in 3.27 is exclusively 'boasting *in the Law*', Jewish boasting, then 3.27 would more naturally follow 3.20, where Paul insists that 'no one will be justified through works of the Law'. The latter statement does not depend on what follows in 3.21-26, but derives from the nature of the Law

---

1 We have already adduced Calvin's comment that Paul discusses 'works *of the Law*' as that class of works that should be expected to provide the grounds for self-justification, *if any* such works existed; an argument *a fortiori* is implicit here.

itself, through which comes the knowledge of sin. But the
solemnity with which Paul announces the revelation of God's
righteousness in 3.21 shows that this passage is not an
incidental digression, but the definitive and unambiguous
manifestation of God's integrity against all challenges. We
must therefore reckon with the possibility that 3.21-26 is
necessary before 3.27; Paul's meaning is that the revelation of
God's righteousness *in Christ*, not simply the nature of the
Law as bearing witness to sin (3.20), excludes human
boasting. That must mean an exclusion of *all* boasting, not
only that of the Jew who is under Law.

Paul's underlying concern in 3.21-26 is not to establish a
new basis for salvation, but to announce how the divine
integrity has 'now' been manifested. If all Paul meant to do in
3.20 and 3.27 was to disqualify the possibility of a *Jewish* boast
on the basis of doing the 'works of the Law', then God's
integrity has been safeguarded against the onslaught of the
boastful Jew *alone*: God's righteousness is *not yet* revealed
against 'all' who have sinned and fallen short of the divine
glory (3.23)—only against the Jews. That Paul rejects this
implication is the point of 3.29: God is *not* the God of Jews
alone, but of all creation, and the righteousness revealed in
Christ is God's claim upon all creation, for in that way God,
who is One, 'justifies the circumcised out of faith and the
uncircumcised through faith' (3.30).

The logic through 3.20-31 becomes clear in the light of this
underlying concern with theodicy. God's righteousness has
been revealed now *apart from* Torah, that is, where there
cannot be even the shadow of a suspicion that God's integrity
is compromised by human success or failure in keeping the
commandments. That shadow has hung over the Law from
2.12, and has been dispelled at last in 3.9-20. The point of 3.20
is that *not even* in the Law (where one might mistakenly
expect to find it) is there any ground for boasting against God,
therefore nowhere. To make just that fact unquestionably
evident God has revealed the divine integrity *outside* the Law,
away from that shadow altogether; and this integrity is
revealed against *all* who have fallen short of God's glory, not
only against those who have (or have not) transgressed Torah.
Therefore there can be *no* boasting (3.27); God's demand for

human trust, revealed in the Law (cf. νόμος πίστεως), is not made conditional on the fulfillment of Torah. It never was, for God is God of Jew and Gentile alike, and lays the justifying claim upon circumcised and uncircumcised alike. 'We thus establish the Law'—but more properly, it is *God* who has now in Christ revealed that the Law has always been the Creator's unadulterable claim upon creation.

The question of the scope of the 'boasting' that is excluded in 3.27 relates to the interpretation of Romans 4 as well. Is the example of Abraham brought forward only to corroborate Paul's polemic against a peculiarly *Jewish* boast? In order to read an 'attack on Judaism' out of this midrashic argument, some interpreters have had first to construct a 'Jewish' appropriation of Abraham contrary to Paul's argument here. When Paul has been seen to oppose Jewish works-righteousness, this required assimilating Abraham into that supposed Jewish perspective. Again, Billerbeck's *Kommentar* provided the matériel for that campaign:

> Die These des Apostels ist: Wenn Abraham auf Grund seiner Werke gerecht erfunden wurde, so hat er Ruhm vor den Menschen, aber darum noch nicht bei Gott; denn vor Gottes Urteil genügt kein menschliches Werkverdienst. Aber Abraham hat seine Gerechtigkeit vor Gott auch gar nicht durch seine Werke erlangt, sondern durch seinen Glauben; denn die Schrift sagt: Abraham glaubte Gott, und es wurde ihm als Gerechtigkeit angerechnet. —Die Gegenthese des Rabbinismus würde gelautet haben: Abraham ist ausschliesslich auf Grund seiner Werke für gerecht anerkannt worden, und darum hat er grossen Ruhm nicht bloss bei Menschen, sondern auch bei Gott. Wenn aber die Schrift sagt: Abraham glaubte Gott, und das rechnete er ihm zu Gerechtigkeit an, so ist der Glaube genau so als ein verdienstliches Werk anzusehen wie irgendeine andere Gebotserfüllung. Der Grundsatz, dass der Mensch durch seine Werke Gerechtigkeit vor Gott erlange, wird also durch die Schriftstelle Gen 15.6 gar nicht berührt, geschweige denn aufgehoben.[1]

---

1 Strack–Billerbeck, *Kommentar*, III, p. 186.

This description of a rabbinic *Gegenthese* is widely accepted.[1] It is nevertheless suspect for being less a historical summary than a projection onto Jewish literature of the categories supplied in Romans 4. To attribute to Judaism the views that Abraham was reckoned just, 'ausschliesslich' on the ground of works, is to indulge in a certain amount of exegetical caprice.[2] In Judaism 'faith' or 'faithfulness' (πίστις; אמונה) and 'works' are interchangeable terms for obedience to God.[3] To speak of 'verdienstliche Werke' is to ignore the prominent theme of joyful obedience in ancient Jewish literature—a theme

1 Barrett (*Romans*, p. 87) asserts that 'according to current Jewish interpretation the "faith" spoken of [in Gen 15.6] was not faith in Paul's sense but a meritorious work'. For corroboration Barrett cites 1 Macc. 2.51f. (which refers not to Abraham 'working' but to his being found 'faithful in trial'), then points the reader to Billerbeck. Cranfield (*Romans*, I, p. 227) declares, 'That Abraham was justified on the ground of his works was indeed what Paul's Jewish contemporaries were accustomed to assume'. He adduces Billerbeck, and cites three references from Billerbeck's treatment. Käsemann (*Romans*, p. 107) pronounces the name 'Billerbeck' as corroboration that in rabbinic Judaism, faith, 'e.g. as a monotheistic confession, becomes one work among others', and that for Jewish interpretation circumcision was 'an indispensable presupposition of justification' (p. 114).

2 As mentioned above, Judaism does not know the phrases δικαιωθῆναι ἐξ ἔργων or ἐκ πίστεως; exegesis of Gen. 15.6 keeps to the idiomatic language (Greek and Hebrew) used there. See Gaston, 'Abraham', pp. 42-52; G. Schrenk, 'δίκαιος, κτλ', *TDNT*, II, pp. 212-19; H.W. Heidland, 'λογίζομαι', *TDNT*, III, pp. 284-92. This verdict stands despite tendentious discussions of 'the righteousness of works in later Judaism' (G. Delling, 'ἔργον, κτλ', *TDNT*, II, pp. 645-52) and of 'the basis of the Rabbinic view', i.e., of justification in which 'the amassing of fulfilments, i.e. of merits, is the goal' (Schrenk, 'δίκαιος', p. 197).

3 This is particularly evident in the aggadot concerning Abraham; cf. *Jub.* 17.15-18, 'the Lord was aware that Abraham was faithful in all affliction': *Jub.* 23.10, 'for Abraham was perfect in all of his deeds before the Lord'. Compare 4 Ezra 9.7, 'everyone who will be saved and will be able to escape on account of his works, or on account of the faith by which he has believed....' Only a tendentious retrojection of the Pauline dichotomy allows construing 'working' or 'doing' righteousness in biblical and Jewish literature as a system of works by which 'man can raise himself up and establish his righteousness' (G. Bertram, 'ἔργον', *TDNT*, II, p. 645).

prominently related to Abraham;[1] the characterization of faith as 'wie irgendeine andere Gebotserfüllung' is similarly tendentious.

The anachronism of speaking of a 'rabbinic *Gegenthese*' to Paul shows the underlying agenda that has skewed Jewish literature here, so much so that in fact Billerbeck's statement can be corroborated from none of the Jewish sources adduced, but only by a mirror-reading of Rom. 4.1-2. One may note, for example, the assimilation of most of the Abraham traditions in ancient Judaism to his notion of 'verdienstliche Werke' where he summarizes the midrashim on Gen. 15.6:

> Erwägt man nun, wie in den obigen Zitaten überall der Glaube Abrahams als ein verdienstliches Werk verherrlicht wird, das Lohn nach sich zieht, so wird man der jüdischen Auffassung wohl am meisten gerecht werden, wenn man in den beiden Targumstellen *zakû* nicht mit 'Gerechtigkeit' [d.h.] 'Rechtbeschaffenheit', sondern einfach mit 'Verdienst' übersetzt. Abrahams Glaube wird von Gott als eine verdienstliche Leistung anerkannt, um derentwillen Abraham nicht bloss diese und die zukünftige Welt in Besitz nimmt... sondern die in mannigfacher Weise auch noch seinen fernen Nachkommen zugute kommt. So steht dann der Glaube Abrahams im Sinn der rabbinischen Schriftgelehrsamkeit als ein vollgültiges Zeugnis dafür, dass der Mensch Gottes Urteil für sich gewinnt und vor Gott etwas gilt nur kraft seiner eigenen verdienstlichen Werke.[2]

Over against Billerbeck's obsession with self-justification through works stand those aggadot, which he himself

---

1 On the התורה שמחת or המצוות see Urbach, *Sages*, I, pp. 390-93. In the early aggadot concerning the patriarch (Targums on Genesis; Jubilees; Philo), Abraham is a paradigm of *joyful* obedience, who 'rejoices' at the promise of Gen. 17.17 (Targum Onkelos; Jub. 15.7); when commanded to observe Sukkoth (Jub. 16.21-31); when commanded to perform the יצחק אכדת (Targums Pseudo-Jonathan and Neofiti); the theme is prominent, also in regard to other patriarchs, in *Jubilees*. Valuable, if not comprehensive treatments of aggadot on Abraham may be found in Schürer, *History*, II, pp. 349-50 (and literature there); G. Vermes, *Scripture and Tradition in Judaism*, Studia Post-Biblica 4 (Leiden: Brill, 1961); S. Sandmel, 'Philo's Place in Judaism: A Study of Conceptions of Abraham in Jewish Literature', *HUCA* 25 (1954), pp. 209-37; 26 (1955), pp. 151-332.

2 Strack–Billerbeck, *Kommentar*, III, p. 201.

adduces, according to which Israel was redeemed *bizekût Abraham*, 'because of Abraham' or 'for Abraham's sake'. That Abraham's faithfulness could be considered efficacious for later generations militates against the notion of a 'commercial' works-righteousness. But such aggadot should not be taken to imply that God was compelled to honor Abraham's faithfulness, so to speak, against the divine will.[1] It is therefore particularly striking that exegetes of Rom. 4.1-2 should seize upon the supposed Jewish doctrine of works-righteousness or of achieved merit as the target of Paul's rhetoric. According to this assumption, in 4.4-5 Paul assigns to the Jew the identity of one who 'works for a reward to be given out of obligation', a view that was condemned by some prominent figures in ancient Judaism.[2]

We come closer to understanding the purpose of Romans 4 when we recognize that the question whether Abraham had a 'boast' on account of 'works' (4.2-5) does not attract Paul's attention for its own sake. The question takes up the declaration in 3.27, which is itself a consequence (οὖν) of the revelation of God's righteousness in Christ (3.21-26); correspondingly the question of Abraham's 'boast' occupies center stage just long enough to introduce the more fundamental question whether God's covenant with Abraham, of which 'we' are beneficiaries (4.1), was a matter of constraint or of God's gracious sovereignty. Once it is established (on the basis of Gen. 15.6) that Abraham could not have compelled God's favor by 'working' for it, the possibility that Abraham might have 'worked' or that he might have gained some 'boast' drop from the discussion. From this point on Paul's theme is the insistence that God's sovereignty in forgiving sins is not

---

1 See Sanders' lucid discussion of the phrase, of the relevant aggadot, and of secondary literature in *Paul and Palestinian Judaism*, pp. 87-101.

2 To Antigonus of Socho is attributed the saying in *m. Abot* 1.3: 'Be not like slaves who serve their master in the expectation of receiving a reward; but be like slaves who serve their master in no expectation of receiving a reward; and let the fear of Heaven be upon you'. 'The reflection may be made that man's good deeds do not of themselves lay God under an obligation; God does not *owe* him a recompense for doing his duty' (Moore, *Judaism*, II, p. 90; see in general pp. 89-111).

compromised in the forgiving of sins (4.6-8), or through the covenant signified in circumcision (4.9-12), or by the Law (4.13-15).

The theological 'risk' for Paul is not that God might be compelled to show favor to people in recompense for their fulfilment of the Law, or (on the alternate view of Paul's anti-Jewish polemic) in recognition of their belonging to the covenantal people; but that *once* God had established the precedent of 'justifying' on the basis of works, subsequent transgressions of the Law would compel God to forfeit the promise (4.14). Romans 4 'rescues' the promise to Abraham from shipwreck on the shoals of human disobedience of the Law, by showing that God had never based the covenant on *human* ability to perform the Law's requirements. Rather it had always been a matter of God's gracious power and human reliance on it (4.16).

This argument constitutes by implication a 'rescue' for Israel as well, since the destiny of Abraham's seed is shown to rest not on performance of the Law (for in that case the promise would be forfeit) but with the same trust in God that Abraham showed, for those who bear circumcision as a sign of that faith as well as for those who, though uncircumcised, also share that faith (4.12). In this aspect of Paul's argument we may see an adumbration of chs. 9–11.

It is a mistake to relate Romans 4 narrowly with 3.27-31, as if Abraham were brought forward only to illustrate Paul's polemical thesis against a peculiarly Jewish 'boasting' or against 'works', or as an illustration that Scripture indeed supported such a thesis. When Paul asks whether Abraham is 'our father according to the flesh', he is taking up again the theme in 3.1-8 and 3.21-26 of God's unswerving loyalty to the divine purposes. Again and again that theme has involved affirming God's sovereignty against possible compromise through human sinfulness, either specifically Israel's unfaithfulness (3.2-9), or more broadly 'former sins that were held in suspense' (3.25-26). By showing that the promise to Abraham was not made dependent on Abraham's prior performance, Paul safeguards the promise to Israel and to the Gentiles alike.

At this stage in the letter, the story of God's dealings with Abraham is related even-handedly to those who through their faith have been made Abraham's seed, Jew and Gentile alike. What is the rhetorical weight of this balance? Is it really directed to counter the perceived *imbalance* of Jewish exclusivism? Is Paul merely being 'diplomatic', 'careful' about Israel's covenantal status out of deference to anticipated Jewish attitudes in Rome (or Jerusalem)?

At a later stage in Romans, the question of Abraham's posterity reenters in a context where Israel's apparent failure to show the 'faith of Abraham' is directly in view (9.6-9). As we shall see in Chapter 3, the argumentation throughout Romans 9–11 poses the unassailable faithfulness of God to the promises given to Israel and regarding the Gentiles against the empirical evidence of Israel's 'unbelief', and insists that, God being God, 'all Israel shall be saved'. The theme of Abraham's faith in God's ability to bring life out of death, even out of his own 'dead' body, is at work in Rom. 4.17-22. Here, of course, the nearest context of meaning for Paul's Gentile-Christian audience may be their own being 'brought to life' out of death (cf. 6.21-23). But in the broader sweep of the letter, the life that is now theirs in Christ is not given them as a possession in which they may boast, but is always the gift of the sovereign God who is able also to bring Israel 'to life again' (11.15!). It is not going too far to suggest that Romans 4 lays the groundwork for the discussion in Romans 9–11 by characterizing Abraham's faith as trust in God's ability to 'do what has been promised' (4.21).

Our reading therefore diverges not only from the 'classical' view that in Romans 3–4 Paul opposes the Christian gospel to Jewish works-righteousness, but also from the more recent view that Paul's purpose in these chapters is primarily to establish and defend the theological legitimacy of the Law-free mission to the Gentiles. The particularity of our view may be brought out in contrast to a paragraph in which John Gager summarizes the argument of Romans 3–4:

> As a final note to Romans 3–4, it is worth emphasizing that the underlying structure of Paul's argument throughout presupposes Israel's election and proceeds through scriptural exegesis to demonstrate that divine election has come finally to include the Gentiles as well. The structure is fully apparent in the series of rhetorical questions that serve as

the backbone of his demonstration: 3.29—'Or is God the God
of Jews only'; 4.9—'Is this blessing pronounced only upon
the circumcised, or also upon the uncircumcised?'; 4.16—
'not only to the adherents of the law, but also to those who
share the faith of Abraham, for he is the father of us all'.[1]

We should prefer to describe the argument in Romans 1–4 in
these terms:

> The underlying structure of Paul's argument throughout
> presupposes Israel's election *and* the salvation of the
> Gentiles through Christ, and proceeds through an apos-
> trophic dialogue with a representative Jew, and through
> scriptural exegesis, to demonstrate that neither Israel's
> election nor the redemption put forward in Christ in any
> way compromise God's righteousness or integrity. The
> structure is fully apparent in the principle of impartiality
> and equal accountability to God, expressed axiomatically in
> 2.6-16 and in the series of rhetorical questions, 3.29, 4.9, 4.16;
> which provides the basis for the analogical argument into
> which the dialogue *with the Jew* is embedded. What is true
> for the Jew is finally true for all human beings, even those
> who stand 'outside the Law': There is no exemption from
> God's claim: what God requires is unconditional trust in the
> divine power to fulfill the promises to Abraham.

The argumentative value of Romans 4 within the letter's
macro-structure, and specifically how Romans 4 functions
between Romans 3 and Romans 5, are questions that must
await the next chapter. It is appropriate here to recapitulate
our findings, however. The underlying exigence of Paul's
argument is a defense of God's unswerving integrity, the
'righteousness of God'. Neither the covenant with Israel
(2.17–3.20) nor the expiation in Christ's blood (3.21-26) compromise God's righteousness: rather they confirm it, for the
covenant never constrained God to tolerate transgression
(2.21–3.9), and the expiation in Christ's blood is God's final
determinative disposition of the sins that previously went
unpunished (3.25-26). But Paul is not content to announce the
revelation of God's righteousness 'apart from the Law' in
Romans 3; he goes on to insist that God showed the same
integrity already with Abraham, so that the destiny of those

1 Gager, *Origins*, p. 220.

who believe, from Israel and the Gentiles alike, should not be jeopardized.

That correspondence holds the key for understanding how the 'dialogue with Judaism' functions within Romans. The courses of Israel and the Gentiles through history have been quite different, and continue to be different (as witnesses also the argument in Romans 9–11); but it is God's unswerving integrity that guides them both and determines them both. Up to now, only God's relation to Israel has been explicit, manifest, open to all to read from (Scriptural) history; in contrast, God's conduct toward the Gentiles has until now been to abandon them to their godlessness (1.18-32), which has meant to hold their rebellion against God 'in suspense', to 'pass over' their sins in temporary silence (3.25). It is the explicit, public character of the covenant with Israel that makes possible the sustained analogy in Romans 1–4. Just as God has related to Israel, so also God relates to the Gentiles as well, for God's judgment is impartial.

What has happened now in Christ (3.21-26) is not only a reversal of the Gentiles' course, but a sharp deflection of Israel's course through history as well, as Romans 9–10 will make clear; but Paul makes it very clear from the first that, for *both* Jew and Gentile, God's righteousness is unconditional and absolute. What has happened in Christ does not change that. In particular, it does not constitute an exoneration of the Gentiles alone while Israel suffers 'shipwreck' on the rocks of the Law.

We have suggested in Chapter 1 that one part of the letter's exigence is Paul's concern to check a Gentile-Christian exultation in the grace shown to them in Christ that shows itself as a 'boast' over their Jewish brothers and sisters, perceived as disbelieving Israel. The preceding paragraphs suggests that the same concern is at work, albeit under the surface, in Romans 1–4 as well. That suggestion cannot be verified until we have examined the rhetorical 'interface' between Romans 1–4 and Romans 6–11 and the argumentation in the rest of the letter body. It is to just such an examination that we now turn.

Chapter 3

THE MODIFICATION OF A RHETORICAL SITUATION
(ARGUMENTATION) IN ROMANS 5–11

We have discussed Victor Furnish's observations regarding
thematic connections between Rom 1.16-32, Romans 6, and
Rom. 12.1-2 as a possible clue to the argumentative macro-
structure of the letter.[1] These connections should warn us
against fragmenting chs. 5–8, 9–11, and 12–15 into discrete
and only tangentially related blocks. They suggest moreover
that the relation between Romans 6 and Romans 12 is more
than mere reiteration. The discussion of baptism in 6.1-13
establishes the possibility of the transformation exhorted in
12.1-2. In Romans 6, then, Paul lays a fulcrum that will allow
him to move his readers from agreement on the christological
premises established at the end of ch. 5 to acceptance of the
paraenesis in chs. 12–15 as the genuine expression of life in
Christ. The connective particle at 6.1, 'What then [οὖν] shall
we say', looking back to the christological formulations in
ch. 5, and the one at 12.1, 'I appeal to you, therefore [οὖν],
through the mercies of God'—that is, God's mercy (ἔλεος) as it
has been described in chs. 9–11; cf. especially 11.32—support
such an interpretation, and encourage us to examine the
argumentative character of chs. 5, 6–8, and 9–11 more
closely.

1. *The Pivotal Significance of Romans 5: Polemical
Christology*
The argumentative coherence of the apostle's rhetoric
throughout the letter has been lost when, as a reflex of systematic theological concerns, Romans 5–8 has been divided

1 See pp. 94ff., above.

into isolated topics on the Christian life, interspersed with a series of precautions, anticipations, and digressions that are not allowed to distract the reader from the letter's presumed dogmatic core. Notwithstanding that observation, Romans 5 has been a large question mark in debates concerning the outline of the letter and the *Mitte* of Paul's theology in general. Does this chapter cohere with the 'forensic' argument in Romans 1–4, corroborating the thesis that 'justification by faith' is the center of the Pauline gospel? Or does it belong with Romans 6–8 in an exposition of the new life in Christ, so that chs. 1–4 may be apocopated as a tactical counter-argument against Judaism and, as such, as a 'subsidiary crater' in the apostle's theology?[1] Related to this question is the broader religion-historical question whether Paul is more at home in the 'judicial' language of Judaism, or in the 'mystical' or 'participationist' language of Hellenistic religiosity.[2]

Our concern is the role of Romans 5 within the letter's argumentative macro-structure. Thematic connections in 5.1-11 with what precedes[3] and in 5.12-21 with what follows[4] indicate that this is a transitional section of the letter. Correspondences on both sides of Romans 5 reinforce the impression: accountability to God's righteous requirement in the Law, 2.1-16, 6.15–8.4; the continuing validity of Israel's covenantal privileges, 2.25–3.8, 9.1–11.36; and the identity of Abraham's children, chs. 4, 9.

In fact, Romans 5 is the pivot on which the letter's argument turns. This chapter channels the force of the opposition generated in chs. 1–4 between divine righteousness and

---

1 See the critical comments by Beker, *Paul the Apostle*, pp. 16-18; Nils Dahl, 'Two Notes on Romans 5', *ST* 5 (1951), pp. 37-48.

2 Beker, *Paul the Apostle*, pp. 67-69; Sanders, *Paul and Pal stinian Judaism*, pp. 447-511.

3 'Justification by faith', 5.1; cf. 1.16-17; 3.21-26; 'boasting', καυχᾶσθαι, 5.2, 3, 11; cf. 2.17; 3.27.

4 The important categories in Rom. 6–8—sin, death, Law, grace—and the central significance of Christ are all very concisely presented here. Dahl ('Missionary Theology', pp. 88-89) has called attention in particular to connections between 5.12-21 and 8.1-39: hope (5.2; 8.20, 24-25), the glory of God to be revealed (5.2; 8.17-21); rejoicing 'in sufferings' (5.3; 8.35-37), the love of God manifested in the giving of Christ (5.5; 8.17, 28-30, 31-32, 35-39).

human boasting into an insistence that Christians boast 'in God' (5.11), specifically in the mode of hope for 'the glory of God' (5.2). The reorientation of christology in 5.12-21 becomes the apocalyptic-theocentric anchor for the extended qualification of the Christian 'boast' in Romans 6–11.

In previous chapters we have argued that the exclusion of boasting in 3.27 involved not only the exclusion of *Jewish* boasting against God, but God's definitive exclusion of *all* human boasting through the atoning sacrifice put forward in Christ. The announcement of the revelation of God's righteousness in Christ (Rom. 3.21-31) and Paul's discussion of the heritage of Abraham's children (4.1-25) applied to those whose sins have been forgiven in Christ (3.25-26) the same verdict to which the Jewish interlocutor assented in 3.9: there is no boast of privilege against God (καύχησις in 3.27, parallel to καύχημα... πρὸς θεόν, 4.2); that is, neither the Jew's possession of Israel's covenantal heritage nor the new status of those who have been redeemed in Christ constitutes a claim of exemption from God's righteous judgment. In this light, Rom. 2.17–3.31 and 4.1-25 appear to be structurally parallel movements from the Jew's corroborative 'testimony' (2.17–3.20; 4.1-22) to the implications for the (Gentile) Christian (3.21; 4.23-25).

In Rom. 5.1-11, Paul brings that extended argument to its conclusion: the Christian's only proper boast is in the gracious saving initiative of the sovereign Lord. The thrice-repeated καυχώμεθα (5.2, 3, 11) shapes the pericope in such a way as to displace an illegitimate boast in one's status in Christ (that is, as one freely forgiven of sins: compare 2.3-4 and 3.25-26), which would be tantamount to a boast against God (3.27), to the proper boast in 'the hope of God's glory' (5.2), which is peace with God (5.1).

Of course the conclusive force of 5.1-11 is greatly enhanced if we accept the textually preferable variant ἔχωμεν at 5.1 and construe καυχώμεθα in 5.2 as a corresponding imperative. The contrary decision is often based on indicatives in the context,[1] as if ἔχομεν were parallel to ἐσχήκαμεν and

---

1 The contrary decision regarding ἔχομεν and the corresponding interpretation of καυχώμεθα is usually made on the basis of 'inter-

ἐστήκαμεν. It appears more likely that the problem of indicative and imperative confronts us already in 5.1, where the Christian's access to God (ἐσχήκαμεν and ἐστήκαμεν) is made the basis of Paul's appeal: 'Let us then be at peace with God'. Reading the passage as an exhortation allows the argumentative coherence in Romans 1–5 to emerge. The exhortation echoes the surrender of a defensive posture before God in 3.9 and the exclusion of human boasting in 3.27. We may bring out this sense in a paraphrase:

> Since, then, we are justified by faith, let us (renounce any counter-claim against God [cf. 3.9] and) be at peace with God... and let us place our boast (neither in our own achievements, nor in a smug reliance that takes divine mercy for indulgence [cf. 3.27]; but) in hope for the glory of God (that is, the coming apocalyptic triumph of God's righteousness).[1]

The apostle pleads for a 'cessation of hostilities' against God, a demobilization of human effort to secure a defense against divine judgment. This surrender is grounded in the divine initiative made 'while we were weak' and impious (5.6), 'sinners' (5.8), 'enemies of God' (5.10). In contrast to any merely devotional contemplation of the breadth of divine love, the stress is on God's sheer undeserved and unilateral initiative. Κατὰ καιρόν (v. 6) points not merely to a particularly advantageous or timely moment, but to God's strategic action 'for the sake of his own name' *just* when no claim of human worthiness could be raised (cf. 3.21-26, χωρὶς νόμου). The sovereign author of this grace, not the good fortune of its recipients alone, is the point (cf. εἰς τὸ εἶναι αὐτὸν δίκαιον, 3.26).[2] The echo of the christological formulations of 3.25-26 in 5.8 places God's love

---

nal evidence' (Metzger, *Textual Commentary*, p. 511; Käsemann, *Romans*, p. 133). On the other hand the reading ἔχωμεν (suggesting that καυχώμεθα be taken as a parallel imperative) has impeccable credentials: Sinaiticus, Vaticanus, and Alexandrinus ($\mathfrak{P}^{46}$ begins at Rom. 5.17).

1 This paraphrase makes sense of the better-attested hortatory subjunctive ἔχωμεν, and there is still no question of 'peace with God as something to be obtained by human endeavor' (Cranfield, *Romans*, I, p. 257 n. 1).

2 See Piper, 'Manifestation of God's Righteousness'.

(5.8) parallel to God's righteousness (3.26) as divine faithfulness to God's own purposes (ἑαυτοῦ in 5.8 has emphatic force).

Two statements *a fortiori* (5.9, 10) relocate the soteriological
fulcrum in the apocalyptic future: the gracious justification
and reconciliation of the impious is made the basis for sure
hope in the salvation to come. These arguments are under-
estimated when they are taken as a figure of speech magnify-
ing the breadth of God's grace to forgive sins,[1] or else as an
assurance to Christians of how secure is their hope.[2] Paul
deliberately distinguishes the justification (from sins) and
reconciliation that Christians have experienced, and the salvation that is awaited in hope, in such a way that the Christians' status as δικαιωθέντες bears witness to that gracious
divine initiative 'while we were yet sinners' that alone is the
ground of hope. The boast of those who are in Christ can *only*
be in the sovereign Lord who will bring to fruition the
reconciliation accomplished in Christ (5.11).

Only when the 'benefits of Christ' have been given their
proper moorings in God's sovereign self-faithfulness (5.1-11)
can Paul formulate this reorientation in a fairly systematic
way (5.12-21). Here, if anywhere in Romans, we can properly
describe the apostle as setting himself deliberately to 'doing
theology', or more precisely 'redoing theology', for his audience.

The section takes shape around his breaking and realign-
ment of typological correlations, which are formed on the
structure 'just as... so also' (ὡς/ὥσπερ... οὕτως).[3] Paul's pur-

---

1 Robin Scroggs (*The Last Adam: A Study in Pauline Anthropology*
  [Philadelphia: Fortress, 1961], p. 81) paraphrases, 'God's act is "how
  much more powerful" than man's'.
2 'The point made is that since God has already done the really difficult thing, that is, justified impious sinners, we may be absolutely
  confident that He will do what is by comparison very easy, namely,
  save from His wrath those who are already righteous in his sight'
  (Cranfield, *Romans*, I, p. 266). Barrett finds in these verses an
  assurance of 'a good hope for the future' (*Romans*, p. 107).
3 The same construction is used in the Adam-Christ typology in 1
  Cor. 15.22, 48, 49, and in the messianic typologies in Jn 3.14 and
  6.58; the structure is used negatively in Jn 6.30-32. On the Johan-
  nine typological constructions see J. Louis Martyn, *History and
  Theology in the Fourth Gospel*, rev. edn (Nashville: Abingdon, 1979),

pose is to extrapolate from the argument up through 5.11 (διὰ τοῦτο, 5.12) a typology of Adam and Christ ('Αδὰμ ὅς ἐστιν τύπος τοῦ μέλλοντος, 5.14). But how is that typology to be understood?

The repeated use of the structure ὡς... οὕτως suggests that Paul is working to supplant an expiatory typology based on the antithesis of sin and forgiveness. The rejected typology might run, 'Just as through one man (Adam) sin entered the world, so also through one man (Christ) sin was forgiven'. It is not accidental that 5.12 begins in the same way—'Just as through one man (Adam) sin entered the world'—but immediately continues quite differently: 'and through sin, death entered, and so death came upon all humanity, since all have sinned'. This is not an anacolouthon. This *would* be an anacolouthon, if Paul had meant to say, 'Just as [ὥσπερ] through man sin came into the world, so also [οὕτως] through one man did forgiveness come into the world....' Against that reading, John Kirby argues that the ὥσπερ/οὕτως syntax in 5.12 is more likely a straightforward structural device as it is in 5.15, 18, 19, 21; 6.4, 19, meaning 'so, also', than an interruption of such a structural device in which οὕτως strangely takes on a new sense.[1] Paul's point is *not* to set Adam and Christ up as opposite representatives of sin, on the one hand, and grace, understood as God's merciful forgiveness of sin, on the other. His point is to declare 'how much more' (πολλῷ μᾶλλον) grace is than the forgiveness of *sins*; it is deliverance from the thrall of *Sin*. The first step in the argument is the declaration in Rom. 5.12, which can be translated: 'Just as through one man [sc. Adam] sin came into the world, and through sin, death, *so too* [sc. through one man, Adam] death came to all men'.[2]

The argumentative force of the Adam-Christ typology is already hinted here. It is not Paul's point simply that the salvation offered in Christ is 'greater' than the sin that entered with Adam (and, incidentally, had fatal consequences). It is

pp. 102-28. Martyn relates the Greek structure ὡς... οὕτως or καθώς ...οὕτως to the rabbinic structure *kî-*... *kak* used in messianic speculation (p. 110).

1 John T. Kirby, 'The Syntax of Romans 5.12: A Rhetorical Approach', *NTS* 33 (1987), pp. 283-86.
2 We have adopted Kirby's translation; 'Syntax', p. 284.

Paul's point that *Death's* leaping through the breach made in creation by Adam's sin is of more consequence than that sin itself, and consequently that the salvation offered in Christ, because it is the overthrow of the thrall of Death, is of more consequence than the forgiveness of sins alone. Paul breaks through a sin-forgiveness typology and supplants it with a deeper death-life typology that comprehends it. Adam's transgression has made necessary not just the countervailing entry of expiation for sin in Christ: it has occasioned the cosmic dominion of Death, calling for the creation of life from the dead in Christ.[1]

This typological reorientation is made explicit in the twin negations of 5.15 and 16: *not* 'as the transgression, so also the grace', and *not* 'as through one sinner, [so also is] the gift'. Both negations are explained by reference to the vicarious-cosmic significance of Adam's sin (cf. εἰς πάντας ἀνθρώπους, 5.12). This means that the divine grace 'in Christ' means much more (πολλῷ μᾶλλον) than release from transgression. The grace 'abounding to many' counteracts the lethal effect 'unto many' of Adam's transgression (5.15). Those receiving the superabundance of grace are no longer under the cosmic dominion of Death occasioned in Adam, but shall reign in life through Christ (5.17). Both of these argumentative subunits, 5.15 and 5.16-17, move by *a fortiori* argument to transcend the strictly judicial-expiatory scheme of sin and forgiveness and to replace it with a more adequate apocalyptic dominion scheme of (moral and cosmic) life and death. They thus carry forward the *a fortiori* argumentation of 5.1-11.

Having negated the inadequate sin-atonement typology, Paul can now (note the logical force of ἄρα οὖν in 5.18) construct in its place an apocalyptic typology in which the cosmic dominion of Death is overcome, and life is created out of death (5.18, 19). Χάρις is not simply the cancelling of transgression (cf. 5.15), but is a cosmic power that deposes Death and

---

1 Rom. 5.13-14 'now appear, not as a digression or interruption, but as the next logical step in his train of thought' (Kirby, 'Syntax', p. 284). Kirby emphasizes that the Adam-Christ typology is *not* 'a one-to-one ratio': 'Paul is at pains, not to balance sin and grace, but to tip the scales decisively in favour of the latter'.

restores 'righteousness', that is, the cosmic 'right' of divine will, and brings to life what was dead.[1]

In broad terms, Rom. 5.12-21 establishes a typology between Adam and Christ, distinguishing the reign of death occasioned by Adam's transgression from the reign of righteousness brought in with Christ's obedience. Paul mentions the Law (νόμος) three times in this chapter (5.13, 20, 21), his primary concern being not to discuss the divine purpose of the Law, but to emphasize that the Law's coming upon the scene did not substantially alter the situation.[2] Death reigned before the Law (5.13, 14); Sin (and Death) reigned after the Law, except that now Sin was marked as transgression (5.20; cf. 3.20; 7.7).

The Law's 'entry' is not derogated, however, as if Paul's point were the impotence of the Law to nullify the power of Sin (cf. 8.3). Rather the Law 'increases the trespass'; it provokes Sin, stirs it up, and by defining it sets a boundary to it, marking it as hostile to God. Through the Law God lays claim to the creation, including the human creature, over whom Sin holds sway. This claim is a condemnation of Sin-as-transgression, but just this condemnation also expresses God's unwillingness to allow Sin to usurp the dominion that is God's

---

1 It bears note that this typological reorientation involves a shift in theological vocabulary: χάρις, χάρισμα, δωρεά, δώρημα are no longer set in opposition to παράπτωμα and ἁμαρτία, but to θάνατος, ἀποθανεῖν, κατάκριμα. 'Sin' (ἁμαρτία) is aligned not with παραβαίνειν/παράπτωμα but with βασιλεύειν. The language of righteousness (δικαιο-) is given a new context as well. Already 3.25-26 shows the collision of meanings: δικαιοῦν no longer means simply 'to forgive sins' (as in δικαιοῦσθαι ἀπὸ τῆς ἁμαρτίας, 6.7), but 'to make righteous' those who have until now been sinners. That is, God's δικαιοσύνη is not just the forgiveness of sins, a merely forensic judgment, but is God's 'right-making power' (Käsemann), manifested in the gracious offering of atonement for sins. So in Rom. 5 'to be made righteous', which might otherwise be taken in 5.9 and 19 in a purely forensic sense, is moved into the apocalyptic antinomy of lethal and life-creating powers (5.17, those who have received 'the gift of δικαιοσύνης' will 'reign in life'; 5.18, εἰς δικαίωσιν ζωῆς).

2 Verses 13-14 only serve to make the point that the absence of law between Adam and Moses did not disturb the basic pattern that death 'reigned because of sin' (Brendan Byrne, 'Living Out the Righteousness of God: The Contribution of Rom. 6.1–8.13 to an Understanding of Paul's Ethical Presuppositions', *CBQ* 43 [1981], p. 561).

alone. In general, it appears to be Paul's intention to shift the weight of the Law's significance away from its function as an index of discrete transgressions (for which expiation is necessary) to its role as God's colors raised in battle against Sin (cf. 7.7-25).

Within the macro-structure of the letter, Romans 5 serves as the pivot, expressly applying the opposition of God's righteousness and human boasting (chs. 1–4) to salvation in Christ in such a way as to disclose the only appropriate human boast as 'hope for the glory of God' (5.1-2). Here Paul's rhetoric comes to bear directly on the immediate constraints of a rhetorical situation that includes Gentile Christians. This christology is argumentative, even polemical; and it bears fruit immediately in the ethical reorientation in Rom. 6.1–8.13.

And yet (we may suppose) Paul could not have begun the letter with Romans 5, before he had laid a foundation for that christology in the righteousness of God. In this light the direct statements of Romans 5 constitute the *propositio* of the letter; being justified out of faith in Christ means being brought into the dominion of righteousness and life by God's free and sovereign grace, and this alone is the ground of the Christian's 'boast'. What precedes may fairly be characterized as an extended and intentionally indirect approach to the subject, an *insinuatio*, made necessary by what Paul may have perceived as a predisposition on the audience's part against his message.[1] In that *insinuatio* Paul is already at work preparing the reader to understanding that God's merciful setting forth of an expiation in Christ in no way compromises God's integrity, as if the blood of Christ could provide the sinner a covering from God's righteous judgment, but instead constitutes the proof, the public manifestation, of that integrity (3.21-26).

---

1 The *insinuatio*, or 'subtle approach', is of use when the cause to be advocated is controversial or discreditable, 'that is, when the subject itself alienates the hearer from us' (*Ad Herennium* 1.9; cf. Cicero, *De Inventione* 1.20).

The extensiveness[1] of the *insinuatio* in Romans 1–4 may be a measure of just how controversial Paul thought his message might be within the context of the Gentile churches with which he was familiar. Beker's comments about Paul's divergence from his Hellenistic Christian environment are provocative. He writes:

> The Antioch church interprets Jesus' death as a sacrificial death, that is, as the forgiveness of the sins that the judgment of the law imposes on a disobedient people. However, Paul radicalizes this confession, because the death of Christ 'for us' (that is, 'for our sins') does not simply mean forgiveness under the law.[2]

Beker argues that in contrast with the Hellenistic Christian κήρυγμα of the Antioch tradition on which Paul relies, the apostle's own interpretation of the death of Christ 'is remarkably apocalyptic':

> The death of Christ now marks the defeat of the apocalyptic power alliance and signals the imminent defeat of death, 'the last enemy' (cf. Rom. 6.7-10; 7.4-6; 8.35-39; 1 Cor. 2.6-8; cf. 15.26). It is therefore an apocalyptic event, and not just an act of sacrificial love that evokes in us a moral sentiment. The author of Colossians interprets Paul correctly on this point: 'He disarmed the principalities and powers and made a public example of them, triumphing over them in him' (Col. 2.15)...
>
> The death of Christ does not refer primarily to the death of an innocent suffering martyr, which evokes remorse and moral cleansing; it does not mean a new moral beginning for the 'old' person, or primarily the forgiveness of his former transgressions so that he can begin again with a clean slate. To the contrary, the death of Christ addresses itself to sin as a cosmic power and slavemaster, that is, to the human condition 'under the power of sin'. It announces the negation of the power of sin that controls the world, and

---

1 The *insinuatio* is considered a form of *exordium*, and our suggestion here is that Rom. 1–4 be considered an extended *exordium* leading to the explicit *propositio* in Rom. 5. To be sure, the more immediately introductory functions are served by 1.1-15, and the thematic introduction of what we have called the underlying exigence is evident already at 1.16-17 and 3.21-27.

2 Beker, *Paul the Apostle*, p. 186.

thus it has not only a moral but also an ontological meaning.[1]

These statements strike at the heart of the argument in Romans; it is not too bold to say that they *are* the argument in Romans. If the exegesis advanced in previous chapters carries conviction, however, we should raise a question about the *direction* of that argument.

Beker opposes Paul's theology to that of the Antioch church, which he assimilates by implication to a Jewish-Christian covenantal theology that proclaims 'a new possibility of obedience under the law'. Instead of this covenantal theology, Paul's theology 'means the termination of the law'. Again, according to Paul's theology, 'Christ died not primarily to enable sins to be forgiven under the Torah but to bring both forgiveness for sins and the end of the Torah'.[2] These statements have much in common with Käsemann's view that in Romans Paul has radicalized a Jewish-Christian theology that celebrates the renewal of Israel's covenant in Christ.[3]

On the other hand, our examination of Paul's rhetoric in previous chapters has suggested that the argumentation in Romans is developed within a communion of meaning that Paul and the Gentile Christians of Rome share. Might Romans involve a theological critique of the Hellenistic Christian κήρυγμα, specifically as this may have been appropriated by *Gentile Christians* who celebrated the forgiveness of sins (cf. 3.21-24) *and* the termination of the Law's validity as aspects of the grace given in Christ (cf. 6.15)? The answer to that question depends on the exegesis of Romans 6–11 in the subsequent sections of this chapter.

2. *Freedom from Law and Obligation to its Requirement:*
Rom. 6.1–8.13
Any segmentation of a text as cohesive as Romans must of course be somewhat provisional and artificial. There are nevertheless formal, thematic, and functional grounds for

1 *Ibid.*, pp. 190-91.
2 *Ibid.*, pp. 186-87.
3 See in particular the treatment of Rom. 3.21-26 in *Romans*, and in his essay, 'Zum Verständnis von Römer 3.24-26'.

identifying Rom. 6.1–8.13 as a rhetorical unit. Although the rhetorical question in 6.1 clearly looks back to what precedes (cf. τί οὖν), the terse christological formulations of Romans 5 have given way now to a discussion of 'the theological basis of the Christian's moral obligation'[1] in 6.1-23, which requires further explication in 7.1-6, 7.7-25, and 8.1-13. The section is bracketed by contrasts in ch. 6 of the old and new life (6.1-13) and of service to sin or to righteousness (6.15-23), and the contrast of life (and obligation) 'according to the flesh' and 'according to the Spirit' (8.1-13). Punctuated with rhetorical questions (6.1-3, 15, 16, 21; 7.1, 7, 13, 24) and dense with logical connectives (γάρ, οὖν, ἄρα, οὖν), this passage is an extensive argumentative progression,[2] the coherence of which is obscured when the passage is broken up into discrete dogmatic topies (e.g., 'freedom from sin', 'freedom from Law', 'freedom from death').[3] The sustained deliberative tone and syllogistic progression evident here were characteristics attributed by the rhetorical handbooks to the figure of conversational reasoning, *ratiocinatio*,[4] which by simulating dialectical reasoning lends to the speaker's handling of a controversial subject the appearance of the self-evident.[5]

1 Cranfield, *Romans*, I, pp. 295-96; similarly Barrett, *Romans*, p. 120.
2 'Paul's method in chapters 5 to 8 is not in each successive section of this division to go back and derive his argument directly from the preceding main division, but rather to lead on from chapter 5 to chapter 6, from chapter 6 to chapter 7, and from chapter 7 to chapter 8' (Cranfield, *Romans*, I, p. 254). For general remarks on 'symboleutische Argumentation' see Klaus Berger, *Form-geschichte*, pp. 93-101.
3 See Anders Nygren, *Romans*, chs. 6–9.
4 Cicero could use the term *ratiocinatio* to describe syllogistic reasoning as such (*De Inventione* 1.57, paraphrased by H.M. Hubbell [Loeb] as '*deduction* or syllogistic reasoning'). The *Rhetorica ad Herennium* uses the term for a rhetorical figure in which 'we ask ourselves the reason for every statement we make, and seek the meaning of each successive affirmation.... This figure is exceedingly well adapted to a conversational style, and both by its stylistic grace and the anticipation of the reasons, holds the hearer's attention' (4.23, 24).
5 Perelman and Olbrechts-Tyteca (*The New Rhetoric*, p. 36) write that 'the importance of dialogue as a philosophical genre' lies 'in the adherence of an individual, no matter who he is, who cannot but be yielding to the evidence of truth because his conviction follows from

The argumentation moves from the rhetorical question in 6.1 ('Shall we continue in sin that grace may abound?') toward the cumulative and definitive answer (cf. ἄρα οὖν) in 8.12-13 ('we are obligated, then, *not* to the flesh, to live according to flesh...'),[1] *through* the discussion of the Law in Romans 7. The simple thematic outline mentioned above— 'freedom from sin, freedom from Law, freedom from death'—fails to recognize how Romans 7 responds to the question raised in 6.14 and given a provisional answer already in 6.15-23, and lays the foundation for 8.1-4. Romans 7 thus forms something of an argumentative apex within chs. 6–8, reflecting the core of the rhetorical exigence within this argumentative unit (see below).

To ask on an abstract level whether the 'indicative' of Romans 5 or the 'imperative' of Romans 6 is primary in Paul's theology is to pose a false dilemma, since 'both indicative and imperative are solidly related to each other. The indicative establishes the imperative and the imperative follows from the indicative with an absolute unconditional necessity'.[2] Nevertheless the question of argumentative *direction* between these two chapters is pertinent.

The rhetorical question in 6.1 is phrased as a possible conclusion (οὖν) that might be drawn from the christological propositions that precede (ch. 5). The question, 'What shall we say then? Are we to continue in sin that grace may abound?', echoes 3.8, 'Why not do evil that good may come?', where

a close confrontation of his thought with that of the speaker'. What the authors say about the privileged status of dialogue as 'a *discussion*, in which the interlocutors search honestly and without bias for the best solution to a controversial problem' and wherein 'the one who gives in should not be beaten in an eristic contest but is supposed to yield to the self-evidence of truth' (p. 37) reveals the strategic value of a figure that *simulates* dialogue and thus imposes adherence with the *apparently* self evident.

1 The anacolouthon in 8.12-14 begins to introduce a new set of themes, or rather reaches back to themes sounded in 5.1-11 (cf. Dahl, 'Missionary Theology', pp. 88-90), that will provide a transition from Paul's discussion of Christian existence in chs. 5–8 to his discussion of Israel in chs. 9–11. This point will be developed below.

2 Günther Bornkamm, 'Baptism and New Life in Paul: Romans 6', *Early Christian Experience*, p. 71.

numerous commentators detect a Jewish objection to Paul's theology of 'freedom from the Law'. But 'Jewish antagonists' are not at all evident in Rom. 6.[1] Paul answers the question on explicitly *Christian* premises: 'How can we who died to sin' (by virtue of baptism into Christ's death) 'still live in it?' Further, the interlocutors addressed in 6.3 are obviously Christians: 'Do you not know that all of us who have been baptized into Christ Jesus were baptized into his death?' The question is *rhetorical* (since Paul is not actually asking whether or not his audience indeed 'knows' something), a figure serving as an appeal to a normative, elite audience, i.e., those who know the full significance of their baptism into Christ,[2] equivalent in sense to an emphatic declaration ('You *ought* to know this...').[3] We need not, however, postulate actual advocates of the position expressed in 6.1 on the scene in Rome or elsewhere on Paul's missionary landscape. This question, like the rhetorical questions in Romans 2, is presented as an obviously false conclusion.

This use of the technique of ridicule and the quasi-logical arguments that follow in 6.2–7.6[4] are designed to consolidate adherence to Paul's christological propositions in 5.12-21 by precluding what might otherwise appear an acceptable alter-

---

1 *Contra* Beker (*Paul the Apostle*, pp. 85-86), who finds in Rom. 6–7 'elaborate replies to Jewish synagogal protests that are aroused by 5.20-21'. Beyond the absence of any direct indication that Jewish protests are in the air in chs. 6–8, it must be objected that Paul's response to such protests as Beker postulates would be rhetorically ineffective. If the Jewish protest were that 'Paul's position [i.e., on the Christian's relation to the Law] is absurd' (*ibid.*), the ensuing answer, grounded on unequivocally christological premises, would hardly remove this obstacle for *Jewish* hearers. Cranfield similarly declares it 'surely clear' that Rom. 6 is 'written to counter the danger of antinomianism in the church' rather than to counter Jewish objections to Paul's gospel (*Romans*, I, p. 297 n. 1).

2 On the rhetorical significance of the question οὐκ οἴδατε; in 1 Corinthians see Wuellner, 'Paul as Pastor', p. 57.

3 Eugene Nida *et al.*, *Style and Discourse, with Special Reference to the Text of the Greek New Testament* (Cape Town: Bible Society, 1983), p. 6.

4 On contradiction, the technique of ridicule, and other quasi-logical arguments, see Perelman and Olbrechts-Tyteca, *The New Rhetoric*, pp. 193-260.

native interpretation of the Christ event, specifically, as an expiatory reality put, so to speak, at the sinner's disposal.[1] If for example the 'grace' offered in Christ (5.15) were *only* proportionate with Adam's transgression, if the 'gift' given in Christ (5.16) merely counterbalanced the sin wrought 'by one man', and was *not* 'much more' (πολλῷ μᾶλλον), then the balanced equivalency of transgression and expiation might yield to the sort of misapprehension that Paul attacks through ridicule in 6.1.[2] In this light, the arguments in 6.1–8.13 may be seen to amplify and corroborate the 'how much more' of 5.12-21.

In Rom. 6.2–7.6 Paul rejects the possibility that those who are in Christ might 'continue to sin' (6.1) by means of three arguments. First (6.1-14a) he appeals to the experience of baptism, which in Christian confession is a 'dying' and 'coming to life' with Christ (6.3-4). Paul establishes by a definition the principle that the death and burial 'with Christ' (συνετάφημεν... αὐτῷ) is a death 'in the likeness of' Christ's death (6.5), so that what is true of Christ's death may be applied transitively to the Christian's participation in that death.[3] So, baptism is a death of the 'old self' (παλαιὸς... ἄνθρωπος), the destruction of the 'body of sin', 'in order that we might no longer do service to sin' (6.6), *because* (γάρ) 'the death [Christ] died, he died to sin' (6.10, RSV). The union with Christ's death corresponds to a union with Christ's resurrec-

1 Bornkamm, 'Baptism and New Lfe', p. 73.
2 It is evident from other passages in the New Testament that belief in the expiatory significance of Christ's death was not immune to the 'libertine' interpretation we have described. The author of 1 John, for example, is compelled to balance the assurance of 3.5 ('You know that he appeared to take away sins': cf. 1.9; 2.1-2) with the assertion that 'No one who abides in him sins' (3.6: cf. 2.5-6; 3.7-10); cf. also Heb. 10.26-31. In light of the antitheses developed in 5.12-21, then, Paul's avoidance of *expiatory* language in Rom. 6–8 becomes understandable.
3 That the passage involves a quasi-logical argument of transitivity (cf. Perelman and Olbrechts-Tyteca, *The New Rhetoric*, pp. 227-31) rather than one of analogy is to be concluded from Bornkamm's observation: 'It already becomes clear that the baptismal event and the Christ-event are not only related to each other in terms of analogy, but are identical with each other. In the baptismal event the Christ-event is present' ('Baptism and New Life', p. 75).

tion, which is identified as release from the dominion of sin. The conviction that 'we shall also live with him (6.8) is justified (εἰδότες ὅτι) by the assertion that 'death no longer has dominion over *him*' (6.9); *he* lives 'to God' (6.10). 'So also *you* consider yourselves dead to sin but alive to God in Christ Jesus' (6.11); 'no longer let sin have dominion' (6.12-13a) but 'present yourselves to God' (6.13b).

The declaration that 'you are not under Law, but under grace' (6.14b) marks a transition to the next section of the argument (6.15-23), being taken up by the rhetorical question in 6.15 ('What then: Shall we sin *because* we are not under Law but under grace?'), and introducing a theme that compels Paul's attention through 8.13. The argumentative coherence of 6.1–8.13 becomes evident once we recognize the problematic relation of Law and grace as one aspect of the letter's rhetorical exigence. The status of Christians as those 'not under Law' threatens the dissociation of sin and life in Christ that Paul has established in 6.1-13. The connection is clarified when interpretation focuses not on the simple opposition of 'Law' and 'grace' as alternative dispensations (cf. 8.2, 4!) but on the peculiar (and from the Jewish standpoint unprecedented) phrases '*under* Law' and '*under* grace' (6.15). The expressions constitute a relationship between two mutually exclusive *spheres of dominion* that comprehensively determine human existence. The realm 'under Law' is the realm in which *sin* (N.B.: not Law) reigns (6.14). It is the opposition of *sin* vs. grace and righteousness that makes the prospect of continued sin in the realm 'not under Law' unacceptable.

That relationship of incompatibility is elaborated in the following verses (6.15–7.6). Existence outside of the sphere of Law (οὐκ ... ὑπὸ νόμον) cannot involve continuing in sin (6.15), *because* such an existence is only possible within the dominion of grace. Paul appeals to the elite audience's knowledge (οὐκ οἴδατε: 'You *should* know') that human existence is inescapably determined by a 'dominion' (6.16). Since the dominions of sin and righteousness are implacably opposed, 'freedom' (ἐλευθερία) from one can only mean 'slavery' (δουλεία) to another.[1] The liaison thus established between 'freedom from sin' and 'slavery to righteousness' (ἐδουλώθητε τῇ δικαιοσύνῃ, 6.18b), corresponding to a liaison between 'slavery to sin' and 'freedom as regards righteousness' (6.20), effectively replaces a purely *'forensic'* understanding of sin as 'transgression' and of existence in Christ as release from penalty with an *apocalyptic* scheme of cosmic spheres of power. Release from the thrall of sin and death is therefore only possible through incorporation into the dominion of righteousness, where 'freedom from sin' means the actual possibility of presenting one's being as the instrument of righteousness.[2] Placing the pericope under the rubric 'freedom from sin' is therefore misleading:[3] in fact the overall effect of the pericope is to *replace* the hierachy of values that prefers 'freedom' to 'slavery' with another that

1 The sequence corresponds to Aristotle's argument from contraries (*Rhetoric* 1397a): Paul must argue that life in Christ is characterized by obligation (δουλεία!) to righteousness, since 'freedom with regard to righteousness' is bondage to sin, which leads to death.

2 See particularly Furnish, *Theology and Ethics*, pp. 143-57, 176-81; Beker, *Paul the Apostle*, pp. 215-16; Käsemann, *Romans*, pp. 171-86. Beker (p. 216) rightly approves Hans Windisch's rephrasing ('Das Problem des paulinischen Imperativs', *ZNW* 23 [1924], pp. 265-81) of the Reformation slogan: *tunc peccator, nunc justus;* see also Byrne, 'Living Out the Righteousness of God', pp. 579-80. Käsemann's protest against Windisch (*Romans*, p. 173) is on target insofar as 'sinlessness' is not to be considered an achievement that might be raised as a counterclaim against God.

3 Käsemann (*Romans*, p. 179) rightly remarks that 'freedom here can only mean 'the determinative relation of Christian obedience vis-à-vis the world. It is presupposed here as elsewhere that a person belongs constitutively to a world and lies under lordship. With baptism a change of lordship has been effected'. But Käsemann fails to realize how fundamental that qualification is to Paul's overall rhetorical purpose, and thus he sunders Rom. 6 from Rom. 7, tying the latter to Rom. 8 under the rubric 'The End of the Law in the Power of the Spirit' (p. 186), and consequently joins other interpreters (especially Nygren) in setting 'freedom from sin' and 'freedom from the Law' beside each other as parallel theologoumena in Paul's dogmatics. In this view the logical subordination of 7.1-6 to 6.15-23 is ignored, and the careful analogical structure of 7.1-6 is obliterated.

contrasts 'slavery *to righteousness*' with 'slavery *to sin*', the first being preferable because 'it pays a better wage' (6.21-23).[1]

Rom. 7.1-6 supports the dissociative argument in 6.15-23 by way of analogy. The broad agreement that this analogy has failed[2] rests on the presupposition that Paul means here to introduce a *new* subject, the Christian's 'death to the Law', as a death *parallel* to the 'death to sin' discussed in Romans 6, and on the consequent effort to align the Torah with the deceased husband in 7.2. But this is not the point of the analogy. Rather we have here a fairly effective explanatory illustration of the preceding discussion of the Christian's death *to sin*, designed to show in what sense the Christian who is 'under grace' can rightly be said to be 'not under Law'.[3] The law relating to marriage determines under what conditions a woman is released from one binding relationship so that she may enter another. It thus serves as an analogy to the Christian's release from the thrall of sin by incorporation into the dominion of righteousness. The common element that sustains the analogy—and that reveals its inseparability from 6.15-23—is the obligatory force of law *in both situations*, an insight missed when Law (Torah) is aligned with the 'dead husband' in 7.1-6.

1 On the so-called 'double hierarchy argument' see Perelman and Olbrechts-Tyteca, *The New Rhetoric*, pp. 337-45. The authors observe that 'the double hierarchy argument makes it possible to base a contested hierarchy', in our case the superiority of obedience to autonomy, 'on an accepted hierarchy', here the superiority of life to death (6.21-23). 'It is therefore most useful', they continue, 'when rules of conduct require justification' (p. 342).

2 So, e.g., Dodd, *Romans*, p. 120 ('gone hopelessly astray'): see Cranfield, *Romans*, I, pp. 333-35, and Joyce A. Little, 'Paul's Use of Analogy: A Structural Analysis of Romans 7.1-6', *CBQ* 46 (1984), pp. 82-90.

3 Sanday and Headlam (*Romans*, p. 172) and Barth (*Church Dogmatics*, II.2, pp. 591-93) consider the passage a tenable allegory once 'the old person' (παλαιὸς ἄνθρωπος) of 6.6 is identified with the 'Former husband'. This rightly interprets Paul's meaning, although Cranfield (*Romans*, I, pp. 334-35) may be right to suggest that the passage is more appropriately taken up as 'a parable rather than as an allegory'; but his judgment that the view put forward by Sanday and Headlam and Barth is 'extremely complicated and forced' (*ibid.*) is unwarranted.

Paul can reject the prospect of continuing to sin 'because we are not under Law but under grace' (6.15), not because Torah has been set aside (cf. 3.31)—nor has the law of marriage ceased to be valid in Paul's analogy—but because a death has sundered the relationship of dominion, to sin in the one case, to the husband in the other, of which law was the obligating force. The binding quality of the divine Law, like that of marriage law in the analogy, remains valid and effectual, but its applicability has changed as a result of the new situation. There is, then, no position of neutral autonomy. The woman is not free to associate herself with one man or another arbitrarily, but is 'bound to her husband by the Law' (7.2).[1] Only by his death is she 'set free' to marry another man, set free, that is, from what continues to be the law's valid judgment regarding adultery (τοῦ μὴ εἶναι αὐτὴν μοιχαλίδα, 7.3). Just so the Christian cannot choose to stand aloof from the opposing dominions of sin or righteousness but must inevitably obey and do service to one or the other (cf. 6.16-20). The Christian has 'died with regard to the Law',[2] not because the Torah is no longer valid, but because the legal obligation to one dominion has ceased through a death (death to sin)[3] and a transfer to another dominion (εἰς τὸ γεγέσθαι ὑμᾶς ἑτέρῳ, 7.4). The two dominions opposed in the analogy are *not* Torah and Christ,[4]

1 τῷ ζῶντι ἀνδρὶ δέδεται νόμῳ. The phrase δέδεται νόμῳ involves a dative of respect, and parallels ὁ νόμος κυριεύει in 7.1 in sense.
2 The construction ἐθανατώθητε τῷ νόμῳ involves a dative of (dis)advantage (Blass–DeBrunner–Funk, pp. 101-102): 'You have died so far as the Law is concerned'.
3 This is evident from a comparison of 7.4 with 6.6, the common term in both being 'that which is achieved through the body of Christ' (7.4): namely, the co-crucifixion of the 'old humanity', the destruction of the body of sin 'so that we might no longer be in thrall to sin' (6.6).
4 Sanders (*Paul, the Law, and the Jewish People*, p. 72) writes to the contrary that in 7.1-6 'the law ... is spoken of as if it were the power opposite Christ'. In part this statement arises from an exegesis of 7.1-6 which Sanders shares with a number of commentators; in part it reflects Sanders' view that in Rom. 5–6 Paul has painted himself into a theological corner by lining up 'Law' and 'sin' on the same side, the side opposed to God and the salvation (righteousness) offered in Christ. Since 'God does not ... "call the shots" within the sphere of sin' (*ibid.*, p. 73), this collusion of sin and Law threatens

but sin-and-flesh and Christ, as 7.5-6 immediately make clear. The Christians' previous existence was ἐν τῇ σαρκί, the sphere in which sinful passions, aroused by the Law's decree, were active in their members; but now Christians have been released from that Law 'because[1] we have died to that in which we were held in thrall', i.e., the dominion of flesh.[2] They are not therefore made free from God's claim: to the contrary, they now may obey that claim by serving God 'in newness of spirit' (7.6). Just as the (marriage) law remains valid in constituting the woman's second marriage as legitimate and not as 'adultery', so, the analogy implies, the sovereign claim established in Torah remains valid (cf. 3.31, νόμον ἱστάνομεν) so as to declare the Christian 'righteous' *within the sphere of Christ's lordship*. So much Paul declares explicitly in 8.1-4: the Law's righteous demand (δικαίωμα) is fulfilled by those who walk by the Spirit (8.4).

the tenet that God gave the Law for a good purpose. Similarly G. Theissen (*Psychological Aspects of Pauline Theology*, trans. John P. Galvin [Philadelphia: Fortress, 1987], p. 179) writes that 'in Romans 5–8, Paul portrays the soteriological change that transposes man from a state of nonsalvation to a state of salvation. In this description, the "law" seems almost to belong to those quantities that stand on the side of nonsalvation'; and Rom. 7 is addressed to refuting that implication. Once it is recognized that Paul's main concern in these chapters is not an exposition of *soteriology* ('how people get righteoused', Sanders), but the category dominant throughout Romans: the 'righteousness' (= integrity) of God, we see that the Law *is* God's 'calling the shots' within the sphere of sin, declaring a verdict upon the rebellious power opposed to divine sovereignty. The Law *remains* God's holy instrument, as it has been throughout Romans.

1 The circumstantial participle ἀποθανόντες has causal sense, equivalent to ὅτι ἀπεθάνομεν (cf. Blass–Debrunner–Funk, pp. 215-16). Byrne's paraphrase, 'Christians are free from the Law and because of this fact are free from sin' ('Living Out the Righteousness of God', p. 565), *reverses* Paul's thought.

2 If [τούτῳ] ἐν ᾧ κατειχόμεθα simply meant the Law, then this participial phrase (ἀποθανόντες) would be superfluous; that meaning could have been expressed more clearly, at any rate, by modifying τοῦ νόμου by a phrase such as τοῦ κατεσχόντος ἡμᾶς. The Law was not the dominion, but God's legal decree *binding* sinners to that dominion (and to its effects, παθήματα, within their members). Thus the passive κατειχόμεθα might be expressed in active voice: ἀποθανόντες [τούτῳ] ἐν ᾧ ὁ νόμος κατεῖχεν ἡμᾶς.

The continuing validity of what we have called the 'binding force of Law', God's discriminative claim upon creation that has come to expression through Torah, is the theme of the 'confession' in 7.7-25. The passage constitutes an 'apology for the Law',[1] shaped on the one hand by the rhetorical questions in 7.6 ('Is the Law sin?') and 7.13 ('Did the good [the Law] become death for me?') and on the other by the crescendo of approval of and consent with the Law from 7.12 ('the Law is holy and the commandment is holy and just and good') to 7.14 ('we know that the Law is spiritual') to 7.16 ('I agree that the Law is good') and 7.22 ('I delight in the law of God in my inmost self').

The interpretation of this passage is burdened with a number of complex problems that we will not attempt to resolve here. Awareness of the rhetorical situation, however— that is, of 'the influence of previous stages of the discussion on the argumentative possibilities open to the speaker'[2]—suggests a productive line of approach. First, the preceding context is concerned with the relation of *Christians* to sin and Law (6.14, 15). The point of the analogical argument in 7.1-6, as we have seen, is the ever-binding force of Law, its character as divine claim, in two aspects: it compels obedience to the 'lord' or 'dominion' one has chosen to serve (7.2, cf. 6.16) and it releases from that compulsion the one who through death has left one dominion 'with the result of becoming obligated to another' (7.3, 6 [δουλεύειν]). That discussion pertains directly to those who as sinners once yielded their members to 'uncleanness and ever greater lawlessness' (ἀνομία: 6.19, 20-21), who, although they were outside the realm of the Mosaic covenant, were nevertheless 'under Law', that is, under God's decree binding them within the thrall of sin (6.16-21; cf. 1.18-32, διὸ παρέδωκεν αὐτούς), but who have 'now' become servants of righteousness through Christ.[3]

---

1 Günther Bornkamm, 'Sin, Law, and Death: An Exegetical Study of Romans 7', *Early Christian Experience*, pp. 87-104; see also Stendahl, *Paul among Jews and Gentiles*, p. 92; Dahl, 'Missionary Theology', p. 84; and Gager, *Origins*, pp. 220-21.

2 Perelman and Olbrechts-Tyteca, *The New Rhetoric*, p. 491.

3 Discussions of Paul's divergence here from Jewish perspectives on Torah are in this light misconceived, since in the present context

The passage describes 'pre-Christian being from a Christian standpoint'.[1] The ἐγώ who speaks is not Paul himself, for as Kümmel has shown, the statement in 7.9, 'I was once alive apart from the Law', would then be unintelligible; further, the contrast between the person who continues to be 'sold under sin' (7.14) and the Christian who is redeemed from sin (Rom. 6) is so stark as to make this 'autobiographical' reading untenable.[2] Salvation-historical correlations[3] are finally less helpful than Käsemann's insight into the paradox of 7.14-25: the 'joyful agreement with the will of God' that is proper only to the 'mind of the Spirit' (cf. 8.7-9) is here attributed 'to the unredeemed'.[4] In fact the ἐγώ represents all those who, while once 'in the flesh', were subjected to 'sinful passions'

Paul's subject is how those who once pursued lives of ἀνομία (cf. 6.14) relate to Law. To appeal to 7.1 ('I speak to those who know Law') as evidence that Paul has shifted to an exclusively Jewish audience is to fragment the argumentative coherence of the passage.

1 Käsemann, *Romans*, p. 192; so W.G. Kümmel in his monograph, *Römer 7 und die Bekehrung des Paulus* (Göttingen: Vandenhoeck & Ruprecht, 1929).

2 Kümmel's insights (*Römer 7*) have been widely accepted. There are occasional voices reviving the autobiographical interpretation: Dunn, for example, sets about to refute Kümmel's conclusions ('Rom. 7.14-25 in the Theology of Paul', *ThZ* 31 [1975], pp. 257-73). But even if the distinction which Dunn tries to draw between 7.1-13, where 'there was no resistance: sin launched its attack, struck him down, and left him for dead with no fight in him', and 7.14-25, where 'we see battle joined', where Paul 'is still defeated, but he is now fighting' (p. 262), were more apparent than it is, we would still have the problem of reconciling these statements with the clear assertions of freedom from sin in Rom. 6.

3 'Methodologically the starting point should be that a story is told in vv. 9-11 and that the event depicted can refer only to Adam... There is nothing in the passage which does not fit Adam, and everything fits Adam alone' (Käsemann, *Romans*, p. 196). Käsemann's exposition proceeds from this sound basis under the more dubious axiom that 'it is to be maintained under all circumstances that the apostle is speaking of mankind under the law, or specifically of the pious Jew' (p. 195). This axiom requires the theory of Paul's rather convoluted appropriation of aggadot concerning Adam, which would have required of Paul's readers even more interpretive acumen than Käsemann requires of his.

4 *Ibid.*, pp. 206-207.

(παθήματα τῶν ἁμαρτιῶν) 'energized by the Law': Rom. 7.8-13 merely amplifies 7.5 through a hypothetical narrative. The ἐγώ brings to speech the perspective of an elite audience, those 'who know Law' (γινώσκουσιν ... νόμον, 7.1), to affirm that 'the Law is spiritual, but I am fleshly, sold under sin' (7.14: note οἴδαμεν γάρ). To confine the scope of this confession to a depiction of the *Jew's* relation to Torah[1] is unnecessarily restrictive; it would then conflict with Paul's own 'robust conscience' as a Pharisee (cf. Phil. 3.6).[2] as with the experience of Paul's Jewish contemporaries.[3] Indeed John Gager has argued that the dilemma described in 7.7-25 was 'uniquely that of the Gentiles. Unlike Jews, they had always been without recourse' to the covenantal relationship established at Sinai, though standing beneath the Law's judgment.[4]

The confessions's rhetorical function, however, does not depend on exact salvation-historical analogue, but consists in the ἐγώ's representative role in expressing a normative perspective on the Law's validity precisely as it exposes and condemns human sinfulness (7.7, 14). This προσωποποιεία brings

---

1 Paul looks 'primarily to people under the Torah ... and Adam is their prototype. This is necessary because Paul wants to depict the work of the Law factually in terms of the recipient of the law and of Jewish piety, and he can exemplify this only through the first recipient of the law' (Käsemann, *Romans*, p. 197).

2 Stendahl, *Paul Among Jews and Gentiles*, pp. 80ff.

3 In fact the only parallel to Paul's 'despair' over the Law to be found in ancient Jewish literature is the 'prophetic' ἐγώ in 4 Ezra (cf. Sanders, *Paul and Palestinian Judaism*, pp. 409-18), and this position is countered by the angelic revealer within the work itself (cf. Räisänen, *Paul and the Law*, pp. 122-24). Käsemann (*Romans*, p. 195) himself admits that 'no Jew experienced the depicted situation of a time without the law and a moment when it came to him'. The resulting tension between his axiom that 'it must be maintained under all circumstances that the apostle is speaking of mankind under the law, or specifically of the pious Jew' and his recognition that this position is only intelligible from *Christian* premises dominates Käsemann's treatment of the passage, revealing the acute need for a deliberately *rhetorical* approach.

4 Gager, *Origins*, p. 222, in accord with Lloyd Gaston's work on the relationship of *Gentiles* to Torah in Jewish thought (*Paul and the Torah*, p. 31, on Rom. 7; and especially chs. 1, 2, and 5 on the status of Gentiles before Torah). On Gaston's hypothesis see above, p. 163 n. 2, and pp. 187-88 n. 6.

to voice the same assent to the divine claim (7.14, 16, 22) that in Rom. 3.4 is put on the lips of the Jewish interlocutor: 'Let God be judged true, though every human being be false', and thus gives expression to that 'submission to God's Law' that is impossible for the sarkic mind (8.7).

By means of this confession, Paul makes it clear that no longer being 'under Law' (6.14, 15) does not mean that the Christian stands aloof from the divine claim expressed in the Law (cf. 8.4). On the contrary, even as one who stands convicted by the Law (7.7, 13), who is thus enabled to recognize the 'law of sin' at work in the bodily members (7.18, 23) and realize the wretchedness of the situation (7.24), that is: as a sinner standing 'under Law', the ἐγώ of 7.7-25 approves of the Law's claim (7.12, 14, 22), acknowledging that the Law's demand is unassailable (7.16; cf. Rom. 3.3-7!).[1] It is sin, not Law, that proves lethal to me (7.13); it is what is 'in me, that is, in my flesh' (7.18) that battles against the Law of God, which I approve (7.23). It is from this rebellious counter-law that I must be saved (7.24).

Rom. 8.1-13 describes the salvation which is 'now' available in Christ as being delivered from the lethal synergism of flesh and Law and being given the 'mind in accord with the Spirit', and thus provides the appropriate conclusion to the argument begun in 6.1. 'There is now no condemnation for those who are in Christ Jesus', *not* because the Christian no longer has any relation to the Law, but precisely because the Christian now *fulfills* the 'righteous requirement of the Law' (δικαίωμα τοῦ νόμου) 'by the power of the Spirit' (8.4). The object of the doxology in 7.25 is shown herein to be not an indulgent God who declares the wrong to be right by a forensic fiat, but the God who has acted in power to redeem men and women from the power of sin at work in the flesh. Christians have been redeemed from the thrall of sin to which the Law bound them

---

1 'Recognizing that the results of his actions do not correspond to his good intentions, the sinner bears testimony to the goodness of the Law—and to his own slavery under sin' (Dahl, 'Missionary Theology', p. 84). 'In Rom. 7 the issue is ... to show how in some sense "I gladly agree with the Law of God as far as my inner man is concerned" (v. 1): or, as in v. 25, "I serve the Law of God"' (Stendahl, *Paul among Jews and Gentiles*, p. 93).

(7.1-6) by being brought into another dominion in which 'the Law of the Spirit of life in Christ Jesus' is in effect (8.2). God's action in Christ does what the Law, impeded by the flesh, could not do: it effectively reverses the moral paralysis described in 7.14-25 so that now 'the just requirement of the Law might be *fulfilled* in us who walk not according to the flesh but according to the Spirit' (8.4).

These verses pick up vocabulary and themes reaching back to Romans 1–3. The Christian is free from divine wrath and condemnation (cf. 1.18; 2.5-6), not (Käsemann) by virtue of a divine mercy that can be conceived as 'separate from its Giver' and that might be presumed upon as a claim against God's righteous judgment (2.3-4), but precisely because in Christ the Christian has been claimed by that God who acts for the sake of the divine righteousness. The Law's righteous requirement is not abolished (3.31: 'Do we then overthrow the Law? By no means!'), but fulfilled in those who live by the Spirit. God's action in Christ is the answer not just to the tortured conscience of 7.14-25, but to the deeper question to which Paul presses his Gentile-Christian audience throughout 6.1–8.13: What can it mean to be 'not under Law but under grace?'[1] Paul's answer is that 'release from the Law' (7.6) can only mean release from the sphere of the flesh in which sin exercizes a lordly influence, corrupting the encounter with God's holy Law so as to inflame the passions toward greater sin (7.5, 7, 8) and bring on the individual the verdict of death (7.10). This, Paul asserts, was the plight of his audience, the Christians of Rome who once 'were in the flesh' (7.5): God's Law stood over them as condemnation, a 'law of sin and death' (7.25; 8.2). Deliverance from the synergism of sin and Law is itself the work of a law, 'the Law of the Spirit of life in Christ Jesus' (8.2), or more precisely, the divine demand for righteousness (δικαίωμα) which when spoken in the sphere of the flesh was subverted by the flesh, but which is now laid afresh on humanity in the sphere of the Spirit, who

1 Byrne ('Living Out the Righteousness of God', p. 564) similarly conceives 6.2–8.13 as an 'integral and necessary element' of Paul's argument, intended to answer the 'ethical question' of 6.1 through a 'skillful vindication of the necessity of obedience in an epoch of grace (freedom from Law)'.

empowers obedience and thus effects the fulfillment of the Law's original and eternal intent, life (8.5ff.; cf. 7.10). 'Freedom from the Law', then, cannot mean autonomy with regard to the demand of righteousness expressed in the Law, for outside of the fulfillment of that demand there is only death (8.6). If it were otherwise, in Paul's perspective, God's righteousness would be annulled; God would not be God.

We may recapitulate the argument up to this point: In Rom. 6.1–8.13 Paul employs argumentative techniques of association and dissociation[1] in such a way as to reconstellate grace, sin, death, and Law for those who are 'in Christ'. The rhetorical question in 6.1 is obviously to be rejected, but it embodies a less tangible and, therefore, a more insidious understanding in which 'sin' and 'grace' are opposed as 'violation' and 'pardon', the magnitude of one being measured by the gravity of the other (ἵνα ἡ χάρις πλεονάσῃ); but neither constituting a radically determinative claim upon human existence. Sin is *not* a merely legal reality applying in the case of infraction (cf. 5.13: 'Sin was in the world before the Law, but is not counted in the absence of Law'), to be reversed by a corresponding forensic fiat. It is rather the means by which death has made a breach in creation to establish its counter-dominion opposed to the sovereignty of God (cf. 5.14, 17), holding sway in the sphere of the flesh and thus determining those who have fallen victim to the moral vulnerability of their corporeality (cf. σῶμα τῆς ἁμαρτίας, 6.6)[2] as 'prisoners of war' ἐν σαρκί and κατὰ σάρκα. Since sin, death, and flesh are linked in this deadly synergism, the Christian cannot escape the power (not only the penalty) of sin except by being removed from the sphere of the flesh, i.e. by 'dying' to it in the death effected through baptism (6.1-13),

---

1 Perelman and Olbrechts-Tyteca (*The New Rhetoric*, p. 190) schematize argumentative techniques into processes of association that 'bring separate elements together and allow us to establish a unity among them, which aims either at organizing them or at evaluating them, positively or negatively, by means of one another', and 'techniques of separation which have the purpose of dissociating, separating, and disuniting elements which are regarded as forming a whole or at least a unified group within some system of thought'.

2 See Beker, *Paul the Apostle*, pp. 286-91.

which is union with Christ's death to the dominion of death (6.9).

The question in 6.14 only develops the *minimization* of the Law's role in this cosmic 'civil war' in 5.13-14 and 5.20. The Law did not generate the power of sin (since sin is not the same as transgression, but a primeval power that comes on the scene *before* Law), but registers it (ἐλλογεῖται, 5.13), provokes it (5.20), forces its manifestation *as sin*, that is, as disobedience and rebellion against God (7.7-8; 13). Once it is recognized that Law is always for Paul God's own sovereign claim upon creation that disposes the rival claim of sin-and-death as a doomed rebellion,[1] then it becomes clear that the question in 6.14 is *already* answered in 6.15-23.

Between these warring dominions there are no pockets of neutral independence, no 'freedom' (ἐλευθερία) from one that is not immediately and necessarily fealty to the other (6.16, 18). This absolute determination of the human situation by the divine claim *is* the Law, which consigns all who serve sin in the realm of the flesh to death (cf. 8.2, τοῦ νόμου τῆς ἁμαρτίας καὶ τοῦ θανάτου) as rebels (cf. 8.7: τὸ φρόνημα τῆς σαρκὸς ἔχθρα εἰς θεόν, τῷ γὰρ νόμῳ τοῦ θεοῦ οὐχ ὑποτάσσεται), but ransoming unto life all those who through Christ are brought into the sphere of the Spirit (νόμος τοῦ πνεύματος τῆς ζωῆς ἐν Χριστῷ Ἰησοῦ), where it is possible to please God (8.8) and the divine Law is fulfilled (8.4), no less a realm of obligation (8.12-13). The illustrative parable in 7.1-6 only makes explicit the material connection of 6.15-23 to 6.14: 'Law' does not function only on one side of the 'sin'–'grace' dichotomy, but rather *constitutes* that dichotomy, from the divine perspective, as the opposition of rebellion against and obedience to God's sovereignty. This polarizing character of Law is explored from the human perspective in 7.7-25.

The argumentation of Rom. 6.1–8.13 effectively substitutes obligation to the δικαίωμα τοῦ νόμου for obligation to νόμος *per se*, that is, to the מצוה of Torah. This substitution reveals an inventional strategy of response to a rhetorical situation in which the validity of Torah is acutely in doubt. Paul never

1 See Karl Barth's penetrating analysis of 'the form of the divine claim', in *Church Dogmatics*, II.2, pp. 583-93.

directly asserts, but rather *presumes* that Gentile Christians are not obligated to observe the מצוה, and can even characterize the Christian who nevertheless does so as 'weak in faith' (14.1-2; 15.1). Yet Paul is concerned to restrain Gentile-Christian freedom *vis-à-vis* Torah so that it is not put into practice in a way that scandalizes the observant (Jewish) Christian (14.13–15.2).

The classical rhetorical handbooks dealt at length with strategy appropriate to cases in which the applicability of specific laws was in question, either because formalized laws did not allow a clear and unequivocal decision in the particular case (the 'legal' issue) or because extenuating considerations weighed against the clear applicability of those laws (the 'juridical' issue).[1] To adopt this distinction, it is clear that Paul does not construe the situation in terms of a *legal* issue. His exhortations do not depend on the citation of מצוה. But neither does he simply rely instead on a value such as 'the good' or 'the just' or 'love', the discernment of which is self-evident and the application of which to the particular situation depends on the commonality of good intentions. That in Romans the righteousness required of those who stand outside of Torah's 'legal' jurisdiction is nevertheless linked again and again to the essence or intent of Torah, as the 'fulfillment of the Law's requirement' (8.4) or of the Law itself (13.8), albeit in 'summary' (ἀνακεφαλαίωσις; cf. πλήρωμα, 13.9-10), shows that Paul cannot relinquish Torah to the status of an ethnic peculiarity.[2] It remains the revelation of the 'will of God' (2.18), for Jews and Gentiles alike, the only question being how, that is, in what manner and by what power, it shall be 'fulfilled' (7.7–8.13). This is because for Paul the validity of Torah's intent coheres with the 'deep exigence' of the letter and of his calling as an apostle, the 'righteousness of God' as God's own integrity and sovereignty, no less than does the continuing validity of the promises spoken to Israel (cf. 3.1-2,

---

1 Aristotle distinguished the legal issue from the issue of 'justice', τὸ ἐπιεικές or τὸ δίκαιον (Rhetoric 1374a). Similarly Cicero distinguished under the 'qualitative issue' (*constitutio generalis*), the 'equitable', *iuridicalis*, and the 'legal', *negotialis* (*De Inventione*, 1.14).
2 See Beker, *Paul the Apostle*, pp. 75, 344.

3. *The Modification of a Rhetorical Situation*   253

9.4-6a). To hold either Torah or Israel in contempt is an affront to the righteousness of God.

The theological cohesion of these two themes, Torah and Israel, is the overarching exigence of the δικαιοσύνη θεοῦ. Their *argumentative* cohesion in the letter to Rome is achieved in 8.14-39. This passage effects a transition from the status of those who 'walk by the Spirit' as the 'children of God' (υἱοὶ θεοῦ, 8.14-17), a status that derives from God's sovereign initiative (8.28-30) and therefore holds firm assurance for the Christian (8.31-39), to a discussion of those to whom the 'sonship of God' is a birthright, Israel (9.1-5). Connections of vocabulary and themes from 8.14-39 to chs. 9–11 show that the latter chapters are not an appendage to the theological 'core' of the letter in chs. 1–8 but represent a climax toward which the preceding argument builds.

3. *The Heritage of the Children of God: Rom. 8.14–11.36*

From the beginning of the letter Paul has emphasized the impartiality of divine judgment *and* the priority of Israel as twin corollaries of God's righteousness.[1] At the outset he declared the gospel to be 'God's saving power for all who believe, the Jew first and also the Gentile' (1.16). Jews and Gentiles alike stand before divine judgment (although the Jew's knowledge of the Law [2.17ff.] means that this judgment is appropriate 'for the Jew first': 2.9-10), 'for there is no impartiality on God's part' (2.11). Jew and Gentile alike are declared to be 'under sin' (3.9), for 'all the world is accountable to God' (3.19). God is the God of Jews and Gentiles alike (3.29), and justifies Jew and Gentile alike ἐκ πίστεως (3.30). David's blessing on those whose sins God forgives is spoken over both Jew and Gentile (4.9). Abraham became the ancestor of all the faithful, Jews and Gentiles together (4.11-12). Indeed, Israel and the nations are inextricably bound up in God's saving purpose, Christ being sent that the promises to the ancestors (of Israel) might be confirmed *and* that the Gentiles might glorify God, 'for the sake of God's truthfulness' (15.7-12).

---

1 See the penetrating discussion by Beker, *Paul the Apostle*, pp. 331-37.

The theme is no less dominant in the discussion of Israel in Romans 9–11. This discussion follows Paul's solemn assurances of God's unwavering love to Christians (8.17-39), in particular Gentile Christian converts (cf. 6.17-19, 7.5), and sets out Israel's fateful course by comparison with the Gentiles (9.24–10.4, 10.19-21, 11.11-12) until it comes to a climax in the solemn warning to Gentiles not to boast over Israel (11.13-36). We should therefore expect *a priori* that more is involved in these chapters than the dialectic of divine predestination and human freedom,[1] or a theodicy that exonerates God in the face of the unbelief of the overwhelming majority of Israel.[2]

The relation of Romans 9–11 to the rest of the letter, and especially to chs. 1–8, remains a vigorously debated question.[3] The abrupt shift from exultation in 8.31-39 to 'great sorrow

---

1 These chapters 'indeed contain statements that raise the issue of predestination and its relation to human responsibility; still, that issue is not Paul's principal concern. Only neglect of the formal composition and of the historical setting has allowed that issue to dominate the discussion of Romans 9-11' (Nils Dahl, 'The Future of Israel', *Studies in Paul*, p. 142).

2 Dahl summarizes a common outline of the chapters that clearly revolves around the exoneration of God ('Future of Israel', pp. 142-43): (1) The failure of Israel is not incompatible with God's promises because in his absolute sovereignty God is free to elect and to reject whomever he wills (Rom. 9); (2) The 'hardening of the hearts' is due to the Jews' own guilt: their lack of faith is at fault (Rom. 10, or 9.30–10.21); (3) The current situation, the Jewish rejection of Christ, will not last forever; at the end, God will show mercy and save all Israel (Rom. 11). It is significant that according to this outline, Paul turns to speak of God's final 'mercy' toward Israel (Rom. 11) only after proving that God's 'righteousness' has been satisfied, despite the unbelief of the vast majority of Israel (chs. 9-10), through the preservation of a remnant, i.e., Jewish Christians (11.2-6).

3 Significant overviews of the issues involved include Dahl, 'The Future of Israel'; Peter Richardson, *Israel in the Apostolic Church* (Cambridge University, 1969), pp. 126-47; W.G. Kümmel, 'Die Probleme von Römer 9-11 in der gegenwärtigen Forschungslage', in *Heilsgeschehen und Geschichte*, II: *Gesammelte Aufsätze 1965-1976* (Marburg: Elwert, 1978), pp. 245-60; Lorenzo De Lorenzi, ed., *Die Israelfrage nach Röm 9–11* (Rome, Hlg. Paulus vor den Mauern, 1977); W.D. Davies, 'Paul and the People of Israel', *NTS* 24 (1977), pp. 4-39; Beker, *Paul and the Apostle*, pp. 63-64, pp. 328-47; most recently Mary Ann Getty, 'Paul and the Salvation of Israel: A Perspective on Romans 9–11', *CBQ* 50 (1988), pp. 456-69.

and unceasing anguish' in 9.1-2 and the introduction of a new theme, Israel's place in God's saving plan, have led some commentators to conclude that the connections between chs. 1–8 and 9–11 is tenuous at best,[1] the later chapters serving as a digression to clean up 'theological difficulties' raised in the preceding,[2] or to indulge the apostle's irrepressible ethnic sentiments.[3] Others holding more positive views of how these chapters relate to the epistolary situation suggest that Paul turns here to defend himself against the accusation that he is a renegade Jew who preaches against the Law and against his people.[4] The proximity to Rom. 5–8 also suggests that God's gracious favor toward Christians, as Paul has discussed this in ch. 8, is imperilled (for Paul, or for his audience, or both) by the perceived failure of God's promises to Israel. So W.D. Davies declares that

1 'Der Neuansatz von Kap. 9 folgt völlig unvermittelt auf den hymnisch-triumphierenden Abschluss von Röm 8. Eine Verbindung oder ein Übergang ist nicht zu erkennen' (U. Luz, *Das Geschichtsverständnis des Paulus* [Munich: Chr. Kaiser, 1968], p. 19).

2 C.H. Dodd considers chs. 9–11 an unnecessary interruption between 8.31-39 and 12.1ff.; the chapters form 'a compact and continuous whole, which can be read quite satisfactorily without reference to the rest of the epistle', and represent 'the kind of sermon that Paul must often have had occasion to deliver, in defining his attitude to what we may call the Jewish question' (*The Epistle of Paul to the Romans*, pp. 148-49). Sanday and Headlam declare that at 8.39 Paul 'has finished his main argument. He has expounded his conception of the Gospel': thus 9–11 were written to address a remaining 'difficulty' that was 'continually being raised by one class of Christians at the time when he wrote' (*Romans*, p. 225), namely, Jewish Christians (cf. Baur, *Paul the Apostle*, I, pp. 308-13).

3 Paul is 'attempting to salvage some remnant of racial privilege for the historic Israel' (F.W. Beare, *St. Paul and His Letters* [Nashville: Abingdon, 1962], p. 97); he 'gives expression to the emotional interest in national hopes which his estrangement from his nation had not destroyed' (Dodd, *Romans*, p. 151).

4 'In Romans... one of the purposes is to refute false rumors that Paul had rejected the Law and his own people. In this letter it is important for him to prove that he is neither an antinomian nor an apostate from Judaism' (Dahl, 'Future of Israel', p. 142; cf. Lietzmann, *An die Römer*, p. 89; Barrett, *Romans*, pp. 175-76; Jervell, 'Paul's Letter to Jerusalem').

the very validity or efficacy of the gospel which he preached was poignantly, even agonizingly, challenged for Paul by the refusal of his own people to accept it... If God who had made the promise to the Jewish people had failed to bring his salvation in Christ to them, what guarantee was there that he would complete the work of the believers' salvation? The failure of the mission to the Jews raised acutely the question of the faithfulness or the reliability of the very God who, Paul had claimed, justified even the ungodly.[1]

Prevalent in these hypotheses is the view that the apostle's main purpose in chs. 9–11 is to explain why the majority of Jews have failed to believe the gospel, without compromising divine impartiality or the righteousness of God that this gospel proclaims.[2] But this 'theodicy' is accomplished in chs. 9 and 10,[3] so that on this view ch. 11 becomes an interesting but nonessential appendage to that argument.[4] So Schmithals regards Romans 9–11 as an appendix ('Nachtrag', 'Anhang') to chs. 1–8,[5] although it does in his view continue to develop the overall theme that 'der Weg zum eschatologischen Heil in Christus ist für [Paulus] in keiner Weise mehr der Weg zum empirischen Judentum', a theme that is 'sein besonderes persönliches Anliegen, die Spitze *seines* Evangeliums'.[6] Schmithals concedes that in ch. 11 Paul does warn Gentiles not to misconstrue 'die faktische Verwerfung der Juden' to

---

1 W.D. Davies, 'Paul and the People of Israel', p. 13. Cranfield (*Romans*, II, pp. 446-47) remarks that at the end of Rom. 8 the need for Paul to discuss Israel's place in the divine economy 'has become urgent, since the very reliability of God's purpose as the ground of Christian hope is called in question by the exclusion of the majority of Jews. If the truth is that God's purpose with Israel has been frustrated, then what sort of a basis for Christian hope is God's purpose?'

2 This view provided the lever with which F.C. Baur (*Paul the Apostle*, pp. 314-17) would have shifted the letter's center of gravity to chs. 9–11.

3 After 10.21, Sanday and Headlam remark, 'Two great steps are passed in the Divine Theodicy' (*Romans*, p. 302).

4 At 11.23, according to Sanday and Headlam (*ibid.*, p. 330), Paul 'turns from the warning to the Gentile Christians, which was to a certain extent incidental, to the main subject of the paragraph, the possibility of the return of the Jews to the Divine Kingdom'.

5 Schmithals, *Römerbrief*, pp. 20-21.

6 *Ibid.*, p. 84.

mean that Gentiles have stepped into the place of the Jews. Nevertheless that warning, like the apostle's defense against the accusation that he denies the election of his people, are only the 'Kehrseite' of the apostle's forceful contention 'dass es keinen Vorzug des empirischen Israel mehr gibt'.

It is our contention, presently to be developed, that epistolary and rhetorical features in Romans 9–11 reveal this section's contact with the constraining exigence of a rhetorical situation; further, that connections in vocabulary and themes *across* the artificial boundary at 9.1 constitute the argumentative integration of Romans 8 and 9, and thereby of the larger segments 1–8 and 9–11; and that the thematic unity of the whole is the hope for the 'glory of the children of God' (8.20-21). This hope precludes a premature boasting in *present* circumstances, because it is founded solely upon 'the depth of the riches and wisdom and knowledge of God', whose judgments are unsearchable, whose ways inscrutable (11.33). The warning against Gentile presumption (11.17-24) is not, in this view, an incidental aside, but is the climax toward which chs. 9 and 10 already build.

'To me', Krister Stendahl announced, 'the climax of Romans is actually chapters 9–11.'[1] This rather impressionistic assertion can be given exegetical substantiation on the basis of Nils Dahl's observations of 'epistolary style' in chs. 9–11.[2] Dahl notices the highly personal address in 9.1, which includes features—the 'oath-like assurance', emotional self-disclosure, and theme of intercession—that are more usually associated with Paul's letter openings. Further, Paul's 'testimony' for his fellow Jews in 10.2 resembles 'a common recommendation', as does the style in 9.4-5. He refers to his audience as 'brethren' as he reveals to them the 'mystery' of 11.25-32; both the address and the disclosure formula are more common in letter openings (cf. 1.13). Gentile Christians, who are deliberately specified as the letter's recipients (cf. 1.6, 13, 14-15), are directly addressed in 11.13; and there Paul discusses his vocation as apostle to the Gentiles (as in the epistolary *exordium* and *peroratio*: 1.1-17; 15.15-33), revealing its

1 Stendahl, *Paul among Jews and Gentiles*, p. 4.
2 Dahl, 'Future of Israel', pp. 139-42.

ultimate purpose to be none other than the salvation of (some) *Jews* (11.14)! Dahl reasonably concludes: 'Attention to such details shows that in Romans 9–11 Paul not only unfolds the theological theme of the letter as a whole, but also addresses the epistolary situation more directly than in most parts of Romans 1–8'. He continues: 'It is only in the light of Romans 9–11 that we are able to understand why Paul had worked so hard for the collection, and why it is so important to him that the Christians in Rome should support him with their inter-cessory prayers'.[1] In accordance with our discussion in Chapter 2 above, Dahl's comment might be modified. It is only in the light of Romans 9–11, particularly as these chapters find their climax in the apocalyptic warning in 11.25ff. that we are able to understand why Paul considers his work for the collections for Jerusalem *and* his pastoral work among his congregations to be justified; why it is so important to him that the Christians in Rome offer each other the mutual regard enjoined in Romans 12–15, and on what basis Paul expects that exhortation to find acceptance.

An important clue to the rhetorical significance of Romans 9–11 is their integration with Romans 6–8. The juncture between chs. 8 and 9 should next attract our attention.

The ethical reorientation of 6.12–8.11 is consolidated (ἄρα οὖν) in 8.12-17, where the negative formulations that were applied to the Christian life in 6.1-11 (death to sin, release from slavery to sin) are replaced by the positive theme of divine 'sonship'.[2] In recapitulation of the arguments of 6.12–8.11, the category of 'freedom from the Law' has now been replaced by 'obligation' to walk by the Spirit, grounded in the stark declaration: 'all else is death' (8.13). It is life in the sphere of the Spirit's power, by which one is enabled to 'put to death

1 *Ibid.*, p. 141. Getty ('Paul and the Salvation of Israel', p. 458) simi-larly emphasizes the importance of Rom. 9–11 for interpreting the letter's purpose, and views 11.25-32 as a key to the meaning of those chapters: the disclosure clause in 11.25 'signals that what [Paul] is about to say is of special importance'.
2 The term 'sonship' is retained here to communicate the valence that υἱοθεσία carried in a patriarchal culture: the υἱός is the heir to the patrimony (in contrast to the 'child', παῖς, who cannot inherit until the period of παιδαγωγία is ended).

the deeds of the body (of flesh)', that constitutes 'sonship' (8.13-17a). But this sonship is not a present possession at the believer's disposal, so that it might provide a καύχημα πρὸς θεόν. It is rather the substance of that eager anticipation and longing which the Spirit inspires.

Indeed, the Spirit's internal testimony creates within the congregation an eschatologically revelatory συμπάθεια with a world that has been subjected to futility and held in the thrall of 'corruption'.[1] By the Spirit, and only by the Spirit, Christians 'suffer with Christ', groaning with the corrupted world in yearning for the glorious consummation of creation, the rightful heritage of God's children (8.17-23); for this is the Spirit's testimony within the congregation, even if it transcends human articulation (8.26-27). As Käsemann and Beker have shown, more is at work here than a pious 'theology of suffering': The apocalyptic coordinates of Paul's gospel are here revealed. We must go further and ask about the rhetorical significance of the 'sonship' theme in its present context.

1 Käsemann's treatment (*Romans*, pp. 229-52) of this pericope, presaged in his essay, 'The Cry for Liberty in the Worship of the Church' (in *New Testament Questions of Today*, trans. W.J. Montague [Philadelphia: Fortress, 1971], pp. 122-37), represents a breakthrough in exegesis. Beker rightly stresses Rom. 8 in his apocalyptic-theocentric reorientation of Pauline theology (*Paul the Apostle*, pp. 135-81, 278-91), declaring the chapter 'the crown of Paul's theological achievement, for here the sighing of the creation is taken up in that of the Christian and in that of the Spirit, as all wait for the glory to be revealed and for the final redemption of the body' (p. 290). The vocabulary of childbearing and travail was the potent and powerful language of theodicy in Jewish apocalyptic literature (cf. Second Isaiah; 4 Ezra 5.46-55 [where the metaphor has already become routinized as a 'steno symbol']; 1QH 3.6-18; cf. the 'birthpangs' of the Synoptic Apocalypse, and the messianic 'salute' from Elizabeth's womb [Lk. 1.41]. Paul plays upon the terrible ambivalence of the metaphor—which after all produced not only the glorious birth of the Messiah, but also stillbirths and monsters as eschatological signs. The creation has been subjected to futility, to the 'dominion of corruption' (δουλείας τῆς φθορᾶς). φθορά, 'corruption' or 'destruction', can also mean 'miscarriage'; and this—so Paul's language implies—would be the result of the cosmic travail were it not for the creative grace of the One who subjected the world to this travail.

The 'sufferings of this present time' are paradoxically related to the identity of God's 'heirs'. The travail imagery of 8.19-23 and the discussion of hope in 8.24-25 make it clear that the 'glory' of God's heirs is not evident in the world now: present circumstances offer not a clue to the identity of God's children ('hope that is seen is not hope, for who hopes for what is seen?'). It is the Lord the Spirit who, by a mysterious and sovereign grace, inspires 'solidarity with the host of those who wait, suffer, and groan,who are not yet redeemed',[1] the hope for 'the redemption of our bodies' (8.23), and for the revelation of the children of God and the liberation of all creation (8.21-22). The deepest longings of human hearts are fathomed by the Spirit who intercedes, within the intimate communion of the divine will (φρόνημα),[2] in the language of heaven.

But while the Spirit may evoke inarticulate utterances within the assembly of those who bear the Spirit, this divine φρόνημα is not beyond human knowledge, for, Paul says, '*we know*' that God is at work to fulfill the divine purpose for redemption (8.28). The congregation of those who bear the Spirit 'know' that God's redemptive purposes (εἰς ἀγαθόν) for the elect are at work 'in all things', even in 'the sufferings of the present time' (8.18), despite 'tribulation, or distress, or persecution, or famine, or nakedness, or peril, or sword' (8.35), despite our 'being killed all the day long' (8.36), despite all the hostile powers of creation (8.38): for God's love in Christ is sure (8.39). What Paul, with the testimony of the Holy Spirit, knows and reveals in chs. 9–11 (note especially the 'apocalyptic' language in 11.25!) is the divine will which only the Spirit can reveal (8.26-27). The inscrutable 'mystery' of God's gracious will (11.33-36) is already anticipated in 8.28ff.: despite present circumstances ('all things', 8.28; cf. Israel's

---

1 Käsemann, *Romans*, p. 242.
2 On φρόνημα as 'aim, aspiration, striving', see the Bauer–Arndt–Gingrich–Danker *Lexicon*. 'The Spirit has a dynamic thrust; its future intent (φρόνημα) is eternal life and eschatological peace (Rom. 8.6). The dynamic energy and movement of the Spirit, however, makes it difficult to define its dual (spatial and temporal) operation, because it not only locates us spatially in a dominion of freedom (Rom. 8.2) but also drives us toward the as yet unfulfilled future' (Beker, *Paul the Apostle*, p. 279).

failure to 'obtain the Law', their rejection of God's righteousness in the sending of the Messiah, 9.30–10.21), God's purposes remain firm ('nothing shall separate us from the love of God', 8.39; cf. 'the gifts and the call of God are irrevocable', 11.29).[1]

The sudden shift in Rom. 9.1 marks neither the beginning of a separate essay on a distinct theme nor an unguarded effluence of personal feeling. It rather capitalizes on the rapturous doxology to the divine will in 8.17-39 in such a way as to reshape and redirect the sympathy of Paul's audience. This unprecedented solemnity and profound intimacy marks an *exuscitatio* aimed to arouse the same feelings in the Roman Christians.[2]

The rhetorical handbooks speak of the potency of the pathetic appeal, and recommend its use in the *peroratio*, when its force is more likely to result in a change of attitude or behavior.[3] Quintilian emphasizes the significance of the affec-

---

1 The theme is already voiced at 3.3-4: 'What if some [Jews] were unfaithful [to the promises of God]? Does their faithfulness nullify the faithfulness of God? By no means! Let God be true, though every human being be false!' It is broached again in 4.14ff.: 'For if those of the Law [the Jews] are the heirs, then the [divine] faithfulness has been made empty, and the promise has been annulled' (4.14)—since from an empirical perspective the Jews are not in possession of any inheritance. The promise to inherit the world (4.13) was nevertheless made to the seed of Abraham, who perceived that his own body was dead, 'yet did not waver in faith' (4.19-20); to those, that is, who trust in the God who makes alive the dead and calls things that are not into being (4.17). So now Christians have been saved 'in hope' for what is not yet visible (8.24-25), and must, by the power of the Spirit's witness, await with endurance the hoped-for glory.

2 On the *exuscitatio*, 'emotional utterance that moves hearers to like feelings', see Richard Lanham, *A Handlist of Rhetorical Terms* (Berkeley: University of California, 1969), p. 122.

3 'When the nature and importance of the facts are clear, one should rouse the hearer to certain emotions—pity, indignation, anger, hate, jealousy, emulation, and quarrelsomeness' (Aristotle, *Rhetoric* 3.19.3). The handbooks *Ad Herrenium, Ad Alexandrinum*, and Cicero and Quintilian all repeat the maxim, 'Nothing dries so quickly as tears', to emphasize that the appeal to affect (*pathos; adfectus*) is intended to be immediately, though temporarily potent. In order to stir pity (*commiseratio; misericordia*), Cicero recommends a solemn tone, and a series of topics expressing the pitiable

tive appeal,[1] and declared that the most direct method for 'exciting' emotions in the audience was to portray them oneself.[2]

Paul's *exuscitatio* in 9.1 is intended to move his (largely Gentile-Christian) audience to compassion for the Jews. This suggestion may be supported by two observations. First, the *exuscitatio* deliberately adapts language and themes from 8.17-39, where the surety of God's grace to those who have been brought near in Christ is in view. So, Paul takes an oath by the witness of the Holy Spirit, the same Spirit who is identified in 8.15 as the 'Spirit of sonship', who elicits in the τέκνα θεοῦ the cry 'Abba'; who evokes eschatological commiseration with an unredeemed world and the anticipation of the glory to come, interceding for the weak who do not know their own need, in accordance with the 'mind' or 'will of the Spirit' (τὸ φρόνημα τοῦ πνεύματος). The oath in 9.1-5 springs from the same internal witness of the Spirit to the divine purpose (φρόνημα) toward redemption, and thus brings to articulate speech—here, as he discusses his Israelite brothers and sisters, no less than in ch. 8—the depths of the divine purpose that remain only unintelligible groans in 8.26.

Second, those on whose behalf Paul might wish himself accursed are identified as 'Israelites, whose are the sonship

---

estate of those who deserve better (*De inventione* 1.106-109; cf. *RhHer* 2.50). Of course the handbooks' orientation toward the courtroom determines the restriction of topics to those especially appropriate to defense or prosecution.

1 'There is scope for an appeal to the emotions, as I have already said, in every portion of a speech. Moreover these emotions present great variety, and demand more than cursory treatment, since it is in their handling that the power of oratory shews itself at its highest.... Few indeed are those orators who can sweep the judge with them, lead him to adopt that attitude of mind which they desire, and compel him to weep with them or share their anger. And yet it is this emotional power that dominates the court, it is this form of eloquence that is the queen of all' (Quintilian, *Institutio* 6.2.2-3).

2 'The prime essential for stirring the emotions of others is, in my opinion, first to feel those emotions oneself.... We must identify ourselves with the persons of whom we complain that they have suffered grievous, unmerited, and bitter misfortune, and must plead their case and for a brief space feel their suffering as if it were our own' (Quintilian, *Institutio* 6.2.34).

and the glory and the covenants and the giving of the Law and the worship and the promises, whose are the Patriarchs, and from whom is the Christ according to the flesh' (9.4-5); that is, to the Jews rightfully belong the 'glory of the children of God' that Paul's Gentile-Christian audience anticipates by the inspiration of the Spirit. Rom. 9.1-5 transforms the assurances of 8.31-39, based as they are in the unshakable divine purpose, into an awed compassion for the people to whom these assurances preeminently belong: 'Nothing shall separate us from God's love' gives way to 'I would wish myself cut off from Christ for their sake'. The recitation of Israel's privileges in 9.4-5 suggests how much greater is the *pathos* of their present distance from the consummation of that heritage. Already implicit here is the contrast of the original and the derivative in 11.17-24 (cf. πόσῳ μᾶλλον, 11.12, 24).[1]

The echoes of 8.17-39 in 9.1-5 suggest that Paul is less concerned to bolster a Gentile-Christian audience's estimate of *their own* salvation-historical status, than to invite them to share his profound and anxious compassion *for the Jews* who have not yet embraced the fulfillment of what is properly *their* destiny. It is just this deeply felt appeal that sets the affective tone for the paraenesis of sober self-estimation and mutual acceptance in 12.1–15.13, for those appeals for proper φρονεῖν are presaged by the Spirit's testimony to the divine φρόνημα.

With the declaration in 9.6, 'it is not as though the word of God'—that is, God's covenantal promise to Israel[2]—'has failed', we are given 'the sum and substance of what Paul wants to say in Romans 9–11'.[3] Related questions in 11.1 ('God has not rejected his people, has he?') and 11.11 ('They have not stumbled so as to fall, have they?') shape these chapters together as a vindication of the divine purpose. So much is clear. What the various segments of that argument mean, however, is the subject of considerable debate.

Rom. 9.1-29 is most often read as the elaboration of a theological principle of discrimination: 'Not all who are descended

---

1 This is a technique of pathetic appeal. Cicero recommends a series of topics expressing the pitiable estate of those who deserve better (*De Inventione* 1.106-109, cf. *Ad Herennium* 2.50).
2 Käsemann, *Romans*, p. 262; Cranfield, *Romans*, II, p. 473.
3 Dahl, 'Future of Israel', p. 143.

from Israel belong to Israel' (9.6b, RSV). In this view, God's righteousness is satisfied through the preservation or redemption of a faithful *portion* of Israel. 'Throughout history a principle of selection has been at work. This has issued in an ever-emerging remnant'.[1] Dahl is right to distinguish this vindication of God's promises from the later Gentile-Christian theory of the 'replacement' of 'old Israel' by a 'new Israel'.[2] Yet Dahl, among others, reads the oppositions in Paul's examples from Scripture ('those from Israel' vs. 'Israel'; 'children of Abraham' vs. 'seed of Abraham'; 'children of flesh' vs. 'children of promise'; Jacob vs. Esau; Moses vs. Pharaoh) as allegorical parallels to the present bifurcation of Israel into those who do and do not accept the Christian gospel,[3] and consequently takes Paul's point to be that 'Not all Israel will be saved, but only a remnant, those among Israel who are vessels of mercy'.[4] This contradicts the apparent sense of 11.26, 'and so *all Israel* will be saved', so that a number of commentators have restricted the scope of the latter passage in various ways,[5] or have perceived an irreconcilable tension between Romans 9–10 and Romans 11.[6] It also casts doubt on the related sayings about the 'first fruits' and the 'root' in 11.16.[7] If, in fact, Romans 9 is intended as a proof that God's righteousness is vindicated in the preservation of a remnant *alone*, then ch. 11 would seem to be gratuitous.

Cranfield concurs with the principle that 'within the elect people itself there has been going on throughout its history a divine operation of distinguishing and separating'; but he insists that 'Paul is not contriving to disinherit the majority of his fellow-Jews'.[8] We contend that, on the contrary, already in

1 Davies, 'Paul and the People of Israel', p. 14.
2 Dahl, 'Future of Israel', p. 146.
3 'Paul puts the non-believing Jews of his time on the same level not only with Ishmael and Esau, but also with Pharaoh and with Babylon' (Dahl, 'Future of Israel', p. 145).
4 *Ibid.*, p. 146.
5 See Cranfield's discussion, *Romans*, II, pp. 576-77.
6 Bent Noack ('Current and Backwater', pp. 165-66) considers it 'inconceivable' that Paul should have written chs. 9 and 10 if he already knew what he would 'reveal' to the Romans in ch. 11.
7 Beker, *Paul the Apostle*, p. 333.
8 Cranfield, *Romans*, pp. 473-74.

Rom. 9.6-29 Paul is asserting the eternal validity of God's promises that *must* extend beyond the present boundaries of the Jewish-Christian 'remnant'. It seems doubtful that Paul's point is to establish from Scripture a principle of *divine discrimination* or *exclusion* ('Jacob I loved, but Esau I hated') to be applied by allegory to the present distinction between 'believing' and 'unbelieving' Jews; when Paul makes such an allegorical move elsewhere, he is much more specific about its aplication (cf. Gal. 3.6-9; 4.21-31). True, Paul draws from the story of the promise to Abraham the principle that 'not all σπέρμα of Abraham are τέκνα of Abraham' (9.7)—the promise goes through Isaac, not through Ishmael—but there ends any possibility of constructing through allegory a dichotomy between opposed *communities*. We hear nothing, good or bad, of Ishmael; Esau is rejected ('Esau I hated') not because of some representative quality he possessed (note v. 11!), but (and this is the point) because of God's sovereign prior decision (which immediately raises the spectre of divine caprice: v. 14). The principle established and maintained throughout this discussion is divine *sovereignty*: God *elects*, God carries out the divine promise by creating life in the barren womb (9.9, 10), God loves, God hardens, God shows mercy, according to the divine will.[1] Not incidentally the Scriptures cited are God's own speech.

---

1 Lloyd Gaston, ('Israel's Enemies', p. 419) likewise finds it improbable that the negative examples here brought forward (Esau, Pharaoh) are meant as coded references to Israel ('Israel's Enemies', p. 419) Getty ('Paul and the Salvation of Israel', p. 459) points out that the 'raising up' of Pharaoh stresses 'not the culpability of Egypt but the freedom of God's election' ('Paul and the Salvation of Israel', p. 459).

Getty argues convincingly that the theme of 9.6-29 is to be located in 9.6a, 'God's word has not failed', rather than in 9.6b, 'Not all of Israel is Israel': she writes, 'What Paul stresses throughout ch. 9 is that the predilection of Israel depends solely on God's mercy (equated with God's justice and freedom) and is not at all related to human activity or striving... [In Romans 9 Paul] clearly insists on the validity of Israel's claim to being God's chosen people. In other words, Romans 9, drawing on the Scriptures, simply restates a basic premise of Israel's theology, viz., the consistent freedom of God's election. Israel was chosen over non-Israel. By "Israel" Paul means, of course, the historical, real, physical Israel, Paul's own

But the sovereignty of Israel's Lord is not like the caprice of Zeus. The summary in 9.16 (ἄρα οὖν) speaks of God's mercy. God both shows mercy and hardens 'whom he will' (9.18); but these are not twin attributes of deity that balance each other in the course of history, but are alternating stages in the working out of God's ultimate *merciful* purpose (9.22-24). The 'mystery' revealed in 11.25ff., 'the surprising wavelike or undulating dynamic of God's salvation-history',[1] is adumbrated in these verses. God's mercy toward the Gentiles is clear in calling those who were 'not a people' to be God's people (9.25-26); God's mercy toward Israel is no less evident in the preservation of a remnant (9.27-29), for the 'vessels of mercy' include Gentiles and Jews together (9.24). These citations of the prophets do not foreclose Israel's role in salvation history, but *reopen* Israel's case.[2]

This does not deny that Paul views Israel's tragic course at present with the utmost gravity. The *pathos* of the paradox in 9.30–10.4 lies in Israel's dismaying failure to realize the goal of the Law, Israel's peculiar treasure, by recognizing the Messiah as the manifestation of God's righteousness.[3] That

kinspeople (cf. 9.3-5). There is no "spiritualizing" of the notion in Romans 9' (p. 465).

1 Beker, *Paul the Apostle*, p. 334.

2 The RSV has amended the citation of Isa. 10.22 to read *'only* a remnant of them will be saved'. But the quotations from the prophets in 9.24-26 'correspond to the promises made at the births of Isaac and Jacob; they confirm that God's promises remain valid' (Dahl, 'Future of Israel', p. 146).

3 Paul Meyer ('Romans 10.4 and the "End" of the Law', in *The Divine Helmsman: Essays Presented to Lou Silberman,* ed. J.L. Crenshaw and S. Sandmel [New York: KTAV, 1980], pp. 59-78) has decisively refuted the notion (cf. Bultmann's *Theology*) that Paul here opposes a legalistic works-righteousness that characterized the Judaism of his day. Yet he interprets Israel's fateful encounter with the Law in these verses by appeal to Rom. 7, rather than to the christological issue that emerges clearly enough in 10.4 (pp. 64-67). While Meyer may be right in suggesting that the 'rock' placed in Zion is Torah, *not* Christ (*ibid.*), there is nothing in *this* pericope that reflects the dialectic of Rom. 7. The midrash in 10.5ff. suggests to the contrary that Torah is intended to point toward Christ ('but what does it say?', 10.8), and that therefore Christ is the *goal*, not the termination (τέλος) of Torah (so also Meyer); and therefore (in contrast to Meyer) Israel's failure with regard to Torah consists only in preferring to

this is what Paul means when he says that Israel 'sought to establish their own righteousness, and did not submit to God's righteousness' (10.3)[1] is brought out in the midrash that follows (10.5-9):[2] the Messiah is not to be 'brought down from

pursue righteousness through Torah *without* recognizing the Messiah to whom the Torah points.

1 E.P. Sanders writes (in *Paul, the Law, and the Jewish People*, p. 37; correctly, in our opinion) that 'Israel's failure is not that they do not obey the law in the correct way, but that they do not have faith in Christ'. He goes on, however, to interpret Israel's 'pursuit of their own righteousness' (10.3) to mean 'the righteousness available to the Jew *alone* on the basis of observing the law' (p. 38). John Gager (*Origins*, p. 224) similarly speaks of 'the position of Jews who are insisting on their collective claim to righteousness to the exclusion of Gentiles as a group'. Against this interpretation it may be observed that Gentiles do not figure at all in 9.31–10.11, suggesting that their appearance in 9.30 only serves as a foil for Israel's tragic story (so Meyer, 'Romans 10.4', p. 62), and that the explanation of 'the righteousness of God' that follows focuses on faith in Christ more than on the equality of Jew and Gentile.

2 There is no reason to see the two passages quoted from Torah in 10.5-6 *opposed* to each other (*pace* Beker, *Paul the Apostle*, p. 246: 'Paul audaciously quotes Scripture against itself'; also Käsemann, *Romans*, p. 284). So Getty ('Paul and the Salvation of Israel', p. 467) remarks that 'if Paul in 10.5 and 10.6-8 quotes Scripture against itself (or more precisely the Torah against itself), he would risk undermining his own credibility'; unfortunately Getty does not provide an interpretation of the passage beyond the declaration that 'the entire passage of Romans 10 is dominated by the theme of the inclusion of the Gentiles rather than by any attack on Israel... Israel is not accused of a "works righteousness" but of an ignorance and blindness born of exclusivity' (p. 467). Our understanding of τὴν ἰδίαν δικαιοσύνην is at variance with this approach. The passages from Torah are not opposed to each other, but are juxtaposed in a midrashic-homiletic technique in such a way that one provides the interpretation of the other. Specifically, what Moses writes about 'the righteousness that comes from Law'—the righteousness which Israel pursued (9.31) under a misconception (10.2), 'not from faith but as if from works' (9.32)—that 'the one who does these things shall live by them' (Lev 18.5)—is given its content through the messianic exegesis of Deut. 30.12-14: faith in Jesus Christ is what Torah itself requires. A third quotation, from Isa. 28.16, confirms Paul's exegesis (λέγει γὰρ ἡ γραφή): 'everyone who believes on him shall not be put to shame'. (For a summary of research and a judicious treatment of midrash see G. Porton, 'Defining Midrash', in *The Study of Ancient Judaism*, I: *Mishnah, Midrash, Siddur*, ed. J.

heaven' or 'brought up from the Abyss' through the keeping of Torah.[1] God has already 'brought Christ up' from the dead (10.9); it remains only to believe in him (10.9-13). Notwithstanding what Paul has said and will say about God 'hardening' Israel, the Jews share the responsibility for their stubborn unbelief (10.21).

Nils Dahl's caveat nevertheless bears keeping in mind:

> It is important to recognize that Romans 10 is not a part of Paul's answer to the question of whether or not God had repudiated his promises to Israel. The chapter is a delayed explanation of the factors which caused him to raise that question. From 10.4 onward Paul digresses from his main line of argumentation, though at the conclusion of the section he returns to it.[2]

One possible reason for including this explanation for Israel's evident disbelief is to exonerate the Torah from culpability. Israel has not believed on the Messiah, *not* because Israel holds the Torah, but because Israel has been blinded to the goal and meaning of that possession.

The question that determines these three chapters is raised again in 11.1: 'I ask, then, has God rejected his people?' The question presumes the preceding quotation from Isaiah: 'All day long I have held out my hands to a disobedient and contrary people' (Isa. 65.2); but is the emphasis to be laid upon

Neusner [New York: KTAV, 1981], pp. 55-92. The specific homiletic technique in view here is discussed by Peder Borgen with relation to Jn 6: *Bread from Heaven* [Leiden: Brill, 1965], esp. pp.59ff.; *idem*, 'Observations on the Midrashic Character of John 6', *ZNW* 56 [1963], pp. 232-40.)

1 The Tannaitic debate whether the Messiah would come in an age of great wickedness or only after Israel as a whole had repented may be relevant here (cf. Schoeps, *Paul*, p. 174 and n. 1; Schürer, *History*, II, p. 524 and n. 36; Moore, *Judaism*, II, pp. 352, 357; Urbach, *Sages*, pp. 668-72); it is especially interesting that Urbach cites Rom. 11.26 as an instance of the former view (*Sages*, p. 670). It is less important to speculate on possible anticipations of that later debate in Paul's time than to elucidate what the apostle implies here: that to continue conscientiously to observe Torah *after* the Messiah has come, and *apart from* recognition of the Messiah (who is the 'goal of Torah'), is a fruitless exercise in self-absorption (τὴν ἰδίαν δικαιοσύνην).

2 Dahl, 'Future of Israel', p. 148.

Israel's contrariness, or upon the divine patience? The answer for Paul is to be found in the community within Israel that has believed on the Messiah, of which he himself is representative ('an Israelite, a descendant of Abraham, a member of the tribe of Benjamin'). And he is not alone: the emphasis in his appeal to the story of Elijah (11.2-5) is on God's *rebuke* of the prophet's shortsightedness.[1] 'So too at the present time there is a remnant, chosen by grace'. This remnant 'does not simply displace the Jewish people and does not represent their fullness; rather, Jewish Christians are the symbol of the continuing faithfulness of God to Israel and thus of Israel's priority in salvation-history and of its future eschatological deliverance as a people'.[2]

The question whether Israel has 'stumbled so as to fall' (11.11) echoes 11.1, confirming that the 'remnant' motif (11.1-6) and the 'hardening' motif (11.7-16) are *both* positively related 'to *one* overriding theme in this chapter: God will save all Israel'.[3] God is faithful, not only *despite* Israel's unbelief, but also *in* that unbelief: for Israel's 'trespass' leads to salvation coming to the Gentiles, and the salvation of the Gentiles will, in Paul's view, increase Israel's jealousy, so that the final outcome—the 'fullness of Israel'—will be even more glorious (11.11-12). Both this argument *a fortiori* and Paul's revelation that his ministry among the Gentiles aims at the salvation of *Jews* (11.14) resound the contrast between Jewish priority and Gentile dependence voiced earlier in the letter (cf. 1.2, 16; 2.9-10; 9.1-5, 11.2), and contribute to an overall

---

1 Käsemann (*Romans*, p. 301) and Dan Johnson ('The Structure and Meaning of Romans 11', *CBQ* 46 [1984], p. 95) both highlight the word spoken to Elijah as significant for Paul. But the point of the comparison is not that Elijah 'seemed to be alone among his people and had to bewail the unbelief of Israel as Paul does in 9.30–10.3' (Käsemann)—to the contrary! Elijah is *rebuked* for his shortsightedness. 'It is very interesting that Paul chooses for typological purposes a prophet whose perception of the situation had become distorted in the heat of theological controversy' (Johnson, p. 95); not, however, because *Paul* has overstated his case (*pace* Johnson), but because in both situations God's gracious preservation of a remnant *surpasses* the loyalty of the apparently solitary individual.

2 Beker, *Paul the Apostle*, p. 335.

3 Johnson, 'Structure and Meaning', p. 92.

dynamic that tends to qualify the significance of the *Gentiles'* salvation by placing it in the context of God's promises to *Israel*.

There is good reasons for understanding the parabolic admonition in 11.17-24 as the climax of Paul's rhetoric, not only in chs. 9–11, but from the beginning of the letter. He addresses his audience in the terms set out so deliberately in the *exordium* (1.6, 13, 14-15) and, more immediately, in terms of the salvation-historical scenario he has just described. He speaks 'to you, *the Gentiles*' (τοῖς ἔθνεσιν), that is, to those who have stumbled onto salvation (cf. 9.30!) because of God's surprising plan to save *the Jews*. The warning to the ingrafted 'branches' not to boast over the branches that 'were broken off' is based on the priority and permanence of Israel's heritage ('it is the root that supports you', 11.18; cf. 11.29) and on God's sovereign power to graft those broken branches in again—'how much more' will those branches fit again into their natural stock (11.24)! The Gentiles' appropriate response, then, is not boasting, but awe (φοβοῦ!, 11.20).

At last Paul invokes the rhetoric of prophecy to reveal to his audience a 'mystery' (μυστήριον):[1] in so doing he discloses the divine will to which the Spirit witnesses (cf. 8.16, 26-27; 9.1) that remains inaccessible to human calculation ('for who has known the mind of the Lord, or who has been his counselor?' 11.34). The hardening of Israel is God's work; its purpose, contrary to appearance, is their salvation.[2]

---

1 On the apocalyptic background of the term see R.E. Brown, 'The Semitic Background of the NT μυστήριον', *Bib* 39 (1958), pp. 218-28; 40 (1959), pp. 70-87; Gerhard Dautzenberg, *Urchristliche Prophetie* (Stuttgart: Kohlhammer, 1975), pp. 152-56.

2 Beker (*Paul the Apostle*, p. 334) argues cogently that 'the hardening motif itself cannot be the mystery, because this has been the presupposition of the argument since Rom. 11.8. Nor is the salvation of "all Israel" the mystery' (note already 11.16); 'Instead, the mystery is the surprising wavelike or undulating dynamic of God's salvation-history, the "interdependence" of God's dealings with Gentiles and Jews' (*Paul the Apostle*, p. 334).

4. Conclusions: The Argumentative Coherence of Romans 5–11

The warning in 11.17-24 is not a precautionary aside to a sub-section of the Roman audience: it touches the heart of the argumentative exigence that constrains Paul's rhetoric throughout Romans 6–15. Rom. 6.1–8.13 is more than an exposition of 'life in Christ'. It qualifies 'freedom from the Law' as obligation to the righteousness required by the Law which is possible only in the sphere of the Spirit (8.1-13). Further, the discussion of Israel in chs. 9–11 does more than provide a salvation-historical anchor for the salvation of the Gentiles.[1] The solidity of that salvation can hardly be in doubt after 8.31-39. But that salvation only is legitimate because of God's righteousness and sovereignty, and this necessarily involves God's integrity regarding the promises to Israel. The salvation of the Gentiles is therefore moved, so to speak, from the center of the spotlight to its periphery.[2] The net result is a qualification of the Gentile-Christian boast (cf. 5.1-11; 11.18-24): neither freedom from the obligation to observe the מצוה of Torah nor the privilege of being 'grafted in' to the place of favor previously occupied by Israel provides any footing for a stand against God's claim (cf. 6.15-23; 11.20-21).

This reconstellation of values *within* the ethos of Gentile Christianity plays a crucial role in the argumentative

---

1 Daniel Fraikin ('Rhetorical Function of the Jews', p. 101) answers the question 'What, then, is the function of [Rom. 9–11] in a discourse aimed at strengthening the Gentile Christians in Rome? Why could Paul not stop in Rom. 8?' by positing that the main problem in these chapters is not Israel's rejection of the *gospel*, but Israel's rejection of *Gentile Christians*. By declaring Israel to be 'in the wrong' (p. 102), Paul defends the election *of the Gentiles* (p. 103). This reverses Paul's rhetoric, turning the argumentative *crescendo* through chs. 9–11 into a *diminuendo e ritardando* after 9.30–10.4.

2 As Beker (*Paul the Apostle*, p. 331) declares, the motif of the unity of Jew and Gentile in the church is for Paul 'not just a strategic move against sectarian fragmentation. It is undergirded by a theological principle: the faithfulness of God to his promises to Israel'. Unless the connection and continuity of the church with Israel are maintained, 'God's faithfulness to his plan of salvation is jeopardized and destroyed. The relation of the church to Judaism is theologically important, because the church cannot be the people of God without its linkage with Israel as the people of God'.

macrostructure of the letter. We have argued above, in part
on the basis of an observed syllogistic structure spanning Rom.
1.18-32, 6.1-23, and 12.1-2,[1] and in part by examining 15.14-
16, that Romans is written to secure the 'obedience' and
'holiness' of the Romans, including the mutual regard and
respect of Jewish and Gentile Christians. Their reception of
his exhortations can ensure the spiritual sanctity of the
'offering of the Gentiles' throughout the world. This is the
immediate epistolary exigence. The argumentation in
Romans 6–11 predisposes their assent to Paul's exhortation in
12–15 as their appropriate response to God's mercies (12.1).[2]
In this light, the argumentative units 6.1–8.13 and 8.14–11.36
may be seen as rhetorical *prolepses* that anticipate objections
arising within the rhetorical situation.[3] They may therefore be
appropriately characterized as elements of a *probatio* (the
christological formulations in Romans 5 constituting a
rhetorical *propositio*); the function of the paraenetic chapters
in distilling and consolidating the argumentative effect of that
probatio into 'creating in the hearers [at least] a willingness to
act'[4] resembles the role of an extended rhetorical *peroratio*,
and is appropriate toward the end of the letter.

We referred above to the letter's reconstellation of values
within the ethos of Gentile Christianity. This point—the
letter's thorough responsiveness to its specific rhetorical situation—bears emphasis. Beker has written that one aspect of

1 See pp. 122-23 above; Furnish, *Theology and Ethics*, pp. 103-106;
  Beker, *Paul the Apostle*, pp. 175, 286-91.
2 Note the overarching theme of 'right understanding': the Spirit's
  revelation within the charismatic congregation of the divine
  φρόνημα (8.18-39) is amplified when Paul unfolds God's plan for
  Israel (9–11), directed against the possible conceit of Gentile Christians ('do not boast', 11.18; 'do not be conceited, but stand in awe' [μὴ
  ὑψηλὰ φρόνει, ἀλλὰ φοβοῦ, 11.20]; 'lest you be wise in your own con-
  ceits' [ἵνα μὴ ἦτε ἑαυτοῖς φρόνιμοι, 11.25]); sober self-estimation
  stands over the paraenesis in chs. 12–13 (μὴ ὑπερφρονεῖν... ἀλλὰ
  φρονεῖν εἰς τὸ σωφρονεῖν, 12.3), providing a foundation for the
  warnings against 'contempt' and 'judgment' of the brother or sister
  in 14-15.
3 See Brandt, *Rhetoric of Argumentation*, pp. 50, 67-68.
4 Perelman and Olbrechts-Tyteca, *New Rhetoric*, p. 45 ('The Effects of
  Argumentation').

the rhetorical exigence addressed by the letter was the presence in Rome of 'a Gentile majority [that] felt that it was in a superior position over the Jewish-Christian section of the church'; but Beker goes on to insist that 'this cannot explain the whole letter, because Gentiles are not warned in other sections of the letter but only in Rom. 11.13-25 and in chapters 14 and 15. To the contrary, the main body of the letter confronts Judaism'.[1] It remains to be seen whether our observations about the argumentative cohesiveness of Romans 6–11— observations that militate against Beker's assessment—can be correlated with a cohesive *historical* situation.

The conviction that the observance of *kašrût* is no longer binding upon Christians (at least not upon Gentile Christians) is obviously a premise Paul shares with his audience (cf. 6.14), to the extent that those who do observe *kašrût* can—*without further elaboration*—be characterized as 'weak in faith' (14.1). It is equally obvious that the failure of Israel to obey the gospel is something Paul must explain (9.30–10.21), but not a proposition he must defend. As Fraikin rightly points out,

> The unbelief of Israel is one of the presuppositions [of Rom. 9–11]. It deserves some comment. What is presupposed is not simply that a great number of Jews, or even the majority, have not accepted the gospel yet, but that Israel, the people of God, have not accepted the gospel. 'Israel' is more than all individual Jews. Somehow, at some point, the rejection of the gospel by individual Jews or synagogues has led to the theological conclusion that Israel has rejected the gospel. It remained only to explain the 'fact'. The fact, of course, is the result of an interpretation. When it came about, and who is responsible for it, are difficult questions to answer, but that it should be considered a major theological event is clear.[2]

Furthermore, these twin attitudes of disregard of the *mişwôt* and the displacement (and disparagement) of Israel were, from early on in the development of Gentile Christianity, related. That is, not only did later generations of Christians 'view Jewish Christianity as a (heretical) minority, and the struggle over the Torah as a debate around ethnicity and

---

1 Beker, *Paul the Apostle*, p. 75.
2 Fraikin, 'Rhetorical Function of the Jews', p. 101.

cultic particularities':[1] for the Epistle of Barnabas and for Justin Martyr, the Law was given to Israel *so that* Israel would forfeit their privilege as the people of God. Torah was the rock upon which Israel suffered shipwreck, and that catastrophe became a warning to the church not to follow in Israel's wake.[2] Even earlier, the 'Paulinist' who wrote Ephesians has abandoned Paul's positive remarks about Torah (Rom. 3.31; ch. 7) and Israel and has declared the basis for unity in the church of Jews and Gentiles to be 'the abolition of the Law of commandments and ordinances' (Christ is ὁ... νόμον τῶν ἐντολῶν ἐν δόγμασιν καταργήσας, Eph. 2.15).[3] Is it

1 Beker, *Paul the Apostle*, p. 75.
2 The *Epistle of Barnabas* divides Scripture into God's reproaches condemning 'them', the Jews, and the divine admonitions that remain valid 'for us', Christians (cf. 2.7-10; 3.1-5). Christians are warned against being 'shipwrecked by conversion to their Law' (3.6) and against saying that 'the covenant is both theirs and ours' (4.6), since Israel forfeited their covenant at the moment when Moses received it (αὐτὴν λαβόντος ἤδη τοῦ Μωϋσέως, 4.7; 14.1-4). According to Justin, the Law given at Horeb was 'for you [Jews] alone' (*Dialogue with Trypho*, 11.2), its provocation being the Jews' 'lawlessness and hardness of heart' (18.2; cf. 21.1; 22.1, 11), its purpose—or rather that of circumcision in particular—being to distinguish the Jews from other nations, 'that you alone should suffer the things you are rightly suffering now' (16.2) and 'that the people should not be a people, and the nation not a nation, as Hosea says' (19.5).
3 A. Lindemann (*Die Aufhebung der Zeit* [Gütersloh: Mohn, 1975], p. 253) can write that Ephesians 'wirkt... beinahe wie eine gezielte "Zurücknahme" von Röm 9–11'. Andrew Lincoln ('The Church and Israel in Ephesians 2', *CBQ* 49 [1987], p. 613) suggests that for the author of Ephesians, 'the law which separated Israel from the Gentiles had also come to separate Israel from God and to hold her in a state of slavery and condemnation', and that the author must have learned this 'as a disciple of Paul'. For Lincoln, Ephesians simply presents the 'logic of [Paul's] position in an unqualified fashion' (p. 612). The 'far more dialectical' treatment of Law and of Israel in Romans is the result of more pressing circumstances (*ibid.*), and therefore must be balanced against Galatians and Ephesians for a picture of 'the canonical Paul' (p. 621). Beker (*Paul the Apostle*, p. 343) is much less sanguine about the 'catholicizing' of Paul in Ephesians into 'an apostle who has lost his anchorage in Judaism and proclaims a timeless gospel that substitutes the church for the eschatological Parousia and applies the promise to Israel to the eschatological reality of the church'.

possible that Romans already addresses a Gentile Christianity characterized not only by *numerical* dominance over Jewish Christians (Beker), but by a growing sentiment that Torah and Israel are together made obsolete by the gospel of Jesus Christ?

Chapter 4

CONCLUSIONS

1. *The Rhetorical Macro-Structure of the Letter*

We are now in a position to hazard a comprehensive understanding of the letter's macro-structure, 'the thought or thoughts that... [determine and control] the choice of words and the construction of the sentences in... a statement or discourse'; that is, to describe how the 'individual parts [of Romans] together contribute to give expression to a coherent meaning, similar to the way in which words together give expression to meaning in a sentence'.[1] Such an explanation will necessarily require integrating the 'dialogue with Judaism' in Romans 1–4 with the more distinctively christological argument in Romans 5–8, with the apocalyptic disclosure of Israel's destiny *vis-à-vis* the Gentiles in Romans 9–11, with the paraenesis in chs. 12–15, and with the epistolary address to the Gentile-Christian congregations in Rome (1.1-15; 15.14–16.27).

In previous Chapters we have observed elements of an overarching macro-structure in the letter. These include the divine calling that impels Paul to secure the 'obedience of faith among all the Gentiles', including the Romans, which we have identified as the 'deep exigence' of the letter;[2] the elements of the 'once–but now' schema of early Christian paraenesis that stretch from 1.18-32 to ch. 6 and 12.1-2,[3] involving the affective dimension of 'shame' toward the previous way of life— elements that may be described as working together in a topical *strategy* that redisposes the rhetorical situation around the

---

1 Boers, 'Problem of Jews and Gentiles', pp. 184-85.
2 Cf. 1.5-6, 13, 14-15; 15.14-16.
3 Furnish, *Theology and Ethics*, pp. 99-106.

'deep exigence' of the divine call to obedience and holiness; and thematic continuities that extend throughout the 'letter body'. These continuities include God's faithfulness to the covenant with Israel (1.2-4; 3.1-8; 4.14-16; 9.1-6, 27-29; 10.21; 11.1-36; 15.8) and to the scriptural promises concerning the Gentiles (4.9-12, 16-17; 9.25-26; 15.9-12); and God's integrity, uncompromised by human failure (2.17-3.9; 4.4-8; 5.6-10; 9.6-29; 11.1-36), which comprises both the absolute accountability ('inexcusability') of all human beings before God, regardless of their status *vis-à-vis* the Law (2.6-16; 3.19-20), and God's sovereignty in determining the destinies of Jews and Gentiles alike, regardless of any presumed merit (9.6-29; 11.23-36).

Our discussion of argumentation in Romans 5–11 (Chapter 3) has helped to clarify the letter's macro-structure. In particular, the correspondence of themes in the diatribal rhetoric in Romans 1–4 and in the paraenesis in Romans 12–15, and the pivotal significance of Romans 5, point toward Paul's redisposition of a rhetorical exigence.

'Judging', which might otherwise appear a reasonable perspective on those who are 'weak in faith' (14.1; 15.1), is roundly condemned as self-judgment and arrogant defiance of God's righteous judgment (2.1-6). The *topos* on the righteousness of God is not simply a 'theme' (1.16-17); it is a central value around which Paul will reconstellate the values and attitudes at play in the rhetorical situation. What is decisive is not one's identity as Jew or Gentile, one's place 'in' or 'outside of', 'under' or 'not under' the Law, but one's standing *vis-à-vis* God's righteousness (Romans 1–3); therefore one's behavior toward others in the community is to be determined not by observance of the *miṣwôt*, but by recognition that each person stands before the Lord (14.4, 6-12). The criterion of conduct is not 'freedom from the Law', but 'fulfillment of the Law's requirement' (8.4), which is love of neighbor (13.8-10).

The reconstellation of values accomplished in Romans has two basic components: (1) An insistence on accountabiliity to God, regardless of standing *vis-à-vis* Torah (Rom. 1–3; 6–8), and (2) an insistence on God's faithfulness to the promises made to Abraham concerning Israel and the Gentiles, regardless of human failure (Rom. 4; 9–11). Both components bear fruit in the paraenesis in Rom. 12–15, which focuses on self-estimation, mutual regard, love as the fulfilment of the Law, and accountability to one's own Lord. Both components disclose some of the potential of the symbolization 'righteousness of God' for Paul, which is at once God's sovereign claim on human obedience, and at the same time God's self-faithful integrity, manifest as faithfulness to the divine promises.

The argumentation in Romans can also be understood in terms of the 'obstacles' it is deployed to address. One of these, the preceding chapters suggest, is a perspective on the Torah as an ethnic peculiarity, at best an obsolete and irrelevant system of obligations, at worst a system for recording transgressions through which Israel has merited God's judgment. Related to this perspective on Torah, we suggest, is a specifically Christian perception that Israel has failed to believe in their Messiah, thus spurning God's salvation, which has surprisingly been embraced by the Gentiles. Of course we should beware the dangers of 'mirror-reading', especially since Paul does not address circumstances in Rome at all directly. Nevertheless, our exegesis in previous Chapters points to the constraining power of these elements in the rhetorical situation, whatever their relation to actual positions held in Rome. Furthermore, these elements are not isolated and disparate attitudes, but could cohere in a single Gentile-Christian perspective, as the Christian literature of the second century makes abundantly clear.

These constraining forces are evident, as well, in the way Paul has gone about approaching his subject. He does not immediately address the status of the Law *vis-à-vis* the Gentile, nor the fate of Israel, nor the character of the redemption offered in Christ (though this is adumbrated in 1.15-17); above all he does not first launch into the admonitions of 14.1–15.13. This may reflect Paul's perception that he cannot exhort the Romans to mutual tolerance and respect across the lines of Torah observance on the basis of an appeal to 'love', even 'love in Christ', before he has redisposed the antagonistic elements of the situation; or it may reflect Paul's own conviction that an ethos that marginalizes Jews as survivors of a *past* covenant is an affront to the righteousness of God. On either account, Paul has chosen to relate the episto-

lary exigence most fundamentally to the underlying exigence
of God's sovereign integrity.

Particularly significant for an understanding of the letter's
character is the relation of the 'proper estimation' and mutual
regard to which Paul exhorts the community (μὴ ὑπερφρονεῖν
παρὺ ὃ δεῖ φρονεῖν, ἀλλὰ φρονεῖν εἰς τὸ σωφρονεῖν, 12.3), which
involves acceptance, even deference to the 'weak' neighbor
rather than judgment (14.1–15.7), to the revelation of the
Spirit's will (φρόνημα) that the heritage of all the children of
God, Gentiles and Jews alike, should be fulfilled (chs.9–11).

The argumentative coherence of the 'theological' and
'paraenetic' sections of the letter has received increasing
attention recently. Wayne Meeks has written that 'Paul's
advice about behavior in the Christian groups cannot be
rightly understood until we see that the great themes of
chapters 1–11 here receive their denouement'. The exhortations in 14.1–15.13 are grounded in God's action in Christ 'to
fulfill promises made in Jewish Scriptures to Jewish patriarchs about Gentiles. This extraordinarily compact statement
[in 15.8-9] constitutes a reprise of the themes Paul has developed in chapters 9–11 and, more than that, in the whole
letter...'[1] In particular Meeks notes the 'striking parallel in
form, substance, and function with the apostrophe... in 2.1...'[2]
Yet Meeks doubts that the exhortations involving *kašrût* in
Rom. 14.1–15.13 are related to 'any present crisis around this
issue in the Roman groups. Paul takes up the topic out of his
experience, not theirs, because it is well suited to show in
behavioral terms the outworking of the main themes of the
letter';[3] he 'chose the topic of his final sample of admonition
with deliberate thought and shaped his rhetorical
presentation of it with great care, as an altogether fitting
conclusion to his great protreptic exhibition of "his gospel"'.[4]

1 W.A. Meeks, 'Judgement and the Brother: Romans 14.1–15.13', in
   *Tradition and Interpretation in the New Testament: Essays in
   Honor of E. Earle Ellis*, ed. G.F. Hawthorne and O. Betz (Grand
   Rapids: Eerdmans, 1987), pp. 290, 292.
2 *Ibid.*, p. 296.
3 *Ibid.*, p. 292.
4 *Ibid.*, p. 297.

In light of our earlier discussion of the letter's *exordium* (1.1-15) and *peroratio* (15.14-32, esp. vv. 14-16), it seems desirable to explain the thematic coherence that Meeks describes in deliberative or paraenetic terms rather than epideictic terms ('sample of admonition', 'protreptic exhibition of "his gospel"'). Although the letter does not present a clearcut picture of circumstances in Rome, perhaps because Paul simply did not know them,[1] it nevertheless appears to be a paraenetic address, perhaps to be understood more as a prophylaxis than as a corrective, written in the conviction that his audience's positive response to it will ensure their own holiness and the sanctity of the worldwide 'offering of the Gentiles' as well. Our interpretation bears out Hendrikus Boers' contention that 'the letter is not a theoretical exposition of the doctrine of justification by faith, but a paraenetic argument based on that doctrine'.[2]

Boers reaches this conclusion on the basis of thematic correspondences extending throughout the letter. Arguing that a 'statement that does not fit smoothly in the surface structure of a text', like the abrupt apostrophe in 2.1, 'may be an important clue to its semantic deep structure or macro-structure', Boers finds that the indictment of *'everyone* who judges' is too broad to be limited to the *Jew*;[3] 'Gentile Christians are removed from their sinful past only by the skin of their teeth, and they would do well to remember that, as he reminds them in 11.19-21...' Warnings against judging others are pitched against presuming upon God's grace in such a way as to hold God's righteousness in contempt (2.1-6; 11.18-24). Boers writes:

> If one takes 1.18–2.29 and 11.13-24 as brackets which set the limits within which the argument of the first eleven chapters of Romans takes place it becomes clear that what Paul is driving at in this part of the letter is that the Christian, specifically the gentile Christian, can neither boast about the

1 Meeks (*ibid.*, p. 292) quite rightly protests against 'mirror-reading' the situation in Rome out of Paul's letter.
2 Boers, 'Problem of Jews and Gentiles', p. 192.
3 'Such an interpretation would strongly limit the applicability of the admonition, providing an easy escape for every hypocrite!' (*ibid.*, pp. 189-90).

> sinfulness of the gentiles, because it is faith alone which
> separates her/him from that sinfulness, nor can she/he
> boast about the disobedience of the Jew, because, once more,
> it is only faith which brought about the reversal of their
> circumstances. In 2.1, thus, Paul apparently got ahead of
> his argument, and therefore had to take a step back again
> with 2.2.[1]

He goes on to draw conclusions about the character of the
letter:

> Paul's letter to the Romans, thus, appears to be as much as
> any of his other letters, directed to what he believed to have
> been concrete pastoral issues of the church... The semantic
> deep structure of the letter, thus, its macro-structure, is not
> his planned visit, but the addressing of the church at Rome
> on the issue of the judgment of others on the basis of the
> security of [one's] own position... According to Paul,
> justification through faith left no basis on which to judge
> others, but the cutting edge of his argument was that Israel
> too was saved by faith, i.e., 'heilsgeschichtlich' by the faith of
> Abraham as its source, that the purpose of Christ was to
> secure the promises to the fathers (15.8). According to Paul
> in Romans, thus, there was no 'new covenant', only a
> reaffirmation of the old one through Christ, and the Chris-
> tian who was justified by faith drew the lifesap of her or his
> existence by having been integrated into the covenant as
> secured by Christ. Therefore the gentile Christian had no
> grounds whatsoever on which to pass judgment on the
> Jews.[2]

Boers' reading of Romans as an admonition to *Gentile*
Christianity challenges the position held, for example, by J.
Christiaan Beker. Although Beker concurs that the central
theological *problematic* of the letter is the tension between
Israel's salvation-historical priority and 'Paul's teaching of
justification by faith [which is] based on the universality of sin
and God's free gift of grace', and contends that Paul has
resolved this tension by emphasizing the 'theocentric foundation' of both themes, in Beker's view this tension is worked out
in Romans mainly against the possibility of *Jewish* presumption: the 'radical contingency' of God's faithfulness that

1 *Ibid.*, pp. 190-91.
2 *Ibid.*, pp. 194-95.

'cannot be captured and possessed by humankind because it originates in His radical freedom and grace' issues in Paul's 'charge against Israel'.[1]

We are confronted with a dilemma. Boers is able to outline a single coherent 'macro-structure' that opposes God's righteousness to Gentile-Christian presumption, but does not integrate the diatribal address to the Jew in 2.17–3.20 within that macro-structure. He calls the apostrophe in 2.17ff. a 'side swipe at [Paul's] Jewish readers, in case they, not being subject to the depravation of the gentiles, think they are exempt from the argument';[2] but in his treatment, that 'side swipe' remains a qualification fairly tangential to Paul's argumentative goal. Beker, on the other hand, gives more attention to Rom. 2.17ff. because of his focus on the dialogue with Judaism in the letter, but the consequent view of a 'convergence of motivations' behind Romans[3] tends toward what must, in contrast to the cohesiveness of the letter in Boers' view, seem a *divergence* of motivations and a diffusion of rhetorical effect.

That dilemma can be resolved only by examining how the interrelationships of Jewish and Gentile 'boasting' and God's integrity are structed in the letter's rhetoric; and that examination must focus on an underlying constraint throughout the letter, the issue of the status of Jew and Gentile before Torah.

2. *The Torah-topos in Romans*

We have argued in earlier Chapters that the 'dialogue with Judaism' contained in Romans 1–4 does not present itself as an attack on Judaism or as an indictment of the Jew. Whatever the purposes of this rhetoric, it does not function to over-

---

1 Beker, *Paul the Apostle*, pp. 335-36. Earlier Beker declares that although 'Romans exhibits a basic apology for Israel' (in 9–11), 'the apology takes a curious form, for throughout Rom. 1.18-8.39 and until 11.11 (except for the interruption at 3.1-4) the apology has the character of a radical polemic [!]... Paul concentrates primarily on the Jewish sins of hypocrisy (2.26-29) and boasting (3.27), whereas typical Gentile sins do not fill the pages of Romans...' (pp. 87-88).

2 Boers, 'Problem of Jews and Gentiles', p. 191.

3 Beker, *Paul the Apostle*, pp. 71-74; summed up as 'the combined factors of the forthcoming debate in Jerusalem, the Galatian crisis, the mixed and troubled character of the Roman church, and Paul's appeal for Rome's intercession' (p. 88).

come an obstacle represented by the Jew; or to phrase the
matter from the opposite perspective, the Jew in Romans 2–3
does not represent an attitude or position that Paul feels must
be 'demolished' or undermined before his gospel can prevail.[1]
Why, then, does he bother with apostrophes to 'the Jew' in a
letter ostensibly addressed to Gentile Christians?

As we have seen, the diatribal mode of rhetoric provides a
somewhat artificial or 'hypothetical' environment in which
values and attitudes can be explored and modified, without
directly confronting the values and attitudes of an audience.[2]
The simulation of dialogue enables the speaker to manipulate
the constraints of an indeterminate rhetorical situation in
such a way that the position for which the rhetor is arguing
appears increasingly self-evident and reasonable; alternative
viewpoints, to the extent that they are not simply ignored,
surface only in caricature as obviousely false conclusions that
the interlocutor is compelled to reject or as illegitimate objections that the speaker can parry with ease.

The characterization of the interlocutor is obviously of vital
significance for the effectiveness of the diatribal strategy, since
the interlocutor must be made plausibly to embody the
attitude to be encouraged or avoided. The characterization
must be plausible, consistent, and straightforward enough
that its *representative* function is clear.[3] We have seen
reasons to doubt that Paul intends the Jewish interlocutor in
Romans 2–3 to personify the pretentious person (ἀλαζών).[4] In
fact the 'psychological' aspect of the Jew's piety as it is
reflected in 2.17-20 is underdeveloped when compared with
the apostrophe in 2.1-5. The first apostrophe focuses on the
arrogant and presumptuous defiance of God's judgment in
somewhat stereotyped terms.[5] In the second, in contrast,

---

1 See the Excursus above.
2 See relevant discussion in Perelman and Olbrechts-Tyteca, *The New
  Rhetoric*, pp. 36-37.
3 See the brief but helpful remarks on 'Argumentation and Diatribe'
  in Berger, *Formgeschichte*, pp. 110-11.
4 Against Stowers, *The Diatribe*, pp. 112-13.
5 Aristotle examines the states of mind of those who do wrong, focusing on those who hope to escape judgment or to find indulgence
  (*Rhetoric* 1372a-b). The *Rhetorica ad Herennium* recommends that

terms related to attitude—'boast in' (καυχᾶσαι), 'rely on' (ἐπαναπαύῃ)—are not used in a negative way (cf. 3.1-2; 9.1-5), but serve rather to set off the rhetorical questions in 2.21-24. The issue is not so much the tone of the Jew's piety as the confirmation of that piety in conduct. These considerations lead us to doubt that the Jewish interlocutor in 2.17-29 is intended to function as a personification of the 'pious person', *homo religiosus*, as such. In fact the Jew's 'personality' here is only relevant as the Jew relates to Torah, and it is *the relation to Torah* that defines the Jew. Torah becomes the fulcrum for the (potential) accusations in 2.21-24.[1] The Jew boasts in Torah; knows the will of God and discerns what is (morally) significant through Torah's instruction; is a guide to the blind, a light to those in darkness, an instructor of the foolish and a teacher of babes *because* the Jew holds the very embodiment of knowledge and of truth in Torah. Yet the Torah calls the Jew to account through the commandments that are the Jew's boast and delight: 'Do *you* steal? Do *you* commit adultery? Do *you* rob temples? Do *you* dishonor God?'

The rhetorical value of the apostrophe to the Jew resides precisely in the Jew's relation *to Torah* as this is already adumbrated in 2.12-13: the Jew is accountable to God 'in Torah' or 'through Torah', that is, on the terms explicitly revealed in Torah. All of 2.17–3.9 can be seen as an extended amplification of 2.12-13 drawing out the implications of the Jew's standing 'in Torah': the very real covenantal privileges which the Jew enjoys (3.1-2) in no way mitigate the Jew's accountability to God through Torah (2.25; 3.9). We are provided a further clue to the rhetorical significance of the apostrophe to the Jew in the juxtaposition of Gentiles who 'sin without regard to the Law' (ἀνόμως), who 'do not have the Law' (2.12, 14), with the Jews who, when they sin, sin 'in (or against) the Law', and are justified when they do what the

the prosecutor address pointed rhetorical questions at the accused (15.22); conventional topics of prosecution are listed in 2.48-49, *Rhetorica ad Alexandrum* 36.
1 'Potential' accusations in that they remain questions in 2.21-22; in v. 23 as well, on the witness of Codex Sinaiticus, and of John Calvin (*Romans*, p. 53); and in that the Jewish interlocutor's confession to these accusations is nowhere presumed in what follows.

Law requires (2.12b-13). Both Jew and Gentile are accountable to God; but while the Jew's position before God is explicit,
definitive, revealed in a sacred history at God's own initiative,
the Gentile's position before God might be perceived as
ambiguous. After all, the Gentiles do what God requires ('the
things of the Law') only incidentally, more or less by accident
(φύσει); and instead of centuries of covenantal relationship, all
the Gentiles have experienced of God (so Paul implies) are
'what is known of God' in creation (1.19-20), and a 'history' of
God's toleration of immorality (cf. χρηστότητος [θεοῦ], 2.4;
πάρεσιν τῶν προγεγονότων ἁμαρτημάτων, 3.25; cf. ἤνεγκεν ἐν
πολλῇ μακροθυμίᾳ σκεύη ὀργῆς, 9.22).

To be sure, for Paul Jew and Gentile are equally accountable
to God (cf. πᾶς in 1.18, 2.1; 'Jew and Greek' in 2.9, 10; οὐ . . .
προσωπολημψία, 2.11; οὐ γάρ ἐστιν διαστολή, 3.22-23). The
Jew, however, is more *explicitly* accountable because of Torah;
by comparison the arraignment of the Gentile is, on 'legal'
terms, elusive. It is striking in this light how frequently Paul
speaks of Gentile accountability in relation to law, νόμος:
although Gentiles sin ἄνομος (2.12a) and are characterized as
'not having νόμος' (2.14), they nevertheless 'do the things of
the νόμος by nature', however occasionally, and thus show
that they 'are a νόμος for themselves' (2.14), the 'work of the
νόμος being written on their hearts' (2.15). In this way they
are included in the axiom, 'Not those who hear νόμος are just
before God, but those who do the νόμος shall be justified' (2.13;
note γάρ, 2.14). Further, the Jew's transgression of νόμος
(2.25) is contrasted with the Gentile's observance of the
'requirements of the Law' (δικαιώματα τοῦ νόμου, 2.26), and it
is on the basis of having fulfilled the Law (τὸν νόμον τελοῦσα)
that the Gentile 'judges' the Jew (2.27). Whatever Paul means
when he says that the Gentiles 'sin ἀνόμως' and 'do not have
νόμος', then, he does not mean that they are not judged on the
same basis as the Jew—that is, specifically *in terms of the
fulfillment of Law*, νόμος.

This is clear as well from the argument in Rom. 6.15–8.13,
where Paul insists that although Christians (including his
Gentile Christian audience) are 'not under Law' (6.15), they
nevertheless should endorse the Law's verdict in harmony
with the ἐγώ in 7.7-25, and in fact should aspire to 'serving the

Law of God with one's intent' (7.25). In fact Paul insists that Christians—by implication, Christians *alone*—fulfill the 'requirement of the Law' since they walk by the Spirit (8.4).

This strange collision of perspectives, in which Gentiles are at once those who do not have the Law and are not under Law, yet are accountable to Law and are judged on the basis of the Law's requirement, can be understood as argumentation once the *paradigmatic* role of 'the Jew' in Romans 2–3 is recognized. By posing for his Jewish interlocutor the possibility that by transgressing the Law the Jew should dishonor God, Paul compels his interlocutor to choose, so to speak, between two alternatives: on the one hand, holding the Law as a possession, a treasure peculiar to the Jew and a privilege against God's reckoning of sin, or on the other hand, submitting to God's righteous verdict spoken in Law, even if it means one's own condemnation by God.

The Jewish interlocutor submits to God's righteous judgment (3.4-9). This is not only what we should expect from a pious Jew as the Psalms give him or her voice; it is also the very purpose for which Paul invoked 'the Jew' in the first place.

Paul calls upon the Jew, not because the Jew is boastful or epitomizes human religion, but because the Jew alone cannot pretend to ignorance of God's will revealed in Torah. The Jew *must* submit to God's righteousness—so Paul manipulates the potentialities in the diatribe—because the Jew has been entrusted with Torah.

The Jew thus becomes a paradigm of trustful assent to God's will. So in Romans 4 Abraham is a model of faith in God's integrity and power to fulfill the divine promises. But the significance of these 'Jewish' models is not restricted to the Jews, as Abraham's faithfulness 'in his uncircumcision' makes clear (4.10-11), and as Paul explicitly asserts (4.23-25). Already in Rom. 3.19 the paradigmatic quality of the Jew's submission to Torah is made clear: what the Law says to those in the Law—namely, that there is none righteous, that no one may make pretense to exemption from God's judgment (3.9)—it says in order to shut *every mouth*, that of the Gentile as well, in order to call *all the world* to account.

The argument in 6.15–7.25 is of immediate relevance for Christians (cf. 6.15), specifically *Gentile* Christians (cf. 6.19), who *previously* were 'in the flesh', subject to the poisonous interaction of sinful passions (παθήματα τῶν ἁμαρτιῶν) and Law (7.5). In the confession in 7.7-25, one who stands in just that position voices assent to God's Law, even as it exposes that person's plight as being 'sold under sin' (7.14). It is just the individual who 'rejoices in God's Law inwardly' and 'serves God's Law with the will' who cries out for redemption from the body of death (7.24-25). The argumentative progression since 3.19 is striking: Paul's rhetoric should have led a *Gentile* Christian audience—those who might distinguish themselves from Jews precisely on the matter of 'belonging to' the Law— to affirm the goodness, sanctity, and validity of Torah as God's requirement of righteousness *for them as well*.

The argument we have described bears resemblance to the discussions in the classical rhetorical handbooks of 'legal' and 'juridical' issues in forensic rhetoric.[1] Aristotle distinguished the legal issue from the issue of justice (τὸ ἐπιεικές or τὸ δίκαιον, *Rhetoric* 1374a). In cases in which the applicability of determinate laws and the question of justice do not coincide, the prosecutor (and the advocate) were encouraged to rely on topics that applied acceptable principles of analogy or precedent toward establishing what is just.[2] In distinctly forensic

1 In forensic rhetoric, the discovery of the point at issue (*status*; Greek στάσις) was at the heart of invention, and was the subject of analysis as early as Aristotle's *Rhetoric*, if not before (Kennedy, *Art of Persuasion*, p. 10). Of the στάσεις or bases of defense identified by Aristotle, only the στάσις of fact concerned whether or not the accused had in fact committed a certain act; the other στάσεις sought to establish whether the accused should be punished for the act or not (*Rhetoric* 1417b). Relevant to all four στάσεις are the topics particular to judicial rhetoric: the motives of wrongdoing, and the character and disposition of the wrongdoer and of the victim (1368b).

2 These topics occupy Aristotle's discussion throughout *Rhetoric* I, 10. Parallel treatments in other handboks tend toward a more practical concentration on the application of τόποι in the δικαστήριον. The *Rhetorica ad Herennium* discusses the 'legal' issue, in which controversy centers around distinguishing the letter from the spirit of a law, or conflicting laws, ambiguous laws, or acts against which no written laws exist (1.19-23), and in which one might appeal, for or against the defendant, to 'natural law', or custom, or to previous

rhetoric, Paul has emphasized the immoral actions of 'the accused' (1.18-32), denying any plea of ignorance (1.19-20, 32; 2.2) and accusing his 'defendant' of willfully presuming on the mercy of the divine 'court' (2.3-5). These rhetorical moves parallel strategies recommended for prosecution in the handbooks.[1]

Interestingly, in the case of a defense plea for mercy (cf. Rom. 2.3-4), the handbooks recommend that the prosecutor appeal to *precedent* in analogous cases in which other people 'have not been pardoned though offering a similar excuse, and argue that they were by comparison more worthy of pardon'.[2] Paul's technique varies only in that his appeal to 'precedent' is at the same time the calling of a witness whose only authority consists in standing beneath the same measure of justice, who indeed is compelled to declare προεχόμεθα; οὐ πάντως (3.9).[3]

judgments in analogous cases, or to contracts, or to 'equity' (*bonum*: 2.13-18). When the written laws were clear enough, the issue was juridical (1.24): one might plead then that the act, though technically illegal, was nevertheless right (an 'absolute juridical' issue), appealing to 'unwritten law'; or one might assume responsibility for the act, but plead innocent by virtue of extenuating circumstances (the 'assumptive' issue); or, conceding guilt, one might plead that the act was not the result of harmful intent, but of ignorance, mistake, or fate or accident (*exculpatio*), or else—as a last resort—one could concede culpability (*concessio*) and throw oneself on the mercy of the court (1.24-25). In each issue, relevant τόποι can be appropriated by the prosecution or by the defense. The *Rhetorica ad Herennium* lists ten topics (*loci*) useful in accusation (2.48-49), and suggests the use of apostrophe and interrogation for provoking indignation toward the defendant (4.22).

1 See *Ad Herennium* 2.48-49, 4.22; *Ad Alexandrum* 1441b, 1443a-b; Cicero, *De Inventione* 2.107.

2 Cicero, *De Inventione*, 2.100; *Ad Herennium*, 2.25.

3 The handbooks discuss the introduction and examination of witnesses in courtroom cases, but do not provide any special insight into the rhetoric of Rom. 2, where a 'fictitious' witness is called. Paul would have been more familiar with the 'prosecution rhetoric' of Israel's prophetic scriptures; in particular, the motif of 'witnesses' in the divine judgment is an apocalyptic motif (cf. 1 Enoch 97–105; Martha Himmelfarb, *Tours of Hell: An Apocalyptic Form in Jewish and Christian Literature* [Philadelphia: Fortress, 1983]. Jews and proselytes are brought forward to testify against Gentile sinners, specifically Gentiles who plead ignorance of Torah, in some later aggadot: see *Pesikta Rabbati: Discourses for Feasts,*

But Paul's use of the Torah-*topos* does more than draw the Gentile hearer toward confessing the rightness of God's verdict in the Law. If the Law remains God's righteous requirement upon all humanity, it is, by implication, not restricted to the Jews alone. More pointedly, Paul's exoneration of the Torah in its involvement in human culpability (7.7-25) and especially with regard to Israel's 'unbelief' (9.30-10.13) implies that the Law is *not* simply the 'rock' against which Israel suffers shipwreck. This is at the same time a vindication of God's elective and redemptive purposes toward Israel, as the larger context of Rom. 9–11 shows. If the 'breaking off' of Jewish 'branches' (11.17-19) is perceived within Gentile Christianity as a 'theological fact',[1] Paul wants to distance that 'fact' from God's purpose in giving the Law, for in fact the Gentile 'boast' against Israel (11.19) coincides with 'contempt' for the keeping of the *miṣwôt* (14.3).

3. *Results: Romans*

At this point we should be able briefly to recapitulate our principal findings concerning Paul's letter to the Roman church, and to discuss at greater length the implications of those findings for a description of Pauline theology.

Our exegetical and rhetorical analysis of Romans leads us to argue strenuously against any view that construes the letter merely as a source lode for a systematic Pauline theology or, more modestly, for isolated theologoumena. All that Paul says here is directed to particular argumentative purposes that arise from his apostolic commission to 'secure the obedience of faith among the Gentiles' (Rom. 1.5).

Romans has a specific paraenetic goal (15.14-16). Paul wills that by their obedient response to his letter, the Gentile Christians in Rome will become participants in the cosmic 'offering of the Gentiles' (15.16), which is symbolized in the collection for Jerusalem, but which is more importantly the 'offering of the Gentiles' to God, the 'spiritual worship' of sanctified minds

Fasts, and Special Sabbaths, trans. W.G. Braude (New Haven: Yale University, 1968), II, p. 674; *The Babylonian Talmud: Seder Nezikin*, vol. 4, ed. I. Epstein (London: Soncino, 1935), pp. 1-7; discussed by E. Urbach, 'Self-Isolation or Self-Affirmation', pp. 269-98.

1 Fraikin, 'Rhetorical Function of the Jews', p. 101.

and bodies (12.1-2). This insight into the paraenetic character of Romans (Boers) means that the letter is misunderstood when it is read as a theological self-introduction to the Roman church (Kümmel), a letter-essay (Stirewalt; Donfried), a theological last will and testament (Bornkamm), an apologetic brief for Jerusalem (Jervell), or in any other way that relates the letter's content to its occasion only loosely as a theological 'cargo' dispatched to a materially irrelevant destination.

The letter includes paraenesis (chs. 12–15) grounded in a sustained enthymemetic argument (chs. 1–11) that disposes the 'mercy of God' (cf. 12.1) as cohering in God's righteousness. The lengthy theological argumentation in these chapters should not be extracted from the rhetorical situation that calls it forth and generalized as 'the gospel according to Paul'. Everything Paul says is oriented toward a particular persuasive goal and constrained by the elements of a particular rhetorical situation. The letter effectively reconstellates principal convictions of the Hellenistic-Christian κήρυγμα, particular among these being the christological-soteriological symbolization of Christ's atoning death 'for us', the ethical status of Gentile Christians as those 'not under the Law', and what has been called the 'replacement theory', that is, the conviction that Gentiles have been incorporated in salvation history in such a way as to supplant Israel, who have rejected their Messiah. Paul's goal is to avert the danger of Gentile-Christian boasting over Israel (cf. Rom. 11.17-24); but this goal is manifest in the macro-structure of the whole letter, not only in the explicit apocalyptic admonition of Romans 11. His use of 'justification' language (δικαιοῦσθαι) and his discussion of the Law (Torah) are integrated into this specific argument, and should not be generalized as 'Paul's debate with Judaism', or cut free from its situational context to serve as the *Mitte* of Paul's theology.

That Romans is nevertheless the lengthiest and most far-ranging of Paul's letters is due to the broad and comprehensive dimension of the apostle's purpose. Although we would not be justified in attributing the letter's sustained and heavily conceptual argumentation to abstractly dogmatic concerns, neither may that argumentation be collapsed into a corrective aimed narrowly at the sociological horizons of the Roman

church. Paul writes to a congregation that he has neither
founded nor visited, although he may be fairly well informed
about its circumstances. He addresses them without regard
for their singularities, but out of his more expansive obligation
to 'the rest of the Gentiles' (1.13). That is, he addresses the
Romans as *Gentile Christians*, and it is precisely as such that
they are to respond to him as the Apostle to the Gentiles. If the
letter is to be appropriated theologically in the modern situation, the exegesis presented above suggests that such appropriation might more properly read Romans along these lines:
Its address to *Gentile Christians as such*, rather than its mistakenly supposed systematic or dogmatic character, should
give Romans whatever catholicity it may enjoy.

4. *Results: Pauline Theology*

The term 'catholicity' may ring odd in ears accustomed to the
contrast of 'the Apostle' and nascent 'early catholicism'. It is
largely on the basis of Augustine's and Luther's reading of this
letter that Paul's writings, and Romans above all, have been
appropriated as the 'canon within the canon' for modern
Protestantism.[1] The heritage of centuries of Protestant appropriation lay a tremendous burden against the interpreter who
would struggle to understand Romans and its author historically (Schmithals). It is tendentious, but perhaps not unac-
ceptably so, to speak of the 'Lutheran captivity' of this epistle.
This dissertation has pointed out only some of the places
where liberation from that captivity is most evidently needed.

In particular, the interpretation of Romans must be
released from the burden of expounding the uniquely Pauline
doctrine of justification by faith alone. Reading Romans
through Lutheran lenses can distort the apostle's rhetoric,
when Rom. 1.16-17 are artifically isolated as the topic paragraph for a treatise, and the dark picture of 1.18–3.20 made
into only a lengthy prolegomenon to the exposition of that
theme in 3.21-26 and chs. 5–8. Romans 9–11 appears tangential to that exposition, and can be related to it only with
difficulty. Under the presumption that Romans shares this

---

1 See Stowers, 'Text as Interpretation'; Paula Fredriksen Landes,
Augustine on Romans (Chico: Scholars, 1982).

central theological theme with Galatians, the contingent character of *this* letter is forfeited, or else reduced to a more cautious and circumspect, albeit also more expansive, echo of Galatians.

The Reformation dichotomy between Law and Gospel, or between faith and works, also requires that Romans be read primarily against the dark background of a Jewish 'counterthesis'. Our second excursus was devoted to exposing the inadequacy of this hermeneutical assumption in interpreting Rom. 1.18–4.25, the supposed heart of Paul's 'debate with Judaism'. The interpretation of those chapters advanced above shows that such an assumption imposes a frame of reference quite foreign to the text.

It is somewhat surprising that this reading of Romans, originally determined by ecclesiastical controversies in the sixteenth century, should find its most eloquent spokesman today in Rudolf Bultmann, who has advocated a thoroughly historical-critical approach to the apostle. After all, Bultmann promulgated Heitmueler's view of Paul's position in the history of early Christianity: 'Standing within the frame of Hellenistic Christianity, he raised the theological motifs that were at work in the proclamation of the Hellenistic Church to the clarity of theological thinking: he called to attention the problems latent in the Hellenistic proclamation and brought them to a decision; and thus—so far as our sources permit an opinion on the matter—became the founder of Christian theology'.[1] Yet Bultmann's exegesis of Romans is determined throughout by the opposition of Paul to *Judaism*, not to Hellenistic Christianity.

Käsemann corrected the individualistic-existentialist skew of Bultmann's demythologizing by recovering the cosmic and apocalyptic coordinates of Paul's theology, and particularly of his doctrine of justification by faith. Yet the main thrust of that doctrine remains oriented polemically against Judaism, and only occasionally and incidentally does Paul's apocalypticism engage Hellenistic-Christian 'enthusiasm' on a second front.[2]

---

1 Bultmann, *Theology*, I, p. 187.
2 See Käsemann's essays, 'The Righteousness of God in Paul'; 'Sentences of Holy Law in the New Testament'; and 'On the Subject

Beker gave Paul's apocalypticism a centrally determinative role in the apostle's theology, and showed that this distinguished Paul from the christocentric theology of the Antioch church;[1] but even here these insights were not allowed to reorient the interpretation of Romans, which remains a 'debate with Judaism', or to pull the description of Pauline theology away from a fundamental opposition to *Judaism* and Jewish Christianity.

Our previous chapters have shown that Paul has channeled the stylized prosecution rhetoric of Romans 1–4 into a redisposition of the christology and *ethos* of Hellenistic Christianity along apocalyptic coordinates. 'Freedom from the Law' and the doctrine of justification by faith alone are not Paul's themes, but the premises he shares with his audience— premises that he seeks to reconstellate around the sovereign claim of the righteous God upon creation. That claim is realized already in those who in Christ have been brought into the dominion of righteousness (6.17-18, 22). Paul makes the slogan 'freedom from the Law' captive to the requirement of *obedience* ('slavery to righteousness'). In this sense, the whole of Romans is written as a *critique* of the Hellenistic-Christian doctrine of justification by faith.

Some more broadly methodological considerations follow. First, the standard practice of writing Pauline theology around the skeleton of Romans (cf. Bultmann's *Theology of the New Testament*) distorts the letter's character, since it is not intended as a comprehensive or systematic representation of 'the gospel', and also mistakenly places justification by faith at the center of that gospel as Paul preaches it (Bultmann, Käsemann). It is preferable to speak with Beker of 'a symbolic structure', of the contingency of Paul's hermeneutic, and of the 'apocalyptic texture of Paul's thought'. Beker uses the language of structuralism to distinguish the 'deep structure' of Paul's thought, 'the Christ-event in its meaning for the apocalyptic consummation of history', from the 'surface structure', 'the contingent interpretation of Paul's Christian

---

of Primitive Christian Apocalyptic'. These views are of course given more sustained elaboration in his *Commentary on Romans*.

1 Beker, *Paul the Apostle*, chs. 8 and 9.

apocalyptic into a particular situation'. This distinction allows him to avoid the periods of identifying a particular symbolization—justification by faith, for example—as the center or whole of Paul's gospel, on one side, and of fixing an apocalyptic worldview as the content of Paul's theology, on the other.[1]

It also (at least potentially) frees interpreters from the restrictive preoccupation with casting Paul's theology almost exclusively in opposition to a Jewish counter-theology that must be manufactured, as it were, from a 'negative' of Romans (Sanders). This is still the preferred method for describing Paul's thought, despite its usually unexamined implications for the description of ancient Judaism;[2] yet it has long outlived its usefulness in anti-Catholic invectiveness. It is just here that our reading of Romans has significant implications for writing Pauline theology, for, as we have argued, the argumentation in Romans is not aimed against Judaism, either directly or by way of bolstering Gentile-Christian self-confidence. The framework of argumentation in Romans (that is, Paul's identification of his audience as Gentile Christians) and the starting point of argumentation (that is, Paul's basis of agreement with his Gentile-Christian audience), no less than the letter's paraenetic exigence suggest that Paul's theology, at least as it is given expression in Romans, might more profitably be elaborated in opposition to the Hellenistic-Christian κήρυγμα. The point of difference is Paul's 'basal language' of Jewish apocalyptic (Beker) as it has determined his interpretation of the Christ event.

---

1 Beker, *Paul the Apostle*, pp. 15-19. Most criticisms of Beker's proposals have objected to his identification of apocalyptic as the hermeneutical key to Paul's theology, either because the apocalyptic perspective is untenable today—an 'objection to apocalyptic' already adequately addressed in Beker's work (pp. 18-19)—or because Beker is supposed to have neglected the 'non-apocalyptic' elements in Paul's thought (cf. V.P. Branick, 'Apocalyptic Paul?', *CBQ* 47 [1985], pp. 664-75). This second objection is addressed by Beker's structuralist approach: elements that are not in themselves patently 'apocalyptic' are nonetheless constellated by an apocalyptic core in Paul's thought.

2 This is true even of Sanders' own work (*Paul and Palestinian Judaism*), which asks *how* and *why*, but not *whether* Paul's theology (at least in Romans) is in fact antithetically related to Judaism.

What most distinguishes Paul from his non-Christian Jewish contemporaries, we suggest, is his conviction that Jesus is the Messiah of Israel. But in this we hardly see the insight of a lone theological genius. Insofar as Paul diverges from his Pharisaic contemporaries—in condoning the entrance of Gentiles into the eschatological community, without requiring the acceptance of the yoke of Torah;[1] in declaring Christ the end, that is, the goal of Torah, and in viewing the Jewish rejection of the Messiah as a refusal to submit to God's righteousness—he is squarely at home within early ('Hellenistic', including Jewish and Gentile) Christianity. Gal. 2.15-16 suggests that even the doctrine of justification by faith was not Paul's exclusive property, but was something he expected Peter to accept *as a Jew*. To discuss these convictions as Paul's theological *proprium* is problematic: they belong to a summary of 'the Hellenistic κήρυγμα'.[2]

We have argued that Romans provides little material for a proposed Pauline critique of Judaism. Paul does not accuse the Jews generally of a self-striving after righteousness through works; nor does he at any time declare either the Torah or Israel's covenant obsolete or invalidated. Nowhere in Rom. 9-11 does he attribute the Jewish rejection of Jesus to any *endemically Jewish* flaw (a perverted legalism, striving for self-righteousness, etc.). Israel failed to realize the purpose of Torah, which is to lead to the Messiah (9.30–10.4), because

---

1 Paula Fredriksen ('Too Many Gentiles, Too Few Jews, and No End in Sight', presented to the Paul Seminar at the SBL Annual Meeting, 1987; see now her valuable discussion in *From Jesus to Christ* [New Haven: Yale University Press, 1988], pp. 165-70) has argued that just this theological move in early Christianity reveals an apocalyptic tradition in Judaism that anticipated the gathering to the God of Israel of *Gentiles* as such; as a sort of eschatological sign, they were not expected to keep Torah or become proselytes.

2 Even Bultmann (*Theology*, I, p. 109) admits that 'the Torah-free attitude of Hellenistic Christianity is by no means simply a result of *Paul's* struggle against the 'Judaizers', and much less was his defense of freedom from the Law either then or later the *only* one in force'; but he nevertheless preserves the doctrine of justification by faith alone for Paul alone, and in classical fashion sets this *proprium* antithetically against Judaism (I, pp. 279-85).

they looked for righteousness not by faith, but 'as if from works', and preferred 'their own righteousness' to the righteousness of God. They failed, that is, not because they sought to obey the Law out of false motives (*contra* Bultmann), but because they have chosen to obey the Law *rather than* accept Jesus as the Messiah. These statements cannot support a phenomenological analysis of the Jew as *homo incurvatus in se* (Luther) or as the paradigm of boastful humanity (Bultmann, Bornkamm, Käsemann), as if Paul described the Jew's relation to Torah *in isolation from* the question of accepting Jesus as Messiah. Nor do the diatribal address in 2.17–3.20 or the stylized 'reminiscence' of 7.7-25 give us material for a Pauline critique of Judaism, as if those passages described specifically *Jewish* standing before Torah in isolation from the question of the Gentile's standing before God's righteous requirement embodied in it.

Our interpretation also has implications in the area of New Testament ethics, where a purely forensic interpretation of Paul's doctrine of justification (Luther, Bultmann) has generated the problematic of 'the relation of indicative and imperative'.[1] A qualitative advance was made when the 'theology of crisis' brought to the fore the gospel's radical demand of obedience. Karl Barth identified 'ethics as a task of the doctrine of God', and discussed 'the command as the claim of God'.[2] Rudolf Bultmann reconstrued ethical action as 'radical obedience', the response of the whole being to God's gracious action[3]—a reconstrual that finds its appropriate issue not in Bultmann's insistent denial that such obedience has any identifiable content, but in Wolfgang Schrage's emphasis upon the concreteness of the ethical demand.[4] This redisposition of the ethical question is echoed in Furnish's

1 Windisch, 'Das Problem des paulinischen Imperativs'; Bultmann, 'Problem of Ethics'; Bornkamm, 'Baptism and New Life in Paul'. Furnish (*Theology and Ethics*, p. 9) declares the relation of indicative and imperative '*the* crucial problem in interpreting the Pauline ethic'.
2 Barth, *Church Dogmatics* II, 2.
3 Bultmann, 'Problem of Ethics'.
4 W. Schrage, *Die konkrete Einzelgebote in der paulinischen Paränese* (Gütersloh: Mohn, 1961).

methodological shift from a starting point in Paul's moral life to a fundamental orientation around Paul's *theology*.[1] Related advances may be seen in Käsemann's reorientation of 'the righteousness of God in Paul' as an apocalyptic category, the sovereign claim of the Creator upon creation,[2] and in Beker's broadening the ethical dimension (against Bultmann's existentialist hermeneutic) to encompass solidarity with an unredeemed creation,[3] and deepening this dimension by revealing its anchorage in the corporeal for Paul.[4]

There is no need to rehearse these treatments here.[5] The contribution of our understanding of Romans is to show that Paul himself was already concerned to address 'hermeneutical difficulties' (Beker) that arise, not from his own theological construction, but from the 'ethical vulnerability' of the Hellenistic-Christian soteriological vocabulary.[6] From beginning to end, the argumentation of Romans is Paul's sustained critique of the Hellenistic κήρυγμα, subordinating the doctrines of expiation of sins in Christ and freedom from the Law to the call for 'the obedience of faith'. Paul has, so to speak, perceived already the problem of generating a positive obligating ethic from the theologoumena of 'freedom', and his solution is to *abandon* that language, at least in Romans, and speak instead ('because of your weakness', 6.19) of 'slavery to righteousness' and the transfer to a new dominion.

From the perspective of ethics, then, Paul's treatment of justification by faith in Romans is not the *problem*, but the first major attempt at a *solution*. In the wake of Käsemann's essay on 'The Righteousness of God', Schrage and Furnish have both emphasized, against Bultmann, the necessary concretization of the sovereign claim for obedience. The rediscovery of Paul's apocalyptic reorientation of ethos and ethics may prove to be fruitful in correlation with newer developments in

---

1 Furnish, *Theology and Ethics*, pp. 9-10.
2 Käsemann, 'The Righteousness of God in Paul'.
3 Beker, *Paul the Apostle*, esp. chs. 13 and 16; see also his *Paul's Apocalyptic Gospel* (Philadelphia: Fortress, 1982).
4 Beker, *Paul the Apostle*, pp. 278-91.
5 See the surveys in Furnish, *Theology and Ethics*, pp. 242-79; Schrage, *Ethik*, pp. 9-20.
6 Beker, *Paul the Apostle*, pp. 264-67.

ethics that reject the nakedly cognitive-volitional Cartesian paradigm for a paradigm that locates the individual agent within a sociopsychological and cultural matrix.[1]

Finally, our interpretation of Romans suggests a corrective to the pervasive Christian chauvinism that is based, historically and culturally, in a triumphalistic christomonism. The recovery of the Pauline gospel's profound rootage in the covenant with Israel points beyond the destiny of particular peoples—'the Jews' or 'the Gentiles'—to the fully cosmic scope of God's redemptive purpose, as this is adumbrated and signified in the history and future of Jesus Christ. The twin slogans of Reformation orthodoxy, *simul iustus et peccator* and *pecca fortiter*, are too often abused, by their inappropriate combination, in a popular piety that exults in identifying with the sinful publican, who relies on God's mercy, while condemning as a hypocrite the 'self-righteous Pharisee'. One result has been the pervasive cultural distortion of Judaism; the misrepresentation of Christian existence as cheap grace, the presumption on the divine mercy in Christ that separates the gift from its Giver, has been another. Only when Romans is released from the 'Lutheran captivity' that chains it to Galatians as a sister exposition of justification by faith may the letter again play its rightful role as a critique of all piety—but especially of all *Christian* piety—that vaunts its privileges as a presumption against God's righteousness. In this way the distinctive voice of the letter's author, who speaks rather as *Paulus contra gentiles*, may again be heard.

1 Alasdair MacIntyre, *After Virtue*, 2nd edn (Notre Dame: University of Notre Dame Press, 1984); Stanley Hauerwas, *A Community of Character* (Notre Dame: University of Notre Dame Press, 1981); *idem, The Peaceable Kingdom: A Primer in Christian Ethics* (Notre Dame: University of Notre Dame Press, 1983). Hauerwas' emphasis (*Peacable Kingdom*, ch. 2) upon the (inevitably cognitivist) narrative structure of ethics should be balanced with the more phenomenological approach of Gibson Winter, *Liberating Creation: Foundations of Religious Social Ethics* (New York: Crossroad, 1981).

BIBLIOGRAPHY

Agnew, Francis H. 'The Origin of the NT Apostle-Concept: A Review of Research'. *JBL* 105 (1986), 75-96.

Applebaum, S. 'The Organization of the Jewish Communities in the Diaspora'. In Safrai and Stern, eds., *The Jewish People in the First Century*, 1.464-503.

Auerbach, Erich. *Mimesis: The Representation of Reality in Western Literature*, Trans. Willard Trask. Princeton: Princeton University Press, 1953.

Aune, David. *The New Testament in its Literary Environment*. Philadelphia: Westminster, 1987.

—Review of H.D. Betz, *Galatians*. *RSR* 7 (1981), 323-26.

Barrett, C.K. *A Commentary on the Epistle to the Romans*. New York: Harper & Row, 1957.

—'Things Sacrificed to Idols'. In *Essays on Paul*. Philadelphia: Westminster 1982.

Barth, Karl. *Church Dogmatics*, vol. II, 2. Trans. Geoffrey W. Bromiley. Edinburgh: T. & T. Clark, 1957.

—*The Epistle to the Romans*. Trans. from the 6th German edition by Edwyn C. Hoskyns. New York: Oxford University Press, 1933.

Bartsch, H.W. 'Die antisemitischen Gegner des Paulus im Römerbrief'. In W. Eckert et al., eds., *Antijudaismus im Neuen Testament*? Munich: Kaiser, 1967.

—'Die historische Situation des Römerbriefes'. *SE* 4/*TU* 102 (1968), pp. 282-91.

Bassler, Jouette. *Divine Impartiality: Paul and a Theological Axiom*. Chico: Scholars, 1982.

Baur, F.C. *Paul, The Apostle of Jesus Christ*. 2 vols. Trans. E. Zeller. London, Edinburgh: Williams and Norgate, 1876.

Beale, Walter. 'Rhetorical Performative Discourse: A New Theory of Epideictic'. *PhR* 11 (1978), 221-46.

Beare, F.W. *Introduction and Exegesis of Ephesians*. IB. Nashville: Abingdon, 1953.

—*St. Paul and His Letters*. Nashville: Abingdon, 1962.

Becker, U. 'Gospel'. In Colin Brown, ed., *New International Dictionary of New Testament Theology*. Grand Rapids: Zondervan, 1976. II, 107-15.

Beker, J. Christiaan. 'The Eschatological Center of the Biblical Message: Paul's Letter to the Romans as Model for a Biblical Theology'. Presented to the Studiorum Novi Testamenti Societas, Göttingen, 1987.

—'The Faithfulness of God and Priority of Israel in Paul's Letter to the Romans'. *HTR* 79 (1986), 10-16.

—*Paul the Apostle: The Triumph of God in Life and Thought.* Philadelphia: Fortress, 1980.

—*Paul's Apocalyptic Gospel.* Philadelphia: Fortress, 1982.

—'Paul's Letter to the Romans as Model for Biblical Theology: Some Preliminary Observations'. In *Understanding the Word: Essays in Honor of Bernhard Word Anderson.* Ed. J.T. Butler et al. Sheffield: JSOT, 1986, 359-67.

—'Paul's Theology: Consistent or Inconsistent?' *NTS* 34 (1988), 364-77.

Berger, Klaus. *Formgeschichte des Neuen Testaments.* Heidelberg: Quelle & Meyer, 1984.

—'Hellenistische Gattungen im NT'. *ANRW* II.25.2 (1984), 1031-1432; 1831-1885.

Berger, Peter. *The Sacred Canopy: Elements of a Sociological Theory of Religion.* New York: Doubleday, 1967.

—and T. Luckmann. *The Social Construction of Reality.* New York: Doubleday, 1967.

Bertram, G. 'ἔργον'. *TDNT* 2.635-55.

Betz, H.D. *Galatians.* Hermeneia. Philadelphia: Fortress, 1985.

—'The Problem of Rhetoric and Theology according to the Apostle Paul'. In *L'Apôtre Paul: personnalité, style, et conception du ministère,* ed. A. Vanhoye. Leuven: Leuven University, 1986.

Billerbeck, Paul. *Kommentar zum Neuen Testament aus Talmud und Midrasch.* Vol. 3. Munich: Beck, 1926.

Bitzer, Lloyd. 'The Rhetorical Situation'. *PhR* 1 (1968), 1-14.

Bjerkelund, C.J. *Parakalô: Form, Funktion, und Sinn der parakalô-Sätze.* Oslo: Universitetsforlaget, 1967.

Black, Clifton. 'The Rhetorical Form of the Hellenistic Jewish and Early Christian Sermon: A Response to Lawrence Willis'. *HTR* 81 (1988), 1-18.

Black, M. *Apocalypsis Henochi Graeci in Pseudepigrapha Veteris Testamenti.* Leiden: Brill, 1970.

Boers, Hendrikus. 'The Problem of Jews and Gentiles in the Macro-Structure of Romans'. *SEÅ* 47 (1982), 184-96.

Borgen, Peder. *Bread from Heaven.* Leiden: Brill, 1965.

—'The Early Church and the Hellenistic Synagogue'. *ST* 57 (1983), 55-78.

—'Observations on the Midrashic Character of John 6'. *ZNW* 56 (1963), 232-40.

—'Paul Preaches Circumcision and Pleases Men'. In Hooker and Wilson, eds., *Paul and Paulism,* 37-46.

Bornkamm, Günther. *Early Christian Experience.* Trans. P.L. Hammer. New York: Harper & Row, 1969.

—'The Letter to the Romans as Paul's Last Will and Testament'. In Donfried, ed., *The Romans Debate,* pp. 17-31. Repr. *ABR* 11 (1963), 2-14.

—'Sin, Law, and Death: An Exegetical Study of Romans', *Early Christian Experience,* 87-104.

—*Paul.* Trans. D.M.G. Stalker. New York: Harper & Row, 1971.

Bousset, W. *Die Religion des Judentums im späthellenistischen Zeitalter.* Ed. H. Gressmann. Tübingen: Vandenhoeck & Ruprecht, 1925.

Bradley, D.G. 'The *Topos* as a Form in the Pauline Paraenesis'. *JBL* 72 (1953), 238-46.

Brandenburger, Egon. *Adam und Christus: Exegetisch-religions-geschichtliche Untersuchung zu Röm. 5,12-21*. Neukirchen: Neukirchener Verlag, 1962.

Brandt, William. *The Rhetoric of Argumentation*. New York: Bobbs-Merrill, 1970.

Branick, V.P. 'Apocalyptic Paul?' *CBQ* 47 (1985), 664-75.

Braude, W.G. *Pesikta Rabbati: Discourses for Feasts, Fasts, and Special Sabbaths*. New Haven: Yale University Press, 1968.

Brinton, Alan. 'Situation in the Theory of Rhetoric'. *PhR* 14 (1981), 234-48.

Brown, Raymond E. 'The Semitic Background of the NT μυστήριον'. *Bib* 39 (1958), 218-28; 40 (1959), 70-87.

—and John P. Meier. *Antioch and Rome: New Testament Cradles of Catholic Christianity*. New York: Paulist, 1983.

Bruce, F.F. *Paul, Apostle of the Heart Set Free*. Grand Rapids: Eerdmans, 1977.

Brunt, John. 'More on the *Topos* as a New Testament Form'. *JBL* 104 (1985), 495-500.

Bultmann, Rudolf. 'αἰδώς'. *TDNT* 1.169-171.

—'Glossen im Röm'. *ThLZ* 72 (1947), 197-202.

—'καυχάομαι'. *TDNT* 3.645-54.

—'Das Problem der Ethik bei Paulus'. *ZNW* 23 (1924), 123-40.

—*Der Stil der paulinischen Predigt und die kynisch-stoische Diatribe*. Göttingen: Vandenhoeck & Ruprecht, 1910.

—*Theology of the New Testament*. 2 vols. Trans. Kendrick Grobel. New York: Charles Scribner's Sons, 1951, 1954.

Bunker, Michael. *Briefformular und rhetorische Disposition im 1. Korintherbrief*. Göttingen: Vandenhoeck & Ruprecht, 1983.

Burgess, Theodore C. 'Epideictic Literature'. *Studies in Classical Philology* 3 (1902), 89-261.

Burkert, Walter. *Homo Necans: The Anthropology of Ancient Greek Sacrificial Ritual and Myth*. Trans. Peter Bing. Berkeley: University of California Press, 1983.

Bussmann, C. *Themen der paulinischen Missionspredigt auf dem Hintergrund der spätjüdisch-hellenistischen Missionsliteratur*. Bern: Herbert Lang, 1971.

Butler, J.T., E.W. Conrad and B.C. Ollenburger, eds. *Understanding the Word: Essays in Honor of Bernhard Word Anderson*. Sheffield: JSOT, 1986.

Byrne, Brendan. 'Living Out the Righteousness of God: The Contribution of Rom. 6.1–8.13 to an Understanding of Paul's Ethical Presuppositions'. *CBQ* 43 (1981), 557-81.

Calvin, John. *The Epistles of Paul the Apostle to the Romans and to the Thessalonians*. Trans. Ross MacKenzie. Grand Rapids: Eerdmans, 1960.

Campbell, W.S. 'The Purposes of Paul in the Letter to the Romans: A Survey of Romans 1–11, with Special Reference to Chapters 9–11'. Dissertation, University of Edinburgh, 1972.

—'Why Did Paul Write Romans?' *ExpT* 85 (1973-1974), 264-69.

—'Christ the End of the Law: Romans 10.4'. *Studia Biblica III*. Sheffield: JSOT, 1978, 73-81.

—'The Freedom and Faithfulness of God in Relation to Israel'. *JSNT* 13 (1981), 27-45.

—'Revisiting Romans'. *Scr* 12 (1981), 2-10.

—'Romans III as a Key to the Structure and Thought of the Letter'. *NovT* 23 (1981), 22-40.

—'Did Paul Advocate Separation from the Synagogue?' A Reaction to Francis Watson: *Paul, Judaism and the Gentiles: A Sociological Approach*'. *SJT* 41 (1988), pp. 1-11.

Charlesworth, James H. 'Jewish Hymns, Odes, and Prayers'. In Kraft and Nickelsburg, eds., *Early Judaism and its Modern Interpreters*, 411-36.

Childs, Brevard. 'The Canonical Shape of the Prophetic Literature'. *Int* 32 (1978), 46-55.

Collins, John. *Between Athens and Jerusalem: Jewish Identity in the Hellenistic Diaspora*. New York: Crossroad, 1983.

Consigny, Scott. 'Rhetoric and its Situations'. *PhR* 7 (1974), 175-86.

Conzelmann, Hans. *The Theology of St. Luke*. Trans. Geoffrey Buswell. Philadelphia: Fortress, 1961.

Cosgrove, Charles. 'What If Some Have Not Believed? The Occasion and Thrust of Romans 3.1-8'. *ZNW* 78 (1987), 90-105.

Cranfield, C.E.B. *The Epistle to the Romans*. ICC. 2 vols. Edinburgh: T. & T. Clark, 1975, 1979.

Crenshaw, James, and Samuel Sandmel, eds., *The Divine Helmsman: Essays Presented to Lou Silberman*. New York: KTAV, 1980.

Dahl, Nils. *Jesus in the Memory of the Early Church*. Minneapolis: Augsburg, 1976.

—'Romans 3.9: Text and Meaning'. In Hooker and Wilson, eds., *Paul and Paulinism*, 184-204.

—*Studies in Paul*. Minneapolis: Augsburg, 1977.

—'Two Notes on Romans 5'. *ST* 5 (1951), 37-48.

Dalbert, P. *Die Theologie der hellenistisch-jüdischen Missionsliteratur unter Ausschluss von Philo und Josephus*. Hamburg: Herbert Reich, 1954.

Dautzenberg, Gerhard. *Urchristliche Prophetie*. Stuttgart: Kohlhammer, 1975.

Davies, Alan, ed. *Antisemitism and the Foundations of Christianity*. New York: Paulist, 1979.

Davies, W.D. 'Paul and the People of Israel', *NTS* 24 (1977), 4-39.

Daxer, A. 'Römer 1.18–2.10 im Verhältnis zur spätjüdischen Lehrauffassung'. Dissertation, Rostock, 1914.

Dibelius, Martin. *James*. Trans. Michael A. Williams. Hermeneia. Philadelphia: Fortress, 1976.

Dodd, C.H. *The Epistle of Paul to the Romans*. Moffat NT Commentaries. New York: Harper & Row, 1932, 148-49.

Donfried, Karl P. 'False Presuppositions in the Study of Romans'. In *The Romans Debate*, 120-48.

—ed. *The Romans Debate*. Minneapolis: Augsburg, 1977.

Doty, William G. *Letters in Primitive Christianity*. Philadelphia: Fortress, 1973.

Dunn, J.G.D. 'The New Perspective on Paul'. *BJRL* 65 (1983), 95-122.

—'Rom. 7,14-25 in the Theology of Paul'. *ThZ* 31 (1975), 257-73.

Ellis, E. Earle. *Prophecy and Hermeneutic*. Grand Rapids: Eerdmans, 1978.

Epstein, I., ed. *The Babylonian Talmud: Seder Nezikin*, vol. 4. London: Soncino, 1935.

Erickson, K., ed. *Aristotle: The Classical Heritage of Rhetoric*. Metuchen: Scarecrow, 1974.

Farmer, W.R., C.F.D. Moule, and R.R. Niebuhr, eds., *Christian History and Interpretation: Studies Presented to John Knox*. Cambridge: Cambridge University Press, 1967.

Feldman, Louis H. 'Jewish "Sympathizers" in Classical Literature and Inscriptions'. *TAPA* 81 (1950), 58-63.

Feine, P. *Der Römerbrief.* Göttingen: Vandenhoeck & Ruprecht, 1903.

Finn, Thomas, 'The God-Fearers Reconsidered'. *CBQ* 47 (1985), 75-84.

Flückiger, F. 'Zur Unterscheidung von Heiden und Juden in Röm. 1.18–2.3'. *TZ* 8 (1952), 154-58.

Fraikin, Daniel, 'The Rhetorical Function of the Jews in Romans'. In Richardson, ed., *Anti-Judaism*, 91-106.

Francis, F.O. 'The Form and Function of the Opening and Closing Paragraphs in James and 1 John'. *ZNW* 61 (1970), 110-26.

Fredricksen, Paula. *From Jesus to Christ: The Origins of the New Testament Images of Christ*. New Haven: Yale University Press, 1988.

Frend, W.H.C. *The Rise of Christianity*. Philadelphia: Fortress, 1984.

Friedrich, G. 'Das Gesetz des Glaubens Röm. 3,27. *TZ* 10 (1954), 401-17.

Friedrich, J., W. Pöhlmann, P. Stuhlmacher, eds. *Rechtfertigung: Festschrift für Ernst Käsemann zum 80. Geburtstag*. Tübingen: J.C.B. Mohr (Paul Siebeck), 1976.

Fuller, R.H. *The Foundations of New Testament Christology*. London: SPCK, 1965.

Funk, Robert. *Language, Hermeneutic, and Word of God*. New York: Harper & Row, 1966.

—'The Apostolic Parousia: Form and Significance'. In W.R. Farmer, C.F.D. Moule, and R. Niebuhr, eds., *Christian History and Interpretation*, 249-68.

Furnish, V.P. *Theology and Ethics in Paul*. Abingdon: Nashville, 1968.

Gager, John G. 'Functional Diversity in Paul's Use of End-Time Language'. *JBL* 89 (1970), 325-37.

—*The Origins of Antisemitism*. New York: Oxford University Press, 1984.

Gamble, Harry, 'The Redaction of the Pauline Letters and the Formation of the Pauline Corpus'. *JBL* 94 (1975), 403-18.

—*The Textual History of the Letter to the Romans*. Grand Rapids: Eerdmans, 1977.

Gaston, Lloyd. 'Abraham and the Righteousness of God'. *HRT* 2 (1980), 39-68.

306   *The Rhetoric of Romans*

—'Israel's Enemies in Pauline Theology'. *NTS* 28 (1982), 400-23.
—'Paul and the Torah'. In Davies, ed., *Antisemitism and the Foundation of Christianity*, 48-71.
—*Paul and the Torah*. Vancouver: University of British Columbia Press, 1987.
Geertz, Clifford. *The Interpretation of Cultures*. New York: Basic Books, 1973.
Georgi, Dieter. *Die Geschichte der Kollekte des Paulus für Jerusalem*. Hamburg-Bergstet: Reich, 1965.
—*Paul's Opponents in Second Corinthians*. English trans. Philadelphia: Fortress, 1985.
Gerhardsson, B. *The Ethos of the Bible*. Trans. Stephen Westerholm. Philadelphia: Fortress, 1981.
Getty, Mary Ann. 'Paul and the Salvation of Israel: A Perspective on Romans 9–11', *CBQ* 50 (1988), 456-69.
Gnilka, J. *Die Verstockung Israels: Isaias 6.9-10 in der Theologie der Synoptiker*. Munich: Kösel.
Goldstein, Jonathan. 'Jewish Acceptance and Rejection of Hellenism'. In Sanders, ed., *Jewish and Christian Self-Definition*, vol. 2, 64-87.
Goodspeed, E.J. *The Meaning of Ephesians*. Chicago: University of Chicago Press, 1933.
Goppelt, Leonhard. *Theology of the New Testament*. 2 vols. Trans. John Alsup. Ed. Jürgen Roloff. Grand Rapids: Eerdmans, 1981, 1982.
Grimaldi, William. 'The Aristotelian Topics'. In K. Erickson, ed., *Aristotle: the Classical Heritage of Rhetoric*. Metuchen: Scarecrow, 1974. Pp. 176-93. Repr. from *Traditio* 14 (1958), 1-16.
Gutbrod, W. 'Νόμος'. *TDNT* 4.1036-1091.
Hahn, F. 'Die christologische Begründung urchristlicher Paränese'. *ZNW* 72 (1981), 88-99.
Hare, Douglas, 'As the Twig Was Bent: Antisemitism in Greco-Roman and Earliest Christian Times', in A. Davies, ed., *Antisemitism and the Foundations of Christianity*, 1-26.
Harnisch, Wolfgang. *Verhängnis und Verheissung der Geschichte*. Göttingen: Vandenhoeck & Ruprecht, 1969.
Hauerwas, Stanley. *A Community of Character*. Notre Dame: University of Notre Dame Press, 1981.
Hays, Richard B. '"Have We Found Abraham to Be Our Forefather According to the Flesh?" A Reconsideration of Rom. 4.1'. *NovT* 27 (1985), 77-98.
—'Psalm 143 and the Logic of Rom. 3'. *JBL* 99 (1980), 107-15.
Heidland, H.W. 'Λογίζομαι'. *TDNT* 4.284-92.
Hengel, Martin. *Judaism and Hellenism*. 2 vols. Trans. John Bowden. Philadelphia: Fortress, 1974.
Himmelfarb, Martha. *Tours of Hell: An Apocalyptic Form of Jewish and Christian Literature*. Philadelphia: Fortress, 1983.
Hooker, M.D. 'Paul and "Covenantal Nomism"'. In Hooker and Wilson, eds., *Paul and Paulinism*.
—and S.G. Wilson, eds. *Paul and Paulinism: Essays in Honour of C.K. Barrett*. London: SPCK, 1982.

Howard, George. 'Romans 3.21-31 and the Inclusion of the Gentiles'. *HTR* 63 (1970), 223-33.

Jeremias, Joachim. 'Zur Gedankenführung in den paulinischen Briefen'. In *Studia Paulina in honorem Iohannes de Zwaan septuagenarii*. Haarlem: Bohn, 1953, 146-53.

Jervell, Jacob. 'The Letter to Jerusalem'. In Donfried, ed., *Romans Debate*, 61-74. Rpt. *ST* 25 (1971), 61-73.

Jewett, Robert. 'The Law and the Coexistence of Jews and Gentiles in Romans'. *Int* 34 (1985), 341-56.

—'Romans as an Ambassadorial Letter'. *Int* 36 (1982), 5-20.

Johnson, Dan G. 'The Structure and Meaning of Romans 11'. *CBQ* 46 (1984), 91-103.

Johnson, Luke T. 'Rom. 3.21-26 and the Faith of Jesus'. *CBQ* 44 (1982), 77-90.

—*The Writings of the New Testament*. Philadelphia: Fortress, 1986.

Karris, R.J. 'Romans 14.1–15.13 and the Occasion of Romans'. In Donfried, ed., *The Romans Debate*, 75-99.

—'The Occasion of Romans: A Response to Professor Donfried'. In Donfried, ed., *The Romans Debate*, 149-51. Rpt. *CBQ* 36 (1974), 356-58.

Käsemann, Ernst. *Commentary on Romans*. Trans. G.W. Bromiley. Grand Rapids: Eerdmans, 1980.

—'Ephesians and Acts'. In L.E. Keck and J.L. Martyn, eds., *Studies in Luke–Acts*. Philadelphia: Fortress, 1966, 288-97.

—'Epheserbrief'. *RGG*, vol. 2, 517ff.

—*Essays on New Testament Themes*. Trans. W.J. Montague. Philadelphia: Fortress, 1982.

—*Exegetische Versuche und Besinnungen*, vol. 1. 6th edn Göttingen: Vandenhoeck & Ruprecht, 1970.

—*New Testament Questions of Today*. Trans. W.J. Montague. Philadelphia: Fortress, 1979.

—*Perspectives on Paul*. Trans. Margaret Kohl. Philadelphia: Fortress, 1971.

—'Zum Verständnis von Römer 3.24-26'. *ZNW* 43 (1950-1951), 150-54.

Keck, Leander, E. 'On the Ethos of Early Christians'. JAAR 42 (1971), 435-72.

—'The Function of Rom. 3.10-18: Observations and Suggestions'. In J. Jervell and W.A. Meeks, eds., *God's Christ and His People: Studies in Honor of Nils Alstrup Dahl*. Oslo: Universitetsforlaget, 1977, 141-67.

—'The Law and "the Law of Sin and Death" (Rom. 8.1-4): Reflections on the Spirit and Ethics in Paul'. In Crenshaw and Sandmel, eds., *Divine Helmsman*, 41-57.

Kennedy, George. *The Art of Persuasion in Ancient Greece*. Princeton: Princeton University Press, 1963.

—*The Art of Rhetoric in the Roman World*. Princeton: Princeton Unviersity Press, 1972.

—*Classical Rhetoric and its Christian and Secular Tradition from Ancient to Modern Times*. Chapel Hill: University of North Carolina Press, 1980.

—*New Testament Interpretation Through Rhetorical Criticism*. Chapel Hill: University of North Carolina Press, 1984.

Kinoshita, J. 'Romans—Two Writings Combined'. *NovT* 7 (1965), 258-77.

Kirby, John. 'The Syntax of Romans 5.12: A Rhetorical Approach'. *NTS* 33 (1987), 283-86.

Klein, Günter. 'Paul's Purpose in Writing the Epistle to the Romans'. In Donfried, ed., *Romans Debate*, 32-49 Repr. *Rekonstruktion und Interpretation: Gesammelte Aufsätze zum Neuen Testament*. Munich: C. Kaiser, 1969, 129-44.

Knox, John. 'A Note on the Text of Romans'. *NTS* 2-3 (1955-1956), 191-93.

—*Romans*. IB9. New York: Abingdon, 1954.

Koskenniemi, H. *Studien zur Idee und Phraseologie des griechischen Briefes bis 400 n. Chr.* (Helsinki: Akateeminen Kivjakauppa, 1956).

Kraabel, A.T. 'The Disappearance of the "God-Fearers"'. *Numen* 28 (1981), 113-26.

Kraftchick, Steven, 'Ethos and Pathos Appeals in Galatians 5 and 6: A Rhetorical Analysis'. Dissertation, Emory University, 1985.

Krauss, Hans-Joachim. *Theology of the Psalms*. Trans. Keith Crim. Minneapolis: Augsburg, 1986.

Kümmel, *Introduction to the New Testatment*, rev. edn Trans. H.C. Kee. Nashville: Abingdon, 1975.

—'πάρεσις und ἔνδειξις, ein Beitrag zum Verständnis der paulinischen Rechtfertigungslehre'. *ZTK* 49 (1952), 154-67.

—'Die Probleme von Römer 9–11 in der gegenwärtigen Forschungslage', in *Heilsgeschehen und Geschichte*, II: *Gesammelte Aufsätze 1965-1976*. Marburg: Alwert, 1978, 245-60.

—*Römer 7 und die Bekehrung des Paulus*. Leipzig: Hinrichs, 1929.

Kuss, O. *Der Römerbrief*. Regensburg: Friedrich Pustet, 1957.

Kustas, G.L. 'Diatribe in Ancient Rhetorical Theory'. In Wuellner, ed., *Diatribe in Ancient Rhetorical Theory*, 1-15.

Lambrecht, J. 'Why Is Boasting Excluded? A Note on Rom. 3,27 and 4,2'. *ETL* 61 (1985), 365-69.

Landes, Paula Fredriksen. *Augustine on Romans*. Chico: Scholars, 1982.

Lanham, Richard. *A Handlist of Rhetorical Terms*. Berkeley: University of California, 1969, 122.

LaPiana, George. 'Foreign Groups in Rome During the First Centuries of the Empire'. *HTR* 20 (1927), 341-93.

Lausberg, Heinrich. *Handbuch der literarischen Rhetorik: Eine Grundlegung der Literaturwissenschaft*. 3rd edn 2 vols. Munich: Max Hueber, 1967.

Leon, H.J. *The Jews of Ancient Rome*. Philadelphia: Jewish Publication Society of America, 1960.

Lietzmann, Hans. *An die Römer*. 3rd edn Tübingen: J.C.B. Mohr (Paul Siebeck), 1928.

Lightfoot, J.B. *Saint Paul's Epistle to the Galatians*. London: Macmillan, 1865.

Lincoln, Andrew. 'The Church and Israel in Ephesians 2'. *CBQ* 49 (1987), 601-27.

Lindemann, A. *Die Aufhebung der Zeit*. Gütersloh: Gerd Mohn, 1975.

Little, Joyce. 'Paul's Use of Analogy (Rom. 7.1-6)'. *CBQ* 46 (1984), 82-90.

Lohmeyer, E. 'Probleme paulinischer Theologie, III: Sünde, Fleisch, und Tod'. *ZNW* 29 (1930), 1-59.

Lorenzi, Lorenzo De, ed. *Die Israelfrage nach Röm 9–11*. Rome: Hlg. Paulus vor den Mauern, 1977.

Lüdemann, Gerd. *Paul, Apostle to the Gentiles: Studies in Chronology*. Trans. F.S. Jones. Philadelphia: Fortress, 1984.

Lührmann, D. 'Christologie und Rechtfertigung'. In Friedrich, Pohlmann, and Stuhlmacher, eds., *Rechtfertigung*, 351-63.

Luz, U. *Das Geschichtsverständnis des Paulus*. Munich: Chr. Kaiser, 1968.

—'Zum Aufbau von Rom I–VIII'. *ThZ* 25 (1969), 161-81.

—*Paulus im ältesten Christentum*. Tübingen: J.C.B. Mohr (Paul Siebeck), 1979.

MacIntyre, Alasdair. *After Virtue*, 2nd edn Notre Dame: University of Notre Dame Press, 1984.

Malherbe, Abraham. 'Ancient Epistolary Theorists'. *OJRS* 5 (1977), 3-77.

—'Exhortation in First Thessalonians'. *NovT* 25 (1983), 238-56.

—'Hellenistic Moralists and the New Testament'. Forthcoming in *ANRW*.

—'Μὴ γένοιτο in the Diatribe and Paul'. *HTR* 73 (1980), 231-40.

—*Moral Exhortation: A Greco-Roman Sourcebook*. Philadelphia: Westminster, 1986.

—*Paul and the Thessalonians: The Philosophical Tradition of Pastoral Care*. Philadelphia: Fortress, 1987.

Malina, Bruce, J. *The New Testament World: Insights from Cultural Anthropology*. Atlanta: John Knox, 1981.

Manson, T.W. "Saint Paul's Letter to the Romans—and Others'. In Donfried, *Romans Debate*, 1-16. Repr. from *BJRL* 31 (1948), 224-40.

Martin, Josef. *Antike Rhetorik: Technik und Methode*. Handbuch der Altertumswissenschaft 2.3. Munich: C.H. Beck, 1974.

Martyn, J. Louis. *History and Theology in the Fourth Gospel*. Rev. edn. Nashville: Abingdon, 1979.

Marxsen, Willi. *Introduction to the New Testament*. Trans. G. Buswell. Philadelphia: Fortress, 1968.

McEleney, Neil. 'Conversion, Circumcision, and the Law'. *NTS* 20 (1974), 319-41.

Meeks, Wayne, A. *The First Urban Christians*. New Haven: Yale University, 1983.

—'Judgment and the Brother: Romans 14.1–15.13'. In Hawthorne and Betz, eds., *Tradition and Interpretation in the New Testament*, 290-92.

—*The Moral World of the First Christians*. Philadelphia: Westminster, 1986.

—'Understanding Early Christian Ethics'. *JBL* 105 (1986), 3-11.

Melanchthon, Philip. 'Römerbrief-Kommentar, 1532'. In *Melanchthon's Werke in Auswahl*, vol. 5. Ed. R. Stupperich. Gütersloh: C. Bertelsmann, 1965.

Metzger, Bruce M. *A Textual Commentary on the Greek New Testament*. New York: United Bible Societies, 1971.

Meyer, Paul, W. 'Romans 10.4 and the "End" of the Law'. In Crenshaw and Sandmel, eds., *Divine Helmsman*, 59-78.

Michel, O. *Der Brief an die Römer*, 13th edn Göttingen: Vandenhoeck & Ruprecht, 1966.

Minear, Paul. *The Obedience of Faith: The Purposes of Paul in the Epistle to the Romans*. London: SCM, 1971.

Mitton, C. *The Epistle to the Ephesians*. Grand Rapids: Eerdmans, 1951.

Montefiore, C.G. *Judaism and St. Paul*. London: 1914.

Moo, Douglas J. '"Law", "Works of the Law", and Legalism in Paul'. *WJT* 45 (1983), 73-100.

Moore, G.F. 'Christian Writers on Judaism'. *HTR* 14 (1921), 197-254.

—*Judaism in the First Centuries of the Christian Era: The Age of the Tannaim*. 3 vols. Cambridge, Mass.: Harvard University, 1927-1930.

Müller, C. *Gottes Gerechtigkeit und Gottes Volk*. Göttingen: Vandenhoeck & Ruprecht, 1964.

Müller, U.B. *Prophetie und Predigt im Neuen Testament*. Gütersloh: Gütersloher Verlagshaus Gerd Mohn, 1975.

Mullins, Y.T. 'Disclosure: A Literary Form in the New Testament'. *NovT* 7 (1964), 44-50.

Munck, Johannes, *Christ and Israel: An Interpretation of Rom. 9–11*. Trans. Ingeborg Nixon. Philadelphia: Fortress, 1967.

—*Paul and the Salvation of Mankind*. Trans. Frank Clarke. Richmond: John Knox, 1959.

Myers, Jacob, *I and II Esdras*. Anchor Bible. Garden City: Doubleday, 1974.

Neusner, J. and E. Frerichs, eds., *New Perspectives on Ancient Judaism*. Vol. 3. University Press of America, 1986.

Nickelsburg, G.W.E., and R.A. Kraft, eds., *Early Judaism and its Modern Interpreters*. Atlanta: Scholars, 1986.

Nida, E.A., J.P. Louw, A.H. Snyman, and J.V.W. Cronjé. *Style and Discourse with Special Reference to the Text of the Greek New Testament*. Cape Town: Bible Society, 1983.

Nissen, A. 'Tora und Geschichte in Spätjudentum'. *NovT* 9 (1967), 241-77.

Noack, Bent. 'Current and Backwater in the Epistle to the Romans'. *ST* 19 (1965), 155-66.

Nock, A.D. *Conversion: The Old Way and the New in Religion from Alexander to Augustine of Hippo*. Oxford: Clarendon, 1933.

Nolland, J. 'Uncircumcised Proselytes?' *JSJ* 12 (1981), 171-79.

Nygren, Anders. *Commentary on Romans*. Trans. Carl Rasmussen. Philadelphia: Muhlenberg, 1949.

Olson, Stanley, 'Pauline Expressions of Confidence in His Addressees'. *CBQ* 47 (1985), 282-95.

O'Neill, J.C. *Romans*. London: Penguin, 1975.

Oravec, Christine. '"Observation" in Aristotle's Theory of Epideictic'. *PhR* 9 (1976), 162-74.

Overman, J. Andrew. 'The God-Fearers: Some Neglected Features'. *JSNT* 32 (1988), 17-26.

Patte, Daniel. *Paul's Faith and the Power of the Gospel*. Philadelphia: Fortress, 1983.

Peake, A.S. 'The Quintessence of Paulinism'. *BJRL* 4 (1917-1918), 295ff.

Pedersen, Sigfred. 'Theologische Überlegungen zur Isagogik des Römerbriefes'. *ZNW* 76 (1985), 47-67.

—ed. *Die paulinische Literatur und Theologie*. Göttingen: Vandenhoeck & Ruprecht, 1980.

Perdue, Leo. 'Paraenesis and the Epistle of James'. *ZNW* 72 (1981), 241-56.

Perelman, Chaim. *The Realm of Rhetoric*. Trans. W. Kluback. Notre Dame: University of Notre Dame, 1982.

—and L. Olbrechts-Tyteca. *The New Rhetoric: A Treatise on Argumentation*. Trans. John Wilkinson and Purcell Weaver. Notre Dame: University of Notre Dame, 1969.

Perrin, Norman, *The New Testament: An Introduction*. 2nd edn revised D. Duling. New York: Harcourt Brace Jovanovich, 1982.

Peterson, Norman. *Rediscovering Paul: Philemon and the Sociology of Paul's Narrative World*. Philadelphia: Fortress, 1985.

Piper, John. 'The Demonstration of the Righteousness of God in Romans in 3.25-26'. *JSNT* 7 (1980), 2-32.

—'The Righteousness of God in Romans 3.1-8'. *TZ* 36 (1980), 3-16.

Porter, Calvin, 'A New Paradigm for Reading Romans: Dialogue Between Christians and Jews'. *Encounter* 39 (1978), 257-77.

Porter, Frank, 'Judaism in New Testament Times'. *JR 8* (1928), 3-62.

Porton, G. 'Defining Midrash', in *The Study of Ancient Judaism, vol. 1: Mishnah, Midrash, Siddur*, ed. J. Neusner. New York; KTAV, 1981, p. 55-92.

Rad, Gerhard von. *Old Testament Theology*. 2 vols. Trans. D.M.G. Stalker. New York: Harper & Row, 1962.

Raisänen, H. 'Legalism and Salvation by the Law: Paul's Portrayal of the Jewish Religion as a Historical and Theological Problem'. In Pedersen, ed., *Die paulinische Literatur*, 63-83.

—*Paul and the Law*. Philadelphia: Fortress, 1986.

Rauer, Max. *Die 'Schwachen' in Korinth und Rom nach den Paulusbriefen*. BT 120. Freiburg: Herder, 1923.

Reumann, J. *Righteousness in the New Testament*. Philadelphia: Fortress, 1982.

Richardson, P. *Israel in the Apostolic Church*. Cambridge: Cambridge University Press, 1969.

—and D. Granskou, eds. *Anti-Judaism in Early Christianity, Vol. 1: Paul and the Gospels*. Waterloo: Wilfried Laurier, 1986. (Vol. 2 ed. by S.G. Wilson).

Ricoeur, Paul. *Interpretation Theory: Discourse and the Surplus of Meaning*. Forth Worth: Texas Christian University, 1976.

Robinson, James M. 'Die Hodajot-Formel in Gebet und Hymnus des Frühchristentums'. In *Apophoreta: Festschrift für Ernst Haenchen*, ed. W. Eltester and F.H. Kettler. Berlin: Alfred Töpelmann, 1964, 194-235.

—'The Historicality of Biblical Language'. In *The Old Testament and Christian Faith*. Ed. B.W. Anderson. New York: Harper & Row, 1963.

Rössler, Dietrich. *Gesetz und Geschichte: Untersuchungen zur Theologie der jüdischen Apokalyptik und der pharisäischen Orthodoxie*. Neukirchen: Neukirchener Verlag, 1960.

Ruether, Rosemary Radford. *Faith and Fratricide*. New York: Seabury, 1974.
Russell, D.S. *The Method and Message of Jewish Apocalyptic*. Philadelphia: Westminster, 1964.
Safrai, S. and M. Stern, eds., *The Jewish People in the First Century*. 2 vols. Compendia Rerum Iudaicarum ad Novum Testamentum, Section One. Philadelphia: Fortress, 1974, 1976.
Sanday, W. and A.C. Headlam. *A Critical and Exegetical Commentary on the Epistle to the Romans*. 5th edn. ICC. Edinburgh: T. & T. Clark, 1902.
Sanders, E.P. *Paul and Palestinian Judaism*. Philadelphia: Fortress, 1977.
—*Paul, the Law, and the Jewish People*. Philadelphia: Fortress, 1983.
—'Puzzling Out Rabbinic Judaism'. In W.S. Green, ed., *Approaches to Ancient Judaism*, vol. 2. Brown Judaic Studies. Chico: Scholars, 1980.
—ed. *Jewish and Christian Self-Definition, Volume 2: Aspects of Judaism in the Greco-Roman Period*. Philadelphia: Fortress, 1981.
Sanders, J.T. 'The Transition from Opening Epistolary Thanksgiving to Body in the Letters of the Pauline Corpus'. *JBL* 81 (1962), 348-62.
Sandmel, Samuel. 'Philo's Place in Judaism: A Study of Conceptions of Abraham in Jewish Literature'. *HUCA* 25 (1954), 209-37; 26 (1955), 151-332.
Satake, A. 'Apostolat und Gnade bei Paulus'. *NTS* 15 (1968-1969), 96-107.
Schelkle, K.H. *Theologie des Neuen Testaments*. Vol. 3. Düsseldorf: Patmos, 1970.
Schiffman, L. *Who Was A Jew? Rabbinic and Halakhic Perspectives on the Jewish Christian Schism*. Hoboken: KTAV, 1986.
Schlatter, Adolf von. *Gottes Gerechtigkeit: Ein Kommentar zum Römerbrief*. 2nd edn. Stuttgart: Calwer, 1952.
Schlier, H. *Besinnung auf das Neue Testament*. Freiburg: Herder, 1964.
—*Der Römerbrief*. HTKNT. Freiburg: Herder, 1979.
—*Die Zeit der Kirche*. Freiburg: Herder, 1956.
Schmeller, Thomas. *Paulus und die 'Diatribe'*. Münster: Aschendorff, 1987.
Schmithals, Walter. 'The Corpus Paulinum and Gnosis'. In A.H.B. Logan and A.J.M. Wedderburn, eds., *The New Testament and Gnosis: Essays in Honor of Robert McLachlan Wilson*. Edinburgh: T. & T. Clark, 1983, 107-24.
—'The Heretics in Galatia'. In *Paul and the Gnostics*. Trans. John Steely. Nashville: Abingdon, 1972, 13-64.
—*Der Römerbrief als historisches Problem*. Gütersloh: Gütersloher Verlagshaus Gerd Mohn, 1975.
Schnackenburg, Rudolf. *The Moral Teaching of the New Testament*. Trans. J. Holland-Smith and W.J. O'Hara. New York: Herder and Herder, 1965.
Schoeps, Hans-Joachim. *Paul: The Theology of the Apostle in the Light of Jewish Religious History*. Trans. Harold Knight. Philadelphia: Westminster, 1961.
Schrage, W. *Ethik des Neuen Testaments*. Göttingen: Vandenhoeck & Ruprecht, 1982.

—*Die konkrete Einzelgebote in der paulinischen Paränese.* Gütersloh: Mohn, 1961.

Schrenk, G. 'δίκαιος, κτλ'. *TDNT* 2.212-19.

—'Der Römerbrief als Missionsdokument'. In *Studien zu Paulus.* ATANT 26. Zurich: Zwingli-Verlag, 1954, 81-106.

Schubert, Paul. *Form and Function of the Pauline Thanksgivings.* Berlin: Alfred Töpelmann, 1939.

Schürer, Emil. *The History of the Jewish People in the Age of Jesus Christ: A New English Edition.* 3 vols. Rev. and ed. by G. Vermes, F. Millar, M. Black, and M. Goodman. Edinburgh: T. & T. Clark, 1973-1987.

Schulz, S. 'Die Anklage in Röm 1.18–3.20'. *TZ* 14 (1958), 161-73.

Schültz, J.H. 'Ethos of Early Christianity', *IDBSup*, 289-93.

Schweitzer, Albert. *The Mysticism of Paul the Apostle.* New York: H. Holt, 1931.

Scroggs, Robin. 'Paul as Rhetorician: Two Homilies in Romans 1–11'. In *Jews, Greeks, and Christians,* ed. R. Hamerton-Kelly and R. Scroggs. Leiden: E.J. Brill, 1976, 271-99.

—*The Last Adam: A Study in Pauline Anthropology.* Philadelphia: Fortress, 1961.

Siegert, F. 'Die "Gottesfürchtige" und Sympathisanten'. *JSJ* 4 (1973), 109-64.

Simon, Marcel. *Verus Israel: A Study of the Relations between Christians and Jews in the Roman Empire.* Trans. H. McKeating. New York: Oxford University Press, 1986.

Smallwood, E.M. 'The Alleged Jewish Tendencies of Poppaea Sabina'. *JTS* 10 (1959), 329-55.

—*The Jews under Roman Rule.* Leiden: E.J. Brill, 1976.

—'The Jews under Tiberius'. *Latomus* 15 (1956), 314-29.

Snodgrass, Klyne. 'Justification by Grace—to the Doers: An Analysis of the Place of Romans 2 in the Theology of Paul'. *NTS* 32 (1986), 72-93.

Snyman, A.H. 'Style and the Rhetorical Situation of Romans 8.31-39'. *NTS* 34 (1988), 218-31.

Steck, O.H. *Israel und das gewaltsame Geschick der Propheten.* Neukirchen-Vluyn: Neukirchener Verlag, 1967.

Stendahl, Krister. 'The Apostle Paul and the Introspective Conscience of the West'. *HTR* 56 (1963), 199-215.

—*Paul among Jews and Gentiles.* Philadelphia: Fortress, 1976.

Stern, M., ed. *Greek and Latin Authors on the Jews and Judaism.* 3 vols. Jerusalem: Israel Academy of Sciences and Humanities, 1974-1984.

—'The Jewish Diaspora'. In Safrai and Stern, eds., *The Jewish People in the First Century,* 1.117-83.

Stirewalt, Martin, 'The Form and Function of the Greek Letter-Essay'. In Donfried, ed., *The Romans Debate,* 175-206.

Stowers, Stanley, *The Diatribe and Paul's Letter to the Romans.* Chico: Scholars, 1981.

—'Paul's Dialogue with a Fellow Jew in Romans 3.1-9'. *CBQ* 46 (1984), 707-22.

—*Letter-Writing in Greco-Roman Antiquity.* Philadelphia: Westminster, 1986.

—'Text as Interpretation: Paul and Ancient Readings of Paul'. In Neusner and Frerichs, eds., *New Perspectives on Ancient Judaism*, vol. 3, 17-27.

Strack, Hermann. *Einleitung in Talmud und Midrasch*. 7th edn by G. Stemberger. Munich: Beck, 1982.

Strecker, G. 'Beifreiung und Rechtfertigung'. In Friedrich, Pöhlmann, and Stuhlmacher, eds., *Rechtfertigung*, 479-508.

Stuhlmacher, Peter. 'Der Abfassungszweck des Römerbriefes'. *ZNW* 77 (1986), 180-93.

—*Gerechtigkeit Gottes*. Göttingen: Vandenhoeck & Ruprecht, 1966.

Suggs, M. '"The Word Is Near You": Rom. 10.6-10 within the Purpose of the Letter". In Farmer, Moule, and Niebuhr, eds., *Christian History and Interpretation*, 289-312.

Theissen, Gerd. *The Social Setting of Pauline Christianity: Essays on Corinth*. Trans. John Schultz. Philadelphia: Fortress, 1982.

—*Psychological Aspects of Pauline Theology*. Trans. John P. Galvin. Philadelphia: Fortress, 1987.

Thompson, Richard. 'Paul's Double Critique of Jewish Boasting'. *Bib* 67 (1986), 520-31.

Thyen, Hartwig. *Der Stil der jüdisch-hellenistischen Homilie*. Göttingen: Vandenhoeck & Ruprecht, 1955.

Tucker, Gene M. 'Prophetic Superscriptions and the Growth of a Canon'. In G.W. Coats and B.O. Long, eds. *Essays in Old Testament Religion and Theology*. Philadelphia: Fortress, 1977, 56-70.

Turner, Victor. *The Ritual Process: Structure and Anti-structure*. Ithaca: Cornell University, 1969.

Tyson, Joseph. '"Works of Law" in Galatians'. *JBL* 92 (1973), pp. 423-31.

Urbach, E. *The Sages: Their Concepts and Beliefs*. 2 vols. Trans. Israel Abrahams. Jerusalem: Magnes, 1975.

—'Self-Isolation or Self-Affirmation in the First Three Centuries: Theory and Practice'. In Sanders, ed., *Jewish and Christian Self-Definition*, vol. 2, 269-98.

Vanhoye, A., ed. *L'Apôtre Paul: personnalité, style, et conception du ministère*. Leuven: Leuven University, 1986.

Verhey, Allen. *The Great Reversal: Ethics and the New Testament*. Grand Rapids: Eerdmans, 1984.

Vermes, G. *Scripture and Tradition in Judaism*. Leiden: Brill, 1961.

Vögtle, A. *Die Tugend- und Lasterkataloge im Neuen Testament*. Münster: Aschendorff, 1936.

Watson, Francis, *Paul, Judaism and the Gentiles: A Sociological Approach*. Cambridge: Cambridge University Press, 1986.

Wedderburn, A.J.M. 'The Purpose and Occasion of Romans Again'. *ExpT* 90 (1978), 137-41.

Weiss, Johannes. 'Beiträge zur paulinischen Rhetorik'. In *Theologische Studien, Festschrift für Bernhard Weiss*, ed. C.R. Gregory *et al.* Göttingen: Vandenhoeck & Ruprecht, 1897.

Wendland, Paul. *Philo und die kynisch-stoische Diatribe*. Berlin: Georg Reimer, 1895.

White, John L. *Form and Function of the Body of the Greek Letter*. Missoula: Scholars, 1972.

—'New Testament Epistolary Literature in the Framework of Ancient Epistolography'. *ANRW* II 25.2 (1984), 1730-56.

Wibbing, S. *Die Tugend- und Lasterkataloge im Neuen Testament*. Berlin: A. Töpelmann, 1959.

Wiefel, Wolfgang. 'The Jewish Community in Ancient Rome and the Origins of Roman Christianity'. In Donfried, ed., *The Romans Debate*, 100-19.

Wilckens, Ulrich. *Rechtfertigung als Freiheit: Paulusstudien*. Neukirchen: Neukirchener Verlag, 1974.

—*Der Brief an die Römer*. 2 vols. Neukirchen-Vluyn: Neukirchener Verlag, 1978-80.

Williams, Sam K. 'The "Righteousness of God" in Romans'. *JBL* 99 (1980), 241-90.

Wills, Lawrence. 'The Form of the Sermon in Hellenistic Judaism and Early Christianity'. *HTR* 77 (1984), 277-99.

Wilson, R.M. 'Gnostics—In Galatia?' *SE 4/TU* 102 (1968), 358-67.

Wilson, S.G. *Anti-Judaism in Early Christianity, Vol. 2: Separation and Polemic*. Waterloo: Wilfrid Laurier, 1986. (Vol. 1 ed. by P. Richardson and D. Granskou).

Windisch, Hans. 'Das Problem des paulinischen Imperativs'. *ZNW* 23 (1924), 265-81.

Wink, Walter. *Naming the Powers*. Philadelphia: Fortress, 1984.

Winter, Gibson. *Liberating Creation: Foundations of Religious Social Ethics*. New York: Crossroad, 1981.

Wrede, William, *Paul*. London: Philip Green, 1907.

Wuellner, William. 'Greek Rhetoric and Pauline Argumentation'. In *Early Christian Literature and the Classical Intellectual Tradition*, ed. W.R. Schoedel and R.L. Wilken. Paris: Beauchesne, 1979, 177-88.

—'Paul as Pastor: The Function of Rhetorical Questions in First Corinthians'. In Vanhoye, ed., *L'Apôtre Paul*, 49-77.

—'Paul's Rhetoric of Argumentation in Romans'. *CBQ* 38 (1976), 33-351. Reprinted in Donfried, *Romans Debate*, 152-74.

—'Toposforschung und Torahinterpretation bei Paulus und Jesus'. *NTS* 24 (1977-78), 463-83.

—'Where Is Rhetorical Criticism Taking Us?' *CBQ* 49 (1987), 448-63.

—ed. *The Diatribe in Ancient Rhetorical Theory*. Berkeley: Graduate Theological Union, 1976.

Yarbrough, D. Larry. *Not Like the Gentiles: Marriage Rules in the Letters of Paul*. Atlanta: Scholars, 1985.

INDEXES

INDEX OF BIBLICAL REFERENCES

OLD TESTAMENT

NEW TESTAMENT

INDEX OF AUTHORS

JOURNAL FOR THE STUDY OF THE NEW TESTAMENT

Supplement Series